PALESTINE AND THE ARAB-ISRAELI CONFLICT

Second Edition

Palestine and the Arab-Israeli Conflict

SECOND EDITION

Charles D. Smith
San Diego State University

ST. MARTIN'S PRESS
New York

Acquisitions editor: Louise H. Waller
Managing editor: Patricia Mansfield-Phelan
Project editor: Robert Skiena
Production supervisor: Katherine Battiste
Cover design: Darby Downey

For information, write:
St. Martin's Press, Inc.
175 Fifth Avenue
New York, NY 10010

ISBN: 0-312-04904-8 (paper)
0-312-06557-4 (cloth)

Library of Congress Cataloging-in-Publication Data

Smith, Charles D., 1936–
Palestine and the Arab-Israeli conflict / Charles D. Smith—2nd
ed.
p. cm.
Includes bibliographical references and index.
ISBN 0-312-06557-4 (cloth)—ISBN 0-312-04904-8 (pbk.)
1. Jewish–Arab relations. 2. Palestine—History. 3. Israel–Arab
conflicts. I. Title.
DS119.7.S618 1992
956—dc20   90-63551
                                                       CIP

Published and distributed outside North America by:
MACMILLAN PRESS LTD.
Houndmills, Basingstoke, Hampshire RG21 2XS and London
Companies and representatives throughout the world.
ISBN: 0-333-57256-4
A catalogue record for this book is available from the British Library.

 The text of this book has been printed on recycled paper.

PREFACE TO THE FIRST EDITION

The 1967 Arab-Israeli War thrust the Middle East into American consciousness and brought about a much greater American political and military involvement there than had previously existed. The more than twenty years since have witnessed strife, wars, and the growth of terrorism which often targeted Americans as victims. There have been various peace initiatives as well, the best known of which resulted in the Camp David accord between Egypt and Israel. These events created certain images, if not necessarily a genuine understanding, of the region and its peoples in the minds of the public. As scholarly and general interest in the Middle East mushroomed, numerous college courses have appeared which deal either directly or peripherally with the Arab-Israeli conflict. Concurrently, a similar proliferation has occurred in research and publications treating various aspects of that conflict, especially Israeli and, to a lesser extent, Palestinian history, as well as the relationship of the Palestinian people to Zionism and to Arab nationalist movements. Other studies have adopted a wider perspective than that of the purely regional approach, examining the Middle East in the light of Great Power struggles for hegemony with its potential for the outbreak of clashes on a global scale.

Despite the prominence of these issues and their urgency, I could not find a satisfactory text to introduce the subject to the college student or general reader. What seemed necessary was a book that gave greater weight to the period before 1948, since it was then that Zionism claimed Palestine and Palestinian resistance began. Understanding the pre-1948 history of Arab-Zionist relations reveals how current Arab and Israeli attitudes, not to mention Jewish and world opinion, have been formed and how contemporary crises are often evaluated with reference to experiences that extend back to World War I and earlier. Not being able to find such a book, I decided to write *Palestine and the Arab-Israeli Conflict*, which, as its title indicates, gives equal emphasis to the modern history of Palestine as well as of Israel. Extended treatment of the period prior to 1948 permits consideration of British policy in Palestine between World War I and 1948 as a point of departure for analysis of Great Power rivalries in the Middle East from the 1950s onward.

Since this book is written as a work of synthesis, to be used by students and to serve as a scholarly reference, I have consulted only works in English and do not claim to have exhausted that material. Limiting myself to these works has meant that I have used many more works published by Israeli scholars than by

Arab scholars on pertinent topics. On the other hand, much of this Israeli scholarship offers insights and a critical perspective regarding Israeli policies, political and military, of which most Americans are unaware.

I have been generally consistent in my spelling of Arab names, but have catered to general usage on occasion. Hence, for example, I refer to Gamal Abd al-Nasser, not Jamal Abd al-Nasir. I also use the "al-" prefix for names from the mandate period, such as al-Husayni, but for figures of the recent past I drop the prefix after the first citation of the name in the text; thus, al-Nasser becomes Nasser, and al-Sadat becomes Sadat. Though "al-" is included in index listings, it is not a factor in the alphabetization of entries.

A word also about the question of balance or fairness when considering subjects that are so controversial and arouse such intense emotions. As a historian, I believe it necessary to examine other peoples and eras in light of the values and historical processes that produced them. This means that opinions and claims considered abhorrent by opponents or partisans removed from the scene may be entirely comprehensible when considered as part of a people's history and interaction with others. I therefore consider Zionist and Palestinian attitudes to be equally understandable in the context of the history and culture of each.

While residing in Jerusalem during the first six months of 1982, my circumstances afforded me opportunities to discuss developments past and current with many individuals. I benefited particularly from conversations with and the hospitality offered by Israel Gershoni, Thomas Mayer, and Itamar Rabinovich of Tel Aviv University, Yehoshafat Harkabi, Matti Steinberg, Emmanuel Sivan, and Daniel Amit of the Hebrew University of Jerusalem, and Salim Tamari and Lisa Taraki of Bir Zeit University in the West Bank. Needless to say, I alone am responsible for the views offered in this book.

I am happy to acknowledge the financial assistance for research provided by a summer faculty fellowship granted by the graduate division of San Diego State University. I also received needed support and research time from Dennis Berge, then chair of the history department at San Diego State, and Robert Detweiler, former dean of the College of Arts and Letters. May I express special appreciation to Paula Tschetter of the History Department staff, who typed many drafts of the manuscript with great skill and good humor and served as co-editor on numerous occasions. This manuscript has benefited greatly from the insightful comments offered by Arthur Goldschmidt, Jr., Pennsylvania State University; Justin McCarthy, University of Louisville; Gene R. Garthwaite, Dartmouth College; Joel Beinin, Stanford University; Donald Quataert, SUNY-Binghamton; Robert S. Kramer, Saint Norbert College; and Stephen McFarland, Auburn University. I was also fortunate to have two perceptive and patient editors at St. Martin's Press, Michael Weber and Andrea R. Guidoboni.

Finally, I wish to recognize the unfailing encouragement given by Julia Clancy-Smith in the midst of writing her doctoral dissertation, and the advice freely offered on how to deal with intractable subjects, including herself, by Elisabeth as she grew in age and wisdom from one to four.

PREFACE TO THE SECOND EDITION

This new edition of *Palestine and the Arab-Israeli Conflict* is essentially identical to the first, except for the final chapter which was rewritten and expanded to include coverage of the Palestinian uprising against Israeli rule (the intifada) and the crisis in the Persian Gulf resulting from Saddam Husayn's invasion of Kuwait on 2 August 1990. Certain sections in other chapters have been rewritten for purposes of clarity or better historical continuity, but in most cases the material is the same. Some footnotes have had their bibliography updated, but the most extensive bibliographical changes have occurred in the "Select Bibliography" at the end of the book in order to take many recent publications into account. As before, this bibliography is suggestive and does not fully reflect the books and articles consulted. These sources are listed in the footnotes for further investigation. There is also a new feature, a historical timeline arranged according to the chapters of the book.

I owe a debt of gratitude to the many colleagues who have offered support for the book and who have suggested changes for future editions. In particular I wish to thank Asad Abu Khalil and Talcott Seelye for their suggestions for improvements, many of which have been adopted. Also, I wish to acknowledge the imagination and encouragement of Louise Waller, my new editor at St. Martin's, and the assistance of Robert Skiena, who served as the project editor. Finally, I again pay tribute to the encouragement and enthusiasm of Julia and Elisabeth.

CHARLES D. SMITH

CONTENTS

LIST OF MAPS

PALESTINE AND THE ARAB-ISRAELI CONFLICT

Second Edition

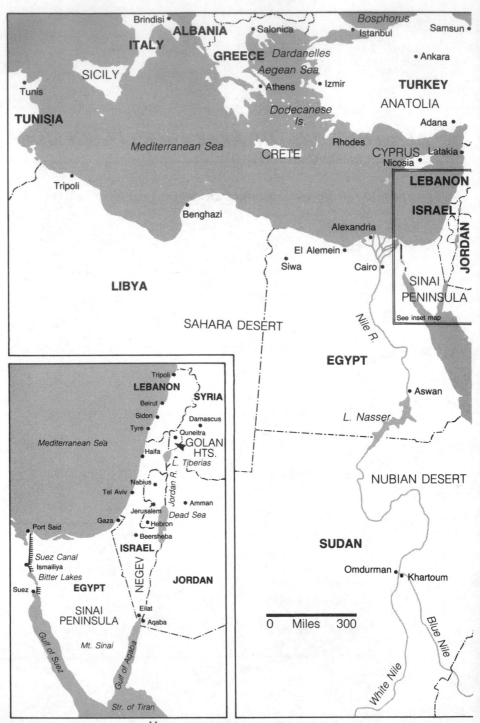

Map I. THE MIDDLE EAST (with insert)

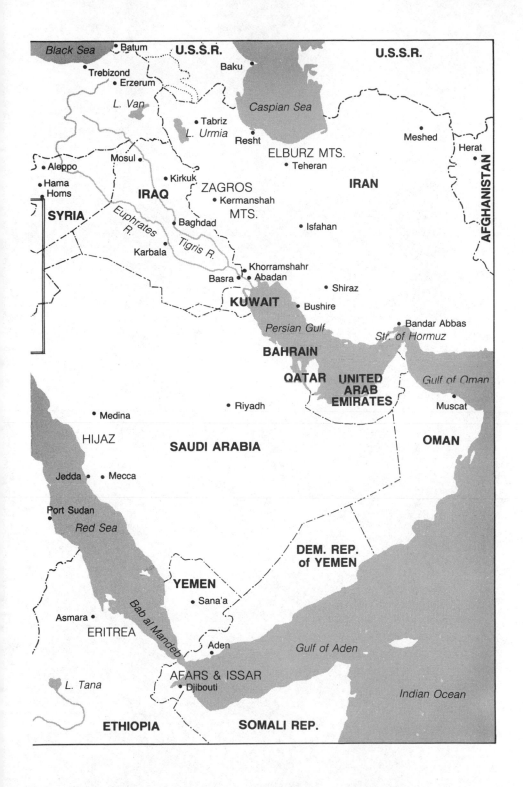

CHAPTER 1

The Middle East and Palestine to 1914:
An Overview

ANCIENT ISRAEL: ITS ORIGINS AND HISTORY TO THE ROMAN CONQUEST

The present state of Israel encompasses a substantial portion of what was once called Palestine. Three thousand years ago it was known to the Jews as Eretz Israel, the "land of Israel," a term they have retained to refer to the region down to the present day. Before the region was Israel or Palestine, it was known as Canaan, after a people who shared a cultural tradition derived from Mesopotamia and the civilization identified with the city of Ebla, southwest of Aleppo in northern Syria. The Canaanites belonged to the northwest Semitic peoples of northern Mesopotamia and Syria, of which the Jews were also a part. The Canaanites inhabited the area for most of the third millennium and the first half of the second; nearly fifteen hundred years. They controlled Palestine west of the Jordan River and parts of Phoenicia (coastal Lebanon) and southern Syria.

The Canaanites made a major contribution to world culture by developing a linear alphabet. It was transmitted to Greece and became the basis of Western writing systems. The Semitic language of the Canaanites, of which Hebrew was a dialect, was the dominant tongue spoken in the region; it reflected a sophisticated, literate culture existing at the time the Jews appeared. As one scholar put it, "the dominant pre-Israelite population was . . . in race and language not different from Israel itself."[1]

What then were the factors that gave Israel its feeling of distinctiveness? It stemmed from the Jews' belief that their God, Yahweh, had chosen them to be His people, superior to and separate from all other peoples. This belief in Yahweh as a single god evolved into monotheism, the idea that one god, their God, was the lord of the universe and that no other gods existed. Faith in Yahweh was quite different from the polytheism, or belief in many gods, that characterized most other cultures at that time, and it formed the basis of what later became Christianity and Islam. For many centuries, however, belief in Yahweh as the God of the Jews coexisted with acknowledgment of the gods of other peoples.

The names *Israel* and *Palestine* derive from peoples that entered the region at approximately the same time, the twelfth century before the Christian era. The Jews, who called themselves "Bnei Israel" (the people or tribe of Israel), believed that the land had been given to them by their God, Yahweh. Palestine refers to the Philistines, a people of Greek origin who settled in the coastal plains of the area at about the same time the Jews took over the hill country in the interior; the first literary reference we have to the region as Palestine is in Herodotus (fifth century B.C.). After nearly two hundred years the Jews united to defeat and subjugate the Philistines and other peoples in Palestine, notably the Canaanites. The establishment of the Kingdom of Israel dates from about 1000 B.C.

Saul and then David were the first kings of Israel, chosen to lead the Jews against the Philistines. It was under David that the Jews triumphed. As part of the conquest he took Jerusalem, until then not in Jewish hands, and made it a religious sanctuary sacred to all who worshipped Yahweh. David, aided by the weak condition of his neighbors, then expanded northward through much of Syria to the Euphrates and created a short-lived empire that did not survive the reign of his son, Solomon. Solomon added to the wealth of Israel by expanding its trading networks, establishing contacts as far south as the Yemen. He also built the first temple to Yahweh in Jerusalem, the focal point of Judaism from that time onward. But Solomon lost Syria, and after his death the united kingdom broke in two as the northern tribes refused to accept the principle of hereditary succession within the family of David. The period of political unity had lasted just over seventy years, from circa 1000 B.C. to 927 B.C.

Eretz Israel was then split into two kingdoms: Israel in the north, which was composed of ten tribes; and Judah in the south, which controlled Jerusalem. The northern kingdom, Israel, survived until 722 B.C. when it was conquered by the Assyrians; thousands of its inhabitants were forcibly resettled in Mesopotamia, and other peoples subject to Assyrian domination were transferred to northern Palestine to replace them. Judah lasted until 586 B.C. At that time it was absorbed into the Babylonian Empire, successor to the Assyrians in Mesopotamia, and many of its state and religious elite were transported to Babylon, an event known as the Babylonian exile.

The nature and stability of the frontiers of these two kingdoms had depended on the relative strength or weakness of the neighboring great powers; Pharaonic Egypt and the warrior states of Mesopotamia. The area called Palestine by biblical scholars more or less coincides with the territory controlled by Israel and Judah around 860 B.C. Its boundaries extended from the base of the Golan Heights in present-day Syria, westward to the Mediterranean Sea; then southward to Gaza where the coast bends west to border the Sinai Peninsula; then directly south again to the harbor at the northern tip of the Gulf of Aqaba; then north to beyond the eastern edge of the Dead Sea; and finally, northwest to touch Lake Tiberias at the foot of the Golan. These borders were not static. Areas east of the Jordan River were often under Jewish rule. The frontiers of Israel extended for brief intervals beyond Damascus to the Euphrates River in northern Syria and, for longer periods, included the Golan Heights. On the other hand, there were centuries when Jewish rule was restricted to the southern part of Palestine, extending from Jerusalem and its environs west to the sea and south to Aqaba.

Jews stayed in Palestine after the fall of Judah, but their lot was difficult and they formed a majority of the population only in the south. The region from that time onward (c. 580 B.C.) was part of a greater empire. Following the conquest of Babylon by the Persian dynasty of the Achaemenids in 539 B.C., those Jews who had been sent into exile were permitted to return. Many chose to do so, though a significant number remained in Mesopotamia. In Palestine the temple was rebuilt, and Jews were permitted to observe their religious tenets, but they remained subject to outside rule for over 350 years. They might have remained in that situation longer but for the interference of their overlords, the Seleucids, who were based in Syria and who decided to implant Greek culture throughout their domain. One ruler rededicated the temple in Jerusalem, the holiest site in Judaism, to the Greek god Zeus. This act inspired a violent rebellion that by 140 B.C. had restored Jewish independence, which lasted for eighty years. This was the revolt of the Maccabees that inaugurated the Hasmonean dynasty. Centered in Jerusalem, Jewish rule expanded to include much of the territory controlled by Solomon nearly eight hundred years earlier. Imbued with religious zeal, the Maccabees forcibly converted the by-now predominantly non-Jewish populations in the northern districts of Samaria and the Galilee. But the achievements of the Maccabees and their successors had been due in part to Roman encouragement of their efforts, which served to weaken Seleucid power and facilitated the Roman advance into the Near East. Palestine, which was known briefly as Judea, was incorporated into the Roman Empire as an autonomous unit. By 63 B.C. Jewish independence was over.

PALESTINE UNDER ROMAN AND BYZANTINE RULE

As part of the Roman Empire, the Jews in Palestine were allowed political and religious autonomy as long as their rulers acknowledged Roman suzerainty. The best known of these kings, a continuance of the Hasmonean line, was Herod the Great (37–4 B.C.), who gained renown for his building efforts, especially his reconstruction of the temple in Jerusalem to its former glory. The emperor Augustus granted Herod mastery over much of southern Syria, extending almost to Damascus, to facilitate Jewish control of pilgrimage routes between Babylon and Jerusalem. Still, there was much discontent under Herod and his successors. Many Jews saw their rulers' collaboration with the Romans as a corruption of Jewish values. Sharp differences arose between those Jews who counseled moderation and cooperation with Rome as a means of preserving the autonomy they did have and those, often known as the Zealots, who considered their subjection to Roman rule to be intolerable.

The Zealots rebelled in A.D. 66 and held out until 73 when their fortress at Masada was taken. Roman retaliation had been fierce; Jerusalem was razed in 70 and the temple destroyed. Autonomy was then restored under stricter Roman surveillance, but Jewish unrest persisted and led to a more carefully planned rebellion that lasted from A.D. 132 to 135. This was the Bar Kokhba revolt. Although initially successful in inflicting heavy casualties on Roman legions, the revolt ended in disaster. The Romans responded by systematically destroying many villages throughout Palestine, killing and enslaving thousands of Jews. Palestine/Judea thereby lost its autonomous status and became a Roman colony known as Syria Palestina. Although a significant Jewish population remained in Palestine, it was concentrated in the Galilee; Jews were forbidden to enter Jerusalem, now in ruins, as punishment for their rebellion. Jews outside Palestine far outnumbered those within it. Jewish communities had sprung up in the Greco-Roman world prior to the Roman conquest, but their numbers were small compared with those that emerged as a result of the dispersions that followed the failed rebellions of A.D. 66 and 132. Nevertheless, Jews still considered Palestine to be Eretz Israel, the land promised them by Yahweh, and Jerusalem remained the focal point of their religious observances.

The Romans eased their restrictions against the Jews in Palestine soon after they had crushed the Bar Kokhba revolt. Jews "were allowed practical self-government in all their internal affairs and were able to set up their own administrative machinery."[2] They were still banned from entering Jerusalem and were forced to pay special taxes which in the long run were not onerous, but they were permitted freedom of religious observance and teaching so long as they did not seek to convert Gentiles. In practice these regulatory laws were not enforced strictly, and Palestinian Jews were relatively free to direct their own affairs, especially during the decline of Roman power in the first half of the third century. But efforts by the emperor Diocletian to restore imperial authority and stabilize the empire at the end of the century had severe repercussions. He imposed harsh tax measures throughout the empire; their application in Palestine led to a significant decline in the Jewish population. By A.D. 300, Jews made up one-half of the total in the Galilee and less than one-fourth in the rest of the region. A new era dawned once Christianity became the official religion of the Eastern Roman Empire, and Palestine acquired an importance for Christian rulers equal to what it had for Jews.

Palestine, as the home of Jesus, was sacred to Christians. Once the rulers of the Eastern Roman Empire, based in Constantinople, accepted Christianity, Palestine—and Jerusalem in particular—acquired a significance totally lacking in the traditional Roman attitude toward the area. Christians considered Jews to be rivals in Palestine, as well as a people who had rejected Jesus as the savior sent by God. As a result, the Byzantines applied existing Roman laws limiting Jewish activities more rigorously and created new ordinances aimed at isolating the Jews. In the fifth century, laws were passed forbidding the construction of new synagogues and defining what types of repairs could be made to those already in existence. These laws were not always applied to the letter, however, similar to what had happened under pagan Rome, and new synagogues were built in the early sixth century, a period when Jews and the Christian majority in Palestine prospered. But the reign of the emperor Justinian saw the passing of new laws that interfered with the internal affairs of the Jewish community, something unknown previously. The articles applying to the building of synagogues were enforced, and mob hostility led to the destruction of many places of worship. Jews returned the favor when they were briefly permitted to rule Jerusalem after the Persian Sassanid dynasty took Palestine during its extended war with Byzantium in the early seventh century: churches were burned and many Christians killed. But Byzantine authority was soon restored and remained in force for the next twenty years before Palestine and the rest of the Middle East fell to Arab invaders from the desert who brought with them a new religion, Islam.

THE ARABS AND THE SPREAD OF ISLAM

The Arab invasion of the urbanized areas of the Near East shattered the balance of power that had existed with interruptions for over two millennia. The region had usually been controlled and fought over by empires situated initially in Egypt and Mesopotamia and later in the northern Mediterranean and southern Mesopotamia/Iran. The last series of wars between Byzantium and the Sassanids, which included the brief Persian occupation of Jerusalem, exhausted the military capacities of both camps and facilitated the Arab conquest.

The Arabs are a Semitic people, ethnically and linguistically related to the northern Semitic tribes out of which came the Canaanites and the Hebrews. The majority of these peoples had become wandering sheepherders in Mesopotamia two thousand years earlier and later settled in the central Near Eastern lands. The people known as the Arabs continued to inhabit the desert; the term *Arab* first occurs in Assyrian texts of the eighth century B.C. referring to camel herders of the desert. Those who could settled in fertile oases with a stable water and food supply, but most had to pursue the wandering life of the bedouin. Arab contacts with the peoples of the settled areas were frequent, through booty raids or when tribes served as auxiliary fighters during campaigns. The Arabs' inclination and ability to invade in force the central Middle East in A.D. 632–633 indicated that major changes had occurred in their social and political organization. These changes reflected the impact of the personality of the Prophet Muhammad and the revelation from God that he delivered to the Arabs and that became the religion of Islam.

Muhammad (c. A.D. 570–632) was born in Mecca, a trading community and religious sanctuary situated near the Red Sea coast along the caravan routes between the Yemen and the central Near East. He was a member of the clan of the Hashim, a subgroup of the Quraysh tribe that controlled Mecca. Mecca's prosperity derived in part from the caravan trade, but also because it possessed a black meteorite that became the focal point of worship for the tribes of the Hijaz. According to Islamic tradition, Muhammad was visited by the angel Gabriel who informed him that he had been selected by God (Allah) to deliver a revelation to his people. Believing he had been chosen to preach God's word, he gave up a secure livelihood and place within Meccan society to challenge the existing religious practices of Mecca and the Hijaz that formed the basis of the prosperity of the Quraysh.

Muhammad began preaching about the year 610. Meccan opposition forced him in 622 to flee with his followers to the oasis of Yathrib (to be known as Medina henceforth). Once there Muhammad took advantage of his prestige and Medinian factionalism to establish himself among the Arab tribes as the recognized leader of the oasis. He also endeavored to gain Mecca's submission, achieved in 630 after a series of inconclusive clashes. By Muhammad's death in 632, he had been accepted as the prophet of Allah in much of central and south Arabia.

Scholars differ over whether Muhammad intended to expand Islam beyond the Arabian peninsula, but such an expansion did take place. By 637 the Sassanian capital of Ctesiphon was taken, and all of Mesopotamia and western Iran were open to Muslim conquest. In Syria and Palestine, Damascus was captured in 635 and Jerusalem fell in 638; Muslim armies conquered Egypt in 640. Expansion eastward and westward continued intermittently for the next ninety years. By 730, approximately a century after Muhammad's death, the boundaries of Islam extended from the Pyrenees in Europe to beyond the Oxus River in Central Asia and to the Indus River Basin in India.

This growth occurred under the direction of the first four caliphs of Islam, those who succeeded Muhammad as heads of the community, and the caliphs of the Umayyad dynasty (661–750). Their successors founded the Abbasid caliphate (750–1258) and moved the capital from Damascus to Baghdad in Iraq, which became the center of a sophisticated culture, but the Abbasids were unable to maintain control over their vast empire. By the tenth century, political life in Islam was characterized by instability and fragmentation, even though Islamic civilization continued to flourish.

In addition, the religion had broken into two major segments, Sunni and Shi'i Islam. The split originated in a dispute over the legitimacy of the claim of Ali, the fourth caliph, to retain his position as leader of the Muslim community. Those who have continued to support the claims of Ali and his family are called Shi'ites. They challenged the formation of the Umayyad caliphate and its successors that was accepted by the Sunni Muslims. Differences in religious interpretation followed from this rift. The Umayyad and Abbasid caliphates were Sunni, as were many of the provincial governors who broke with the Abbasids, but a major Shi'i dynasty, the Fatimids, established itself in Egypt in 969 and lasted until 1171. For a time it even threatened the continuance of the Abbasid caliphate as head of Sunni Islam in Baghdad. We shall return to our discussion of political authority in Islam in our treatment of Palestine under Muslim rule.

ISLAM AND ITS RELATIONSHIP TO JUDAISM AND CHRISTIANITY

The word *Islam* means submission to the will of Allah; those who profess faith in Allah as the only God are called *Muslims*, "those who submit." Muhammad was selected by Allah to be His messenger. He was a human being who became a prophet—to Muslims a messenger of God analogous, though not identical, to the selection of Abraham by Yahweh to deliver a covenant to the Jews. Allah's covenant was the Quran, the revelations that Allah delivered to the Arabs of the Hijaz through the mouth of Muhammad, who believed that Allah was speaking through him. These recitations were written down after Muhammad's death and have been the basis of Muslim life to this day. The Quran is believed to be the word of Allah sent to guide all Muslims in their lives. Along with the compilation of Muhammad's sayings and examples, it became the basis of Muslim law, the *sharia*. The sharia contains also the interpretations and elaborations by Muslim legal scholars, similar to the Jewish Talmud with its body of legal interpretation and commentary reflecting the divine wisdom found in the commandments and the Torah.

Muslims consider Islam to be the culmination and perfection of the Jewish and Christian traditions; Allah is also the God of the Jews and Christians. According to Islam, Allah gave His revelation to prophets He chose to establish both religions (Jesus is revered but not considered divine in Islam), but in both cases the believers failed to adhere to His commands. This led to the fragmentation of the Jewish and Christian communities. Allah then sent a final revelation to Muhammad. Muslims believe that the black meteorite in Mecca, which Muhammad made the place of pilgrimage for Muslims, was initially a shrine of Abraham, thus establishing a link between earliest Judaism and Islam.

To Muslims, Jews and Christians are "People of the Book of Revelation," recipients of a divine message that they corrupted. As such, they were to be tolerated because of their place in the lineage of Islam, but they were nevertheless inferior to Muslims because of their treatment of God's messages to them. Islam was the perfection of that revelation, and Muslims were superior to Jews and Christians who, though permitted to keep their religious beliefs, were to be kept in a humble status appropriate to their denial of God's gift. At the heart of the relationship was Islam's award of protection to non-Muslims, including their right to worship, in return for payment of specified taxes, the *jizya*, a poll tax paid by non-Muslims, and the *kharaj*, a property tax that was later paid by Muslims as well. Jews and Christians became known as *dhimmis*, those who were granted protection in return for their submission to Muslim rule and their payment of the jizya.

Muslim treatment of non-Muslims was consistent with, and in some ways an improvement upon, the policies of Byzantium and the Sassanids toward Jews and Christians, respectively. Byzantine laws prohibited the construction of new synagogues, required the destruction of unsafe ones rather than their repair, interfered in Jewish doctrinal matters at times, and in general aimed at relegating Jews to eternal subordination in the probable hope that they would disappear; schismatic Christian groups were treated harshly also. Sassanian rulers permitted Jews to regulate their own affairs but watched Christian sects more closely and forbade the construction of new churches. These rules, with modifications, were incorporated into Islam's policies toward Christians and Jews. The construction of new churches and synagogues was banned, and the repair of existing houses of worship had to be approved. Dhimmis were forbidden to wear clothing identical to that worn by Muslims, in order to preserve visible signs of differentiation, or to build houses that overlooked the inner areas of Muslim dwellings. Later, rules were imposed forbidding dhimmis to ride animals as large as those ridden by Muslims. The enforcement of these regulations varied considerably according to place and historical circumstances. Under Islam, Jews experienced a lessening of control in certain aspects of their lives. Unlike the Byzantines, Muslim authorities did not interfere in doctrinal matters and allowed Jews to visit and inhabit Jerusalem. Indeed, Christians felt more debased by Muslim policies because they were now equated with Jews, after having ruled them and discriminated against them for over two centuries.[3]

As a rule, dhimmi security or insecurity reflected that felt by Muslims. The Crusades and the later European economic and political penetration of the Islamic world, especially during the nineteenth century, threatened the ongoing stability of Muslim society. In these situations tolerance declined, and regulations were imposed more harshly. In general, Muslims discriminated against non-Muslims but did not persecute them, although persecution was not unknown. Intolerant by modern Western standards of racial and religious equality, Muslim policies were consistent with and often an improvement on the prevailing treatment of Jews and Christians as subject peoples in an age when equality was unknown and inconceivable. Similar legal protection for religious minorities in Europe did not appear for another millennium. Official tolerance and protection of dhimmis in a pluralistic society survived numerous dynastic changes from the seventh century onward to confront ultimately in the eighteenth and nineteenth centuries European claims for dhimmi equality with Muslims backed by Western military might.

PALESTINE UNDER MUSLIM RULE TO 1517

The place of Palestine in Islamic history down to the modern era was generally a minor one, the exception being the period of the Crusades which created a European presence in parts of the eastern Mediterranean littoral from 1097 to 1291. But Palestine was not unimportant to Islam. Jerusalem, as a holy city to both Jews and Christians, was thus sacred to Muslims as the heirs and perfectors of the Judeo-Christian tradition. It became the third holiest city in Islam, surpassed only by Mecca and Medina, its sanctity reinforced when, according to Islamic tradition, Muhammad stopped there briefly during his night journey to heaven. The place where he set foot is a rock on the Temple Mount, the site of the Jewish temples, and an Umayyad caliph built a shrine over the stone, completed in 691 (the Dome of the Rock), to commemorate the event.

The Umayyad caliphs situated in Damascus showed concern for Jerusalem and endowed several buildings in the city in addition to the Dome of the Rock. But the Umayyads ruled for less than a century (661–750). Once the Abbasids shifted the capital to Baghdad, official attention waned, although during the ninth century Harun al-Rashid did permit the Frankish emperor Charlemagne and his son Louis to endow several hostelries there to house Latin pilgrims. Caliphs were frequently unable to retain control of provinces adjacent to Iraq, let alone those more distant. Palestine fell under the sphere of those who controlled Egypt, whether Sunni Muslims such as Ahmad ibn Tulun (868–883) or the Shi'i Fatimid dynasty, which held Palestine from 969 to 1099, when the Crusaders took Jerusalem.

The inhabitants of Palestine seem to have prospered during much of this period from the Muslim conquest to the appearance of the Crusaders. A majority of the population was now Muslim, but there were many Christians and Jews. Palestine, especially Jerusalem, remained a center of pilgrimage for members of all three faiths. Muslim rule was generally unobtrusive, to the point that new churches and synagogues were permitted to be constructed. Friction among the religious communities and the official sanction of violence against one group or another were infrequent.

The Crusaders took Jerusalem in 1099, subjecting much of its citizenry, Muslim, Jewish, and Eastern Christian, to a bloodbath. The Crusaders saw themselves as wresting the most sacred city in Christianity from heathen Muslim rule. Jerusalem became for a time "a Christian city where no Muslim or Jewish cult was permitted and no non-Christian could take residence permanently."[4] It took several years before Muslims and Jews were allowed to pray in the city. But effective Christian control of Jerusalem lasted less than a century. Saladin recaptured the city for Islam in 1187, and it resumed its Muslim character, interrupted by a struggle between rival Ayyubid princes in Cairo and Damascus that influenced the return of Jerusalem to Christian governance between 1229 and 1244.

From 1250 onward Palestine was under the Mamluks, a Muslim military elite centered in Cairo and Damascus. The province was administered by those ruling from Damascus, but Jerusalem was considered a separate entity under Cairo's authority, where the Mamluk sultan resided, in order to protect the holy places of the three religions. A weakening of Mamluk authority in both Cairo and Damascus in the early sixteenth century permitted bedouin raids to disrupt the stability of the area, a situation that persisted down to the taking of Palestine by the Ottoman Turks in 1516–1517. The Ottomans then ruled Palestine almost continuously until 1918.

OTTOMAN RULE TO 1800: AN OVERVIEW

In 1453 the Ottoman Turks conquered Constantinople and ended the existence of the Byzantine Empire. Descendants of tribal warriors who established themselves in western Anatolia after the Mongol invasions of the thirteenth century, the Ottoman sultans inherited an imperial legacy they sought to expand for Islam. Vast areas of Eastern Christendom fell under Muslim authority. By the end of the sixteenth century, Ottoman rule extended westward in Europe to Budapest and beyond; Vienna was nearly taken twice, in 1529 and 1683. Ottoman power extended along the southern rim of the Mediterranean into Algeria. By taking greater Syria (including Palestine), Egypt, and the Hijaz in 1516–1517, the Ottomans acquired the responsibility to protect pilgrims traveling to Mecca and assumed more directly the mantle of authority held by Muslim rulers.

Still, Ottoman power did not easily translate into security for the inhabitants of the Arab world. During much of the sixteenth century, the sultans concerned themselves principally with military expeditions into European territory. Administrative reforms and the taking of several censuses testify to the extension of Ottoman authority, but its effectiveness seems to have waned by the end of the century. Scholars differ on the stability of life in Palestine during this period, but there is general agreement that bedouin encroachment increased during the seventeenth and eighteenth centuries and that land formerly cultivated fell into disuse.

Palestine under Ottoman rule was eventually divided into districts known as *sanjaks*, incorporated within the province of greater Syria governed from Damascus for much of this period. These were the sanjaks of Gaza, Jerusalem, Nablus, Lajun, and Safad. Jerusalem was granted to the governor in Damascus as a source of income that sometimes led to the imposition of excessive taxes. In general, life in the towns and villages in the hill country was secure. The bedouin were a constant threat to travelers and cultivators in the coastal area. Urban inhabitants and peasants often suffered more from exorbitant demands for revenue by local Ottoman officials left unsupervised by a faltering imperial government in Istanbul. The Ottomans gradually began to rely on leading Arab clans to perform local governmental functions for them. During the late seventeenth and eighteenth centuries, a number of prominent Palestinian families first became established as tax collectors, guardians of charitable endowments, and the like; among them were the Khalidis, Nusaybas, Alamis, Husaynis, and Nashshashibis.

Ottoman society was pluralistic, similar in its inclusion of different peoples and faiths to its Byzantine and Arab predecessors but on a larger scale. In the words of a recent evaluation:

> Remarkably this polyethnic and multireligious society worked. Muslims, Christians and Jews worshipped and studied side by side. . . . The legal traditions and practices of each community, particularly in matters of personal status—

death, marriage, and inheritance—were respected and enforced throughout the empire. . . . Opportunities for advancement and prosperity were open in varying degrees to all the empire's subjects. . . . For all their shortcomings, plural societies did allow diverse groups of peoples to live together with a minimum of bloodshed. In comparison with the nation-states which succeeded them, theirs is a remarkable record.[5]

The restrictions of the dhimmis were similar to those mentioned before: special clothing, denial of the right to build new churches or synagogues, and restrictions on the types of animals they could ride and the arms they could own. As Sunni Muslims, the Ottomans viewed the dhimmis with disdain as inferiors but accepted responsibility for their protection and usually acted swiftly when mobs threatened their safety. Their status was far better than that of the Jews in medieval and early modern Europe. Indeed, the Ottoman Empire became a haven for Iberian Jews who fled the persecution that became rampant in Spain following the reconquest. Ottoman Jews were able to advance and prosper during the sixteenth and seventeenth centuries, in part due to their economic contributions, such as the textile industry at Salonica, and in part because the Ottomans permitted non-Muslims to hold certain positions that involved contact with foreigners. But this situation began to change in the eighteenth century. Jews were replaced by Christian rivals, not because of Ottoman policy but because of European influence. European patronage of Christian minorities was an extension of efforts by European powers to expand their commercial and political influence in the Ottoman Empire and to undermine Ottoman authority. Ottoman attempts to resist these pressures failed and led to a redressing of the nature of Muslim–non-Muslim relations in the middle of the nineteenth century, with serious repercussions for the empire and for the attitudes of Muslims toward their former subjects.

THE OTTOMANS AND EUROPE, 1500–1800

The treaties that ultimately weakened Ottoman sovereignty had their origin in agreements made at the height of Ottoman power. During the sixteenth century the sultans offered privileges to several European states that permitted their agents to trade within the empire. The Ottomans saw these agreements as a convenient means of regulating their relationships with Christians who were not their subjects. They were made from a position of strength and did not pose a threat to Ottoman authority until the middle of the eighteenth century. By this time the balance of power had shifted. Western Europe had made tremendous strides in developing its domestic economies and its military technology while the Ottomans had stagnated. In addition, the seventeenth and eighteenth centuries witnessed great European commercial expansion as a result of overseas conquests and the exploitation of foreign markets.

Hampered by internal disarray and court intrigue, the Ottoman rulers were unable to respond effectively to the challenges they began to face toward the end of the seventeenth century when various European rivals initiated campaigns to recover lands and trade routes lost two centuries earlier. The Treaty of Karlowitz in 1699 was the first in which the Ottomans were forced to deal with Europeans as equals and cede territory to them. From this time onward the sultans were continually faced with the territorial ambitions of Austria and the newly emerging power of Russia to the north. And, henceforth, military reverses were often accompanied by European demands for greater influence in the affairs of Christian subjects of the Ottomans as a means of expanding their own authority at the Ottomans' expense.

The first treaty exhibiting these tendencies was that between the French and the Ottomans in 1740. The French were granted the right to protect Roman Catholics in the empire and to represent their interests before the sultans. In addition, French priests were given privileges and permitted to build new churches in Palestine. As a means of extending their influence through the protection of minorities, the French arranged for the Maronites of Lebanon to recognize papal authority and thus be designated as Roman Catholics in return for papal permission for the Maronites to retain their own language for the mass, their own rites, and their own priestly orders. As Roman Catholics, the Maronites thus qualified for French tutelage in the Lebanon where the French had extensive commercial interests. Finally, the French acquired the right to grant special status (the *barat*) to Ottoman subjects that gave them trading privileges and legal immunity formerly reserved for foreigners. This set in motion a process whereby dhimmis could escape Ottoman control by gaining the protection of a European power. Naturally, the French, and later other powers, awarded this status to Christians who represented their interests, often at the expense of other minorities. For example, in the seventeenth century an Armenian replaced a Jew as a customs official in Aleppo, at the behest of the French consul there.

Equally significant was the Treaty of Kuchuk Kanarji of 1774, signed after the Russians had driven the Ottomans out of the Crimea and gained access to the Black Sea. The treaty acknowledged Russian control of the north coast of the Black Sea and Russian rights of commercial navigation on it, but it also included clauses that affected the non-Muslim subjects of the Ottomans. The Russians demanded and received the right to build in Istanbul a Greek Orthodox church under its protection. They could intercede on behalf of the clergy and patrons of that church and, by inference, all Greek Orthodox in the city. Russian pilgrims were permitted greater access to Palestine, and Russian Orthodox clergy were allowed to build hostels and churches there. These considerations were similar to those given the French in 1740 and led to an acrimonious rivalry among clergy of different faiths for possession of certain Christian holy places in Palestine. One such clash between Roman Catholic and Russian Orthodox monks, backed by their respective government sponsors, was the catalyst for the Crimean War of 1854–1856.

As a corollary of these developments, trade came increasingly under European control during the nineteenth century, often handled by non-Muslim Ottoman subjects who gained the protection of the countries they represented and thus became free of Muslim-imposed restrictions. A mutuality of interests flourished, as the European nations were eager to claim protection of these minorities as a pretext for extending their diplomatic and commercial interests. As the century progressed, the Ottoman Empire became a focal point of larger imperial rivalries, with the European powers eager to use trading rights and control of non-Muslims as tools to wield influence against their competitors as well as against the Turks. For much of the period, the major protagonists were Great Britain, France, and Russia.

THE OTTOMANS AND EUROPE, 1800–1914

In contrast with France and Russia, Great Britain did not seek initially to use protection of minorities as a wedge to expand its influence and weaken Ottoman power. The British wished to maintain the political stability of the region and, if possible, the territorial integrity of the Ottoman Empire in order to ensure the safety of their routes to India, the centerpiece of their own empire, across Ottoman lands. Consequently, they strove for most of the nineteenth century to prop up the Ottomans in order to block the ambitions of their European rivals and keep open their own lines of communication to the East. As part of this policy they joined the Ottomans in successfully opposing Napoleon Bonaparte when he landed with a French army in Egypt in 1798, seeking to interdict these routes and weaken British power in Europe as well as Asia. Likewise, the British strove during the 1830s to block the expansionist tendencies of the Ottoman governor of Egypt, Muhammad Ali, who in 1833 took over Greater Syria, including Palestine, and threatened to overthrow the Ottoman sultan. They were finally successful in 1841 following a new international crisis in which Muhammad Ali's son and deputy, Ibrahim, once more seemed on the verge of taking Istanbul.

Britain's policy was part of what has been called "The Great Game in Asia," a contest in which it saw itself pitted primarily against the Russians, whose southward expansions threatened the security of India's frontiers. Britain's actions in the Middle East were designed to keep the Russians out of Istanbul in order to forestall the prospect that a Russian fleet stationed there with access to the Mediterranean could cut Britain's imperial lifeline to India. Muhammad Ali's challenge to Ottoman power established a pretext for Russian intervention at Istanbul's behest in 1832–1833, illustrating how local rivalries could undermine or abet imperial strategies.

Britain's success in achieving its goals depended on European cooperation, which was generally forthcoming following the Congress of Vienna in 1815. British diplomats encouraged Ottoman officials to undertake administrative and legal reforms (to be discussed more fully later), in the hope of stabilizing the regime and forestalling further European inroads. But Ottoman reform efforts, though relatively successful, were hampered by internal opposition and rising nationalist sentiment that fostered separatist movements backed by European nations. The Greek Rebellion of 1821 ultimately succeeded because of joint Anglo-Russian intervention. More blatant interference in local matters followed the withdrawal of Egyptian forces from Syria and Lebanon in 1840–1841, when fighting broke out between Druze and Maronite Catholic elements in Mount Lebanon. A far more serious eruption in 1860 led to the deaths of thousands in Lebanon and the massacre of similar numbers of Christians in Damascus by Muslims aroused by the specter of European intrusion into Ottoman Muslim affairs. Here the French were arming the Maronites and the British the Druze, the latter determined to block French hegemony through its own protégés.

The Crimean War of 1854–1856, itself sparked by religious rivalries in Palestine between Catholic and Orthodox monks backed by France and Russia, respectively, resulted in a major Russian defeat at the hands of France and Great Britain. From this time onward the tsars sought to fan Balkan separatist movements in order to acquire influence against both the Ottomans and Russia's major European rival in Eastern Europe, Austria-Hungary, which itself strove to dampen nationalist ardor. Even Russian setbacks contributed to regional instability. Russian victories in the Russo-Turkish War of 1877–1878 led to concerted European diplomacy at the Congress of Berlin (1878) that reduced the extent of Moscow's territorial gains, but at Istanbul's expense as well. The congress granted independence to Serbia, Romania, and Montenegro, while the Austrians were allotted Bosnia-Herzegovina, all former Ottoman possessions. Mutual dissatisfaction at this dividing of the spoils contributed to further conflict: Austro-Hungarian–Serbian enmity over the status of Bosnia-Herzegovina resulted ultimately in the assassination of the Austrian Archduke Ferdinand on 28 June 1914 in the Bosnian capital of Sarajevo, setting in motion the diplomatic exchanges and ultimatums that caused the outbreak of World War I.

Elsewhere, in their Arab lands, the Ottoman Turks also lost extensive territory from the 1870s onward. Great Britain continued to encourage internal Ottoman reforms and to discourage outside threats to Ottoman territorial integrity until a series of developments led it to participate in the carving up of the empire. In 1869 the Suez Canal had opened, creating a direct sea route to India through the Mediterranean. Alarmed initially because construction of the canal was a joint French-Egyptian venture, London soon decided to become involved in the Suez Canal Company and in 1875 bought the shares of the Egyptian ruler, the Khedive Ismail. Most British diplomats gradually came to see the security of the canal as vital to their imperial interests, an association that created greater concern for Egypt's financial and internal stability. As part of this concern, the British acquired the island of Cyprus from the Ottomans at the Congress of Berlin, viewing it as a potential naval base able to protect the Suez Canal if the

Ottomans crumbled. Then when Egyptian anger at European interference in its financial affairs threatened to topple Ismail's successor, the British invaded Egypt in 1882; they remained until 1956.

The British absorption of Egypt, though not decided on for several years, contributed to a scramble for African territories by the French and the Germans, who hoped to establish a balance of power abroad commensurate with their ambitions in Europe. In North Africa the French, having taken Tunisia in 1881, gained control of Morocco in 1912 following a series of crises with Germany. The Italians invaded Libya in 1912. Ottoman efforts to oust the Italians were stymied by the outbreak of further Balkan wars in 1912–1913. By 1914 Istanbul controlled only a small strip of land in Europe. What remained secure were the Turkish heartland, Anatolia, and the Arab provinces of the Middle East down to the Sinai Peninsula. The Germans were now the Ottomans' major ally, as a result of British and French involvement in the carving up of the empire that occurred in the aftermath of the Congress of Berlin.

NOTES

1. John Bright, *A History of Israel*, 3rd ed. (Philadelphia, 1981), p. 116. I rely principally on Bright for my discussion of ancient Israel.
2. Michael Avi-Yonah, *The Jews of Palestine: A Political History from the Bar Kokhba War to the Arab Conquest* (New York, 1976), p. 83.
3. C. E. Bosworth, "The Concept of *Dhimma* in Early Islam," in Benjamin Braude and Bernard Lewis, eds., *Christians & Jews in the Ottoman Empire: The Functioning of a Plural Society*, vol. 2, *The Arabic-Speaking Lands* (New York, 1982), pp. 37–54.
4. S. D. Goitein, "al-Kuds," *Encyclopedia of Islam*, vol. 5 (Leiden, 1980), p. 330.
5. Braude and Lewis, *Christians and Jews*, vol. 1, *The Central Lands*, p. 1.

CHAPTER 2

Ottoman Society, Palestine, and the Origins of Zionism, 1800–1914

OTTOMAN SOCIETY IN THE ARAB LANDS IN THE NINETEENTH CENTURY

The progressive diminution of Ottoman power in the nineteenth century affected the stability of Muslim society, especially Muslim-Christian relations, which began to change as a result of European intervention and Ottoman responses to these incursions. The customary Muslim view of a world in which dhimmis remained in inferior positions befitting their status began to be shaken. The improved position of the Christian dhimmis seemed to many Muslims to result from a loss of Ottoman power at the hands of hostile forces that sought to weaken Muslim control over lands they considered to be theirs. The situation in Palestine remained relatively stable—more so than in areas of Syria and Lebanon—as did Muslim attitudes toward Jews until the appearance of Zionists who claimed that Palestine was inherently Jewish and should revert to Jewish rule.

Ironically, the impact of French and Russian rights of protection over Christian sects was made known to many Arab Muslims by a Muslim ruler, Ibrahim, the son of Muhammad Ali of Egypt. Ibrahim governed Syria, Palestine, and parts of Lebanon for nearly ten years. Eager to exploit the local populace to finance the costs of occupation, he sought to modernize the administration and enforced tax policies that had been ignored for generations. Faced with the opposition of the area's Muslim population, Ibrahim turned to dhimmis, usually Christians, whom he placed in high administrative posts. It was not uncommon for a Christian official to assess taxes on well-to-do Muslim families in cities such as Damascus and Aleppo. Egyptian actions were motivated also by the desire to acquire allies in the midst of a Muslim population generally loyal to the Ottoman sultan and opposed to the imposition of levies they had not experienced previously. Ibrahim encouraged European trade and the influx of Christian missionaries into Lebanon and Syria as a means of gaining European backing against Ottoman demands for Egyptian withdrawal. As part of these tactics, Ibrahim granted Christians and Jews effective political and religious equality with Muslims, overturning the foundations of the structure on which intercommunal relations had been based for centuries. The Muslim masses, traditionally exploited by Ottoman officials, suddenly found themselves subject, not merely to harsher taxes, but also to military conscription from which non-Muslims, their supposed equals, were exempt.

Muslim resentment against Christians in particular intensified because European consuls and traders hired Arab Christians to represent them in the selling of European goods which were cheaper, being mass-produced, than those indigenous products sold by Muslim merchants. The local market on which Muslims relied was thus undermined to the benefit of Europeans and their Arab Christian protégés, who usually acquired protective status (*barat*) and became exempt from Muslim authority. What made matters worse was the manner in which some Christian clergy flaunted their newfound equality by holding public processions in elaborate vestments and having church bells rung, practices forbidden under Muslim ordinances for centuries. In contrast with the Christian ostentation, Jews accepted their official equality cautiously and without fanfare. This contributed to the greater stability of Muslim-Jewish relations during a period of Muslim-Christian enmity. Indeed, the major threat to Jewish communities during much of the century came from Christians who were their rivals in trade. The blood libel against the Jews in Damascus in 1840 was inspired by the Christians, though they tried to enlist Muslim mobs in their cause. Conversely, when the Muslims rioted against the Christians in Damascus in 1860, the Jews were reported to have encouraged them.[1]

Muslim self-regard was further undermined when edicts issued by the Ottoman sultans reaffirmed the hated practices instituted by the Egyptians, the result of the great power pressures just noted. Following Sultan Mahmud II's disastrous attempt in 1839 to drive Ibrahim out of Syria, only British intervention had kept Ibrahim from marching on Istanbul. Mahmud died the same year. Four months after his death, his young successor, Sultan Abdul Medjid, issued the Hatti Sharif of Gulhane (1839), an imperial edict proclaiming principles derived from Western liberalism that dealt with equal rights for all Ottoman subjects, reform to the justice system, and the like. In part this declaration was the work of Ottoman statesmen who believed that implementation of reforms in education, the economy, and military technology required the application of these principles. As such, the Hatti Sharif was the beginning of the *Tanzimat*, or the reordering of society, the creation of a new system that should enable the Ottomans to strengthen themselves internally and to resist further threats to their frontiers. But the Hatti Sharif was also the work of the British ambassador in Istanbul, Stratford de Redcliffe, who believed that these reforms were the only means by which the Ottomans could become strong enough to prevent the Russians from ultimately gaining control of the straits. He saw the document as an appeal to British opinion and that of other European countries, thereby justifying a concerted anti-Russian effort on behalf of the Ottomans.

Likewise, the conclusion of the Crimean War saw similar British efforts to draft a document reaffirming Ottoman adherence to the Hatti Sharif before the Congress of Paris in 1856 in which penalties against the Russians would be imposed. The new declaration, the Hatti Humayun, proclaimed unequivocally the equality of dhimmis with Muslims in the empire in education and in administration of justice; freedom and openness of worship were also guaranteed. Orders sent out to provincial governors to implement these policies were often met with hostility, but their anger was directed mostly at the European powers, who were seen as forcing the sultans to issue the decrees. As a consequence, Muslim animosity toward Ottoman Christians flared, the most explosive example being the massacre of thousands in Damascus in 1860 which reflected particular local rivalries (to be discussed later). There had also been anti-Christian riots in Aleppo in 1850 and in Nablus in northern Palestine in 1856, the latter instigated by the accidental killing of a Muslim by an English missionary.[2] The interrelationship of local sectarian rivalries and outside interference was crucial to the course of events in the Lebanon during this period and left a legacy of distrust that has lasted to the present.

THE LEBANON TO 1860

Lebanon in the early nineteenth century was essentially Mount Lebanon, rugged terrain that dominated the shallow coastal plain between it and the sea. It had long served as a haven for people seeking refuge. The two groups that predominated in the Mountain, the Maronites and the Druze, were heterodox offshoots of Christianity and Shi'i Islam, respectively. The Maronites had established themselves in the north, the Druze in the south.

The period from the mid-sixteenth to the mid-nineteenth centuries witnessed major social upheavals coupled with the often successful attempts of various chiefs to establish dynasties that went beyond the Lebanon to control northern Palestine as well. A Druze dynasty, that of the Ma'nids, lasted from roughly 1590 to 1697. Its greatest leader, Fakhr al-Din II, united Mount Lebanon and introduced an era of Druze-Maronite cooperation that strengthened the region and guaranteed its independence from direct Ottoman authority, although Ottoman suzerainty was acknowledged. Fakhr al-Din joined Mount Lebanon in apparent harmony under Druze rule, preached religious tolerance, and opened the coast to European traders and missionaries.

The Ma'nids were succeeded in 1697 by the Shihab dynasty, which lasted until 1840. Originally Sunni Muslims, the Shihabs often portrayed themselves as Druze so as to further communal harmony and the allegiance of the still-powerful notables. Then in 1770, members of the Shihab family who had converted to Maronite Catholicism became the amirs of Mount Lebanon. Their conversion was in part the result of factionalism within the extended Shihab clan, but it also indicated recognition of the shift in the Druze-Maronite power balance that had begun a few decades earlier. The opening of Lebanon to European trade under Fakhr al-Din II had been a boon to the Maronites, who traditionally sought to align themselves with European allies. The Maronites welcomed trade and the increased Catholic missionary activity sponsored by the French that accompanied it. As a result the Druze began to lose influence to the

Maronites, a process that accelerated during the reign of the Maronite Bashir II, who reigned from 1788 to 1840.

Initially Bashir's authority was limited in that he, like his predecessors, had to respect the power of the local rulers in northern Palestine who intervened frequently in the affairs of Mount Lebanon. He had to contend with Ahmad al-Jazzar whom the Ottomans appointed pasha of Sidon in 1775 and who involved himself in Shihab politics. Bashir II emerged as the dominant force in the Lebanon only after al-Jazzar's death in 1804. By playing off rival Druze families against one another and then crushing them, he acquired hegemony over the region but incurred the lasting enmity of the Druze in the process.

Eager to establish total independence from Ottoman rule, Bashir backed the Egyptian invasion of Syria in 1831, but his alliance with Ibrahim ultimately proved his undoing. Ibrahim extended his tax reforms and conscription orders to Mount Lebanon, arousing hostility among Druze and Maronites alike, along with resentment toward Bashir who had to implement these decrees. Insurrection finally erupted in 1839–1840, inspired in part by Ibrahim's demand that both Christian and Druze communities hand in their arms, a challenge to the traditional autonomy of these enclaves. The European powers intervened, forcing Ibrahim to retreat to Egypt and Bashir to flee into exile. Mount Lebanon reverted to communal violence. Only Ottoman intercession kept Druze-Maronite animosities from escalating in 1841, but the fundamental causes of their antagonism remained.

The roots of Druze-Maronite animosity lay in the Maronites' gradual assumption of power at Druze expense, culminating in Bashir II's defeat of the major Druze families. A crucial factor in sustaining hostilities was the question of land ownership in the south, the traditional preserve of the Druze. During the eighteenth century, Maronite peasants had migrated into the south. This was accepted at the time in the afterglow of the reign of Fakhr al-Din II. Then Bashir II, after smashing the Druze families in battle, transferred Druze lands in the south to Maronites. This led to a greater infusion of Maronites, now in the guise of lords taking over land that had been Druze for centuries. Following Bashir II's death, his successors refused to return this land to the Druze and were backed in their stance by the French. As a result the British decided to support the Druze diplomatically and militarily. The situation was exacerbated by economic grievances. Ottoman efforts to resolve hostilities and reassert their influence in the Mount Lebanon area met with little success. Finally, there was the alarm felt by Muslims once the Ottomans proclaimed the Hatti Humayun of 1856. This led many Sunni Muslims in the Lebanon to side with the Druze when violence erupted on a larger scale in 1859–1860. The Druze gained control over the south, with thousands of Maronites killed and many more forced to flee.

Despite the violence, European intervention seemed unlikely. The Ottoman governor in Beirut acted swiftly to prevent that prospect by reaching a settlement agreed to by both Druze and Christian leaders that accepted Druze territorial gains. Then the Damascus riots occurred on 9 July 1860, three days after the Christian-Druze agreement, with the Ottoman troops there participating in the killing. Although the Ottomans punished many soldiers and government officials with death, including the governor of the province, European alarm led to the landing of French soldiers outside Beirut in order to protect the Christian population there. An international commission was formed to decide the future of Mount Lebanon, with agreement reached in the spring of 1861. It became a separate Ottoman province with autonomous status, to be administered by a Catholic chosen by the Ottomans from outside Lebanon. The coastal strip from Tripoli south through Beirut to Sidon was separated from the new province, as was the fertile Biqa' valley east of the Mountain. This solution stressed the predominantly Maronite-Druze composition of the area and excluded regions with heavier Sunni and Shi'i Muslim populations. This arrangement lasted until the end of World War I and provided peace for the region.

Beirut continued to grow as a commercial center for several more decades, with silk the major export industry. Trading houses arose, fortunes were made, and the search for profits led several Beirut families to invest in land in Palestine, a matter we will examine shortly. Maronite national aspirations remained. Fearful of Muslim domination and restricted in their influence by the Statute of 1861, the Maronites still looked to France as their protector. France in turn viewed the Maronites as loyal allies who could assist achievement of its ambitions in the Levant. The World War I settlements that gave Syria and Lebanon to France were welcomed by the Maronites as a step that would guarantee their ascendancy in the Mountain and beyond.

PALESTINE IN THE NINETEENTH CENTURY

Palestine was still divided into several administrative entities in 1800, and it underwent various transformations as the century progressed. The officials primarily responsible for the area were the pashas of Sidon and Damascus. The pashas of Sidon resided in Acre, within Palestine; on occasion they controlled areas of Lebanon up to and including Beirut, the Galilee in northern Palestine, and parts of the northern Palestinian coastal region. The pashas of Damascus, in addition to their responsibilities in Syria, were concerned with the administration of central Palestine on a north-south axis, including Jerusalem. These *pashaliks* were divided into *sanjaks*, or districts, where local notables appointed by the Ottomans were responsible to them for security and the collection of taxes. There were further sudivisions extending down to the village level, where the small area known as a *nahiya*, made up of several villages, was represented by a dominant local family.

The most heavily populated region was the central mountain terrain which was more easily defended against bedouin incursions and invasions by outside powers. The area was dotted with villages and several large towns. Political authority lay in the hands of notables or chiefs, heads of prominent families who became the tax collectors of their regions. In some areas one or two families might dominate, in others, such as Nablus, there were eight or nine families vying for power whose fortunes waxed and waned according to their willingness to serve Ottoman interests and the strength of their opponents. The countryside was dominated by village coalitions grouped together by clan loyalties. Around Jerusalem the situation was different, in that Jerusalem notables did not control land and the collection of land revenues at this time. Their authority rested on their possession of religious offices, as the Muslim hierarchy in Jerusalem appointed functionaries in the Palestinian towns. Nonetheless, these functionaries could derive a good deal of wealth from these offices, along with their control of the many charitable endowments (*waqfs*) in the area, their collection of taxes and security payments from the dhimmis, and the constant flow of pilgrims, most of them Christian, to holy places in the city and its environs. As in rural areas, there existed intense competition among Jerusalem families for these posts.

A crucial issue affecting social relations and power in the latter half of the century was the question of land ownership and the impact of the Ottoman land reform laws passed in 1858 and 1867. As we have seen, the Ottomans issued the Hatti Humayun in 1856 in the hope that a guarantee of equal rights for all Ottoman subjects would reduce the separatist tendencies of non-Muslim minorities and thus stabilize the empire. Equally important to this process of stabilization in Ottoman eyes was their reassertion of authority over Anatolia and the Arab provinces whose revenues had been lost to Istanbul because of inefficient administration and the Egyptian occupation of Syria. Ottoman officials began applying Tanzimat principles in earnest in Syria and Palestine. The goal of the land laws, applicable throughout the empire, was to regularize the structure of land ownership and the cultivation of land. By establishing clear proof of title to possession or use of land, the Ottomans could make the holders of these titles liable to taxes and thus increase state revenues. The law of 1867 granted foreigners the right to own land, but only in return for their agreement to pay taxes on it to the Ottoman government. The aim of this law was to lessen the scope of the capitulations and to force foreigners, mainly Europeans, to submit to Ottoman jurisdiction in return for their investment in land in the empire.

In Palestine the inconsistent application of these laws opened the way for extensive outside investment without much Ottoman success in controlling the revenues derived. A great deal of land in Palestine was state land (*miri*). Some of it had been uncultivated for decades because of the insecurity of life in the area. Some had been taken over by landowners who exploited it as private property (*mulk*) without the Ottoman government's benefiting from either the revenues paid for the use of state land or from either the taxes they could assess on private landholders. Finally, a large amount of land, state and private, was cultivated by peasants who assumed traditional rights to it and practiced a form of communal ownership of the soil they tilled (*musha'a*).

When the Ottoman land laws were passed, peasants were often unable or unwilling to pay the taxes owed either for the use of state land or for the title to land they held by custom. Indeed, the peasants were frequently in debt and owed considerable amounts of back taxes. The peasants' resistance to the imposition of taxes was well known, and officials in Damascus had on occasion destroyed whole villages that had openly defied attempts to collect revenues from them.[3] In addition, many peasants able to pay to establish title were afraid to do so because they or their sons would become subject to military recruitment once their names appeared on the tax rolls. Consequently they, as well as the indebted peasants, were quite willing to have their lands registered in the names of individuals who assumed the tax burdens and became large landholders in the process. The peasants continued to farm the land as they had before and seem to have assumed that they retained rights to it on the basis of custom, whatever its new legal status.

Some of those who purchased land in this manner were Palestinian notables, many of whom served as tax collectors for the Ottomans. Included among these were families from Jerusalem who had not previously been landowners. Others were merchants, local Christian, Lebanese, or Europeans who began to invest in land in Palestine. Among these were Christian merchants from Beirut. The most prominent was the Sursuq family, Greek Catholics who owned a silk factory there and exported textiles. The Sursuqs bought land from peasants or uncultivated state land that the Ottoman government offered for sale. They purchased a total of 230,000 dunams, approximately 57,500 acres (1 dunam = ¼ acre), in the Galilee, mostly in the Marj ibn Amir (Plain of Esdraelon) and near Nazareth where much of the land they bought had belonged to nearby villages. This latter sale violated a provision of the 1858 land law that forbade the possession of the lands of a village by an individual, but the Ottoman interest in revenue prevailed. Extensive Jewish investment and colonization did not begin until after 1882.

It is clear that a major transformation of landholding patterns had occurred in Palestine before Zionist immigration began, with the beneficiaries being either Palestinian notables or outsiders, usually Christians from the coastal areas. As a result, title deeds to extensive areas of land had been acquired by a relatively few people or families while the peasants on much of that land still assumed they had customary rights to its use. One estimate from the turn of the twentieth century is that "only 20 per cent of the land in Galilee and 50 per cent in Judea was in the hands of the peasants."[4] Nevertheless, peasant village holders retained possession of the bulk of cultivable land. For example, one observer noted that nearly one-third of the cultivable land, amounting to 3 million dunams was held by only 144 families. But two-thirds of that amount belonged to tribes who cultivated the coastal plains of Gaza and Beersheba. This leaves 1 million dunams for the Sursuqs, the Sultans, and other great families. The remaining two-thirds of cultivable land, 9 million dunams, remained in village and peasant hands. What had changed was the amount of land under cultivation, as much of the property bought by the Sursuqs in the Marj ibn Amir had not been tilled for years because of local strife.

What then of the land's productivity? Estimates again are not totally reliable, but it seems that a major expansion of productivity occurred following the Crimean War and the restoration of Ottoman authority and greater security in the region. We see more land cultivated, by peasants and tribes as well as large holders, mainly in response to demands from markets in the Middle East and Europe. For example, Gaza became an important grain-producing region at this time, initially because Russian exports declined during the Crimean War. One estimate placed the amount of land added for cultivation in Gaza during the 1850s at 600,000 to 800,000 dunams. Cotton production expanded greatly to meet rising European prices during the early 1860s owing to the loss of American cotton during the Civil War, but this market did not last beyond the mid-1870s. More successful and much better known was the extension of citrus cultivation and production, especially oranges. A British report of 1873 estimated the orange crop then at 33 million oranges, five-sixths of which were exported, mainly to Egypt and Turkey. Production continued to increase in response to European demand. Around Jaffa from the 1880s to 1914, the orchard area for oranges multiplied over seven times, from 4000 to approximately 30,000 dunams, with exports nearly quintupling. By 1913, Jewish colonists at Petah Tikva near Jaffa were exporting about 15 percent of Palestine's total.[5]

These figures indicate a phenomenon that was occurring elsewhere, namely, the discrepancy between Palestinian methods of production and those introduced by European colonists, whether Jewish or others such as the German Templars who brought with them more efficient methods of cultivation. The great expansion of Palestinian Arab productivity began before the appearance of Europeans in large numbers who introduced more modern agricultural techniques; their per-capita output was thus lower than that of the colonists. The same dichotomy existed in industries such as the manufacture of soap and olive oil, in which Arabs continued to use traditional methods of production, as opposed to the rise of factories using imported machinery that were run by immigrants from abroad.

An important source of revenue for several cities in Palestine, especially Jerusalem, Bethlehem, and the ports of Jaffa and Haifa, was the tourist and pilgrim traffic to the Holy Land which grew rapidly during the nineteenth century along with antiquarian interest. Most of the surveys of Palestine during the century "were concerned with the geography of the region in relation to its past"[6] and in identifying biblical sites. In addition to British travelers and expeditions, various Christian groups organized tours from the 1850s, and travel agents began touting excursions from the 1870s. During the 1870s between ten and twenty thousand pilgrims visited Jerusalem annually, the largest contingent being Russian. Conditions for travel improved, and Muslim hostility to the influx of foreigners, remarked upon by travelers during the first half of the century, seemed to abate somewhat.

Other visitors to Palestine came with the intent to establish a presence there. French Catholics participated in what they called "the peaceful crusade," visiting holy places and donating sums to build religious institutions. The German Templars established agricultural colonies with the idea of settling in Palestine and Christianizing it if possible. Finally, Protestant missionaries from England and America came to Palestine. They sought converts among members of other Christian sects and encouraged Jewish migration. As evangelical Christians who considered the end of the world to be at hand, they hoped to bring Jews to Palestine and convert them to Christianity in the Holy Land prior to the Day of Judgment. Similar aspirations can be found today among Christian fundamentalists in the United States and forms one component of their support of Israel. But during most of the century, those Jews who came to Palestine did so for their own religious motives. They were making their pilgrimage to the land of ancient Israel, many in order to die there. They settled in several cities, but especially in Jerusalem where Jews comprised the majority of the population by 1890. Another town where Muslims lost their majority was the port of Haifa which expanded greatly from the 1850s onward; Christians made up the largest single group, many of them probably of Lebanese origin, traders taking advantage of the commerce and pilgrim traffic that passed through Haifa. And between 1895 and 1914 forty thousand Jews entered Palestine, often not for religious reasons but to seek to colonize it and establish a base for the future restoration of Palestine as Israel. As Zionists they were more interested in establishing agricultural colonies than in settling in the cities.

Our discussion of immigration raises the question of the nature of the population of Palestine during this period and the reasons for its increase to about 650,000 by 1914: natural causes or the settlement of foreigners? This is an important issue and one critical today to both Palestinian Arabs and Zionists. One sensationalist study argues that very few Arabs in Palestine in the late nineteenth century were born there; most had immigrated into Palestine from other Arab areas. Similarly, Amos Elon states that the Arab population in Palestine "increased mostly as a result of Arab immigration from neighboring countries."[7] These conclusions place Jewish immigration to Palestine on an equal footing with Arab during approximately the same period and deny the existence of a significant *Palestinian* Arab population that would be deprived of its land by the creation of a Jewish state.

But claims that the Arab population of Palestine increased mainly through the influx of Arabs from outside Palestine are suspect. There was some settlement of Circassians and Algerians, the latter then in Damascus, in the northeast corner of Palestine around Tiberias and Safad, encouraged if not forced by Ottoman administrators seeking to establish greater security in areas not well protected by Ottoman authorities. This settlement was not large, and many Circassians left soon after. There was also an infusion of Egyptians into the Gaza area, the legacy of the passage of Muhammad Ali's armies in the 1830s. This too was small in number. There are in fact no statistics that are absolutely certain, including the estimate of the population of Palestine at 650,000 in 1914.

Israeli and other scholars who have examined aspects of the question conclude that a natural increase in the overwhelmingly Arab population of Palestine from the 1840s would account for a Palestinian Arab component of the total, estimated at 650,000 in 1914, of between 555,000 and 585,000. The figure of 650,000 includes a Jewish population of about 80,000, the majority of whom had entered Palestine after 1860. Taking the lower figure of 555,000 for the Palestinian Arab population and adding the Jewish population of 80,000, we still have leeway for probably between 25,000 to 40,000 settlers, whether other Europeans or Arabs. Arabs undoubtedly did migrate to Palestine from other areas during the period, but they likely made up no more than 8 percent of the Arab population of Palestine in 1914.[8]

Nevertheless, to assume a predominantly Palestinian Arab population does not permit us to postulate the widespread existence of a Palestinian Arab national consciousness at this time. The idea of nationalism was a European phenomenon, just beginning to be known in the Arab world, that often collided with the regional and family loyalties that predominated. Nationalism was, however, part of the Zionist ideology, held by about 25,000 of those Jews who came to Palestine from the 1890s to 1914. They hoped to reclaim Palestine as Eretz Israel, the land of the Jewish people. We shall now examine the nature of Zionism and how it became a national, as opposed to a religious, cause in Europe that inspired migration to Palestine and aroused Arab opposition by 1914.

ZIONISM: ITS ORIGINS AND DEVELOPMENT TO 1914

THE JEWS OF WESTERN EUROPE

The modern Zionist movement dates from the second half of the nineteenth century, inspired by secular nationalism and anti-Jewish prejudice in Western and especially Eastern Europe. Underlying modern Zionism was the wish to establish an independent Jewish existence in Palestine, the ancient land of Israel, which the Jews had last governed nineteen hundred years before. Modern Zionism differed from the traditional Jewish yearning for their return to Zion, Eretz Israel, in that religious Jews viewed the matter as one to be decided by Yahweh. Just as their exile reflected Yahweh's punishment of Jews for their transgressions of His laws, so should their return indicate that He had granted redemption to them, a redemption that many believed could occur only when the end of the world was at hand. In contrast, modern or political Zionism was activist and predominantly secular. It was a movement of Jews who were disenchanted with their religious culture but who rejected the idea of assimilation into European society. This seemed impossible because of the persistence of hostility toward Jews despite the passage of laws in Western Europe granting them equality. The situation was much worse in Eastern Europe, where the persecution of Jews intensified as the century drew to a close.

Until the Crusades the Jews had suffered sporadic persecution in Western Europe balanced by long periods of relative tolerance. Christianity, like pagan Rome, allowed Jews to retain their religious autonomy, the only community permitted to do so. Christian laws prohibited Jewish proselytization or expansion, including the building of new synagogues, but ordered the protection of existing institutions. As we have seen, these rules were later taken over into Islam. With the Crusades the haphazard expression of Christian hostility toward Jews became more focused. Intended to recapture Jerusalem from Islam, the Crusades aroused intense feelings of hostility toward all those who denied the divinity of Jesus and gradually established a climate of hysteria in which the Jews came to be considered as a people seeking to subvert Christian security.

Latent religious hostility was reinforced by the competition that the Jews presented to a newly emerging Christian bourgeoisie often allied with monarchs eager to acquire wealth to bolster their power. As a result Jews were expelled from England in 1290, not to return until the end of the seventeenth century, and from France in 1306, although small communities did remain there. Protestantism was no less hostile to Jews in regions under its control. The most extreme example of Christian fear of subversion arose in Spain where the Spanish reconquest led to the expulsion laws of 1492 that ensured the demise of these communities and caused an exodus of Spanish Arab Muslims to North Africa and of Jews into the Mediterranean world, especially the Ottoman Empire, as noted earlier. During the eighteenth century, Jews were readmitted to the northern European countries of England and France under state sponsorship. There, with growing prosperity and security as mass outbreaks diminished sharply, a process of assimilation at the higher levels of society in France, England, and some German states had begun even before the French Revolution, the catalyst for the legal emancipation of Western European Jewry during the nineteenth century.

The French Revolution of 1789 and its Declaration of the Rights of Man proclaimed the equality of all people as the basis for true citizenship. Jews were specifically offered the opportunity to assimilate as individuals into French society. The idea of assimilation meant that Jews would presumably give up their commitment to retain their distinctiveness as a separate community adhering to Jewish laws and, with that, their commitment to the idea of a return to Eretz Israel, a hope that had bound them together for centuries. It was an exchange that the majority of West European Jewry opted for during the nineteenth century as barriers broke down gradually in Germany, Austria, England, Hungary, and later, Italy and France. By mid-century, Jews were permitted to stand as candidates for Parliament in England. In France, and especially in Germany, assimilation proceeded rapidly. Intermarriage and a declining birthrate led to a sharp decrease in the original German-Jewish community, but the Jewish population there remained distinctive because of the influx of Jews from Eastern Europe.

In sum, great strides toward legal and social equality had been made by the end of the nineteenth century, but latent and sporadic open hostility toward Jews remained. It was during this period, the 1880s, that the term *anti-Semitism* was coined by an anti-Jewish German author to emphasize the nature of his antipathy as racial and thus "modern," as opposed to the traditional religious antagonism toward Jews. Anti-Semitism went hand in hand with Jewish efforts to assimilate. Still, most Western European Jews strove to merge more fully into society. When an active Zionist movement emerged, its initial impulse and main support came from Eastern Europe where legal equality, let alone assimilation, seemed increasingly unattainable.

EASTERN EUROPEAN JEWRY AND THE RISE OF ZIONISM

At approximately the same time that Jewish equality with non-Jews was declared in Western Europe through the French Revolution, Eastern European Jewry was entering a century-long phase of increased hostility and segmentation from Polish and Russian society. The future of East European Jewry was decided by the partition of Poland that occurred in three stages in 1772, 1793, and 1795. Portions of the country went to Russia, Prussia, and Austria. As a result, Russian Jewry, heretofore a small community, expanded significantly and created in Russian eyes a question they had to deal with in a decisive manner. Their response was both harsh and contradictory. They attacked Jews for their separatism but usually imposed laws forbidding their right to participate freely in Russian society unless they converted. In 1790 and 1791 they passed laws creating the Pale of Settlement. These decrees stipulated that Jews could not live in the major Russian cities of the interior. They were confined to the former Polish territories and certain other areas of southwest Russia where they were supposed to live in the larger cities, and even here they were later barred from cities such as Kiev and Sebastopol. These laws were not always strictly enforced, but they reflected an official attitude of suspicion and hostility that led to repeated attempts to isolate Jews from Russians, whether inside or outside the Pale.

Isolation and concentration of habitation ensured the continuity of strong religious and communal bonds among East European Jewry during the nineteenth century, a time when adherence to those traditions was fading in the West. Thus it "was the Jew whose attachment to tradition was loosening who found the condition of Jews intolerable," whereas the leadership of Eastern Jewry sought to preserve the strength of the community which lay in its adherence to traditional values and practices.[9] Modern Zionism found its roots among Russian Jews who had already broken with communal life in the Pale, many of whom had hoped briefly for the opportunity to assimilate into Russian society. The bases of these aspirations lay in the modernist movement among Russian Jewry called the *haskala* which arose in the 1850s. Their members were attracted to Western European literary models and the idea of legal equality with non-Jews that was occurring there. The reign of Tsar Alexander II inspired optimism among the modernists as many of the restrictive laws were relaxed and Jewish students, for example, were allowed to attend universities in Moscow and elsewhere. But the assassination of Alexander II in 1881 signaled the reimposition of a conservative regime hostile to modernization and Jewish integration. Equally alarming to Alexander III and his chief adviser, Pobedonostsev, was the specter of peasant unrest, especially in southern Russia. A means of diverting peasant hostility from the government lay in tolerating, if not encouraging, attacks on Jewish communities, the catalyst for the decision of some Jews to seek a haven in Palestine.

The first series of attacks, or *pogroms*, erupted in 1881 and lasted until 1884. They consisted of assaults on Jewish quarters accompanied by rapes, looting, and some killing. Rioters were brought to court and some were punished by exile, but the peasants believed they had the tsar's approval and the pogroms continued, encouraged by the tacit support of local officials. The impact of these pogroms lasts to the present day. They signified to many Jews that Russia would never grant them legal emancipation. The result was the beginning of a vast emigration movement which between 1900 and 1914 saw 1.5 million Jews leave Russia. The great majority headed for the United States, but some, especially Jewish students whose hopes for greater equality had been raised during the reign of Alexander II and who had broken with their communal traditions, directed their attention toward Palestine.

This movement became known as BILU, an acronym taken from a passage in Isaiah that inspired the group. Its founders were students from Kharkov who decided to establish agricultural settlements in Palestine. Their success was meager, as most of those who actually settled there soon left. But the ideals of the members of BILU were to leave a lasting impression on later Zionists. They envisaged a Jewish state in Palestine founded on the principles of Jewish agriculture and Jewish labor. And they were quite specific about the need to return to Palestine, the ancient home of the Jews, rather than to seek a haven elsewhere. All these factors would later be part of Zionist labor ideology. Their vision of agricultural communes led ultimately to the forming of the *kibbutzim*, which many saw as the embodiment of Zionist principles.

A more diffuse but longer-lasting organization that arose in 1881–1882 would later be known as Hibbat Zion (The Love of Zion). Circles whose members called themselves Hovevei Zion (Lovers of Zion) began to meet in various cities, including St. Petersburg. They agreed that life in Russia was intolerable and that emigration to Palestine was the only answer. Unlike the BILU, the Lovers of Zion did not undertake immediate practical steps to implement their ideals by founding agricultural settlements in Palestine, but they did expand greatly in numbers in Russia, so that by 1895 they had approximately 10,000 members. The Hovevei Zion included many diverse types who envisaged the restoration of Eretz Israel, including Y. L. Pinsker whose book *Autoemancipation* was published in 1881.

Pinsker was not a firm adherent of a return to Palestine. He believed that Jews had to acquire territory somewhere in order to escape the persecution they experienced in Europe. Although Pinsker wrote his book in response to the Russian pogroms and the plight of East European Jewry, he had little faith in the assimilation process under way in the West. To him Jewish security in Europe was a mirage. A key to his thesis was that Jews had to emancipate themselves rather than relying on non-Jews, an argument that had great appeal to the Lovers of Zion, even though they disagreed with Pinsker's lack of specific commitment to Palestine. Pinsker had written his book as an appeal to German Jews in the West to save their Russian brethren, but he found his audience only in the East. He agreed in 1883 to become head of the Lovers of Zion in Odessa and ultimately became leader of the Hibbat Zion movement until his death in 1891.

In Palestine itself the expansion of Jewish settlements owed little to the Hibbat Zion movement. Indeed, the majority of the Jewish immigrants in the first wave following the pogroms of 1881–1884 were not technically Zionists. They were inspired by religious more than nationalist motives and settled in urban areas. Whereas between twenty and thirty thousand Jews entered Palestine as part of this first wave of immigrants (Aliya), fewer than three thousand settled in the new villages that were established. These agricultural enterprises survived not because of funds from Russian Jews but primarily because of the philanthropy of wealthy Western Jews, such as Moses Montefiore and particularly Baron Edmond de Rothschild of the great banking family, who between 1883 and 1889 gave 1.6 million English pounds sterling to the settlers.[10] But whatever de Rothschild's role was in preventing the collapse of Zionist efforts during this period, he was not a leader of a movement. That task fell to Theodor Herzl, an assimilated Viennese Jew, whose efforts produced the formation of the World Zionist Organization in 1897.

THEODOR HERZL AND THE ZIONIST MOVEMENT TO 1914

The contribution of Theodor Herzl to the development of Zionism was seminal, as many scholars have noted, but they have also stressed that Herzl did not instigate the idea of Zionism. Indeed, for years he was unfamiliar with the strands of Zionist thought and activity current in Eastern Europe. In many ways he was self-inspired in his decision to seek a solution to the question of the Jews in Europe. He had dreamed of being the leader who liberated them even while, as a journalist for a prestigious Viennese paper, he appeared to be well integrated into European culture. The catalyst for his decision to commit himself to the cause of European Jewry was the Dreyfus case, the trial of a French-Jewish officer falsely accused of treason and sentenced to Devil's Island. The trial brought out the vengeance of the French right at what they saw as the undermining of the nation by the liberalization of its laws which included the granting of equality to Jews. It became a *cause célèbre*, with violent anti-Semitic overtones that caused the French left to take up Dreyfus's defense. Herzl had lived in Paris from 1891 to 1895 and was aware of the depth of French anti-Semitism before the Dreyfus case, but it led him to write *Der Judenstaat (The State of the Jews)* which established him as the principal leader of world Zionism.

In *Der Judenstaat*, Herzl called for the creation of a Jewish state that would absorb European Jewry and thus end the anti-Semitism that still prevailed even in Western Europe and proved that assimilation was impossible. Though he was vaguely aware of the plight of Eastern European Jewry and of the intellectual currents then prevalent there (he read Pinsker's *Autoemancipation* after completing *Der Judenstaat*), he directed his appeal to European statesmen and wealthy Jews in the West. He hoped that these Jews would provide financial assistance for the formation of an organization, perhaps a company, that would arrange the transference of Jews to their new home. They could also help persuade European leaders of the validity and feasibility of the idea. Like Pinsker, Herzl was not committed to Palestine, although he did not discount it as the ideal solution. Rather, he preferred to accept empty territory that might be offered, such as sections of Argentina. In this, as in his eagerness to seek the aid of prominent Europeans, Herzl's aspirations were quite different from those of the Lovers of Zion, who emphasized self-help within the Jewish community and stressed the need to reestablish the Jewish state in Palestine. These differences proved to be crucial to the ultimate direction of the Zionist movement. When Herzl called a congress to meet in Basel in 1897 to establish a Zionist organization, he expected to gain the support of the leading Jews of the West. But in fact most stayed away out of fear that his efforts would endanger the status of the newly assimilated Jews in the West. The majority of delegates were from the East, Lovers of Zion who were attracted to Herzl's ideas if not in total agreement with them. At Basel, the World Zionist Organization was formed with Herzl as its president. Its program declared that the goal of Zionism was "the creation of a home for the Jewish people in Palestine to be secured by public law."[11] The real objective was a Jewish state, but it was deemed advisable not to declare that openly because of Ottoman objections to the idea of a new nationality seeking self-rule in its territory.

The question before the first and later congresses was how to pursue their objectives. Herzl favored diplomacy and sought continually to acquire Ottoman approval for Jewish settlement and the idea of a Jewish state in return for Jewish repayment of the by then substantial Ottoman national debt. He wanted official recognition of the Jewish right to have Palestine as a prelude to extensive settlement there and consequently opposed the efforts of East European Zionists to create a de facto Jewish presence in the area. Herzl was alarmed by such practices because he feared they would undermine his diplomatic endeavors. The Ottomans had passed laws forbidding Jews from purchasing land in Palestine, but Zionists evaded them with the aid of foreign consuls and Ottoman Jews sympathetic to their cause. Ottoman officials informed Herzl that Jews could settle in designated areas of Syria and Iraq but not in Palestine, and they could enter Ottoman territory only as individuals, not as a distinct community with political ambitions.

Herzl devoted himself to diplomacy. He visited Constantinople on several occasions and met Sultan Abdul Hamid in 1901. Herzl turned to the British in 1902, seeking the al-Arish area in the Sinai Peninsula because it was adjacent to Palestine and could serve as an opening for future demands for expanded migration to the area. Joseph Chamberlain, then British colonial secretary, replied by suggesting land in British-controlled East Africa, now part of Kenya. Though initially hostile to this idea, Herzl later saw it as granting a temporary haven that might give the Zionists leverage in their demands for Palestine. This led to a major clash with the representatives of East European Jewry who remained steadfast in their commitment to Palestine as the sole objective. They suspected Herzl of being willing to abandon Zionism, a suspicion encouraged by Herzl's secretiveness in diplomacy and his aloof personal style. Herzl's death in 1904 ensured the failure of the project as leadership of world Zionism passed to the Russian Lovers of Zion who stressed the need for practical achievements in Palestine as the prerequisite of political recognition.

Herzl had been unable to gain international recognition of the Jewish right to a state of their own. Toward the end he encountered strong opposition from East European Zionists who stressed the need for continual settlement in Palestine. But the success of their efforts in coming years was to a large degree the result of his endeavors. With his encouragement the World Zionist Organization created its own bank in 1899, and in 1901 the Jewish National Fund was established for the express purpose of purchasing and developing land for Jewish settlement in Palestine. The fund played a major role in the acquisition of land that became inalienably Jewish, never to be sold to or worked by non-Jews, as part of the program to establish a dominant Jewish presence in the area.

Equally important, however, was the ideological commitment of the second wave of immigrants who came to Palestine between 1904 and 1914, among them David Ben-Gurion (née Green) who later became Israel's first prime minister. Many were socialists nurtured in the revolutionary atmosphere then prevalent in Russian intellectual circles. But they were also Zionists who were determined to achieve their socialist ideals within a separate Jewish environment rather than as part of a world movement. Their vision of a new Jewish society entailed a commitment to the land and to the creation of a socialist agricultural basis for the future Israel. In this they fused their socialist ideals with the agricultural vision found in the writings of David Gordon. This new society was to be based on Jewish labor alone, a fact that caused these new immigrants to look down on the earlier generation of Jewish settlers whose farms employed Arabs. The latter's willingness to work with Arabs violated Jewish socialist ideals, as it was class exploitation that included working with non-Jews. Jewish socialism meant to them an egalitarian Jewish society from which Arabs were excluded, a basic tenet of their Zionism. They formed two groups, Poale Zion (Workers of Zion) and Hapoel Hatzair (The Young Worker), both of which strove to create new settlements that reclaimed the land and in which Jews lived a communal life based on socialist principles. They were helped in their efforts by the Jewish National Fund. By 1914, of the forty-four existing Jewish agricultural settlements, fourteen had been sponsored by the World Zionist Organization, the nucleus of Zionist efforts in Palestine from that time onward. Jews owned over 400,000 dunams, of which slightly more than half was under cultivation. Out of the approximately 85,000 Jews then in Palestine, 12,000 lived on the land. Nevertheless, the Zionist drive to purchase land and the openness of their commitment to a separate Jewish entity in Palestine had already aroused Arab fears, which had become well known to Zionist leaders in Palestine by 1914 but were ignored or downplayed by Zionist leaders in the West.

THE ARAB RESPONSE TO ZIONISM

At the turn of the century, Palestine was divided into two principal districts: the northern sector, composed of the sanjaks of Acre and Nablus, was part of the vilayet (Arabic: *wilaya*) of Beirut; the independent governorate of Jerusalem, overseen directly by the Ministry of the Interior in Istanbul, encompassed most of central Palestine. Jerusalem's direct link to the Ottoman capital likely reflected the increased pace of tourism and immigration into southern and central Palestine during the latter half of the nineteenth century, developments that necessitated closer surveillance by the Ottoman authorities of Jerusalem and surrounding areas.

The Arab population of Palestine was overwhelmingly Sunni Muslim. Sixteen percent were Christian, with the Greek Orthodox the dominant sect. Despite local rivalries, there was a sense of community, especially among the Muslims, because of the religious festivals that brought them together from various parts of Palestine and also because of the influence of the highest religious official, the mufti of Jerusalem, whose authority extended into the northern vilayet. The al-Husayni family controlled the post of mufti from the mid-nineteenth century and consequently "was able to win national status" which was buttressed by their hold over various administrative posts in Jerusalem as well.[12] Their ongoing prominence led to British recognition of the then mufti, Hajj Amin al-Husayni, as the leading Arab representative during the Mandate following World War I, but it also contributed to resentment among rival Jerusalem families and in prominent clans in other areas.

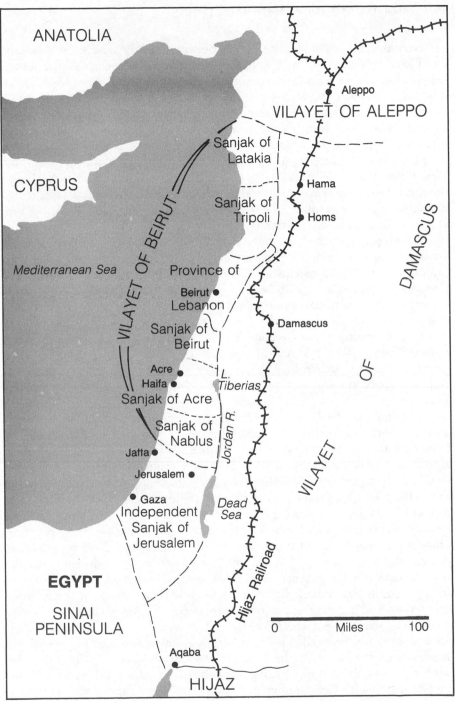

ANATOLIA

CYPRUS

Mediterranean Sea

EGYPT

SINAI
PENINSULA

Aleppo

VILAYET OF ALEPPO

Sanjak of
Latakia

Hama

Sanjak of
Tripoli

Homs

Province of
Lebanon

Beirut

Damascus

Sanjak of
Beirut

Acre
Haifa

L.
Tiberias

Sanjak of Acre

Sanjak of
Nablus

Jordan R.

Jaffa

Jerusalem

Gaza
Independent
Sanjak of
Jerusalem

*Dead
Sea*

VILAYET OF BEIRUT

DAMASCUS

OF

VILAYET

Hijaz Railroad

0   Miles   100

Aqaba

HIJAZ

Map 2. OTTOMAN PALESTINE and SYRIA, 1910

Arab conceptions of identity varied. Beyond local and family ties, Muslims considered themselves to be Ottoman subjects giving allegiance to the sultan/caliph as head of the Islamic community. Christians, especially the Greek Orthodox, seem to have been more aware of themselves as living in a specific region called Palestine, and it is among them that there emerges the dominant journalistic opposition to Zionism. Nevertheless there seems to have existed a general awareness of Palestine as an area distinct from Syria, even if considered part of it for administrative purposes, as reflected in the Ottoman government's term "the land of Palestine."[13] What is clear is that Zionism, with its goal of establishing a dominant Jewish presence in Palestine, revised significantly the Arab conception of the Jews and their place in a Muslim society. Zionists and Zionist claims changed completely the traditional Muslim conception of Jews as occupying dhimmi status, protected by, but subordinate to, Muslims, a role that most Ottoman Jews had continued to play despite the legal equality they had been granted along with Christians as a result of Tanzimat reforms. Zionism, as a European movement, came to be seen initially as another attempt by Western imperialism to subordinate Muslims to Europeans and became even more threatening once it was realized that the Zionists wished to take part of what had been Arab lands for centuries and remake it into a Jewish homeland. Arab opposition emerged before World War I in response to Zionist immigration and land purchases and was shared by Muslims and Christians, despite their sometimes different conceptions of identity as either Ottoman subjects or inhabitants of Palestine.

As noted previously, official Ottoman policy remained consistent toward Zionism from 1881 onward: "Jewish immigrants will be able to settle as scattered groups throughout the Ottoman Empire, excluding Palestine. They must submit to the laws of the empire and become Ottoman subjects."[14] The Ottomans feared the creation of another "national" problem similar to those found in the Balkans which continued to erode their hold on territories they had controlled for hundreds of years. But official Ottoman policy was not effectively realized in Palestine. Jewish immigrants entered Palestine as tourists or pilgrims. Once there, they acquired the protection of foreign consuls, as the European powers were eager to protect their own rights under capitulations laws. Restrictions on land sales to foreigners were circumvented by having Ottoman Jews or foreign consuls buy the land for them. As a result, concern about Jewish immigration and land purchases existed in certain circles in Palestine before the World Zionist Organization was created in 1897. In that year an Arab commission was formed in Jerusalem, headed by the mufti, to examine the issue of land sales to Jews, and its protests led to the cessation of such sales for several years. Jewish agents discovered that it was much easier to buy land in the northern vilayet, and in 1900 the Jewish Colonization Association opened an office in Beirut. Purchases were facilitated both by the fact that many large landholders in northern

Palestine resided in Beirut and by the willingness of the Ottoman officials there to ignore regulations. Similar practices occurred in and around Jerusalem from 1901 onward as the appointed Ottoman governors permitted Jews to buy land in return for financial favors. For example, the Anglo-Palestine Company, the first Zionist organization to be established in Palestine, found that despite Ottoman laws, local Ottoman authorities would permit land sales in return for loans from the company to the governor.

Although Ottoman regulations and protests by Arab officials were often ineffective in blocking Jewish purchases of land, general Arab opposition did not arise during the 1890s and early years of this century. Arab peasants had initially opposed Jewish land purchases, and in cases where they were ousted from their homes, violence and armed resistance did result. Most peasants gradually accepted Jewish landowners, however, because the latter usually permitted them to work the soil and receive income from it, a practice that was condemned by labor Zionists.[15]

Arab protests were infrequent and often seemed to reflect individual rather than general opinion, although it is clear that Arabs outside Palestine were also aware of Zionism. Thus the Syrian Christian-owned journal *al-Muqtataf*, based in Cairo, published an article in 1898 warning against Jewish hopes to control trade in Palestine. The next year Yusuf al-Khalidi, a prominent Jerusalemite, wrote to the chief rabbi of France, telling him that although "historically it is your country" and Zionism could be understood in theory, in practice its implementation would require "brute force," and he pleaded with the rabbi to "let Palestine be left in peace." Rashid Rida, a Muslim reformer born in the Beirut vilayet but living in Cairo, published in 1902 an article in his journal, *al-Manar*, stating that Jews entering Palestine sought national sovereignty there, not simply a haven from persecution. Finally there was the book published in 1905 by Naguib Azoury, a Maronite Catholic, *Le Réveil de la Nation Arabe (The Awakening of the Arab Nation)*, which called for the separation of Arab provinces from Ottoman rule and predicted violent clashes in Palestine between the Arabs and Jews for control of the area. Azoury's call for Arab independence reflected a Christian's, as opposed to a Muslim's, concern for the future of the region. Muslim opinion was still loyal to Ottoman authority, even though some circles were becoming increasingly critical of it. Azoury's discussion of Palestine also reflected the intrusion of European anti-Semitic arguments into the discussion of Jewish aims in Palestine, the result of the Dreyfus affair and French Catholic propaganda.

These protests can be characterized as individualistic, with the exception of the Jerusalem commission of 1897. But they presumably reached an audience receptive to them, especially because *al-Muqtataf* and *al-Manar*, although totally different in character, circulated throughout the Arab world and were read in Christian and Muslim circles respectively. More significant is the nature of the opposition that emerged from 1908 onward, presumably in response to the more strident calls of labor Zionism which openly opposed Jewish employment of Arabs and called for the establishment of a separate Jewish entity in Palestine. These arguments, espoused in the Zionist press and translated into Arabic, became known to increasing numbers of Palestinian Arabs, especially once a Palestinian Arab press appeared in 1908.

Both the editors of the papers most emphatically opposed to Zionism were Greek Orthodox Christians. The papers were *al-Karmil*, created in 1908, and, significantly, *Filastin* (Palestine), founded in 1911; the former was published in Haifa, the latter in Jaffa. *Al-Karmil* was openly pro-Ottoman in its loyalties, although it became increasingly critical of the Committee of Union and Progress, following the Young Turk Revolt of 1908, for failing to protect Palestinian interests. *Filastin* backed the Committee of Union and Progress, but as its name indicates, it stressed local nationalism rather than Ottoman allegiance; it referred to Palestine as an entity and to its readers as "Palestinians."[16] The importance of the press is indicated by the fact that when *Filastin* was first founded, Jews— under Arab pseudonyms—submitted articles to it supporting Zionism. But after 1912, the paper published no such articles.

The fact that most Palestinian Muslims remained loyal to Ottoman authority did not prevent them from agreeing with those Palestinian Christians who led the public opposition to Zionist immigration, land purchases, and, in a general way, Jewish exclusiveness. What the editors of *Filastin* and *al-Karmil* argued in their papers was echoed in the debates in the Ottoman parliament in Istanbul where Arab Muslim representatives from Palestine called for greater Ottoman vigilance against Zionist activities. Consequently, Zionism contributed to a growing sense among educated Muslims and Christians in Palestine of a common identity as Palestinians. This was at a time when Muslim suspicion of Christians because of Ottoman territorial losses in the Balkans was increasing elsewhere in the empire. The rising tensions in Palestine led to outbursts against foreign Christians and Jews, but they usually reflected socioeconomic circumstances in which Muslims found themselves progressively at a disadvantage with respect to outsiders. According to one scholar, most urban disturbances from 1860 onward "broke out in towns where Muslims had originally been in the majority [especially Haifa and Jaffa], but where their majority status either had been obliterated or was seriously threatened by the influx of foreigners and non-Muslims, . . . [and where] poverty, disappointment, jealousy, and exposure to new and unfamiliar ways of life, all combined to produce social instability."[17] By 1914 and the outbreak of World War I, Arab Palestinian suspicion of and opposition to Zionist goals were established, and Zionist officials in Palestine were well aware of Arab fears. The coming of the war presaged new developments of the utmost importance to the expectations of both Arabs and Jews as to the ultimate fate of Palestine.

NOTES

1. Discussion of these matters can be found in two works by Moshe Ma'oz, *Ottoman Reform in Syria and Palestine* (Oxford, 1968); and "Changes in the Position of the Jewish Communities of Palestine and Syria in the Mid-Nineteenth Century," in Moshe Ma'oz, ed., *Studies on Palestine During the Ottoman Period* (Jerusalem, 1975), pp. 142–163. See also the overview by Bernard Lewis, *The Jews of Islam* (Princeton, 1984), pp. 154–159 ff.
2. David Kushner, "Intercommunal Strife in Palestine During the Late Ottoman Period," *Asian and African Studies* 18 (1984): 197.
3. Two travelers' accounts mentioning the destruction of villages are Henry Light, *Travels in Egypt, Nubia, Holy Land, Lebanon and Cyprus in the Year 1814* (London, 1818), pp. 158–159; and William C. Prime, *Tent Life in the Holy Land* (New York, 1857), p. 220.
4. Alexander Schölch, "European Penetration and the Economic Development of Palestine, 1856–82," in Roger Owen, ed., *Studies in the Economic and Social History of Palestine in the Nineteenth and Twentieth Centuries* (Carbondale, 1982), pp. 23–24. My discussion of economic development and land transfers in Palestine is drawn primarily from Schölch and from E. R. J. Owen, *The Middle East in the World Economy, 1800–1914* (New York, 1981), pp. 153–179, 264–272.
5. Owen, *The Middle East*, p. 271.
6. C. Gordon Smith, "The Geography and Natural Resources of Palestine As Seen by British Writers in the Nineteenth and Early Twentieth Century," In Ma'oz, ed., *Studies on Palestine*, p. 90.
7. Amos Elon, *The Israelis*, 2nd ed. (New York, 1983), p. 89. See also Joan Peters, *From Time Immemorial* (New York, 1984), who relies on inadequate data and her own imagination.
8. Haim Gerber, "The Population of Syria and Palestine in the Nineteenth Century," *Asian and African Studies* 13 (1979): 58–80; Yehoshua Ben-Arieh, "The Population of the Large Towns in Palestine During the First Eighty Years of the Nineteenth Century According to Western Sources," in Ma'oz, ed., *Studies on Palestine*, pp. 49–69; Alexander Schölch, "The Demographic Development of Palestine, 1850–1882," *International Journal of Middle East Studies* 17 (November 1985): 485–505, which is an excellent overview of the literature; and Justin McCarthy, *The Population of Palestine: Population Statistics of the Late Ottoman Period and the Mandate* (New York, 1990), an important addition to the literature.
9. David Vital, *The Origins of Zionism* (Oxford, England: Oxford University Press, 1975), p. 74. I rely mainly on Vital for my discussion of Zionism. See also Walter Z. Laqueur, *A History of Zionism* (New York, 1972).
10. Ibid., p. 214.
11. Ibid., p. 368.
12. Y. Porath, *The Emergence of the Palestinian Arab National Movement, 1918–1929* (London, 1974), p. 14.
13. Neville J. Mandel, *The Arabs and Zionism Before World War I* (Berkeley and Los Angeles, 1976), p. xix.
14. Ibid., p. 2.
15. For early Zionist colonization of Palestine and Arab resistance, see two studies: Gershon Shafir, *Land, Labor, and the Origins of the Israeli-Palestinian Conflict, 1882–1914* (Cambridge, England, and New York, 1989); and Rashid Khalidi, "Palestinian Peasant Resistance to Zionism before World War I," in Edward Said and Christopher Hitchens, eds., *Blaming the Victims: Spurious Scholarship and the Palestinian Question* (New York, 1988), pp. 207–233.
16. Mandel, *The Arabs*, p. 128. See also Porath, *Emergence*, pp. 7–8.
17. Kushner, "Intercommunal Strife," p. 199.

CHAPTER 3

World War I, Great Britain, and the Peace Settlements

The outbreak of World War I on 1 August 1914 ended an extended period during which the European Powers had avoided outright conflict. Since the Franco-Prussian War of 1870 and the Russo-Turkish War of 1877–1878, potential great-power clashes had been settled by diplomacy. Past grievances and resentments remained strong, however. The French still hoped to avenge their defeat at Prussian hands in 1870 and remained deeply suspicious of British imperial ambitions. Russia continued to view Constantinople and the straits as its chief prize. Britain strove to maintain the status quo and hence the territorial integrity of the Ottoman Empire, if only because this situation permitted it to guard areas of great strategic importance to Britain, such as southern Iraq and the Suez Canal area, without challenge from other European powers.

Despite their mutual mistrust of one another's motives, Britain, France, and Russia were allies in 1914, having created an Entente that reflected fear of a common enemy more than sincere friendship. The foe was Germany, whose industrial and military expansion since the 1880s, coupled with its aggressive involvement in the race for colonies in the 1890s, aroused general alarm. The British were also wary of Germany's intentions in the Ottoman lands. Germany had gained many concessions from the Ottomans, the most significant in British eyes being that for a railway from Constantinople through Baghdad to Basra and the Persian Gulf. British officials considered southern Iraq as a sphere of military and commercial influence, as well as part of a defense perimeter protecting allies in the Gulf and the oil fields discovered in southwest Iran in 1907. Britain controlled these fields, which were now vital to its military position in Europe as well as Asia: the British navy had gone over to oil in 1912, and the Iranian reserves were the source of its supply. In addition, British agents were investigating potential oil deposits in northern Iraq around Mosul. These matters, plus the growing number of Indian Shi'i Muslims who made the pilgrimage to the shrine at Karbala near Baghdad, made the British extremely sensitive to the threat of German incursion.

Defense of Ottoman territorial integrity was not absolute, however. It served as a means to maintain a European power balance that might otherwise collapse. Thus, the British ambassador in Constantinople wrote to the foreign secretary, Sir Edward Grey, in 1913 that "all the powers including ourselves are trying hard to get what they can out of Turkey. They all profess to the maintenance of Turkey's integrity but no one ever thinks of this in practice."[1] The

European Powers worried about being omitted from the future division of the spoils. If European stability depended for the moment on maintaining Ottoman territory intact, so did future harmony rely on guaranteeing an equitable parceling of Turkish-controlled land according to recognized geopolitical interests. These diplomatic criteria, well grounded in the traditions of nineteenth-century diplomacy, were the bases of British actions in the Middle East once war broke out. They were later altered to meet demands advanced by politicians and British officials in the field who sought to advance Britain's strategic interests at the expense of its allies. It is in this context that one can analyze the nature of the promises and pledges made to the Arabs and Jews during the war that radically transformed the nature and future of the region.

WORLD WAR I: THE OTTOMAN EMPIRE AND THE POWERS TO JULY 1915

Germany's declaration of war on Russia on 1 August 1914 obligated the Turks to enter the hostilities on Germany's side. They had concluded an alliance promising this on the same day. Instead, the ruling officers of the Committee of Union and Progress declared neutrality and maintained it until 2 November. During this interval the Entente powers tried to persuade the Ottomans to remain neutral. Turkish neutrality would be necessary if the straits were to remain open to commercial shipping; this was Russia's lifeline through which it could receive military equipment and export grain, a major source of Russian foreign exchange.

The Entente countries were hampered in their wooing of the Turks by their long-standing policies regarding Ottoman territorial integrity. Their commercial and political involvement in Ottoman lands required that they support the continuation of the capitulations whereby foreigners were free of Turkish law on Ottoman territory. In contrast, the Germans backed the Ottomans when they abolished the capitulations unilaterally on 9 September, an act that drew the muted ire of all three Entente members. British efforts to ensure Ottoman neutrality were further weakened when the government canceled delivery of two cruisers that had been contracted for construction in Britain by the Ottoman government; instead they were diverted to duty with the British fleet to confront the Germans. The Germans seized the opportunity to enhance their status with the Turks by presenting them with two German cruisers, the *Goeben* and the *Breslau*, then on station in the Mediterranean, which avoided British surveillance and steamed into the Sea of Marmora. There they were ostensibly handed over to the Turkish navy, although they retained their German officers and crews. Russia declared war on the Ottomans on 2 November, following an incident in which the *Goeben* shelled Russian installations along the Black Sea while accompanied by Turkish destroyers. The British and French followed suit, and the Ottomans closed the straits to foreign shipping. By the end of the year, Russian munitions supplies were seriously depleted, and the British and the French were concerned about their ally's ability to maintain a formidable presence on the eastern front.

With the Ottoman Empire officially in the war, the British took swift action to ratify their existing occupation of Ottoman territory. In December they declared Egypt a British protectorate and annexed Cyprus. The Russians were pleased, as these actions established a precedent for acquiring Ottoman lands that could be used by Britain's allies as well. British forces sent from India had already landed in southern Iraq in November, taking Basra by the end of the month. Their immediate goal was to secure the oil fields in southwest Iran and territory adjacent to them. British officials in India, commanding the operation, were also eager to establish a British presence at least as far north as Baghdad, with a view to its incorporation into the empire after the war. Security arrangements also were made with tribes in eastern Arabia to secure their cooperation against Turkish forces.

Here India Office officials anticipated future strategic arrangements that London had not yet considered in any specific terms. British statesmen had declared as early as November that the Ottoman Empire should be dismembered because of its entry on the side of Germany, but just how that would be done was unclear, along with what would be claimed by the Entente allies. Grey, the foreign secretary, believed that the Muslim holy places of Mecca and Medina should be independent under an Arab sovereign after the war. Otherwise he was inclined to postpone consideration of the disposition of territories. Thus when Herbert Samuel, later the first British high commissioner in Palestine, submitted a memorandum in November 1914 suggesting that Palestine be considered as the home of the Jewish people, he received little sympathy. Palestine was not viewed as of strategic importance when compared with British interests in Iraq and their concern for the security of the Suez Canal. These attitudes changed, however, as the war progressed and as conditions for harmony among the Entente demanded recognition of individual spheres of interests.

Of particular importance to the fate of Ottoman territorial holdings in Asia was the conduct of the Gallipoli campaign that was approved by Britain and France in January 1915. The idea was to have the fleet storm the Ottoman defenses guarding the Dardanelles and break through to Constantinople. The seizure of the Ottoman capital, ending its involvement in the war, would open the Bosphorus Straits to Allied shipping that could bring badly needed supplies to Russia. The British cabinet already feared that Russia might withdraw, thereby enabling Germany to divert all its forces to the western front against the British and French armies. Keeping Russia in the war was of the utmost importance both in 1915 and with respect to the motives behind the Balfour Declaration of 1917. In addition, the Foreign Office saw the plan's potential for enhancing Britain's postwar bargaining position with Russia, because the British would control Constantinople and the straits. This idea occurred to Russian officials also. In early March they presented London with the demand that at the end of the war Russia be granted control of the straits, Constantinople, and adjacent territory surrounding both. The British were forced to concede the issue, given the war needs of the moment. The result was the Constantinople Convention of March 1915, giving Russia what it had requested. In return, Russia recognized Asiatic Turkey and the Arab lands under Ottoman rule as the special sphere of British and French interests. The following month the Treaty of London was signed whereby the Allies, in return for Italy's entrance into the war, recognized its claims to Libya and to the Dodecanese Islands off the Turkish coast and promised Italy a portion of southern Anatolia to be specified after the war.

In light of these agreements and the obvious disarray within the British war cabinet as to what course it should take, the cabinet appointed a special committee chaired by Maurice de Bunsen in April 1915 to explore a range of options defining potential areas of interest to Great Britain in the Middle East. The de Bunsen Committee delivered its report on 30 June. It identified four possible dispositions of Ottoman territory, ranging from outright partition of the empire into areas controlled by the European powers to a decentralized Ottoman state containing the autonomous provinces of Anatolia, Armenia, Syria, Palestine, and Iraq under nominal Ottoman sovereignty. The committee preferred the latter, a statement that has led some scholars to present the British as essentially not interested in annexing Ottoman territory.[2] Nevertheless, even the decentralization scheme provided for the Russian annexation of Constantinople and the straits, as established in the Constantinople Convention, and for the British annexation of Basra. In addition, the decentralization alternative also advocated the designation of the supposedly autonomous provinces of Iraq and Palestine as special zones subject to British influence exclusively. This recommendation took account of British wishes to build a railway from Haifa in Palestine to Baghdad and Basra in Iraq, creating a direct link between the Mediterranean and the Persian Gulf across British-controlled territory; this would bolster the security of both the empire in India and the Iranian oil fields. Two other proposals offered by the committee reproduced this plan for Britain to control Palestine and Iraq, either outright or as a sphere of exclusive influence; France would be given Syria, including Lebanon, from just south of Damascus into southern Anatolia.[3]

The de Bunsen Committee's alternative recommendations were intended to clarify future discussions on the subject of partition. Its suggestions formed the basis of British policy for the rest of the war, especially with respect to French claims. The committee's schemes stipulated that Mosul and its oil fields be included within Iraq, under direct British control or subject to its influence. The French were to be permitted to have extensive holdings in central and northern Syria, including Lebanon and southern Anatolia, to compensate them for losing Palestine which, as the committee was well aware, the French considered part of their rightful claim within Greater Syria. Palestine with its holy places was to be internationalized so as to avoid complications arising from great power competition and conflicting Christian claims to the area. International status was also a means of blocking French efforts to incorporate Palestine into its sphere. At this point, de Bunsen and British officials in general showed little interest in controlling Palestine, but the committee did recommend that Haifa and Acre be recognized as British enclaves in order to ensure the linkage of imperial communications from Haifa to Iraq. In the words of a British imperial historian, "Britain had thus, only a few short months after the outbreak of the war with Turkey, completely changed its views on the desirability of maintaining Ottoman territorial integrity. Considerable areas of Asiatic Turkey were to be completely detached from Turkish rule and the rest retained only under stringent terms. Even Grey accepted the inevitability of dissection however long he might prefer to delay it."[4]

With the de Bunsen Committee proposals in hand, Grey could now turn to the demands of the French, whose interests in Syria, including Palestine, had been made clear to him in March 1915 when he discussed the matter with the French ambassador in London. But before official talks with France began, Arab claims came to the fore, transmitted by British officials in Cairo acting with some degree of independence from London. Arab aspirations and the need to accommodate them with French interests, or appear to do so, dominated British discussion of the Middle East for nearly a year. Indeed, the consequences of their promises to both remain the basis of Arab grievances to the present.

BRITAIN, THE ARABS, AND THE HUSAYN–McMAHON
CORRESPONDENCE, JULY 1915–JANUARY 1916

In February 1914, Sharif Husayn of Mecca sent his second son, Abdullah, to Cairo to request British aid against the Turks. Sharif Husayn, a member of the clan of the Hashim to which the Prophet Muhammad belonged and the official guardian of the holy places of Mecca and Medina, was an Ottoman subject and held his post by their approval, but he was eager to retain as much autonomy as possible. Alarmed by Ottoman plans to extend the Hijaz railway to Mecca, Husayn deputized Abdullah to seek British support to keep them out of the Hijaz. The British response was negative. Lord H. H. Kitchener, then consul general in Cairo, informed Abdullah that Great Britain would not supply arms to be used against a friendly power. But ten months later when Britain declared war on Turkey, Kitchener, now secretary of war in the British cabinet, cabled Ronald Storrs, oriental secretary at the British Agency in Cairo, with instructions concerning Husayn. Storrs was to inform Husayn that in return for any assistance that the Arab nation might give to the British, they would defend the Arabs against external aggression, protect Husayn against internal threats, and support the principle that an "Arab of true race" might become caliph in Mecca. This message, with embellishments by Storrs, was delivered to Husayn and created the basis for a relationship that lasted throughout the war.

The reasons for the British interest in Husayn and the Hijaz were clear. They believed that Husayn might inspire an Arab revolt that at the least could divert the Ottoman troops from positions threatening the Suez Canal. At the most, as envisaged a year later, such a revolt might entail a massive uprising throughout the Arab Middle East that would completely undermine Ottoman security in the area. In return, Kitchener and Storrs promised British protection and the installation of the caliphate in Mecca with Husayn presumably as caliph. These promises were not made out of regard for Husayn alone. Indeed, the British were endowing Husayn with more prestige than he had within the Arab Middle East. His power was confined to the Hijaz, and he was challenged by Arab tribes in eastern Arabia, especially by the Wahabbi reform movement identified with Ibn Saud, who himself was being funded by British officials in India.

Nevertheless, the British were eager to spur Arab aspirations for freedom from Turkish rule. They were aware of separatist sentiments among Arab officers in the Ottoman army and presumably wished to encourage them to look to the British rather than the Turks for fulfillment of their hopes. As a result, British officials in Cairo, without apparently consulting London, sent a letter to Abdullah in December 1914, the contents of which were also distributed in the Arab world generally. In it Storrs addressed the "natives of Arabia, Palestine, Syria, and Mesopotamia" and promised them that Great Britain had no designs on their territories after the war. He then stated that if the Arabs rebelled and drove out the Turks, the British would recognize and help establish Arab independence "without any intervention in your internal affairs."[5]

The sincerity of such statements was clearly questionable. British officials in Cairo as well as London were uncertain as to what form or extent any independent Arab entity should have after the war. All accepted Grey's conception of an independent Arabia, meaning the peninsula, with the caliphate in Mecca. Kitchener and Storrs apparently hoped that this caliphate could rule a British-protected Syria despite their knowledge of French ambitions, which they hoped to reward elsewhere. Their wartime alliance notwithstanding, British officials looked with suspicion upon French territorial claims in the Middle East as threats to their legitimate spheres of interest; the feeling was mutual. Grey might consider a division of the spoils to be necessary and proper, but Kitchener saw France as a potential postwar enemy that should be thwarted in its demands for any territory adjacent to the Suez Canal and Arabia. He and others saw Palestine as occupying the crucial position of a buffer between potential French-held areas and Egypt. Initially, an internationalized Palestine with British enclaves would suit British imperial needs; later, a Palestine promised to the Zionists seemed to do the same.

Once under way, the Husayn–McMahon correspondence embraced issues that went beyond the reservations and contingencies that London believed necessary. The exchange began with a letter from Sharif Husayn to Storrs in

Cairo, dated 14 July 1915. Husayn demanded a great deal, namely, that Great Britain recognize the "independence of the Arab countries" whose boundaries encompassed all of Greater Syria, including Palestine, Lebanon, Iraq, and the Arabian Peninsula. The only exclusion would be Aden, to which Britain's rights were acknowledged. The British would proclaim an Arab caliphate as well. In return, the sharif would grant the British "preference in all economic enterprises in the Arab countries."[6] Husayn also requested an answer within thirty days, or he would be free from all obligations suggested in his letter.

The British were annoyed by Husayn's claims but unwilling to reject them out of hand. Henry McMahon, now high commissioner in Cairo, seems to have acted with some latitude despite suggestions sent to him by the Foreign Office and by officials at the India Office. The latter were backing Ibn Saud and questioned whether Husayn had support in Arabia for his claims to the caliphate. McMahon sent a response to Husayn, dated 30 August, which was far more encouraging than London intended. He affirmed with pleasure Husayn's view that British and Arab interests were the same. He then declared that "we hereby confirm to you the declaration of Lord Kitchener [November 1914] . . . in which was manifested our desire for the independence of the Arab countries and their inhabitants and our readiness to approve an Arab Caliphate upon its proclamation." McMahon also noted British willingness to have the caliphate in the hands of "a true Arab born of the blessed stock of the Prophet."[7] Beyond this, McMahon deferred consideration of the specific boundaries on the advice of London, arguing that the war and Arab passivity under Turkish rule precluded a discussion of the details. Nevertheless, McMahon had gone beyond London's instructions and even what Kitchener had written to Abdullah in November 1914. Kitchener had never promised "the independence of the Arab countries" but, rather, had referred to the freedom of the Arabs. McMahon's reference to this independence, omitted from some studies of the correspondence and its implications, seemed to acknowledge Husayn's demands in almost identical language while avoiding mention of the boundaries in question.[8]

Husayn replied on 9 September 1915. He stressed his unhappiness at British hesitancy to acknowledge the "essential clause" in his first letter, namely, the matter of boundaries. Nevertheless, he indicated his eagerness to have Britain's response, intimating that an Arab revolt in Turkish-occupied territory awaited a favorable reply. Although Husayn had dispatched his elder son, Faysal, to contact Arab nationalist circles in Damascus, his ability to instigate a rebellion seemed exaggerated. Then coincidentally, his promises seemed to be supported by a Syrian officer in the Ottoman army who defected to the British and arrived in Cairo in September 1915. Muhammad Sharif al-Faruqi impressed British officials there with his knowledge of Husayn's demands; apparently members of his circle had been in contact with Husayn and probably inspired his first letter to Storrs in July.[9]

Al-Faruqi's appearance, coupled with Husayn's letters, created a sense of urgency among British officials in Cairo, perhaps encouraged also by the disasters of the Gallipoli campaign, in which Britain and France suffered a major defeat at the hands of the Ottomans, causing British officials to worry about a loss of face in Arab eyes. At the same time al-Faruqi intimated that Husayn's requests might be modified. In imparting their alarm to London, British officials noted that the Arabs apparently wished for autonomy in Palestine and Iraq under British guidance and that they would resist the French occupation of Syria.[10] What emerged, as McMahon cabled Grey, was the idea of including the "districts of Aleppo, Damascus, Hama, and Homs," Syrian cities regarded as purely Arab, in the area to be promised to the Arabs. Grey instructed McMahon to tell Husayn that the Arabian Peninsula and the Muslim holy places would be independent. But he cautioned that the British would probably want to control most of Iraq, a sphere in which Husayn and al-Faruqi proposed British guidance, not total authority. Grey did not refer to Syria except to warn against any general encouragements that might alarm the French. Still, Grey emphasized the need to "prevent the Arabs from being alienated" and left McMahon to decide the exact phraseology of his response.

With this leeway and feeling the need to encourage the Arabs to side with the British, McMahon wrote to Husayn on 24 October 1915 with promises that became the basis of Arab claims that Great Britain betrayed them after the war. McMahon acknowledged Husayn's concern about the definition of boundaries and outlined British recognition of Arab areas of independence subject to reservations, which he left in some cases deliberately vague. He argued that northwest Syria (Mersin and Alexandretta) and "portions of Syria lying to the west of the districts of Damascus, Homs, Hama, and Aleppo" were not "purely Arab" and would be exempted from Arab areas of postwar self-rule. The provinces of Baghdad and Basra in Iraq were to be placed under British administrative supervision, presumably with Arab autonomy, in order to safeguard British interests, and Britain's arrangements with shaykhs along the coast of the Persian Gulf would remain in force. Other than that, and with the stipulation that the Arabs seek only British assistance to establish their government(s), McMahon stated that in the areas "where Great Britain is free to act without detriment to the interests of her ally France," it pledged "to recognize and uphold the independence of the Arabs in all the regions lying within the frontiers proposed by the Sharif of Mecca" and would protect the holy places against external aggression. These areas appeared to include, at the least, central Syria, including Damascus, Homs, Hama, and Aleppo, northern Iraq, and Arabia.

This declaration, though apparently specific in certain instances, was intended to promise more than it would fulfill. A bone of contention has been the use of the word *district* to refer to Damascus, Homs, Hama, and Aleppo. The Arabic word used was *wilaya* which usually meant province and was employed in that sense with respect to Basra and Baghdad in the same letter. But when referring to the four Syrian cities, it signified to McMahon "cities" and adjacent environs, a meaning clear in McMahon's own references to the term and the areas involved.[11] The importance of this distinction lies in what was intended to lie west of these "districts." If they meant cities, as McMahon felt at the time, then the areas west of them would incorporate an area from the Lebanon, including Beirut, in the south extending north beyond Alexandretta, already omitted from the region that Husayn had demanded. In this interpretation, Palestine, unmentioned in the letter, was not specifically excluded from the Arab territory to be independent after the war. The British later claimed, however, that the term *wilaya* signified administrative district when applied to Damascus. According to this interpretation, the *wilaya* of Damascus included eastern Palestine, the land across the Jordan River, and hence omitted western Palestine, which by this time had been promised to the Zionists by the Balfour Declaration. It is clear from subsequent developments that the British never intended to cede Palestine to the Arabs, despite private acknowledgment by some officials that McMahon's letter seemed to include it.

Later confusion over the place of Palestine in the Husayn-McMahon correspondence can be attributed to oversight and incompetence, but no such excuse can explain McMahon's evasiveness regarding his reference to French interests in the 24 October letter. As explained to Grey, McMahon was careful not to be precise regarding areas France might seek: "While recognising the towns of Damascus, Homs, Hama, and Aleppo as being within the circle of Arab countries, I have endeavoured to provide for possible French pretensions to those places" by simply referring vaguely to areas "where French interests might exist."[12] In other words, whatever the apparent specificity of McMahon's pledges to Husayn concerning Damascus, Homs, Hama, and Aleppo, he was deliberately leaving their disposition open to future French claims. British officials in Cairo did not feel bound by the promises implicit and even apparently explicit in McMahon's first two letters to Husayn; they felt that terms like statehood and independence were meaningless to the Arabs. At the same time they used these terms to attract Arabs to the British side. McMahon's letters of 30 August and 24 October 1915 seemed to promise independence, subject to the Arabs' rebelling, whatever the interpretations he and his aides preferred to place on them. Such independence, when applied in light of the proclamation sent to Abdullah in December 1914, included Palestine, Syria, and Iraq.

McMahon was careful in the remaining letters of the exchange to emphasize the closeness of French-British relations and the need for the British to accommodate French interests at the end of the war, though he mentioned only Beirut and Aleppo specifically. Husayn reiterated his belief that the two cities were Arab and emphasized his opposition to French control of any Arab land. The correspondence ended on a note of agreement to disagree until the end of the war with regard to Lebanon and northern Syria. Husayn acknowledged British interests in Iraq and accepted their temporary occupation of it in return for their assistance of Arab development there. The issue left outstanding was that of French demands which by this time, January 1916, British diplomats in London knew that they had to curtail, not out of concern for Husayn, but to protect their own interests in the region.

THE SYKES-PICOT AGREEMENT AND THE HUSAYN-McMAHON CORRESPONDENCE

British diplomats had long known of French aspirations in Syria and Palestine and had discussed the matter informally with their French counterparts in the spring of 1915. On 21 October, one day after he advised McMahon to give Husayn sufficient assurances to bind him to the British side, Grey proposed to the French that they appoint a representative to discuss the prospective partition of Ottoman lands. He did so not out of concern for potential obligations to the Arabs but because he assumed, mistakenly, that British troops were about to enter Baghdad. Assuming that Iraq, considered vital to postwar British interests, had been effectively secured, Grey felt able to discuss with France the disposition of other areas.

The principal negotiators were Georges Picot, a diplomat with wide experience in the Middle East, and Sir Mark Sykes, a member of Parliament seconded to military service, an Arabist who had no official diplomatic experience but whose closeness to Kitchener enabled him to gain access to policymaking circles. Picot insisted initially on all of Syria, Lebanon, and Palestine, from the Egyptian border in the Sinai to the Taurus Mountains in Turkey. Sykes, influenced by the de Bunsen Committee report, was determined to create a belt of English-controlled territory from the Mediterranean to Iraq and the Persian Gulf. He also wished to block French ambitions in Palestine by having it granted international status, again in keeping with the de Bunsen recommendations. But to accomplish this, Sykes decided to cede Mosul to the French sphere of influence to be created in Syria and northern Iraq, contrary to the de Bunsen report. Finally he gained Picot's agreement to have Damascus, Homs, Hama, and Aleppo "included in the territories administered by the Arabs under French influence."[13] Here Sykes operated on the basis of the assurances given to him by al-Faruqi during their conversation in Cairo in November 1915, ignoring Husayn's known opposition to French advisers.

The Sykes–Picot Agreement, officially ratified in May 1916, defined areas of direct and indirect British and French control in Arab lands and southeast Turkey. The British would occupy Iraq from Baghdad south to the Gulf; they would have indirect authority in a region designated as their exclusive sphere of influence that ran from the Egyptian border through eastern Palestine into northern and southern Iraq, thus protecting the Baghdad-Basra axis and establishing the linkage to the Mediterranean recommended by the de Bunsen Committee. The French were allotted Lebanon and coastal Syria as their areas of direct control, along with southeastern Turkey (Cilicia); their sphere of indirect influence included the rest of Syria from just west of the "districts" of Damascus, Homs, Hama, and Aleppo through northern Iraq, including Mosul, to the Iranian border. In the areas of direct authority, both countries would have the right "to establish such direct or indirect administration as they desire and as they think fit to arrange with Arab State or Confederation of Arab States." In the spheres of indirect influence, each would "have priority of right of enterprise and local loans . . . and shall alone supply advisers or foreign functionaries at the request of the Arab State or Confederation of Arab States."[14] The terminology indicates the degree of control presumably assigned, to be imposed as each power should "think fit" in the areas of direct authority, to be asserted "at the request" of the Arab state(s) in the latter. Palestine was internationalized, the type of administration to be determined after discussions with Russia, other allies, and Sharif Husayn. The British were given the ports of Haifa and Acre as enclaves under their authority and gained the right to build and control a railway from Haifa to Baghdad.

For the most part, the Sykes–Picot Agreement met British more than French territorial objectives. Sykes's willingness to grant the French a sphere of influence across Iraq to the Iranian border reflected Kitchener's desire, based on nineteenth-century strategic principles, that Britain should never share a frontier with the Russians; the French thus served as a buffer in that Russia had been granted land in northeastern Turkey. Some scholars view the agreement as compatible with McMahon's pledges to Sharif Husayn, reached "in order to obtain international recognition for and confirmation of McMahon's promises to the Sharif."[15] This seems doubtful. Both British and French officials seem to have assumed that they would have what amounted to protectorates throughout their respective territories, whatever the Arabs' expectations. McMahon could promise Husayn in his letter of 13 December 1915 that "Great Britain does not intend to conclude any peace whatsoever, of which the freedom of the Arab peoples and their liberation from German and Turkish domination do not form an essential condition."[16] But he could also defend himself against charges of promising too much to Husayn, by arguing that

> I do not for one minute go to the length of imagining that the present negotia- tions will go far to shape the future form of Arabia or to either establish our rights or to bind our hands in that country. . . . What we have to arrive at now is to tempt the Arab peoples into the right path, detach them from the enemy and bring them over to our side. This on our part is at present largely a matter of words and to succeed we must use persuasive terms and abstain from haggling over conditions.[17]

In short, if there were no specific contradictions between the pledges given to Husayn and the areas demarcated in the Sykes–Picot Agreement, it was only because McMahon did not intend to be precise in his letters to Husayn.

On the other hand, British officials soon came to view the Sykes–Picot Agreement itself as a temporary wartime collusion. As we shall see, they hoped to take advantage of their superior military presence in the Arab Middle East at

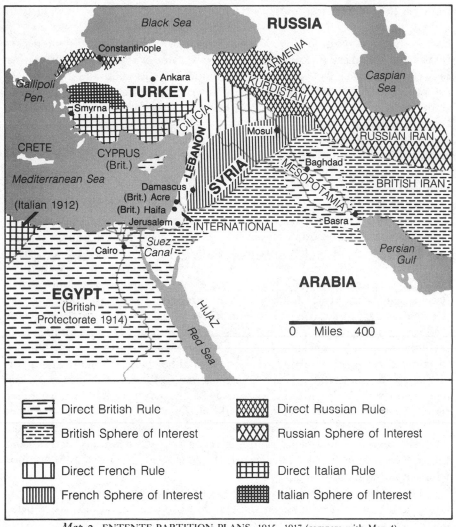

Map 3. ENTENTE PARTITION PLANS, 1915–1917 (compare with Map 4)

the end of the war to gain total control of the area, either through direct occupation or through sponsorship of an Arab state in Damascus. At this time the pledges to Husayn became a means of blocking British obligations to the French under Sykes–Picot, and vice-versa; neither European power saw the two sets of promises as compatible. The discrepancy between promise and intent widened as the war progressed, and Great Britain and France issued more assurances of independence to the Arabs while Britain awarded Palestine to the Zionists as their national home.

PALESTINE AND THE BALFOUR DECLARATION

For the first two years of the war, Palestine was of little strategic interest to British policymakers in London. Its primary value was as a potential buffer between French-controlled territory in Syria and Lebanon and British-held Egypt. Hence Mark Sykes advocated the internationalization of Palestine while reserving Haifa and Acre for British suzerainty. Even when British statesmen began to pay more attention to Zionist urgings to support the idea of a Jewish state in Palestine, they did not necessarily consider Britain as the logical protector of Palestine. Some, including the foreign secretary, Arthur Balfour, wished to hand over authority in Palestine to the United States if internationalization were no longer the accepted procedure.

British interest in Zionism and Palestine increased as 1916 drew to a close. The Asquith government fell, and David Lloyd George, long sympathetic to Zionism, now became prime minister. He was eager to involve himself in all aspects of foreign policy, to the frequent alarm of the Foreign Office. Also, 1917 saw the beginning of revolutionary ferment in Russia that soon toppled the tsarist regime and ultimately brought the Bolsheviks to power. Concern that Russia might withdraw from the war, permitting the Germans to concentrate all their forces against France and Britain in the West, led to efforts to promote Zionism as a means of persuading Russian Jews—believed to be influential in revolutionary circles—to support Russia's war effort. Finally, the British hoped to gain American aid and troops to assist them. They believed that their support of Zionism would lead American Jews to encourage President Woodrow Wilson to enter the war on the side of the Entente. All these factors, added to a concern for the fate of European Jewry, led to the Balfour Declaration of 2 November 1917 that promised a national home for the Jews in Palestine. Though this did not meet Zionist requirements totally, it went a long way toward recognition of a future Jewish state in Palestine and was recognized as such by those in London who supported its proclamation.

The issuing of the Balfour Declaration was the result of intense activity and lobbying by several leading Zionists, the most prominent and persuasive being Chaim Weizmann, who became the first president of the state of Israel. Weizmann was born in the Pale of Settlement, in southern Russia. His family was relatively well-off. This and his intelligence enabled him to leave Russia for Switzerland, where in 1904 he received his doctorate in chemistry from the University of Geneva. In 1908 he left Switzerland for England and a post at the University of Manchester, where he remained until 1916 when he took up special work in the employ of the British government: he was engaged in experiments leading to advances in munitions manufacture. An ardent Zionist, Weizmann had been deeply involved in World Zionist Organization activities in Europe from the turn of the century. Once in England, he soon acquired prominence inside and outside Jewish circles. A persuasive speaker and conversationalist, he converted several prominent Manchesterites to his cause, most notably C. P. Scott, editor of the *Manchester Guardian*. In one sense, British willingness to issue the Balfour Declaration was largely due to Weizmann's efforts. During the war he established ties with important personalities within the British government, including Mark Sykes, who supported Zionism. But the Balfour Declaration would not have come about without the blending of Weizmann's arguments regarding the value of Zionism to British interests with the emergence of events that seemed to prove him right and that caused British officials to decide that they wished to control Palestine rather than permit it to be internationalized.

Before the change of governments in London in December 1916, British policy toward the Middle East had been designed generally in accordance with the idea of an equitable division of the spoils among the allies. Consequently, Herbert Samuel's memoranda in November 1914 and January and March 1915 advocating British sponsorship of a Jewish Palestine were for the most part ignored. British control of Palestine did not suit a division of the spoils in which Russian and French interests were balanced, whereas internationalization of the region and its holy places did. Nevertheless, Weizmann and others were active in their lobbying efforts during this period, and various British officials pursued the idea, especially because of its potential value to the British war effort. Thus Lord Crewe, personally sympathetic to Jewish aspirations, instructed the British ambassadors in Paris and Petrograd on 11 March 1916 to discuss with host government representatives the idea of an appeal to world Jewry to support the Entente war effort in return for Britain's backing of Zionism. In his view, the "Zionist idea has in it the most far-reaching political possibilities, for we might hope to use it in such a way as to bring over to our side the Jewish forces in America, the East and elsewhere which are now largely, if not preponderantly hostile to us."[18] British sympathy at this time did not indicate a willingness to assume control of Palestine as the Zionists wished; rather, they still favored an international administration of the area.

Lloyd George's accession to the prime ministership in December 1916 coincided with a reassessment of Britain's war objectives by the military command. As the trench warfare dragged on with appalling casualties on the western front during the spring and summer of 1916, British statesmen and generals began once more to look favorably upon a campaign in the East. The General Staff proposed a campaign into Palestine, to be undertaken in the autumn of 1917, and it met with the full approval of Lloyd George and his cabinet in January 1917. Along with the military criteria, however, there was now a political one associated with American policy. President Woodrow Wilson, in a speech on 18 December 1916, called for "peace without victory," an ending to the conflict in order to stop the carnage. The Lloyd George cabinet opposed this idea, but they were in a difficult situation in that they were becoming increasingly reliant on American goods and were eager to bring the United States into the war militarily on the side of the Entente. Aware that Wilson would oppose a

British occupation of Palestine in principle as indicating imperialist tendencies, it was then proposed to link the British campaign with the support of Zionism. If done, then American Jews close to Wilson might persuade him to support the occupation. The advocate of this idea was C. P. Scott, not only a confidant of Weizmann's but very close to Lloyd George as well. Sympathetic to Zionist aspirations, he also saw a British-controlled Palestine as a vital strategic asset guarding the Suez Canal and thus Britain's imperial lifeline. Linking support of the Jews to Britain's interests was thus a means of furthering Britain's immediate wartime needs while ensuring its long-range imperial goals.

Also eager to assist the Zionists was Mark Sykes, for much the same reasons. He too sympathized with Zionist hopes to regain Palestine and was now converted to the idea that Palestine—rather than being internationalized as stipulated in the Sykes–Picot Agreement—should be taken over by the British. Sykes was in a key position in that Lloyd George had appointed him assistant secretary to the war cabinet to oversee Middle Eastern affairs. He was aware that to occupy Palestine would require that the French be finessed. Sykes thus hoped to amend the Sykes–Picot Agreement to get Palestine for Great Britain. An alliance with British Zionism "provided a way to outmanoeuvre the French without breaking faith [sic], and a useful card at the future peace conference to play against any move by Germany to rally the German-oriented and Turcophile Jews to buttress her claim" for a role in the region.[19] But the Foreign Office was still wedded to the idea of the Entente and the Sykes–Picot Agreement, whatever Balfour's personal sympathy for Zionism. Sykes thus undertook his own diplomacy without consulting the Foreign Office, but with the blessings of Lloyd George.

Sykes's efforts bore fruit because of new developments that threatened the war effort. In March the first Russian Revolution produced developments that foreshadowed Russia's possible withdrawal from the war. At the same time, the new Russian government denounced imperial schemes for dividing up territories after the war. In addition there was Woodrow Wilson's campaign for nonannexation and his known sympathy for the principle of self-determination, to be officially promulgated with his declaration of the "fourteen points" in January 1918. Zionism now seemed even more attractive, for to support it was to back the idea of Jewish self-determination in Palestine. It thus "provided a cloak under which Britain could appear free from any annexationist taint" while ensuring for itself control of the area.[20] Sykes felt pressure to gain a declaration also because of rumors that the Germans were considering a pro-Zionist declaration. This was particularly threatening because most American Jews were inclined toward Germany rather than Great Britain, if only because of the latter's alliance with Russia. Nevertheless, Weizmann and Sykes were aware of Wilson's sympathy with Zionist aspirations, communicated to them by Louis Brandeis, Supreme Court Justice, who headed the Zionist organization in the United States and who was close to the American president. The immediate problem was France. Sykes, in consultation with British Zionists, pressed for French recognition of

Zionist aims. In June, Jules Cambon, the French foreign minister, gave assurances that the French supported "the renaissance of Jewish nationality" in Palestine, in part because they saw it as a means of encouraging Russian Jews to press the provisional government to stay in the war. Nevertheless, the French statement permitted the British, in their view, to proceed with the formulation of a statement acknowledging Jewish claims to Palestine without going into the question of their own planned control of the area, a matter the French opposed strongly. Lord Walter Rothschild, titular leader of the British Jewish community, was invited in June 1917 to submit a draft proposal outlining Jewish goals for consideration by the government.

The process resulting in the Balfour Declaration reflected disagreements within the British Zionist community as well as opposition to the idea in the cabinet. Weizmann favored a version that declared British support for "the reconstitution of Palestine as a Jewish State and as the National Home of the Jewish People." This draft, written by Harry Sacher, contained the phrase "Reconstitution of Palestine as a Jewish State" rather than "in Palestine" because the latter might enable the Arabs in Palestine to control the state administration: "give the Arabs all the guarantees they like for cultural autonomy; but the State must be Jewish."[21] The London Zionists disagreed. They thought Sacher was demanding too much too soon, although a state was certainly the Zionist objective. Hence Lord Rothschild submitted a draft that requested British recognition of Palestine "as the National Home of the Jewish People" and acceptance of the Zionist Organization in Palestine as an autonomous, self-governing body representing the Jews there until they achieved a majority. By early August a statement incorporating Rothschild's criteria was prepared for Balfour's signature. British and French leaders now feared even more acutely that Russia might withdraw from hostilities, and British officials sought more American aid, both economic and military. Although the United States had declared war on Germany in April, only a token military force had been sent; large military detachments would not arrive until January 1918. The temporary mutiny of French troops in the spring had presented the specter of Britain's being forced to fight the Germans alone, bereft of French as well as Russian aid. A favorable response to the Zionist request could be used as the basis of a propaganda push in both Russia and the United States. But no decision was immediately forthcoming, in part because of substitutions made by cabinet members and in part because of the concerted effort by the secretary of state for India, Edwin Montagu, the only Jew in the cabinet, to block the declaration altogether.

Montagu's objections stemmed mostly from his feeling that a declaration in support of a Jewish state in Palestine, defining the Jews as a separate nation, would threaten the position of assimilated Jews in countries where they had established themselves as citizens. It would raise the question of loyalties and might well result in demands that English Jews, for example, renounce their citizenship and go to the new Jewish state. He saw Jews and Judaism as comprising a culture but not a nation and believed that granting national status to Jews would arouse European anti-Semitism by emphasizing Jewish distinctiveness. Montagu's campaign, though disruptive, alone did not delay the declaration. Bureaucratic inertia also played a part, along with the time taken to consider drafts from cabinet officials that modified the proposed August statement accepting Rothschild's letter. Of vital importance to the final version of the Balfour Declaration were the modifications made by Lord Milner. He favored a statement supporting "the establishment of a home for the Jewish people in Palestine," a version that omitted the idea of nationhood and the concept that such a nation or a home should possess all of Palestine. He did so out of concern both for the fate of the Arab population and for the security of British interests, notably in India and Egypt.

Finally, renewed alarm about Russian intentions and rumors that the Germans were considering a pro-Zionist proclamation in order to persuade the Russians to withdraw from the war led to cabinet debate over the Zionist request. On 31 October the war cabinet met with Balfour speaking in favor of a declaration. He argued that

> from a purely diplomatic and political point of view, it was desirable that some declaration favorable to the aspirations of the Jewish nationalists should now be made. The vast majority of Jews in Russia and America, as indeed all over the world, now appeared to be favorable to Zionism. If we could make a declaration favorable to such an ideal, we should be able to carry on extremely useful propaganda both in Russia and in America.

In Balfour's view, the term *National Home* was acceptable, but he clearly envisaged it as signifying the ultimate accomplishment of "an independent Jewish State." The cabinet approved a draft known as the Balfour Declaration, issued as a letter to Lord Rothschild on 2 November 1917. It stated:

> His Majesty's Government view with favour the establishment in Palestine of a national home for the Jewish people, and will use its best endeavours to facilitate the achievement of this object, it being clearly understood that nothing shall be done which may prejudice the civil and religious rights of existing non-Jewish communities in Palestine, or the rights and political status enjoyed by Jews in any other country.

The last clause took account of Montagu's fears concerning the place of Jews in Western society. The preceding clause incorporated Milner's concern for the future of the then Arab majority of 90 percent in Palestine, but it was modified to specify that their civil and religious rights would be respected. This ensured that political rights would be allotted only to the prospective Jewish community once it attained a majority.[22]

With the Balfour Declaration announced, propaganda commenced. Leaflets were dropped over German and Austrian troops, urging the Jews to look to the Entente powers because they supported Jewish self-determination. American

Jewish groups undertook publicity designed to encourage greater commitment to the war effort. Great celebrations erupted in Russia but had little effect on events. The Bolsheviks had gained power on 7 November, denounced wartime treaties, and entered peace negotiations with the Germans in December. Without the Russian contribution, Britain and France might well have lost the war if it had not been for the decision of the United States to commit itself more fully to the Entente and to send large detachments of troops, beginning in January 1918.

The Balfour Declaration was not based solely on British evaluations of self-interest and immediate war aims. Key British statesmen had a deep sympathy for Zionism, sparked both by a Christian interest in the land of the Old Testament and by a sense of guilt at Europe's treatment of the Jews. Balfour, Lloyd George, and Sykes all were Zionists in part because of these feelings, sentiments that Weizmann exploited masterfully in private interviews in which he addressed the question of Zionism in light of his listener's concerns, religious fulfillment, or strategic interests.[23] These innate affinities for Zionism played an important role in that the Jews, unlike other "small nationalities" who were seeking self-determination, were not a majority in the land they claimed. Rather, they had to acquire recognition of their right to the land based on history, namely, their possession of it two thousand years before. Once this right was recognized, Palestinian Arabs were automatically denied the same right, an assumption derived both from sympathy for the Jews and, in Britain's case, from an evaluation of which group would better suit its imperial desiderata. Sympathy alone would not have resulted in the Balfour Declaration.

THE GREAT POWERS, ZIONISM, AND THE ARABS, 1917–1918

British Middle East policy continued to be influenced by individuals eager to extend British power in the region despite apparent contradictions in promises made to different parties. Many pledges already made had been given with an eye to postwar negotiations. Mark Sykes backed Arab, Jewish, and Armenian claims for independence. He apparently assumed that conflicts among them could be ironed out after the war; the important thing was to have Britain appear to back self-determination in order to negate attempts by rival European powers to extend their own influence in the area. Impulsive by nature, Sykes then wrote several more statements that promised independence to various Arab groups, even though they contradicted other arrangements he had previously helped formulate. Nevertheless, his ideas were backed by the war cabinet, at times over the objections of officers in the field.[24]

In March 1917 British forces took Baghdad. The cabinet issued a declaration written by Sykes that told the Iraqis they should look to Sharif Husayn of the Hijaz who had "expelled the Turks and Germans" and concluded by encouraging them to collaborate with "the Political Representatives of Great Britain . . . so that you may unite with your kinsmen in the North, South, East, and West in realizing the aspirations of your race."[25] British representatives in Iraq thought such a statement went beyond the political awareness of most Iraqis, but it was designed to encourage the Iraqi officers with Faysal to look to the British, apparently to ensure their cooperation after the war. Admittedly and intentionally vague, the statement did suggest a future independent status quite different from that intended for them by the British.

In May, Sykes and Picot went to the Hijaz to discuss the Sykes–Picot Agreement with Sharif Husayn. Here Husayn rejected French claims to inner Syria as a sphere of influence along with control of the Lebanon. He changed his mind only after being informed, falsely, by Sykes that the French role in the Lebanon would be the same as that of the British in Baghdad, that is, as advisers only. This was the basis of Husayn's acceptance of the Sykes–Picot Agreement, even though his understanding of it was wrong regarding Baghdad as well as the Lebanon. That is, Baghdad was within the zone of direct British control, not that of influence dependent on consultation with the sharif.[26]

Once the Balfour Declaration was issued, instructions were sent to the Arab Bureau in Cairo that further "assurances" be transmitted to Husayn. Sykes again wrote a declaration referring to the Arab race's achieving independence as a nation and proclaimed the British government's support for Jewish aspirations to return to Palestine only "in as far as is compatible with the freedom of the existing population, both economic and political. . . ."[27] This statement, with assurances of political freedom for Palestinian Arabs clearly not contained in the Balfour Declaration, led Husayn to indicate his unconcern. David Hogarth, the British agent delivering the message, reported that Husayn "left me in little doubt that he secretly regards this (Palestine) as a point to be reconsidered after the Peace, in spite of my assurance that it was to be a definitive arrangement."[28] Husayn welcomed Jews to Arab lands, said Hogarth, a formula that recalls previous Ottoman policy. But as Hogarth noted, "the King would not accept an independent Jewish State in Palestine, nor was I instructed to warn him that such a State was contemplated by Great Britain. He probably knows little or nothing of the actual or possible economy of Palestine and his ready assent to Jewish settlement there is not worth very much."[29] Husayn's acceptance of Jewish immigration in Palestine was thus part of their immigration into Arab lands in general, but he opposed a Jewish state, a Zionist goal that Hogarth refrained from imparting to him. It seems that Husayn, having been informed—with deliberate omissions—of the various arrangements made by the British, assumed that they would amount to nothing: "he has real trust in the honour of Great Britain . . . and is more assured than ever both of our power to help him and the Arabs, and of our intention to do so, and . . . he leaves himself confidently in our hands."[30] This of course was unwise.

To a degree Husayn was deluding himself. He had initially claimed rulership over the entire Arab Middle East, had left areas subject to dispute in his exchange with McMahon, and had been informed of various agreements undertaken by the British with France and the Zionists. His awareness of these agreements bolstered later British arguments that they had been open with him and that he and Faysal had no right to claim that they had been deceived by the British. Yet whatever Husayn's delusions of grandeur, he had been deliberately misled in the Husayn–McMahon correspondence as to France's goals; he had been intentionally misinformed by Sykes as to the exact terms of the Sykes-Picot Agreement; and he had been assured by Sykes, through Hogarth, that Zionist immigration would not compromise the political and economic freedom of the Arab population of Palestine. This had happened because the British needed Husayn and the continuance of the Arab revolt, even though they realized that Husayn's position in the Arabian Peninsula was shaky, let alone the doubtfulness of his appeal to Arabs in Syria, Iraq, and Palestine. In return, Husayn needed the British to facilitate creation of his kingdom in these areas, which made him more than willing to accept British explanations of the meaning of their arrangements. British actions were in keeping with Reginald Wingate's analysis of the overtures made to Husayn in 1915: "After all what harm can our acceptance of his proposals do? If the embryonic Arab state comes to nothing all our promises vanish and we are absolved from them—if the Arab State becomes a reality we have quite sufficient safeguards to control it."[31] Thus Wingate, though overruled, proposed in January 1918 to counter Ottoman propaganda by advising Husayn that the inhabitants of Syria, Palestine, and Iraq could control their destinies after the war. And in June of that year he lied to Husayn by telling him that the Sykes–Picot Agreement no longer existed, a statement made without London's approval but later accepted by officials there.

Wingate's overtures in 1918 were part of a British reaction to a propaganda offensive undertaken against them in the first half of the year. The Bolsheviks' publication of the secret agreements dividing up the Middle East gave most Arabs their first news of them. The Ottomans seized the opportunity to publicize the treaties, advising the Arabs that British promises were meaningless. In addition, President Woodrow Wilson proclaimed his fourteen points in January 1918: their advocacy of self-determination received immense publicity in the Middle East as elsewhere. Finally, these developments occurred at that moment when British forces had occupied most of Palestine and were planning their assault on Syria where they hoped to meet a receptive populace. Jerusalem had been taken in December 1917, at which time General Edmund Allenby announced that in the East, Great Britain sought "the complete and final liberation of all peoples formerly oppressed by the Turks and the establishment of national governments and administrations in those countries deriving authority from the initiative and free will of those peoples themselves."[32] These promises were repeated in June 1918 in a statement issued by British officials in Cairo to a delegation of Syrians, then residing in Cairo, who asked what British intentions were with regard to Arab territories. The Syrians were apprehensive not only about British motives but also about the possibility of being placed under the rule of Sharif Husayn, whom they viewed as an upstart. The British responded with the "Declaration to the Seven," which promised the following: in Arab territories independent before the war or liberated by Arab forces, Great Britain recognized the "complete and sovereign independence of the Arabs." In regard to those areas freed from Turkish rule by Allied military action, the British called the Syrians' attention to the Baghdad proclamation of March 1917 and Allenby's Jerusalem declaration of December: the future government of such lands should be based on the consent of the governed. This condition presumably applied to the southern half of Palestine, including Jerusalem and Jaffa, and Iraq from Baghdad south. As for regions still under Turkish domination, namely, northern Palestine, Syria, and northern Iraq, the British promised to work for the "freedom and independence" of their inhabitants.[33]

The expectations aroused by these promises were considerable once they became known. The French, on the other hand, strongly suspected the British of trying through such proclamations to justify excluding them from Syria. Their fears were confirmed when Damascus was taken in the autumn of 1918. Allied troops destroyed Turkish resistance, but Faysal and his Arab forces were permitted to be the first detachment into the city. Damascus was thus "liberated" by the Arabs, presumably ensuring that it would be independent. Allenby allowed Faysal to establish himself in Damascus where he proceeded to set up an Arab administrative system and government. Allenby interpreted the Sykes–Picot Agreement to mean that French military officials could occupy only Lebanon, west of the districts of Damascus, Homs, Hama, and Aleppo. Though correct in the strict interpretation of the accord, Allenby's decision did not fulfill French expectations of their rights to inner Syria, especially when Faysal's creation of an Arab government led the British to try to undermine Sykes–Picot by a *fait accompli*. An independent Arab state under British sponsorship would preclude French occupation of the area and align the British with Arab nationalist aspirations. Lloyd George pursued this tack until August 1919 when he finally acceded to French insistence on their right to Syria. In the meantime British and French officials made one final pledge of freedom to the Arabs following the Armistice of Mudros, signed on 30 October 1918, when the Ottomans capitulated. In this announcement, dated 7 November, which was posted throughout Palestine, Syria, and Iraq, the two powers promised once more to support the creation of national governments in Syria and Iraq derived from "the initiative and choice of the indigenous populations" and elected by their free will. This statement, which contradicted British and French intentions, was designed to calm the inhabitants and facilitate occupation of the region.[34]

The war was now over in the East, and the armistice in the West was imminent. The Arabs had been promised much more explicitly and publicly in 1918 what had been only implied to Sharif Husayn. Anticipation ran high in Damascus, but there was already unease in Palestine, where British statements seemed to conflict with Zionist aspirations as embodied in the Balfour Declaration. Reports from officials in Palestine of Arab unrest inspired the British to send a Zionist delegation led by Weizmann in the spring of 1918. Once there, he met with Palestinian notables and later with Faysal. In both instances he told his opposites that the Zionists did not intend to create a Jewish government in Palestine or "to get hold of the supreme power and administration" there.[35] Though untrue, this declaration served to allay Arab fears and protests about Zionist goals which had been inspired largely by Zionists in Palestine; with the Balfour Declaration they had immediately begun to proclaim statehood as the Jewish dream. But if the Arabs in Palestine were alarmed about the Zionists' intent, Weizmann was himself fearful of what the British might do, when confronted with Arab protests, to undermine the Balfour Declaration. As he saw it, British administrators in Palestine were "distinctly hostile to Jews" because in trying to be fair to both sides, they threatened to undermine Jewish prospects. The British were acting according to "the democratic principle, which reckons with the relative numerical strength, and the brutal numbers operate against us, for there are five Arabs to one Jew. . . ."[36] Indeed, Weizmann believed that British fairness played into the hands of "the treacherous nature of the Arab" who exploited it to seek to gain the advantage.

Insofar as Palestinian Arab and Zionist feelings were concerned, the lines were drawn, although Weizmann hoped to gain Faysal's recognition of Zionist aims in Palestine in return for the latter's support of Faysal against the French. This seemed a possibility on the eve of the Peace Conference in January 1919 when Faysal and Weizmann signed an agreement embodying these principles, but Faysal then appended a statement repudiating his support of Zionist immigration into Palestine unless he gained his independent Arab state in Syria. With this both men entered the Peace Conference, in which Faysal was abandoned by the British and Weizmann and the Zionists gained further confirmation of their right to Palestine.

THE PEACE SETTLEMENTS

The British found themselves at the end of the war in a far more advantageous position than the French in regard to their respective Middle East objectives. British forces had occupied Palestine, Syria, and Iraq. French efforts to guarantee recognition of Palestine's international status had failed. In Syria Faysal had been installed as head of what became a Syrian Arab government, and French officials had been denied access to Damascus. On the other hand, French leaders felt in December 1918 that they had acquired British recognition of their claims to Syria. As noted earlier, the British were eager to revise, if not abrogate, the Sykes–Picot Agreement. On 1 December 1918 Georges Clemenceau, the French prime minister, and Lloyd George met in London to seek to settle potential areas of dispute before the Peace Conference began. When Clemenceau asked what the British sought from France, Lloyd George responded that he wanted Mosul incorporated into Iraq plus British control of Palestine. Both these points significantly changed the status of the affected areas as established in the Sykes–Picot Agreement. Clemenceau agreed immediately. Thus an understanding was reached, although it was made orally and in private, apparently so that both parties could not be held accountable for opposing self-determination when they met with Woodrow Wilson. France did not come away empty-handed. In return, Lloyd George apparently agreed to Clemenceau's demands that the remaining portions of the Sykes–Picot Agreement be upheld, with the important proviso that Aleppo and Damascus be included with Lebanon in the area under direct French control. And it is certain that the French were promised a share of Middle East oil in return for ceding Mosul to the British zone.[37] Lloyd George had gained Palestine, but apparently at Faysal's expense.

Having made this private agreement with Clemenceau, Lloyd George, with Foreign Office encouragement from Lord George Curzon, tried to break it with respect to Syria. Their idea, approved during December 1918, was to establish exclusive British sway in the French sphere of influence as delineated in the Sykes–Picot Agreement. This meant backing Faysal in Damascus on the basis of self-determination for the Arabs while giving the French only the Lebanon and the Syrian coast, including their much-desired port of Alexandretta. This policy seemed to have a chance of success, given the predominance of British forces in the region, but it infuriated the French during the ensuing negotiations that occupied much of 1919. On at least one occasion Clemenceau and Lloyd George nearly came to blows.

In the meantime, British support for Faysal was further weakened by their backing of Zionist claims to Palestine which were rejected by the Syrian National Congress; this in turn caused Faysal to repudiate outright his tentative agreement with Weizmann of January 1919 and to claim that Palestine had been promised to the Arabs in the Husayn–McMahon correspondence. Faysal's arguments were recognized as having some validity, especially by Curzon, but only in the sense that there seemed to be contradictions in the promises made to both Arabs and Jews throughout the war. On the other hand, the Zionist delegation to the Peace Conference had submitted a memorandum to the British before the conference began, asking that Palestine be acknowledged as the Jewish National Home and that its administration be by Great Britain during a period in which immigration would permit its development "into a Jewish commonwealth . . . in accordance with the principles of democracy."[38] The delegation also defined the boundaries of Palestine to include southern Lebanon up to and including the Litani River, the east bank of the Jordan, and the Sinai Peninsula to al-Arish. And the Jewish communities in Palestine were to be allowed as much self-government as possible, presumably meaning that the British administration sought by the Zionists was to oversee the Arab community alone. These demands were later scaled down significantly.

The dilemma faced by the British government during the first half of 1919 was one that its members recognized clearly. They approved in principle the idea of self-determination, if only to mollify Wilson's suspicions regarding European ambitions in conquered lands. They were now backing Faysal's call for an Arab state in Damascus on the basis of self-determination, in order to block French claims that the British had supposedly acknowledged as valid. But when faced with Palestinian Arab demands for the right to self-determination, Britain rejected them in favor of Jewish proposals. This, according to Balfour, was morally right: "Our justification . . . is that we regard Palestine as being absolutely exceptional; that we consider the question of the Jews outside Palestine as one of world importance and that we conceive the Jews to have an historic claim to a home in their ancient land; provided that home can be given them without either dispossessing or oppressing the present inhabitants."[39]

These arguments were made in the context of discussion on the type of rule that the powers would impose on the territories given to them. Woodrow Wilson had consistently opposed the annexation of land as spoils of war; he had also advocated the creation of a League of Nations after the war to provide a forum for settling international disputes peacefully. The Covenant of the League of Nations, reluctantly accepted by the British and French, included Wilson's fourteen points and provided a formula whereby former German or Ottoman territories could be taken over temporarily by the world powers. This was the mandate system. The country awarded a mandate over a given area accepted it with the understanding it would encourage the development of political, economic, and social institutions to the point that self-government would result and the mandatory power would withdraw. It was thus a system of tutelage, although British and French officials viewed it principally as a means of legitimizing their control of desired territories while satisfying Wilson's concerns for the application of the principle of self-determination. In theory, however, the opinions of the regions' inhabitants should be ascertained. The Arab lands were designated class A mandates, meaning that they were judged to have "reached a stage of development where their existence as independent nations can be provisionally recognized subject to the rendering of administrative advice and assistance by a mandatory power until such time as they are able to stand alone. The wishes of these communities must be a principal consideration in the selection of a mandatory power."[40]

It was the last sentence that created the problem. The United States proposed forming a commission to ascertain the desires of the inhabitants of Syria, Iraq, and Palestine as to the power that should guide them to independence. The French and the British, already at odds over Syria, attempted to block any delegation from going to the Middle East. The British then finally agreed, in part to force the hand of Clemenceau who refused to appoint French delegates, thus giving the British the excuse to back out. In the end, American envoys, designated as the King–Crane Commission, set out for the Middle East to ask the preferences of the inhabitants, while the British and French continued their acrimonious discussions in Paris and London. The commission interviewed Arabs and Jews in Palestine as well as inhabitants of Syria and Lebanon but did not go to Iraq. It concluded that one Arab state of Greater Syria, including Lebanon and Palestine, should be created, with Faysal as its king and the United States as the mandatory power; the second choice was Great Britain. A majority of the commission favored a drastic curtailment of the Zionist program which should be limited to an expanded Jewish community within the Arab state. The report was submitted to the Peace Conference but was not published or considered by the diplomats there. There is little doubt, however, that the commission's findings accurately reflected both Zionist hopes and Palestinian Arab fears and opposition to Zionism as well as the Syrians' anti-French sentiments.[41]

As the summer wore on, Balfour reviewed Britain's apparent obligations set against the wishes of the resident populations in the Arab world. The Sykes-Picot Agreement bound the British, rightly thought Balfour, to give Syria to the French despite Faysal's and the Syrian Arabs' obvious preference for either independence or the United States or Great Britain as the mandatory power. The Anglo-French Declaration of November 1918 had promised to build governments in accordance with the inhabitants' wishes, principles found also in the criteria for mandates enshrined in the Covenant of the League of Nations. But in Balfour's view, these promises could not be reconciled with others: Palestine was a "unique situation" in which "we are dealing not with the wishes of an existing community but are consciously seeking to re-constitute a new community and definitely building for a numerical majority in the future." In this light, the opinions of the Palestinian Arabs were not important, however understandable they might be. The Allies were violating the principles of the Covenant because the powers (including the United States) were "committed to Zionism. And Zionism, be it right or wrong, good or bad, is rooted in age-long traditions, in present needs, in future hopes, of far profounder import than the desires and prejudices of the 700,000 Arabs who now inhabit that ancient land." That, in Balfour's view, was also "right," although he recognized that "so far as Palestine is concerned, the Powers have made no statement of fact which is not admittedly wrong, and no declaration of policy which, at least in the letter, they have not always intended to violate."[42]

Confronted with domestic problems resulting from demobilization and from the cost of maintaining troops in postwar ventures, Lloyd George decided in September to withdraw from Syria and let Faysal deal directly with the French. This in essence meant giving the French a free hand there once they had sufficient troops. In the meantime the Allies agreed to distribute the mandates as decided upon in the Lloyd George–Clemenceau conversation of December 1918. This occurred at the San Remo Conference in April 1920 where the French were given mandatory rights in Syria and Lebanon, the British in Palestine and Iraq. The Balfour Declaration was included in the obligations for the mandatory power in Palestine, thus binding Great Britain to establish conditions whereby the incoming Jewish population would be assisted in their path toward ultimate dominance in Palestine. The mandates were ratified by the League of Nations in July. French-Arab skirmishing had begun in May. Determined to oust Faysal, whose presence symbolized Arab nationalist aspirations, the French commander in Beirut presented him with a series of ultimatums and then marched on Damascus, even though Faysal accepted them. Damascus fell to the French on 24 July, and Faysal was escorted to British Palestine; the British later installed him as the king of Iraq.

The ratification of the mandates by the League of Nations confirmed the agreements finally reached by Great Britain and France after bitter recriminations. Yet the powers, especially the British, found themselves still mired in the Middle East while trying to restore a semblance of normalcy to life at home. In Turkey the British backed the Greeks whom they had permitted to land in Asia Minor in the summer of 1919. But the Greek occupation of Asia Minor and subsequent invasion of Anatolia spurred Turkish resistance which culminated in the complete collapse of the Greek offensive in August and September 1922. The Greeks were driven into the sea by Turkish national forces who occupied most of Anatolia and precipitated a near confrontation with Allied troops in Constantinople. The British were forced to back down, and Turkish independence in Anatolia was acknowledged in the Treaty of Lausanne, signed on 24 July 1923.

The British also found themselves facing armed resistance in the Arab Middle East. A rebellion broke out in Iraq in May 1920 and lasted through the summer. There were many casualties, and reinforcements from India had to be sent. British officials, civil and military, were alarmed primarily about the expenditures that their commitments were requiring at a time when British citizens were demanding a return to peacetime standards of living. Winston Churchill was particularly concerned. He had been appointed secretary of state for war in 1919 and became colonial secretary in January 1921. He had been awarded responsibility for Palestinian and Iraqi affairs, with a specific Middle East department established under his authority. Churchill was determined to try to stabilize the British position in the Middle East while drastically cutting expenditures at the same time. He and advisers such as T. E. Lawrence arranged the Cairo Conference of March 1921 to pursue such goals. It was here that they agreed to install Faysal in Baghdad, "the best and cheapest solution," and decided to grant to his brother Abdullah eastern Palestine which now became Transjordan.[43] This was done over Zionist objections, though they were made privately. Churchill acted on the advice of Lawrence, who declared that the Damascus *wilaya* included eastern Palestine. While this permitted western Palestine to be allotted to the Zionists according to the Husayn-McMahon correspondence, it also legitimized the awarding of eastern Palestine to the Arabs. Neither the Arabs nor the Jews were entirely satisfied with this arrangement, but it remained in force. It permitted the British to withdraw troops from eastern Palestine and cut expenses. With the Cairo Conference, the British

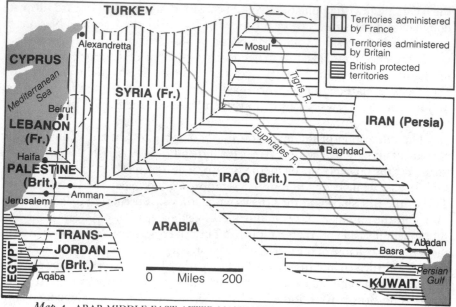

Map 4. ARAB MIDDLE EAST AFTER MANDATE ALLOCATION AT SAN REMO

distribution of land and titles ended. Then began the process of striving to lower imperial costs while maintaining a strong presence in the face of growing Arab nationalism, a tightrope act that did not end until 1954.

Our focus on the Middle East must be balanced by the awareness that many of the decisions affecting it were made during the war with a view to their European and worldwide impact, not to their implications for the region's inhabitants. The Gallipoli campaign, designed to save Russia, led to the Constantinople Convention of 1915 which set in motion events resulting in the Sykes–Picot Agreement, itself intended to harmonize Allied relations by satisfying mutual aspirations in the region. Promises of independence and later of governments based on the consent of the governed were products of wartime expediency and, in the latter case, the desire to show conformity with Wilsonian principles and ensure American support and cooperation. The Balfour Declaration, whatever the Old Testament inspiration of Lloyd George, was essentially granted because of its long-range promise of a stable bastion governed by a people friendly to British imperialism, and a short-term advantage believed to be the attraction of world Jewry to the side of the Entente.

What emerges most clearly is the nature of the great powers' decision-making process which, in the words of one student of the Eastern Question, was "exceedingly informal, flexible, and by design almost, amateurish." Individuals rather than governments or united cabinets made decisions and "where senior statesmen floundered, the influence of pressure groups or unofficial grey-eminence confidants could sometimes be decisive."[44] This was less so in Britain and France than among the Central European powers, but it clearly existed, especially as evidenced in the waning role of the British Foreign Office under Grey during 1915–1916 when the initiative passed to men in the field and it appeared "that Grey felt totally out of his depth."[45] With the accession of the Lloyd George government, the influence of the Foreign Office lessened further as the prime minister took an active and decisive part in Middle East policy. Here the personal access of Weizmann was crucial to convincing British officials that Zionism was in the interests of the British and did not challenge their imperial aspirations, a benefit that was less sure to be derived from support of the Arabs.

Finally, there was the natural assumption of European statesmen that they had the right to dispose of foreign lands as they wished, conditional on the agreement of their rivals rather than the wishes of the lands' inhabitants. Imperialism and the security of imperial interests were the crux of nineteenth-century great power relations, based on the economic as well as military and political advantages to be derived from direct or indirect control of territory. Here Zionism melded with British assumptions of their right to deal with territories as they saw fit. Zionism was also "right" because it was part of a European experience—the persecution of the Jews—that had to be redressed. That it was admittedly a unique situation was part of its appeal, and this in turn meant, at least in the beginning, that Palestinian Arab opposition was of little import.

But to Jews and to Palestinian Arabs, the struggle was really just beginning. Each rejected the idea that the British had an obligation to the other. The idea of fairness under the mandate, of encouraging the development of self-governing institutions, could apply only to themselves, not their rival. For the British to attempt to balance the scales was, to the Arabs, a denial of their basic rights, to the Jews the same, and to some signifying the anti-Semitism of the British administrators in the bargain. There was to be no harmonizing of these conflicting conceptions of "right," a gap reflected also in the vastly disparate circumstances and habits of an incoming population schooled in Europe and a native, Eastern people living in a nearly traditional society. If the Palestinian Arabs believed that their right to the land stemmed from historical precedent acknowledged by the powers for other peoples and found in Allied promises made during the war, the Jews believed that they had a right because of history, both Middle Eastern and European. They had lived there as a majority two thousand years before, and their pariah experience in Europe justified their achievement of independence and normalcy in the land of their distant origins. This too had been recognized during the war, by a power that was able and willing to impose its will in favor of Zionism. That will would be tested severely as the mandate took shape.

NOTES

1. Marian Kent, "Constantinople and Asiatic Turkey, 1905–1914," in F. H. Hinsley, ed., *British Foreign Policy Under Sir Edward Grey* (Cambridge, England, 1977), p. 155.
2. Isaiah Friedman, *The Question of Palestine, 1914–1918: British-Jewish-Arab Relations* (New York, 1973), p. 21.
3. This division recognized French wishes to possess the port of Alexandretta in northern Syria. The fourth proposal placed Alexandretta in a British zone giving direct access to Iraq.
4. Marian Kent, "Asiatic Turkey, 1914–1916," in Hinsley, ed., *British Foreign Policy*, p. 444.
5. Elie Kedourie, *In the Anglo-Arab Labyrinth: The McMahon–Husayn Correspondence and Its Interpretations, 1914–1939* (Cambridge, England, 1976), p. 21.
6. The complete correspondence can be found in George Antonius, *The Arab Awakening* (New York: Capricorn Books, 1965), pp. 413–427.
7. Ibid, pp. 415–416.
8. Kedourie, *Labyrinth*, pp. 69–70, omits the reference to "the independence of the Arab countries" from his quotation of the passage and from his discussion of it, focusing his attention on the promise of the caliphate to Husayn.
9. Ibid, pp. 74–75.
10. Ibid, p. 81. But al-Faruqi told Mark Sykes in November that the Arabs might accept French advisers.
11. Ibid, pp. 99–103.
12. Ibid, pp. 98–99.
13. Jukka Nevakivi, *Britain, France, and the Arab Middle East, 1914–1920* (London, 1969), p. 33.
14. Ibid, p. 261.
15. *Labyrinth*, p. 198. See also Friedman, *Palestine*, p. 112.
16. Antonius, *Arab Awakening*, p. 424.
17. Quoted in Kedourie, *Labyrinth*, p. 120.
18. Friedman, *Palestine*, p. 57.
19. Ibid, p. 126.
20. Ibid, p. 175.
21. Ibid, pp. 252–253.
22. Ibid, pp. 275–280, traces the final stages of approval of the Balfour Declaration.
23. Friedman, p. 283, quotes from Sir Charles Webster, *The Art and Practice of Diplomacy* (London, 1961), pp. 5–6, in which Webster recalls how Weizmann "with unerring skill . . . adapted his arguments to the special circumstances of each statesman. . . .".
24. Elizabeth Monroe, *Britain's Moment in the Middle East, 1914–1956* (London, 1963), pp. 40–41. For the Foreign Office's and Chaim Weizmann's impressions of Sykes, see Zara Steiner, "The Foreign Office and the War," in Hinsley, ed., *British Foreign Policy*, p. 526; and Weizmann, *Trial and Error* (New York: Schocken Books, 1966), p. 181.
25. Quoted in Monroe, *Britain's Moment*, p. 41.
26. Kedourie, *Labyrinth*, pp. 165–177, has a long discussion of this meeting and Sykes's maneuvers.
27. Quoted in ibid, pp. 189–190. On pp. 282–284, Kedourie disputes the claim of Antonius that Hogarth's message was a significant reduction of the commitments made by the British to the Zionists in the Balfour Declaration because it recognized the political rights of the Palestinian Arabs, not simply their civil and economic rights as stated in the declaration. Kedourie rejects Antonius's analysis as "worthless" and concludes that the paragraph in question "is no more than a reiteration of the Balfour declaration. . . ." Given the evidence we have on the British intent to grant political rights in Palestine only to the Jews, Hogarth's message was clearly not "a reiteration of the Balfour Declaration," and Kedourie's contemptuous dismissal of Antonius can be applied more justly to his own conclusions. On the other hand, Antonius's claim that Hogarth was reducing the scope of the Balfour Declaration (*Arab Awakening*, pp. 267–268) is probably not true. Hogarth, following Sykes's lead, was stringing Husayn along. As shown below, he refrained from telling Husayn, in the same conversation, that the Zionists intended to form a state. Nevertheless, Antonius is correct to argue that what Husayn could have understood about the Balfour Declaration from Hogarth's version was indeed a significant misrepresentation of what the declaration actually entailed. Friedman, p. 328, follows Kedourie's argument.

28. Kedourie, *Labyrinth*, pp. 189–190.
29. Quoted in Leonard Stein, *The Balfour Declaration* (London, 1961), p. 633.
30. Quoted in Kedourie, *Labyrinth*, p. 191.
31. Quoted in ibid, p. 46.
32. Quoted in Doreen Ingrams, *Palestine Papers, 1917–1922: Seeds of Conflict* (London, 1972), p. 20.
33. The text is in Antonius, *Arab Awakening*, pp. 433–434.
34. Ibid, pp. 435–436. Palestine was mistakenly included in the distribution of the leaflets.
35. Ingrams, *Palestine Papers*, p. 30.
36. Ibid, p. 32.
37. Nevakivi, *Arab Middle East*, pp. 89–93. Equally if not more important was Lloyd George's pledge to come to French aid if the Germans attacked.
38. Ingrams, *Palestine Papers*, p. 53.
39. Written on 19 February 1919 and quoted in ibid, p. 61.
40. Paul C. Helmreich, *From Paris to Sevres: The Partition of the Ottoman Empire at the Peace Conference of 1919–1920* (Columbus, 1974), p. 27.
41. The standard source for the history of the commission is Harry N. Howard, *The King–Crane Commission: An American Inquiry in the Middle East* (Beirut, 1963).
42. All quotations are from Ingrams, *Palestine Papers*, p. 73.
43. Martin Gilbert, *Winston S. Churchill*, Volume 4: *The Stricken World 1916–1922* (Boston, 1975), p. 546. For more extended discussion of the Cairo Conference and British concern about expenditures, see Aaron S. Klieman, *Foundations of British Policy in the Arab World; the Cairo Conference of 1921* (Baltimore, 1970).
44. Both quotations are from G. D. Clayton, *Britain and the Eastern Question: Missolonghi to Gallipoli*, London History Studies, no. 8 (London, 1971), p. 245.
45. Steiner, "The Foreign Office and the War," p. 528. See also Marian Kent, "Great Britain and the End of the Ottoman Empire, 1900–1923," in Kent, ed., *The Great Powers and the End of the Ottoman Empire* (London, 1984), pp. 188–189. Friedman, *Question of Palestine*, attributes far too much importance to Grey's warnings about annexation as indicative of the actual course of British policy.

Palestine between the Wars: Zionism, the Palestinian Arabs, and the British Mandate

The Palestine that the British forces entered in December 1917 was quite different from what had existed in 1914. It had served as a staging area for Ottoman troops throughout much of the war and finally as a battleground. Many foreign residents and recent immigrants had either left or were forcibly deported at the outbreak of war. The Turks conscripted thousands of Arab peasants and confiscated their crops. There was extensive deforestation as the occupation progressed and wood was needed for fuel. These developments, coupled with locust plagues and poor crop yields owing to bad weather and labor shortages in villages, led to the impoverishment of sectors of the Arab peasantry, accompanied by malnourishment and susceptibility to disease spreading into the cities among the poorer inhabitants, Christian and Jewish as well as Muslim. The immediate task of the British government was to provide food and medical supplies to the destitute and to restore social and economic order to the region.[1]

In the midst of these efforts, British officials found themselves confronted almost immediately with Arab hostility toward Zionism, inspired both by awareness of the Balfour Declaration and by the actions of many Jews in Palestine who believed that the achievement of a Jewish state was imminent. The Zionist Commission arrived in April 1918 to act as the representative of the Zionist movement. Granted status as a semi-independent body by the Foreign Office, the commission could either request concessions from British military and civilian authorities in Palestine or intervene in London to countermand decisions made by these authorities if it thought them unfavorable. Soon after their arrival, members of the commission asked military officials to grant the Hebrew language equal status with Arabic in all official proclamations, appoint Jews as government officials, appoint a Jew as mayor of Jerusalem, and move to ensure that half the members of the municipal council of Jerusalem were Jewish. British officials complied with the first two demands and also acceded to the Zionist Commission's request that Jewish government employees be granted higher pay than Arabs, in that as Europeans, they needed higher salaries to live on. Zionists were permitted to fly the Zionist flag, symbol of their aspirations to sovereignty, but Arabs were prohibited by government order from flying theirs.

These actions had a devastating effect on the Palestinian Arabs still recovering from the war. Traditional Ottoman society had defined the places of Christians and Jews vis-à-vis Muslims, as we have seen. Prewar Zionist activities had not disrupted the traditional political and social order, but this was now threatened by the appearance of militant Jews demanding and receiving equal status with Arabs, granted by a British government apparently fulfilling Zionist wishes. Knowledge that during 1919 certain Jewish papers were calling for the forced emigration of Palestinian Arabs to Faysal's Arab state in Syria also roused alarm.[2] Arab fears were only partially tempered by British reassurances. Zionist celebrations on 2 November 1918, the first anniversary of the Balfour Declaration, led to several clashes between Arabs and Jews, followed by a petition to the British authorities protesting Zionist immigration and the idea that Palestine was to belong to the Jews and not to the Arab population. The Anglo-French Declaration of 7 November, inadvertently publicized in Palestine, temporarily mollified Arab unrest, but such unintended assurances were soon countered by Zionist activity. As a result, joint Muslim-Christian groups, initially formed in early 1918, now coalesced into the Muslim-Christian Association that first appeared in Jaffa and then Jerusalem in November of that year. Made up of leading notables among the Muslim and Christian Arab communities, the association became for a while the leading Palestinian nationalist forum and, as such, was encouraged by the British military authorities who wished to create a balance to Zionist activities.[3]

British military officials in Palestine were clearly sympathetic to the Palestinian Arabs, in part because of what they saw as Zionist abrasiveness in demanding Jewish rights immediately and going behind their backs to London if they were not satisfied. In addition, they saw Zionist calls for statehood as threatening the stability of the British imperial presence in Palestine, which required a country free from the strife that compliance with Zionist wishes would bring. In this they were at odds with British politicians in London, many of whom saw Zionism as the primary cause of Britain's presence in Palestine that enabled it to justify its occupation of the region.[4] A pattern emerged that continued throughout the 1920s. Most local British authorities and those who came to investigate the disturbances invariably began to sympathize with Arab views, whereby the British government, out of concern for its imperial presence as well as sympathy for Jewish needs and awareness of domestic political considerations, sided with the Zionists.

High British officials continued to back Zionism until Britain's imperial position seemed threatened by the resentment of other Arab countries at the onset of World War II. These officials then issued a White Paper in 1939 that essentially repudiated the Balfour Declaration and seemed to ensure Arab domination of a future Palestinian state. This shift, even more than the Balfour Declaration, was dictated by expediency and resulted in armed conflict between the British and Zionist forces, the subject of the next chapter.

THE FIRST PHASE: HOPES FULFILLED AND DASHED, 1918–1920

During this period, the Zionist leadership, headed by Chaim Weizmann, was concerned principally with acquiring great power recognition of the Zionists' right to Palestine. Although Weizmann told the delegates to the Peace Conference that he envisioned Palestine's becoming as Jewish as England was English—a statement that further added to Arab alarm in the country—he was himself disturbed by local Zionist enthusiasm and claims of immediate statehood and sought to downplay their "undue exuberance," referring to demands that included the possible deportation of Palestinian Arabs to Syria.[5] The Palestinian Arabs, on the other hand, had fewer options and less scope for their pursuit. The end of 1918 found Palestine united under a single administration, for the first time in centuries. But unity brought with it the potential for rivalries among different families and groups whose traditional bases of power and prestige might not be recognized at a national level. Disagreement arose as to what policy to pursue with respect to the British and Zionism, with differences often reflecting the status of one's family before the war. The al-Husayni family, for example, controlled in 1918 the two most important posts in the Jerusalem administration, as befitting their preeminence: Musa Kazim al-Husayni was mayor and Kamil al-Husayni was mufti. Both, but especially Kamil, welcomed British rule and cooperated with the administration in its early stages. Both opposed Zionism but recognized that their positions of prominence were not threatened by the British assumption of power. It was through them and members of other notable families that the Muslim-Christian Association was founded in November 1918.

Younger Arabs, though not unsympathetic to the British as potential administrators of Palestine, looked to Faysal in Syria and the hope of union with him as the best means to foil Zionist goals. There emerged the idea of Palestine as "southern Syria," with Palestinian Arabs among the most ardent pan-Arab nationalists in Damascus during the heyday of Faysal's rule in 1918 and 1919. Among these young Palestinians was Hajj Amin al-Husayni, younger brother of Kamil al-Husayni, who headed a society called the al-Nadi al-Arabi. A rival society, the al-Muntada al-Arabi, was dominated by members of the al-Nashshashibi family. Nationalist fervor reached its height in March 1920 when the Syrian National Congress, which included Palestinians such as Hajj Amin, proclaimed Faysal as the king of a united Syria. This in turn had profound repercussions in Palestine.

The Syrian National Congress had always been anti-Zionist and had actually forced Faysal to back off from his tentative support of Zionist goals. Once the congress crowned Faysal, demonstrations broke out in Palestine in which Musa Kazim al-Husayni, the mayor of Jerusalem, played a role. Tensions escalated as the festival of Nebi Musa (Prophet Moses) was scheduled for 4–5 April. A celebration that traditionally brought Muslims together from throughout Palestine, the festival was also an occasional source of religious friction in that it often coincided with both Passover and Easter. Nationalist fervor led to plans for anti-Zionist riots which occurred during the Nebi Musa observances, encouraged in part by speeches in which Hajj Amin al-Husayni, returned from Damascus, declared that the British would support the idea of Faysal's rule over Palestine.[6] Muslims attacked the Jewish quarter in old Jerusalem. In the melee prior to the intervention of British forces, 5 Jews were killed and 211 wounded, whereas Arab casualties were 4 killed and 32 wounded.

British reaction was swift but, to the Zionists, belated, in that they felt the British authorities had facilitated the Arab attacks, a charge the latter angrily denied. Ronald Storrs, governor of Jerusalem, summarily dismissed Musa Kazim al-Husayni as mayor for having ignored Storrs's directive to stay out of politics. He replaced him with Raghib al-Nashshashibi, head of the less-prominent but ambitious Jerusalem family that hoped to acquire power at al-Husaynis's expense. Al-Nashshashibi's willing accession to the mayoralty was to encourage a growing split within Palestinian Arab ranks that dominated and fragmented nationalist activity throughout the mandate. As the al-Nashshashibis moved closer to the British, the al-Husaynis distanced themselves somewhat, although they were always careful during this period to maintain ties with the mandatory power. The rivalry became all the more significant as pan-Arab hopes were dashed soon after the Nebi Musa affair. The mandate, including the Balfour Declaration, was confirmed on 24 April at San Remo, and a declaration to that effect was read in Palestine on 28 April. The British military administration was summarily dismissed, and Herbert Samuel inaugurated civilian rule as of 1 July. On 20 July, Faysal's government collapsed, and the Arabs' hopes of independence ended. The Palestinian Arabs would now have to turn inward to deal with a high commissioner determined to fulfill British responsibilities toward both Arabs and Jews under the terms of the mandate.

THE FIRST DECADE, 1920–1930

PALESTINIAN ARAB LEADERSHIP

Herbert Samuel was a dedicated Zionist, but he also believed that he had to take account of Arab grievances while not reversing Britain's basic obligation to assist the fulfillment of Zionist goals. He hoped to gain Arab participation in mandatory affairs and to guard their civil and economic rights while simultaneously refusing them any authority that could be used to stop Jewish immigration and purchase of land in Palestine. His efforts were "subtly designed to reconcile Arabs to the . . . pro-Zionist policy" of the civil administration.[7] On the other hand, Samuel felt that Great Britain should establish conditions in which Zionist activity could flourish, but he would not intervene directly on their behalf. His tactics led ultimately to recriminations from both sides.

The Third Palestinian Arab Congress was held in December 1920. It established an executive committee headed by Musa Kazim al-Husayni, ousted mayor of Jerusalem, to represent the congress in dealings with the mandatory power. To a great extent the congress reflected the membership of the Muslim-Christian Association, but it was boycotted by the al-Nashshashibi family. Samuel tried to establish contacts with the Arab Executive (AE) and in general acted in a conciliatory manner toward those who represented Arab nationalist feelings. When the mufti, Kamil al-Husayni, died in the spring of 1921, Samuel agreed with those of his advisers who recommended Hajj Amin al-Husayni for the post, even though he had been disqualified by the elections held in accordance with existing regulations and the candidate backed by the al-Nashshashibis had come in first in the balloting. Amin al-Husayni would ultimately emerge as the unquestioned leader of the Palestinian Arab resistance. He established the Supreme Muslim Council (SMC) in January 1922 which oversaw all appointments to religious offices in the Islamic community in Palestine.

Conciliation could not repress the Arab dislike of Zionism, however. With the end of the war, Jewish immigration had resumed, comprising what became the third Aliya (1919–1923). These immigrants were "young, enthusiastic, penniless workers," socialists for the most part, who were eager to contribute to the building of a Zionist society.[8] In their manners and their ideology, they were the antithesis of the norms of Arab culture, and many Arabs, and others also, saw them as signifying the introduction of communism into Palestine. Over 10,000 Jewish immigrants entered Palestine in 1919–1920, most of them part of this worker influx; another 8294 entered in 1921.[9] Rivalries among factions of these workers led to renewed outbreaks of Arab-Jewish strife. On May Day 1921, riots erupted in Tel Aviv between Jewish communists, parading in support of a Soviet Palestine, and socialists who opposed them. The fighting spread into adjacent areas of Arab Jaffa and led to Arab attacks on Jews and Jewish reprisals. One of the main targets of the Arab attacks was the Jaffa Immigrants Hotel where many incoming Zionists stayed.[10] In this fighting, 14 Arabs and 43 Jews were killed, and 49 Arabs and 143 Jews were wounded. Further violence occurred almost immediately as the Nebi Musa celebrations began. Arabs attacked Jewish settlements, which were armed, and the British responded with air attacks on the Arab rioters. In these clashes, 47 Jews and 48 Arabs were killed, and 146 Jews and 73 Arabs were wounded.

The May 1921 riots had a profound impact on Samuel, who immediately halted the immigration, albeit temporarily, and assured the Arabs that the British government "would never impose on [the people of Palestine] a policy that people had reason to think was contrary to their religious, their political, and their economic interests."[11] This speech led many Zionists in Palestine to view Samuel as having betrayed his official obligations. It encouraged the Arab leaders to believe that British concessions might be forthcoming. An Arab delegation composed of members of notable families went to London in July 1921 and stayed until November. They demanded that the Balfour Declaration be repudiated and that Britain agree to build an Arab national government. Their claims were rejected consistently by British officials, including Churchill, who offered them a representative assembly with an Arab majority but denied it effective power to block British support of the Zionist cause. Determined to mollify Arab feelings, the British government issued a White Paper in June 1922 that declared that Britain did "not contemplate that Palestine as a whole should be converted into a Jewish National Home, but that such a home should be founded in Palestine." This statement regressed not so much from the letter of the Balfour Declaration as its spirit, which to Zionists and their British allies embodied the idea of ultimate Jewish statehood in all of Palestine. Although not pleased by this modification of previous statements, the Zionists accepted it, if only to appear cooperative with the mandatory power. And with official approval of the mandate by the League of Nations in July 1922, they could feel they had the right to pursue their objectives to the utmost.

With these documents in hand, Samuel now turned to the task of trying to create a legislative body in Palestine that would incorporate the different segments of the community. Britain had drafted a constitution for Palestine which was officially promulgated on 10 August 1922. It provided for a consultative body that would advise the high commissioner and his subordinates on matters of concern to them. This council would be composed of twenty-three members, eleven selected from the government (the high commissioner and ten government officials) and twelve to be elected from the population in proportion to the size of the respective communities (eight Muslims, two Christians, and two Jews). This was an improvement over the advisory council that Samuel had created in October 1920 which had four Muslims, three Christians, and three Jews, a ratio that significantly underrepresented the Muslim community, given its share of the population of Palestine. Nevertheless, both Muslims and Christians, through the Arab Executive (AE), decided to boycott the elections for the new council because the AE was specifically denied the right to discuss matters pertaining to British obligations to the Zionists. The al-Nashshashibi camp had quietly favored the idea of the legislative council but would not say so publicly out of fear of reprisal by their opponents. Zionist efforts to create more amenable parties through bribery, especially to the National Muslim Society, failed because their members lacked credibility; that is, their reliance on Zionist financial support was known.

Samuel tried again in the spring of 1923, this time to create a council with the same proportion of representatives, but with all its members appointed by the high commissioner. Failing in this effort, Samuel attempted to gain Arab agreement for creation of an Arab Agency that would presumably represent Arab interests in the same manner as the Zionist Executive did for the Zionists. But there were differences. The Executive was a self-selecting institution whose membership was outside British control, whereas members of the Arab Agency would be selected by the high commissioner. By restricting the Arab Agency's concerns to the affairs of the Arab community, which precluded consideration of Zionist policies, the British isolated its proposed scope of responsibility from matters that were of greatest concern to the Arabs. This too failed to gain Arab backing and with it ended British efforts to bring Arab leaders into official contact with the government. Later Arab willingness to participate in such institutions would be foiled by the course of events and Zionist opposition. The Arabs' refusal to cooperate with the mandatory regime by participating in these councils prohibited them from being able to present their views from within the administration of Palestine. But for Arab leaders to have done so would have meant recognition of the mandate and the Balfour Declaration, and thus accept- ance of the right of the Jews to immigrate freely into Palestine. Such acknowl- edgement would have itself undermined the foundation of their claim that they should be granted the right of self-determination in Palestine.

On the other hand, the Arabs' rejection of Samuel's proposal did not mean that all segments of the community opposed it. The al-Nashshashibi faction privately favored participation, presumably in the hope of establishing a rapport with the high commissioner by displaying a cooperative attitude toward his efforts. As mayor of Jerusalem, Raghib al-Nashshashibi needed and sought a close relationship with Samuel, but it was also known that he would generally approve what the al-Husaynis opposed and vice versa, often as a matter of principle rather than support of a specific policy.[12] Here the al-Nashshashibis benefited, as the 1920s progressed, from the growing Muslim resentment at the al-Husayni family's control over the Arab Executive and the Supreme Muslim Council. Some Arab Christians, though opposed to Zionism, were wary of Hajj Amin al-Husayni's prominence as a Muslim leader, though he, unlike some more radical associates, always strove to maintain Muslim-Christian ties as the basis of a national Arab coalition opposing Zionism. These factors enabled the al- Nashshashibi party to collect enough support to gain a majority of the seats in the 1927 municipal elections held throughout Palestine. Its success was encouraged by Zionist donations, as several members of the Jewish Executive were eager to promote opposition to the al-Husaynis. Some funding went also to the two major independent newspapers, Filastin and al-Karmil, which in 1926 switched their backing to the al-Nashshashibis.[13] The extent of the opposition was such that the AE, headed by Musa Kazim al-Husayni, closed its offices in 1927, a step that indicated also the AE's inability to secure any concessions from the British that might weaken their commitment to Zionism.

In fact, hopes of achieving such concessions were unrealistic: "no British cabinet would have sanctioned the establishment . . . of a government really representative of the Arab majority and possessing effective powers."[14] Arab leaders thus turned inward during the mid-1920s to seek to expand their influ- ence against one another, encouraged perhaps by a sharp decrease in Jewish immigration that lessened their sense of urgency regarding the likelihood of Zionist success: Jewish emigration was higher than immigration in 1927. The moderate al-Nashshashibi party felt secure enough from 1925 onward to espouse openly the idea of Arab participation on a legislative council, especially after the arrival of the new high commissioner in midyear, Lord Plumer. Aware of its declining influence, the AE decided to back the project in 1927, but it was not until June 1928, when the Palestine Arab Congress met for the first time since 1923, that the two coalitions agreed to push for representative institutions. Talks were begun with both Raghib al-Nashshashibi and Musa Kazim al-Husayni following the arrival of Plumer's successor, Sir John Chancellor, in late 1928 and his announcement in January 1929 that he would consider proposals for a legislative assembly.

These discussions were interrupted, however, by the outbreak of new riots in August 1929, the outgrowth of Muslim-Jewish tensions stemming from the question of access to and control of the Wailing Wall in old Jerusalem. These riots and the ensuring furor over British policy recommendations ultimately reinforced British bonds to Zionist policies and undermined the possibility of creating legislative bodies on the lines that had been considered likely of success in mid-1929. They reflected ongoing as well as immediate points of conflict, the result of Arab-Jewish interactions that we will consider before turning to the riots.

ZIONIST LEADERSHIP IN PALESTINE AND ABROAD

Zionist leadership in Palestine existed at several levels, reflecting the concerns of international Zionism and the struggles for control of Palestinian Jews by local Zionist leaders. Zionism in Palestine was represented initially by the Zionist Commission sent out by the World Zionist Organization in 1918 to act as a semi-independent authority in dealing with British officials. Its activities were overseen by the World Zionist Organization, now based in London and led by Chaim Weizmann. In 1921 the Zionist Commission was replaced by the Palestine Zionist Executive (PZE), meaning those members of the World Zionist Organization Executive residing in Palestine and acting in accordance with directives from London. The PZE oversaw the activities of the major organizations created to secure a Zionist presence, such as the Keren Hayesod, the foundation fund or key financial institution for financing projects in Palestine, or the Jewish National Fund which sought to purchase land that would then become inalienably Jewish.

Weizmann hoped to broaden the scope of world Jewish support for the Zionist cause by creating a commission that would include non-Zionist as well as Zionist Jews. His major incentive was financial, striving to increase donations for use in Palestine that would be controlled by official Zionist groups. Throughout the 1920s, contributions funneled through Zionist channels were only a small portion of the total infusion of Jewish capital into Palestine. Between 1919 and 1926, 22 out of 28 million English pounds brought into Palestine were capital seeking a return on investment for corporations abroad or money devoted to private enterprises.[15] This type of funding sought immediate results, not to serve overall Zionist or socialist goals; managers speculated in land and hired cheaper Arab labor, not Jewish workers. Differences over the philosophy of such funding had led a bloc of American Zionists, represented by Justice Louis Brandeis, to withdraw from the World Zionist Organization in the mid-1920s. Brandeis wanted immigrants with sufficient capital to be productive on arrival, whereas Weizmann and the European members of the WZO believed it necessary to encourage anyone to settle in Palestine if only to increase the Jewish population. If Jews of independent means were unwilling to do so through Zionist auspices, then poor workers should be encouraged, sponsored by Zionist funds. But this approach required a good deal of money, and Weizmann spent six years, between 1923 and 1929, seeking commitments from wealthy European and American Jews who were not necessarily committed personally to Zionism. And such promises meant that the donors wished to be involved in overseeing the use of their contributions.

In 1929 Weizmann succeeded in gaining agreement for the creation of a new governing body for the Zionist movement in Palestine, the Jewish Agency, which supplanted the Palestine Zionist Executive. The agency's headquarters were located in Jerusalem, with a branch office in London directed by its president, Chaim Weizmann, who took the post by virtue of his leadership of the World Zionist Organization. The bylaws provided for non-Zionists to have equal representation with Zionists on the agency's major committees. This arrangement was designed to satisfy the desires of non-Zionists to oversee the finances of the Zionist undertaking. Also, the joining of the agency and the World Zionist Organization under Weizmann's leadership would help coordinate the pursuit of Zionist objectives in Palestine and the representation of their interests before the British government in London and the League of Nations which supervised the mandate.

However, the new arrangement also established the basis for future rivalries between Weizmann and the leadership of the Zionist movement in Palestine which resented outside control. They decided to increase their influence in world Zionist circles through elections to the newly created Jewish Agency. They did this by taking over the seats on the major committees, including the Executive Council, that were allotted to non-Zionists. This proved simple to do, as technically a non-Zionist was anyone not nominated for a post by the World Zionist Organization run by Weizmann. The success of the Palestinian Zionists in this effort set the stage for later confrontations between the leadership of the Yishuv, the Jewish community in Palestine represented by David Ben-Gurion, and the world Zionist leadership centered in Weizmann, as to the nature of the policy to be pursued in the area.

The manner in which the Palestinian Zionists gained influence in world Zionist councils illustrates the nature of intra-Jewish relationships in Palestine as well as Jewish assumptions about the Arab community. The Jewish community in Palestine on the eve of World War I was divided into three main sectors. First there were the Orthodox Jews, still a majority at that time, who rejected Zionist pretensions because they clashed with their own vision of a universe controlled by divine will. Second, there was the private Jewish sector, predominantly landowning, which was the offshoot of the early colonizing efforts of Hibbat Zion and the later donations of Baron de Rothschild. These landlords used Arab labor and had in many ways become part of the Palestinian landscape, as opposed to identifying themselves solely with a separatist Jewish cause. Third, there were the labor Zionists, the offspring of the second Aliya in the first decade of the twentieth century. They were ardent socialists, reared in the revolutionary fervor of Russian collectivism and devoted to the idea of establishing a singular Jewish presence in the land of ancient Israel. They attacked Jewish landlords for using Arab labor, both as socialists on the grounds of exploitation and as Zionists on the grounds that these Jews were undermining the Zionist idea of a self-governing Jewish community devoted to restoring Palestine to Jewish control.

Though there were always splinter groups, there were two main factions among the labor Zionists during this period and later. Poale Zion (Workers of Zion) retained ties with its parent labor-Zionist organization in Europe and for years identified with European revolutionary socialism in principle, even though its own nationalist views contradicted basic socialist ideology. Though leaders of Poale Zion like David Ben-Gurion supported the idea of Jewish settlement on the land, they focused their attention on the cities of Palestine because it was there that most Jewish immigrants settled. In contrast, Hapoel Hatzair (The Young Worker), inspired by the writings of David Gordon, stressed the need for collective settlement of the land as the foundation for the building of a Jewish nation. Both groups adopted the idea of "conquest of labor" which signified the victory of Jewish labor in creating a new society. This in turn meant that Jewish investment and capital were meaningful only when Jewish labor was used. For many years, neither group controlled a majority of the workers. When construction of Tel Aviv, the first all-Jewish city, began in 1909, financed by the Jewish National Fund, Arab labor predominated.[16]

Both Poale Zion and Hapoel Hatzair were to a degree political as much as labor groups, the former especially as it seemed to espouse the idea of class conflict. In 1919 Poale Zion expanded by incorporating many unaffiliated unionists and a small number of Hapoel Hatzair to form a new party, the Ahdut Ha'Avodah. It and Hapoel Hatzair encouraged the worker immigration following the war that amounted to over ten thousand by the end of 1920. Though penniless, these immigrants were highly motivated and were more committed to labor ideology than to a specific political identity. Their socialist ideals pushed the Ahdut Ha'Avodah to agree with Hapoel Hatzair to form a single workers' organization to control Jewish labor. This was the Histadrut, created in December 1920 and destined to become the dominant force in Jewish affairs in Palestine. The Histadrut was technically an all-embracing labor movement devoted to the enhancement of Zionist goals through the infusion of Jewish labor and ownership of the land. As a workers' group it supposedly subsumed the political activities of the Ahdut Ha'Avodah and Hapoel Hatzair. In fact both parties retained their separate identities and competed to control the Histadrut executive, a contest eventually won by Ben-Gurion and the Ahdut Ha'Avodah.

As the dominant party in the Histadrut, Ben-Gurion and his colleagues were able over time to control the fortunes not only of Jewish labor but of world Zionism as well. Histadrut funds had been dispensed initially by the World Zionist Organization which designated areas for their use. By the mid-1920s the WZO agreed to permit Histadrut to decide their allocation, thus aiding Ahdut Ha'Avodah fortunes. For example, incoming workers were assigned jobs through labor exchanges sponsored by the Histadrut but actually controlled by the party. Nevertheless, political and organizational strife throughout the 1920s led Ben-Gurion to decide to merge the two parties.

Most immigrants during the 1920s were from the middle class, mainly from Poland. They settled in cities and became part of the private economy outside Histadrut control. Then an economic crisis in 1927–1928 caused massive unemployment among the workers sponsored by the organization.[17] These problems led the Histadrut to push its attacks on Jewish enterprises that employed Arabs, actions seen by many Jewish merchants as a threat to their livelihood. From this perspective, unifying the labor movement politically would increase the Histadrut's effectiveness in dealing with its opponents within the Jewish community in Palestine. But the creation of the new party, the Mapai, in December 1930 had other goals as well—to forestall further capitalist inroads into Palestine by increasing labor's influence in world Zionist councils.

From the perspective of the labor Zionists in Palestine, Weizmann's success in gaining non-Zionist membership in the new Jewish Agency posed a threat to them. Most were wealthy capitalists who would presumably encourage the agency's backing of private projects outside the Histadrut's authority. Consequently, once the Ahdut Ha'Avodah and Hapoel Hatzair merged to become the Mapai, the new party's leadership undertook an energetic campaign in Europe and America to gain support for representation on world Zionist councils. They gained 40 percent of the votes for delegates to the 1931 Zionist Congress and 44 percent in 1933. The Mapai also gained access to the Jewish Agency through election to the "non-Zionist" seats, and by 1933 its members were the most powerful bloc within the agency. The merger thus enabled the Histadrut and the Mapai, under Ben-Gurion's direction, to increase its influence over Zionist politics in Palestine and to gain a major voice in world Zionist policymaking.

Still, the ascendance of labor Zionism did not go unchallenged. Its main opponents inside and outside Palestine were followers of Vladimir Jabotinsky, who in 1925 founded the Revisionist party. Jabotinsky, a forceful writer and speaker, believed that Zionism should focus its attention solely on the creation of a Jewish state. Ideally this would be done in conjunction with Great Britain. Indeed, Jabotinsky was willing to offer the services of Jewish legions to ensure order not only in Palestine but also in the greater Middle East. On the other hand, if Britain were unwilling to act decisively in this matter, then Jewish forces should be mobilized to attain this goal of statehood by military means against the British. The immediate achievement of a state outweighed all other considerations. Consequently, Jabotinsky viewed the Histadrut and labor Zionism in general "as a cancer on the national body politic."[18] Arguments about social goals and class structures weakened the Zionist effort. Furthermore, the Zionist experience showed that private investment and middle-class immigration were the true foundations of Zionist state formation; the Histadrut's emphasis on socialism and collectivity thus threatened rather than contributed to the likelihood of Zionist success.

The directness of Jabotinsky's appeal had a major impact on young Jews, especially in Europe where he formed youth groups (*Betar*) whose practices, patterned after the tactics and symbols of fascism, included wearing brown shirts and using special salutes.[19] These exercises emphasized the idea of strength and unity, as opposed to the weakness and factionalism of the Zionist leadership and labor Zionism. Jabotinsky demanded the union of Palestine both east and west of the Jordan, thus incorporating into the prospective Jewish state the region of Transjordan. The fact that Weizmann had acceded to its separation from Palestine indicated his willingness to bow before British demands. Betar groups were formed in Palestine during the latter half of the 1920s, while Revisionist Zionism gained increasing strength in Europe. From four delegates to the Zionist Congress in 1925, they went to twenty-one in 1929 and fifty-two in 1931.

In the process, antagonism and hatred developed between the labor Zionists and the Revisionists, memorialized in the murder of perhaps the leading labor Zionist of his day, Chaim Arlosoroff, in 1933. Revisionists were arrested and charged with the crime. Although they were ultimately released for lack of evidence, labor Zionists continued to believe that Revisionists were responsible for Arlosoroff's murder, enshrining a bitterness that has continued to the present. Indeed, Menachem Begin, self-styled inheritor of Jabotinsky's mantle of leadership, tried to reopen the trial in 1982 to prove that the Revisionists were innocent of the crime. In general, labor Zionist and Revisionist rivalry persisted. The Histadrut's efforts to force Jewish employers to use only union members and its incitement of strikes were countered by Revisionist strikebreaking tactics and offers to supply their own workers to the Jewish bourgeoisie of Palestine, who often backed the latter against the Histadrut. These rivalries led Jabotinsky to break with the World Zionist Organization in 1935. He formed his "New Zionist Organization" which, at its first congress in Vienna, welcomed delegates who had been elected by 713,000 Revisionist voters, compared with the 635,000 voters for the WZO's nineteenth congress.[20]

Another group of some significance was the Agudat Israel, composed of Orthodox Jews who believed political Zionism to be heretical. It was quite active in the 1920s in its anti-Zionist activity, which included contacts with Palestinian Arabs and with British parliamentarians who were anti-Zionist, and it sent messages to the League of Nations attacking the British mandate's obligation to fulfill the Balfour Declaration. To the Zionists, the Agudat Israel's actions gave the "impression of treacherous fraternization with the greatest enemies of Zionism," and hostility to the Agudat Israel culminated in the assassination of its most ardent opponent of Zionism, Dr. Israel DeHahn.[21] The 1929 riots, in which Arab assaults were mostly against Orthodox Jews, who were unarmed, pushed the Agudat Israel to affiliate itself with the Zionist movement by 1931.

THE ZIONIST LEADERSHIP, THE BRITISH MANDATE, AND THE ARAB COMMUNITY, 1920–1931

Unlike the Arabs, the Zionists were not isolated in a direct interaction with the mandate officials in Palestine. And whereas the Arabs were primarily concerned about the Zionist component in Britain's mandatory role, the Jews were much less concerned about an Arab threat to their position for most of this period. From the Zionist perspective, the Arabs would naturally object to Zionism. That was understood, but it was a problem for the British, not the Jews. The latter should be able to proceed with the building of the Jewish state; the British should take on the task of keeping the Arabs at bay and ensuring that they did not become either a military or, more importantly, a political threat to the development of the Zionist program. Zionist leaders such as Weizmann were thus far more interested in British than Arab policy, whereas Palestinian Zionist leaders such as Ben-Gurion were far more involved in internal matters regarding power within the Zionist community than with Jewish-Arab problems.

This did not mean that Zionists were unaware of Arab opposition. Ben-Gurion told fellow Zionists in 1918 that "there is no solution to the question of relations between Arabs and Jews. . . . And we must recognize this situation. . . . We as a nation want this country to be ours; the Arabs, as a nation, want this country to be theirs. . . ."[22] Resistance was to be expected. When arguing for a Jewish military force at the Zionist Congress in Prague in 1921, Jabotinsky declared succinctly that "I don't know of a single example in history where a country was colonised with the courteous consent of the population."[23] It was necessary that the Arabs be kept in check by the British so that the Jewish community could expand. This meant also keeping the Arab economy as separated as possible from the Jewish. As early as 1913, this goal was expressed by Arthur Ruppin, who foresaw the "creation of a Jewish milieu and of a closed Jewish economy in which producers, consumers, and middlemen will all be Jewish."[24] There was no intent to create a joint society with the indigenous Arabs nor to give them access to the modern Jewish economy that would emerge. The fact that this goal could not be easily implemented did not undermine its currency as a basic tenet of Zionist ideology. Ben-Gurion envisaged any possible agreement with Palestinian Arabs on the nature of Palestine to be possible only through Arab acquiescence to Zionist hegemony. That would result from Arab recognition of the absolute nature of Zionist power and Arab weakness, a relationship that should be continually impressed on the Arabs, as Ben-Gurion did in talks with prominent Arabs in the 1930s. By 1936 he, like Jabotinsky, called for a Jewish state including Transjordan in conversations with Arabs who sought his opinion. Ben-Gurion viewed the Palestinian Arabs as part of a broader Arab nation deserving independence, but not in Palestine.[25] Thus British paternalism toward the Arabs and attempts to assist them to develop political resources were viewed with concern but not outright alarm so long as the nature of Arab institutions did not threaten the basic Zionist interests, especially immigration but also land purchases. And it was precisely here that the Palestinian Zionists had a great advantage over the Arab community, because of their influence in the British mandatory government and the sympathetic ear they could generally rely on, especially in London.

Both communities in Palestine served the British with divided loyalties, their primary allegiance being to their own groups, but there were differences. The Arabs were a majority, but the percentage of their representation in government posts was less than the ratio of their size to total population, reflecting their more traditional educational experience. Furthermore, their inclusion was designed to "emasculate Arab nationalist opposition to the mandatory system" while excluding them from positions in which they might be able to exert influence against that system.[26] No Arab was nominated to be head of a government department. This policy was backed by many British officials in subordinate posts who, to many Jews, were pro-Arab because they were critical of Zionist policies. But their paternalism toward the Arabs contained the implicit assumption of their own superiority and open unwillingness to deal with the Arabs on an equal basis in government. When one qualified Arab was given a responsible position, it was only after British officials decided to save money, as they could pay him a lower salary than they would have had to pay an Englishman.[27]

The Jews, on the other hand, did not experience either the psychological or the economic disadvantages felt by the Arabs in the mandatory government. Their salaries were higher, and their participation was a means of furthering Zionist objectives that they themselves espoused. And in situations in which the mandatory power had to decide major issues, the Jews could often rely on an official who was at least sympathetic to Zionism if not a committed member of the movement. Norman Bentwich, for example, was deeply involved in Zionist activities; he was also the senior judicial officer during the military administration and retained his high legal status as attorney general in the mandatory government. As such, he pushed successfully for the assignment of supervision of the Land Registry Department to the chief legal adviser and "enjoyed unparalleled influence over land matters until High Commissioner Chancellor included these offices under his purview in 1929."[28] Leopold Amery, colonial secretary from 1924 to 1929, was himself an ardent Zionist, as was William Ormsby-Gore, colonial secretary from 1936 to 1938.

In addition, the Zionist organization was far superior to the rudimentary and factionalized Arab effort to influence British opinion. Both Arabs and Jews in the mandatory government passed information, but "Jewish intelligence gathering was more systematic, pervasive, and centralised."[29] Zionist officials had access to nearly all secret documents that were formulated both in Jerusalem and in the Colonial Office in London, either through their own spies or through British officials sympathetic to their cause. When British policies were formulated in 1930 that tried to restrict Zionist activity in Palestine, leading Zionists wrote the rebuttal that the British prime minister issued to counter that policy. In the Palestine gendarmerie, only Jews were allowed to serve along with British soldiers; Arabs were excluded because of their anti-Zionist attitudes. Jews used their positions in the force to steal arms which they transferred to the Hagana, the Jewish defense force under Histadrut control. By these means and by extensive arms smuggling, aided by Jewish customs officials, the Yishuv became fairly well armed, especially as compared with the Arabs who had few weapons.

From the Zionist perspective, this was and should have been the natural order of things. Palestine was their country, and the role of the British was to facilitate their acquisition of it. In such circumstances, concern for legality focused on British adherence to the terms of the mandate, not the means by which the Yishuv could be consolidated. From the Arab perspective, the expansion of the Yishuv posed a recognized threat that they should try to resist but that many realized could not be done through legal processes. Adherence to administrative procedures as established under the mandate guaranteed the progressive loss of Arab Palestine. Eventually violence became the only recourse.

In the meantime, the efforts of Arab notables to oppose Zionist strategy were undermined by both their own rivalries and British policies that undercut their economic position. Intra-Arab antagonisms encouraged, as we have seen, the al-Husayni–al-Nashshashibi split and the rival parties that developed from them. During the mid-1920s, some members of the Palestine Zionist Executive exploited these differences and paid stipends to the moderates to encourage their opposition to the al-Husayni party. In some cases they approached the Arabs, and in others, the Arabs approached the Zionists. On occasion Musa Kazim al-Husayni, president of the Arab Executive, received funds from H. Kalvarisky, head of the PZE's Arab Department.[30] By this method Zionist leaders could hope to influence those Arab leaders who were regarded as being in the forefront of opposition to Zionism. The most important area where Arabs seemed willing to undermine their own proclaimed hostility to Zionism was land sales to Jews, a process that reflects the complexity of the process of intra-Arab as well as Arab-Jewish interaction.

THE LAND QUESTION, 1920–1931

To both Arabs and Jews, land was crucial to either the retention or attainment of their respective national existences. Palestinian Arab society, especially its Muslim component—which was 90 percent of the total—worked on the land. Although only a relatively small percentage of Jews in Palestine ever actually farmed, the possession of land was seen as essential to the foundation of the future Jewish state. Zionists had recognized this issue from the beginning. The Jewish National Fund had been established at the fifth Zionist Congress in 1901 for the purpose of coordinating and centralizing Jewish land purchases and ensuring that land thus bought would never again be available for sale. This conception of the inalienable nature of land purchased by the Jewish National Fund became central to Zionist policy, even though the actual amount bought by it—as opposed to other sources of Jewish land capital investment—remained relatively small throughout the first third of the century. The key differences between the policies of the national fund and other Jewish groups did not lie in the principle of inalienability, however. Rather, the distinction lay in the willingness of Jewish capitalists to hire cheaper Arab labor, whereas to the national fund only Jewish workers were acceptable. Until 1948, private Jewish capital played the major role in land purchase and development as well as industry. By 1914 Jews owned slightly over 420,000 dunams, 20 percent of all the land registered as owned by Jews in 1948. Only 4 percent of this amount belonged to the Jewish National Fund. The remainder, slightly over 400,000 dunams, was in private hands, 275,000 dunams of which had been settled and developed as a result of Baron Edmond Rothschild's financial assistance, which amounted to some 40 million francs by 1900 when he turned over his properties to the Jewish Colonisation Association. Without this massive infusion, of both private capital and Western specialists in modern agricultural techniques, Jewish settlements would have failed, and it was precisely this access to outside funds that distinguished Jewish from Arab land practices following World War I. [31]

Arab landholdings varied considerably in size and nature of ownership or assumption of right to the land. The most common form of holdings for village peasants was called *musha'a*, or collective village ownership. Each shareholder was allotted a fixed share of the total property for cultivation, and fields were redistributed periodically to give all shareholders equal access to the best land held under common ownership. It was assumed that those holding shares would be able to work the land. Musha'a-owned land, or land worked according to musha'a principles, amounted to between 4 and 5 million dunams after the war, situated in the plains and valley regions for the most part; individual ownership of land was the norm in the hill country. [32] Yet by 1923, approximately 75 percent of all musha'a lands were owned by absentee landlords living in towns. This was due to the escalation of peasant indebtedness, which was always endemic but increased during the war because of the devastation that Palestine suffered. As a rule, the former peasant shareholders remained on the land as tenants of those owning the right to the land in the village. Most musha'a land was deliberately unregistered in order to avoid taxes. This practice continued under the British mandate, reflecting traditional distrust of central authority. In short, peasant society predominated in Arab Palestine, but many farmers did not own the land they tilled, although they might have originally "owned" it through the musha'a system. They had rights of cultivation only, but they often assumed it was a legal right, as opposed to one of sufferance. As a result,

> the Zionist ability to create a national home was significantly aided by the poor economic status of the Palestinian peasant during the Ottoman and Mandatory periods. Insufficient rainfall and draft animals, inefficient management of agricultural lands, small parcel size, lack of investment capital, indebtedness, and a general disillusionment with government aided Jewish nation building. Lack of interest in the majority of the fellaheen agricultural population by a socially distanced Palestinian Arab landowning elite also aided the development of the Jewish national home. The Palestinian Arab community was unquestionably a numerical majority throughout the Mandate, but its own financial distress gave the Zionist minority a distinct advantage in the struggle to control Palestine.[33]

This was particularly the case in the 1930s when the peasants' sale of land to Zionists increased sharply. Until then the majority of sales were made by nonresident absentee landlords and resident large landholders.

As was discussed in Chapter 2, changes in land laws in the second half of the nineteenth century had led peasants to transfer their titles of ownership so as to avoid conscription and tax assessments. This encouraged the purchase of land by Arabs residing outside Palestine and by leading urban families in the area. The number of large landholders cannot be ascertained, but it is clear that they controlled directly or indirectly a significant amount of the cultivable land in Palestine. Excluding the Gaza and Beersheba districts in the south, where large tribal holdings were concentrated in family units, 116 families owned 1.131 million dunams as of 1915. This averages 9750 dunams per family. The size of these family holdings varied widely, especially when we consider the Sursuq properties which amounted to 230,000 dunams and were concentrated principally in the Esdraelon Plain. Lands belonging to resident families might be distributed in various sectors of the region. The al-Husayni family was reputed to own about 50,000 dunams, the Abd al-Hadi family in the realm of 60,000.[34]

The disparities in landownership can be shown by the following statistics for 1936. Though they are incomplete and account for only about two-fifths of all property holdings, they do indicate the huge gap between large and small landholders. One hundred and fifty families owned 1000 or more dunams. These properties were only 0.2 percent of all individual plots listed, but they took up 27.5 percent of the land area. In contrast, property holdings under 100 dunams were 91.8 percent of the total but comprised 36.7 percent of the area. This leaves another 35.8 percent of the land taken up by holdings of between 100 and 1000 dunams. In sum, plots over 100 dunams were only 8.2 percent of all plots but encompassed 63.3 percent of the cultivable land. The situation of the peasants was even more precarious if we consider that a majority of those owning plots under 100 dunams actually had 40 or fewer, when 80 to 90 was considered necessary for subsistence. In contrast, there were some immense properties. The land owned by the 150 families who had plots of 1000 dunams or more amounted to 895,124 dunams. Thirteen of these families owned an aggregate of 624,435 dunams, 70 percent of these holdings, which incorporated 19.2 percent of the land area evaluated for all properties.[35]

The Zionists were well versed in the intricacies of Arab landownership even before World War I, and British officials relied on them for information as they began to draft land laws in 1918–1919. At this time nonresident owners held significant portions of Palestinian land, about 500,000 dunams. Zionist land agents focused on them, especially the Sursuqs with whom they had been negotiating since before the war. In general the Zionists hoped to buy large properties, both for reasons of efficiency in terms of integrating Jewish-held lands and for political reasons. Norman Bentwich, when drafting the first Land Transfer Ordinance issued in 1920, calculated that Zionist purchases from the Palestinian notables would weaken their political and social prestige and thus undermine Arab opposition to Zionism by discrediting its leadership.

Zionists were immediately successful in arranging for the purchase of approximately 240,000 dunams in the Esdraelon Plain (to be called the Jezreel), primarily from the Sursuq family, between 1921 and 1925. The buyers were the Jewish National Fund and the American Zion Commonwealth, a private company. The cost was £800,000, compared with an initial cost to the Sursuqs of £20,000.[36] But Zionists also succeeded in buying land from Palestinian Arab notables, some of whom were prominent in the nationalist movement, especially from 1927 onward. Tables listing Zionist land purchases from 1878 to 1936, admittedly restricted to 55.4 percent of total acquisitions, indicate that during this period 90.6 percent was bought from large landowners and only 9.4 percent from peasants. When broken down further, the statistics indicate that although nonresident landowners sold 80 percent of the land bought by Jews between 1920 and 1927, they sold only about 30 percent of the land bought between 1928 and 1936. The difference in the latter period was made up by Palestinian Arab landlords, who sold about 50 percent of the properties bought by Jews, and the peasants, who sold about 20 percent.[37]

The reasons for the increasing willingness of the Palestinians, whether large or small holders, to sell land to Zionists were primarily economic. As the Muslim-Christian Association recognized in 1920, "the Jewish population was the only financially viable segment of Palestine's population at the conclusion of World War I."[38] Zionist organizations, though registered in Palestine and staffed by Jews living there, had access to external sources of capital, the only source of their financing. In contrast, Palestinian Arab families lacked capital and had no ready access to outside funds. Their wealth was in land, and the major means of maintaining or seeking to increase it was through land speculation. This meant ultimately the sale of land to Jews, to gain cash that enabled the notables to preserve their economic and political status in the Arab community. As a consequence, only Zionist organizations could afford to buy large land areas owned by nonresident Arabs who themselves, at least initially, were forbidden by the Land Transfer Ordinance of 1920 from purchasing more land in Palestine. Arab notables retained possession of most of their land, but the fact that they might sell portions to the very Zionists they condemned fueled Zionist optimism about the success of their endeavors.

The procedures followed in the sale of such lands varied and often required the circumvention of existing regulations. There was, however, an ongoing problem for both sides, the question of the fate of those who worked the land, whether tenants—peasants who often assumed customary rights to work the land—or a larger class of agricultural laborers. Stipulations in the Land Transfer Ordinance of 1920 required that the peasants (tenants) be left an area sufficient for their sustenance in case the land changed hands. But the Jewish purchasers wanted land without tenants when they took possession, so that it could automatically revert to inalienable Jewish ownership. They thus frequently had clauses inserted in the sales agreements stating that the property would be free of tenants when handed over to them. The Arab sellers, whether actual owners or agents, were often anxious to comply, and the tenants usually had little leverage, being indebted to their landlords or money lenders. Thus they were willing to accept monetary compensation from buyers or could be forced to do so, with little recourse. As a result, the right of these tenants to be given maintenance areas was ignored despite their supposed protection, whose weakness was reflected in the fact that the status of a "tenant in occupation" was not legally defined until 1929. As for other workers on the land, "the overwhelmingly larger classes of agricultural laborers and small owner-occupiers were not entitled to any legal protection. . . ."[39]

Thousands of Arabs who worked the land for livelihood were thus forced to leave, many of them without any compensation because they did not qualify as tenants; the compensation itself averaged about an estimated wage for one year. In some cases in which the land area sold was extremely large and many tenants were involved, they were given the option to stay on a portion of the property. For example, 688 tenant families lived on the Sursuq lands. The total amount of compensation was £39, or about $195 per family. Some accepted land instead of money, with the option to purchase it after six years, something that would have been impossible for them to do, as they had no capital. Most left, meaning a displacement of about three thousand people among the tenant families. Many estimate the total displacement to have been about eight thousand.[40] When efforts were made in 1930–1931 to determine the extent of the landless Arab problem, the British government accepted in essence the Jewish Agency's definition of what constituted a "landless Arab," one that referred to tenant cultivators only. Consequently, a much larger category of persons who were actually landless as a result of Jewish land purchases was automatically not considered, especially "owners who habitually let their lands, ploughmen and persons who, from debt or bad seasons or other causes, had ceased to be cultivators and had become laborers etc."[41] In consequence, the Landless Arab Inquiry of 1931–1933 accepted fewer than nine hundred claims of displacement out of a total of nearly four thousand, a major propaganda victory for the Jewish Agency.

The Landless Arab Inquiry was itself the outgrowth of a major investigation of conditions in Palestine ordered by London following the riots in August 1929 that left many Jews and Arabs dead. This explosion of Arab hatred and frustration against the Jews, the first since 1921, stemmed from both the Arab fear of Jewish infringement on their territory in general and specific resentment over what they saw as a threat to the most sacred Muslim site in Jerusalem; it was also a place holy to Jews. The pressures brought to bear on the leaders of both camps indicate the complexity of relationships within both communities as well as between them. Because of the riots the Arab community lost its chance to be represented politically in the mandate structure, a goal that had seemed within reach in early 1929.

THE CONFLICT OVER THE WESTERN WALL (WAILING WALL), 1928–1929, AND ITS REPERCUSSIONS

To the Jews, the Western Wall was the last remnant of the outer wall that had surrounded Herod's temple, itself built on the site of Solomon's temple. It was thus a relic of the sanctuary of ancient Israel, a focal point of religious and national pride. To the Muslims, the wall was the outer perimeter of the Haram al-Sharif, the third-holiest site in Islam, the temple mount on which they had built the al-Aqsa Mosque and the Dome of the Rock. The latter commemorated the place from which, according to Muslim belief, the Prophet Muhammad had ascended to heaven on his night journey. The wall was itself holy to the Muslims because Muhammad had tethered his horse, al-Buraq, to it before his ascension; the Muslims gave the wall the horse's name. The wall was administered by funds from a charitable estate that made it part of a religious foundation, the Maghrebi waqf, named after the Moroccans who inhabited the area.

Jews had always prayed at the wall, which abutted onto a narrow lane separating it from the houses of the Muslims of that quarter. During the nineteenth century as the Jewish population of Jerusalem increased and they began to acquire protection from foreign consuls, the Jews began to attempt to change long-standing practices by bringing chairs to the wall for the elderly to rest on and a screen to divide male and female worshipers. Muslim leaders opposed such amendments, fearful that any alteration of the status quo could be then used to argue for further changes, with Jewish demands backed in Istanbul by foreign influence, a natural response in an environment in which different Christian groups sought to gain control of certain holy places at the expense of rivals.

With the British assumption of power, matters became increasingly politicized. Various Zionist leaders, including Weizmann in 1919, proposed buying the wall from the Maghrebi waqf. One such suggestion in 1926, by Colonel Frederick Kisch of the PZE, had behind it the intent to force the Moroccans out of their houses in the area adjacent to the wall and to demolish the buildings in order to create a broader area for the worshipers (this was finally done after the 1967 War). In his memo Kisch added that the "political effect would be very great," meaning that Palestinian Muslims would be forced to recognize Zionist power.[42] Muslims viewed Jewish attempts to buy the wall as an example of the Zionist wish to take over Palestine. Once the Supreme Muslim Council was established in 1922, Hajj Amin al-Husayni stressed the sacred Muslim character of the property and challenged Zionist attempts to modify the conditions of prayer permitted to Jews. British officials backed Muslim claims to supervision of the entire area, but in an atmosphere of increasing tension. Al-Husayni sent emissaries to seek financial aid from other Muslim countries, helped by the discovery of a painting done in the latter part of the nineteenth century which showed the Dome of the Rock crowned by the Star of David, the symbol of Jewish nationalism. At the same time Weizmann pursued efforts to buy the wall and had collected £61,000 by December 1928. By then the friction had intensified.

On the Jewish Day of Atonement (Yom Kippur), 24 September 1928, Jews brought with them to the wall a screen to divide male and female worshipers. The screen blocked the eleven-foot-wide alley along which the inhabitants of the quarter passed daily. The incident was not unique in the history of contention for greater Jewish access to the wall and Arab resistance to it. Arab protests to the British authorities brought from them a request that the screen be removed. When it remained there into the next day, 25 September, further Arab complaints led the police to remove the screen, which had to be done forcibly because of some resistance by the worshipers. From here matters escalated. Jewish reaction was swift, not only inside Palestine, but outside as well. Leading Zionist officials and the chief rabbi protested to the British government in London and the League of Nations. Claims of police brutality were spread about, and one Jewish paper compared the Muslims with the Russians who participated in pogroms, even though no Muslims had taken part in the events at the wall. The matter had suddenly become a conflict beyond the scope of earlier protests, and the chief administrator in Palestine at the time noted that "Jewish public opinion in Palestine has quite definitely removed the matter from the purely religious orbit and has made it a political and racial question."[43] Jewish outrage included mob action seeking the police officer who had actually removed the screen.

Muslim response came at the beginning of October when Amin al-Husayni, as head of the Supreme Muslim Council, reacted to Jewish demands that the wall be turned over to them. His official defense of the Muslim position to British administrators was accompanied, however, by public calls to the Muslim community to be alert to the threat to al-Buraq, and a committee to defend the wall was formed, presumably with his encouragement. The crisis did permit him to enhance his position within the Arab community, but Jewish threats and political and religious propaganda sparked Muslim concern and seemed to validate his claims. Chaim Weizmann wrote to the Yishuv in an open letter published in November 1928 that the only feasible solution to the problem of access to the wall was to "pour Jews into Palestine" and gain control of their ancient homeland, thus implicitly resolving the wall issue because Jewish sovereignty would have been established. This letter may have been intended to soften Yishuv unrest by suggesting that the matter would not be resolved immediately, that creation of a Jewish majority might take a while. But the linkage of the wall question with Jewish sovereignty was to Muslims proof of their initial suspicions. For both communities the matter was now thoroughly politicized.[44]

No major incidents occurred for nearly a year, until July 1929 when the mufti resumed building activities around the wall, apparently hoping to pressure the British government to issue a statement supporting Muslim ownership of the property. This aroused a furor in Zionist ranks, especially in Jabotinsky's Revisionist party, which formed a committee for a defense of the wall to match the Muslims'. One rightist paper called for rebuilding the temple, and Rabbi Kook, spiritual leader of the Jewish community, lauded young Jews "willing to sacrifice their lives in the cause of their Holy Place."[45] On 15 August members of Betar, the Revisionist party's youth organization, marched to the wall, raised the Zionist flag, and sang the Zionist anthem. The next day was a Friday, the Muslim sabbath. Thousands of Arabs marched to the wall and burned prayers inserted into it by Jews. Sermons calling on Muslims to defend the wall aroused strong emotions.

Matters came to a head on Friday, 23 August, as rumors spread that Jews were planning an attack on the mosque. Militants poured in from outlying areas and, inspired by radical speakers, prepared to defend the Haram al-Sharif. When the mufti tried to calm the mob, some accused him of betraying Islam. Arabs then poured out to attack Jewish quarters, initially in Jerusalem and later in other towns. Orthodox Jews suffered the most, as they were unarmed, 64 being killed in Hebron and others in Safad. Zionist groups retaliated, at one point invading a mosque in Jaffa to kill a religious official and 6 others. The rampage lasted nearly a week, with 133 Jews and 116 Arabs killed and many more wounded. Most Arab casualties were inflicted by British reinforcements called in to bolster the undermanned British police force. The ancient Jewish community of Hebron was evacuated, even though many of its inhabitants had been saved by Arab neighbors and the bravery of the one British policeman there.

Attribution of responsibility for the outbreak has varied, some accusing the mufti of direct responsibility and others considering the Betar demonstration of 15 August as the catalyst for what followed. What seems clear is that the struggle for control of the Western Wall evolved from a purely religious matter of long standing into a political confrontation in which both the hopes and the fears of the respective populations were fused. Rumors fueled alarm on both sides, a classic response in quarters where each sector felt threatened by the other. Ironically, the ultimate result of the outbreak was to entrench Hajj Amin al-Husayni as leader of the Palestinian Arabs while at the same time weakening Arab ability to influence British policy.

YISHUV EXPANSION, ARAB REBELLION, AND THE BRITISH RETHINKING OF THEIR OBLIGATIONS, 1930–1939

INVESTIGATIONS AND RETRACTIONS, 1930–1936

The British reaction to the 1929 riots was to appoint a commission, led by Sir Walter Shaw, to investigate the causes of the riots and to propose policies to prevent their recurrence. A majority of the commission absolved Hajj Amin al-Husayni of direct responsibility and went on to present what they saw as the underlying causes of Arab unrest. The Shaw Report, published in March 1930, identified Zionist immigration and land practices as the reasons for the 1929 outbreaks. It declared that "a landless and discontented class is being created" and called for limitations on the transfer of land to non-Arabs.[46] This had also been suggested by the high commissioner in a long memorandum that Chancellor sent to the Colonial Office in January 1930; he too concluded that Arab landlessness as a result of Zionist policies was at the root of Arab disaffection. The accord between Chancellor and the Shaw Commission was best expressed in the latter's conclusion: "The fundamental cause [of the outbreak] is the Arab feeling of animosity and hostility towards the Jews consequent on the disappointment of their political and national aspirations and fear for their economic future. . . . The feeling as it exists today is based on the two-fold fear of the Arabs that by Jewish immigration and land purchases they may be deprived of their livelihood and placed under the economic domination of the Jews."[47] The report called for a much more explicit British policy regulating matters pertaining to land and immigration that would in effect sharply curtail the Jews' ability to pursue their national goals.

The British government in power, the minority cabinet of Ramsay MacDonald, felt extremely uncomfortable with these proposals. With regard to Palestine, the curtailment of land transfers to Jews would mean the loss of tax revenues and the influx of Jewish capital brought by immigrants. This in turn would place a greater economic burden on the British themselves and ultimately the taxpayers, as Jewish revenues and tax payments helped fund social services and administrative costs, allowing the British to allot a comparatively small amount of their own money to military needs. The financial cost of administering Palestine would rise. Thus one of the ironies of the dilemma was that Jewish immigration and the capital generated by it permitted the British to maintain their imperial presence at comparatively little expense, whereas this same immigration aroused Arab alarm and violence which threatened the security of the British position there. With regard to domestic considerations, the MacDonald cabinet was confronted by a formidable opposition to any change in the mandatory system, led by the authors of Britain's Palestine policy who were now in the conservative opposition and in close contact with the Zionist leadership in London. Calls were made for the formation of a new commission to reverse the Shaw findings. MacDonald compromised by creating an investigatory committee to examine the economic issues pertaining to land and immigration, headed by Sir John Hope-Simpson. This, along with a government statement on the duality of its obligation to both Arabs and Jews in Palestine, enabled the cabinet to avoid any commitment to policy, but it did issue a White Paper on 27 May that reaffirmed the Shaw Commission's conclusions. At the same time it avoided any call for specific steps until Hope-Simpson completed his inquiry. Nevertheless, Jewish immigration was suspended temporarily, leading the Zionists to prepare for a struggle to confront MacDonald if Hope-Simpson's conclusions ratified those already expressed in the Shaw Report.

In the meantime, Zionist officials in Palestine tried to persuade Hope-Simpson that the landless Arab question was insignificant; some hoped also that he might consider the unilateral transfer of Arabs to Transjordan, since he had directed Greek-Turkish population exchanges following the Treaty of Lausanne in 1923.[48] He, however, became increasingly sympathetic to the Arab case and reached conclusions as threatening to Zionist hopes as were those of Shaw and Chancellor. Hope-Simpson asserted that 29.4 percent of Arab rural families were landless and presumably displaced by Jewish land purchases. This conclusion, based on statistics that did not suggest it, ignored aspects of Arab rural life that also contributed to landlessness.[19] Hope-Simpson attacked Jewish exclusionary labor policies and viewed them as contributing to Arab unemployment. He pointed out that although Article 6 of the mandate required British permission for "close settlement of the Jews on the land," it also demanded that "ensuring the rights and positions of other sections of the population" not be "prejudiced by Jewish immigration and settlement."[50] Jewish labor policies and their practice of making Jewish-bought land inalienable were seen as violating the second clause of the article, which should have been given equal if not more weight than that referring to Jewish settlement. Hope-Simpson's analysis and recommendations were incorporated into the Passfield White Paper of October 1930. In it Lord Passfield, the colonial secretary, criticized Jewish colonization policies and the immigration practices of the Histadrut which focused on Jewish labor, arguing that concern must be given to all unemployed in Palestine. The White Paper called upon Jewish leaders to make "concessions . . . in regard to the independent and separatist ideas which have developed in some quarters in respect of the Jewish National Home." It asked the Arabs to recognize "the facts of the situation" which presumably meant accepting the Jews then living in Palestine.[51]

The Passfield White Paper aroused a furor that seemed to threaten the stability of the MacDonald government. Weizmann resigned as head of the World Zionist Organization and the Jewish Agency. Other leading Zionists followed suit. Conservative parliamentarians attacked the White Paper and called for its repudiation. The MacDonald cabinet was on shaky ground and was alarmed at the threat of Jewish pressure on the American government to bring economic sanctions against Great Britain. The insecurity of the Labour government and the strength of Jewish objections led MacDonald to enter discussions with Weizmann, the intermediary being MacDonald's son, Malcolm, an ardent Zionist himself. MacDonald then issued a letter to Weizmann repudiating the Passfield White Paper after extended negotiations during which Weizmann told the prime minister, "We want it made clear that the letter to me containing the authoritative interpretation of the White Paper shall be the basis of the law in Palestine."[52] MacDonald's letter was in effect dictated by Weizmann and his colleagues. The British government's capitulation ensured that the Jewish community would expand, aided during the 1930s by European events— most specifically the rise of Adolf Hitler in Germany and the ensuing exodus of many German Jews to Palestine.

Adolf Hitler was sworn in as chancellor of Germany on 30 January 1933. He quickly had laws passed that barred Jewish participation in many professional and commercial activities. In July 1935 the Nuremberg laws restricted citizenship to Aryans and banned marriage or any type of sexual relationship between Germans and Jews. German Jewish emigration then began, although a majority of those leaving did not go to Palestine. Those who did were able to transfer much of their money, thanks to agreements reached between Zionist leaders and the Nazi government.[53] Indeed, the Nazis were so eager to get rid of the Jewish population of Germany that they permitted the Zionist organization to establish vocational training camps in Germany to train future immigrants. The SS officer in charge of facilitating these arrangements was Adolf Eichmann.[54] German Jewish immigration to Palestine coincided with increased Jewish immigration from Eastern Europe, especially Poland. Between 1933 and 1935 the Jewish population in Palestine doubled, nearly a majority of the immigrants being Polish and about one-fifth being German. This influx, far more middle class than worker in its composition, brought a major infusion of capital into Palestine, whose urban and Jewish sectors underwent an economic boom in the mid-1930s despite the world Depression. Most immigrants settled in the cities, which grew rapidly. Tel Aviv, including Jaffa, expanded from 46,000 inhabitants in 1931 to 135,000 in 1935; Haifa's Jewish population went from 16,000 to 40,000 in the same period. Encouraged by German Jewish funds, industry expanded as the number of industrial firms increased from 6000 in 1930 to 14,000 in 1937.[55] The Yishuv was thus able to consolidate itself during the mid-1930s to a point that it was much more stable than it had been in 1931 and in a stronger position to argue against continuing Arab requests for a legislative council on which they would be represented, requests that Chancellor had been supporting on the eve of the 1929 riots.

The question of a legislative council had been mentioned in the Passfield White Paper. The new high commissioner, Sir Arthur Wauchope, who assumed office in 1931, delayed bringing up the matter until 1933, at which time it became clear that Zionist opposition remained, especially that of the Yishuv in Palestine. On the other hand, Arab leaders seemed favorable to the idea, al-Nashshashibi openly and the al-Husayni faction privately. What the Arabs wished in return was that the British might declare the Jewish National Home to have been achieved, thus freezing immigration and the scope of the Jewish community in Palestine. Wauchope finally announced a specific proposal in December 1935, albeit in the face of the opposition of the Zionist Congress, which had rejected the idea two months earlier and had called for the resettlement of Palestinian Arabs elsewhere, especially Transjordan. The legislative council would have five official members, eleven nominated (three Muslim, four Jewish, two Christian, and two British, all commercial representatives) and twelve elected (eight Muslim, three Jewish, and one Christian). As in 1922, the high commissioner would have veto power over the council's proposals. With Jewish opposition in the open, the British government invited Arab leaders to London to discuss the matter. But before they left Palestine, the matter was taken up in both the House of Lords and the House of Commons on the initiative of British parliamentarians favorable to the Zionist cause. They scuttled the proposals, leaving the British government with nothing to present to the Arabs when they reached London.

British parliamentary rejection of the council idea, at a time when Arab leaders were leaning toward participation in it with recognition of the mandate as it then existed, confirmed to them the Zionists' power and influence in the British government, even though Zionist officials had not initiated or requested the action. Nevertheless, the motions put forth by British legislators sympathetic to the Zionist cause reflected Weizmann's wish to delay discussion of the matter to enable continuing Jewish immigration and land purchases to further consolidate the Jewish presence in Palestine. It was precisely these concerns that had led Arab leaders to move toward acceptance of the legislative council idea, in the hopes of influencing British decisions that might stem the tide of immigrants. But British legislators were more concerned with conditions in Germany and Eastern Europe that caused Jews to flee, not the impact of the Jewish plight and emigration on Arabs in Palestine. For the Arabs, however, this was one final rejection, coming at a time when the surrounding Arab populations seemed to be moving toward greater self-rule under either British or French sway. More radical Arabs had already been advocating armed resistance. Now it erupted into what became known as the Arab Revolt, which began in April 1936.

THE ARAB REVOLT, ITS ROOTS AND IMPACT ON PALESTINE

If the early 1930s were a time of triumph for the Zionists, they marked a continuation of divisiveness and economic disarray for the Palestinian Arabs. The Zionists had not only thwarted the Passfield White Paper through the MacDonald letter; they had also written the terms of the Landless Arab Inquiry so that fewer than nine hundred claims were deemed valid, permitting them to argue that Zionist settlement efforts had little or no impact on Arab peasant society. Initially eager to resolve the landless Arab question, which it saw as a cause of unrest that required further expenditures to maintain public order, the British government had backed down in 1933 in the face of carefully concerted Zionist efforts to respond to any and all charges brought before British officials investigating the issue. Arab leaders were not able to respond decisively to British findings, as Lewis French, head of the Landless Arab Inquiry, disclosed that a number of leading Arab families had been involved in selling land to Jews. This disclosure intensified the antagonisms between Hajj Amin al-Husayni and the more moderate faction led by the al-Nashshashibis and Musa Kazim al-Husayni, head of the Arab Executive until his death in 1934. As head of the Supreme Muslim Council and leader of the fight to preserve the Western Wall under Muslim control, Hajj Amin had gained a great deal of prestige during 1929 and used it to enhance his political stature and influence from that time. His followers publicized the news of Arab land sales to Jews and castigated the Arab Executive for its apathy in confronting this situation. At the same time, Hajj Amin retained correct relations with British officials in order to preserve his own position as mufti and to be in a position to deal with the British to try to stop Zionist gains in Palestine.

Yet even though Arab concern about land sales to Jews was increasing, economic conditions during the 1930s were forcing more Arabs, often of the smaller landholding class, to sell portions of their land just to survive. Indeed, "in the early 1930s, Arab land sales and Jewish land purchases contributed to the evolution of an Arab landless class,"[56] precisely during that period when the Landless Arab Inquiry concluded that the landless Arab problem was negligible. As we have noted, Palestine experienced something of an economic boom during the 1930s, but it was due to the influx of Jewish capital and benefited the Jewish economy almost exclusively, although there was some spin-off to the Arab urban economy and to Arabs who left the land to work in construction trades in the rapidly expanding cities. Many of these workers became part of an expanding Arab proletariat surviving on the edge of Jewish urban centers. One report stated that in Haifa in the mid-1930s, 11,160 Arab workers were living in 2500 gasoline-can huts.[57] Arab access to certain jobs was restricted by British policies. In the public works sector, the Jewish Agency gained British agreement to employ Arabs and Jews on a fifty-fifty basis rather than on that of population ratios, which would have been approximately 70 percent Arab to 30 percent Jewish.

The justification was that Jews provided 50 percent of the tax revenues in Palestine. This reflected the modern European economy installed by the Jews, but the rationale contributed to Arab unemployment.

As noted, the majority of the Arab population, and nearly 90 percent of the Muslims, lived on the land. As peasants and small landholders, they had seen their economic situation deteriorate continually since the end of World War I. In addition, the status of Palestine as a mandate under European control placed it in a disadvantageous economic position, able to be exploited in classic colonial fashion. Article 18 of the mandate established that Palestine could not create discriminatory tariffs against members of the League of Nations. It thus became an open market into which countries with excess surpluses could dump both agricultural and industrial goods, a frequent practice after the onset of the Depression.[58] This worked totally to the disadvantage of the Arab economy in Palestine. Wheat production dropped in the early 1930s as imports increased and peasants went further into debt to Arab money lenders, often doubling as grain merchants, who demanded cash rather than kind.[59] As a result, many peasants seem to have left the land for possible work in the cities or with Jewish citrus-grove owners, themselves under attack by the Histadrut for using non-Jewish labor. Equally significant was the fact that from 1931 onward we see the increasing number of land sales to Jews by smaller holders in need of capital and willing to sell portions of their land to try to survive in adverse times. This pattern continued throughout the 1930s in keeping with the weakening economic condition of much of the Arab peasantry. These circumstances may partially explain why the peasants formed the basis of support for the Arab Revolt when it erupted in 1936.

Equally important to the growth of more overt Arab resistance was the emergence of a younger generation of Arabs educated under the mandate and advocating more open defiance to British authority. Many had ties with Hajj Amin al-Husayni and backed his more hostile stance against Zionist policies which increasingly incorporated Islamic themes. Some were influenced by the example of organized youth found in Italy and Germany, as were Jabotinsky's Betar members, and encouraged the formation of Boy Scout troops and branches of the Young Men's Muslim Association as a means of creating cadres ready to confront Zionist immigration or British authority. A Congress of Arab Youth met for the first time in January 1932, but it could not escape the imprint of the al-Husayni–al-Nashshashibi rift. Especially notable was the formation of the Istiqlal party in August 1932. It advocated pan-Arab unity as the only solution to the Arab plight in Palestine and harked back to the greater Syria themes prominent during Faysal's rule in Damascus from 1918 to 1920. The Istiqlalists were primarily from northern Palestine, especially Nablus, indicating an aversion to the factionalism rampant among the leading Jerusalem families in the early 1930s. Raghib al-Nashshashibi had established the National Defense party in December 1934 to represent his opposition to the al-Husayni bloc which created in turn the Palestine Arab party in March 1935. In June, Husayn al-Khalidi, scion of another leading Jerusalem family and victor over Raghib al-Nashshashibi in elections for mayor of Jerusalem in late 1934, formed the Reform party. Although both al-Khalidi and al-Nashshashibi opposed the power of Hajj Amin al-Husayni, they were rivals themselves, and al-Nashshashibi sought to undermine al-Khalidi at every opportunity.[60] But both agreed in their preference for political rather than militant opposition to British policies whereas Hajj Amin, though considering the Istiqlal a challenge to his authority, seems to have sympathized with its call for active armed resistance to Zionism. And his use of Muslim ideology to seek external Islamic assistance to confront Zionism blended at times with the pan-Arab ideas of the Istiqlal.

Several secret societies were formed during the early 1930s, one led by Abd al-Qadir al-Husayni, the son of Musa Kazim who personally identified with al-Nashshashibi moderation and sought an accommodation with the mandatory authorities; generational cleavages were beginning to appear. The younger al-Husayni founded an organization called Holy War and began buying arms in preparation for open resistance. Finally, there was a group led by a Muslim shaykh, Izz al-Din al-Qassam, and two founding members of the Istiqlal. Al-Qassam called for rejection of the influences of modern culture as a precursor to open resistance against the British. He preached for years in Haifa and its environs, calling for strict adherence to Muslim principles and finding an audience among a population becoming progressively impoverished in the face of an influx of Jewish immigrants and the great expansion of Haifa itself under their impact. Al-Qassam and two followers were killed in November 1935 after themselves killing a Jewish policeman whom they encountered as they were preparing for open resistance.

Al-Qassam's death occurred shortly after a major Jewish arms smuggling operation had been discovered at the Jaffa port. This, and the inability of British officials to locate the addressee, aroused Arab alarm. But their arms purchases were apparently rudimentary compared with Jewish efforts which resulted in a stockpiling of weapons and ammunition sufficient to arm an army of ten thousand, according to an official British estimate in 1937.[61] These developments, coupled with increasing Arab unemployment, led to calls for a strike and demands for greater vigilance by the mandatory authorities over Jewish arms smuggling. Though concerned, High Commissioner Wauchope felt that the granting of a legislative council would satisfy Arab grievances, as he knew that Hajj Amin al-Husayni, along with the al-Nashshashibis, was willing to accept the proposal. Zionist opposition and its rejection by the British Parliament provided the spark for open revolt. These developments came at a time when demonstrations in both Egypt and Syria in late 1935 led to British and French willingness to negotiate new treaties with Egyptian and Syrian nationalists in early 1936. The lesson of resistance seemed obvious, especially once the legislative council proposals had been jettisoned.

With the outbreak of Arab attacks on Jews in April 1936, the feuding Arab factions joined together in a temporary display of unity to form the Higher Arab Committee. The committee called for a general strike by all Arab workers and government employees, a boycott of Jewish goods or sales to Jews, and attacks on Jews and Jewish settlements as well as British forces. This first stage of the revolt lasted from mid-April to early November 1936. In many ways it was unsuccessful. For example, Arab workers in major Jewish enterprises often could not strike effectively because they would simply be replaced by Jewish workers. For Arab government employees to strike would mean a loss of any ability to influence government policies; they pledged a tenth of their salary instead. And where a strike was sustained, as in the closing of the port of Jaffa, then the only large port for Palestine, the Agency leadership petitioned successfully to have Tel Aviv developed as a port for Jewish goods. Here, as in other instances, the strike encouraged further Zionist self-reliance.

Fighting shifted gradually to the countryside, where armed bands mined roads and sought to disrupt transportation. Palestinian groups were aided by other Arabs, most notably Fawzi al-Qawuqji, Lebanese born and an officer in the Iraqi army, who led occasional attacks on British forces. By early fall almost 20,000 British troops had arrived, and offensive actions quickly quelled Arab resistance. In early November the leaders of the Higher Arab Committee were willing to call off the strike, in part because of its relative failure and in part thanks to mediation by the ministers of surrounding Arab states who tried to achieve a peaceful settlement of the matter, albeit one favorable to the Palestinian Arab cause.[62] In apparent reward, the Colonial Office approved only 1800 Jewish entry permits for the period between October and March 1937, 17 percent of the 11,200 requested by the Jewish Agency.[63]

With hostilities ended, the Peel Commission, appointed in May to investigate the motives for Arab resistance, arrived and received testimony as to the underlying causes of unrest from both Jewish and Arab sources. The Zionists called for unlimited immigration and the purchase of land as a matter of right, whereas Hajj Amin demanded that Palestine be declared an Arab state in which there would be no place for those nearly 400,000 Jews who had immigrated since World War I. The commission published its findings in July 1937. It concluded that the Palestine Mandate was impossible to sustain because of its terms and the unyielding mutual hostility reflected in the conflicting demands for statehood made by the Arabs and the Jews. According to the stipulations of the mandate, Arab objections to Jewish immigration and land purchases were unwarranted, but given the fact that the drive for Jewish statehood could come about only by imposing it on a hostile Arab population, this too was contrary to the mandate which was supposed to guard the interests of the Arab population. It was, in the end, a case of "right against right," a situation that the Peel Report believed could be resolved only through the partition of Palestine into separate independent Arab and Jewish states. Great Britain would remain as a mandatory power in a

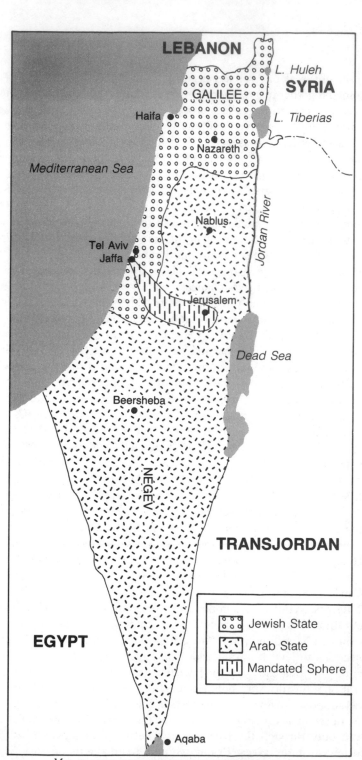

LEBANON

SYRIA

L. Huleh

GALILEE

Haifa

L. Tiberias

Nazareth

Mediterranean Sea

Jordan River

Nablus

Tel Aviv

Jaffa

Jerusalem

Dead Sea

Beersheba

NEGEV

TRANSJORDAN

EGYPT

Aqaba

	Jewish State
	Arab State
	Mandated Sphere

Map 5. PEEL COMMISSION PARTITION PLAN, 1937

zone including the holy places. The Peel Commission awarded to the proposed Jewish state about 20 percent of Palestine, comprising the northern region of the Galilee and the Jezreel Plain (Esdraelon), south of Nazareth, and the coastal plain from the Lebanese border to a point south of Jaffa which itself would remain Arab. The Arabs were granted the remainder of the area, which meant central Palestine from slightly below Nazareth, and the Negev; the commission envisaged Arab Palestine's being united with Transjordan. Jerusalem and Bethlehem would be under British mandatory control with access to the sea.[64]

Arab opposition to partition was swift. Though the Arab state would comprise about 80 percent of post-1922 Palestine, the most fertile area had been granted to the Jews, and 250,000 Arabs of the Galilee would have to be evacuated. The area awarded to the Jews contained a nearly equal number of Arabs, whereas the Arab area was 90 percent Arab in composition. Neighboring Arab governments joined the Higher Arab Committee in condemning the proposals, and an Arab congress was held in Bludan in September 1937 to call for united Arab resistance to world Jewry and its efforts to establish a state in Palestine. Palestine was becoming an Arab, as opposed to a purely Palestinian Arab, issue.

The Zionist response to the partition proposal was mixed, if finally cautiously favorable. In the face of strong opposition, Ben-Gurion and Weizmann found themselves united in tentatively accepting partition in principle but demanding larger, if unspecified, borders. For them the issue was one of sovereignty. They would have an independent state with rights to unlimited immigration, a crucial point at a time when more and more Jews were beginning to flee anti-Semitism in Central and Eastern Europe. Whatever the original applicability of the Zionist claim that Palestine would be a haven for world Jewry, it now seemed to be justified. Furthermore, Weizmann and Ben-Gurion did not feel they would be limited by the borders set. These could be considered temporary boundaries, to be expanded in the future. As one British member of Parliament favorable to the Zionists declared, "I hope that the Jews will treat it merely as a stepping-off ground for further advance." And Ben-Gurion announced at the World Zionist Congress in August that although "there could be no question . . . of giving up any part of the Land of Israel, . . . it was arguable that the ultimate goal would be achieved most quickly by accepting the Peel proposals."[65] The congress authorized Zionist leaders to negotiate for borders more favorable than those allotted.

Aware of Zionist tactics and totally opposed to the initial partition plan, Arab leaders despaired of retaining control of Palestine. The ensuing tensions led to the second and much more violent stage of the Arab Revolt, from September 1937 to January 1939. For the first time, British officials became targets, and the acting district commissioner for Galilee was murdered on 26 September. The violence continued, even though the Higher Arab Committee had disbanded after Hajj Amin Al-Husayni's flight to Lebanon and then to Iraq, barely escaping British efforts to capture him because he opposed partition. The al-

Nashshashibis initially backed the partition plan but reversed themselves when faced with assaults from opponents. They then discovered that their patron, Amir Abdullah of Transjordan, backed partition, as he viewed it as an opportunity to take over Arab Palestine, later the strategy he followed in 1948.

With the Higher Arab Committee in disarray, leadership of the revolt devolved to individual commanders in the field. Peasant despair at their lot and hatred of the great landowners caused the revolt to last a year and a half and to include retaliatory attacks on leading Arab families, not just on Jews and British troops. Armed bands roamed much of central Palestine during 1938 and for a time controlled most major lines of communication and many towns: "By September 'the situation was such that civil administration and control of the country was to all practical purposes non-existent.' "[66] Raghib al-Nashshashibi fled to exile in Egypt following assassination attempts ordered by the mufti.

Attacks on Jews led to Jewish reprisals. The Hagana counseled self-restraint, but from 1936 onward this meant selective retaliation rather than purely defensive measures, a move undertaken to placate restive members who wished to strike back at the Arab attackers. Once the Arab Revolt became widespread in 1938, the Hagana and British forces cooperated. The Hagana was permitted to arm itself legally, and special Jewish units were formed under the direction of a British officer, Orde Wingate, that carried out night attacks on guerrillas were dynamited, a practice adopted by the Hagana and later by the Irgun began its own operations. The Irgun advocated terrorist tactics equal to those used by Arabs who attacked individual Jews. In three weeks in 1937, Irgun bombs planted in Arab marketplaces killed seventy-seven Arabs.

British forces were harsh in their treatment of the Arabs. Over one hundred were hanged between 1937 and 1939, and many more were killed by British troops in acts of unofficial retribution. Houses of families suspected of harboring guerrillas were dynamited, a practice adopted by the Hagana and later by the Israeli government after 1948. But when the British tried to curb Irgun acts, by hanging a member of Betar for an attack on an Arab bus, it seemed to the Jews to be discriminatory, an attempt to indicate fairness to the Arabs rather than a penalty consonant with the supposed crime. This in turn appears to have encouraged the Irgun to undertake more intensive actions against Arabs and to prepare for resistance to the British.[67]

In such a conflict, many Arab villagers were placed under great pressure by both guerrillas demanding assistance and British forces seeking information. They might be tortured by Arab resistance groups or have their houses blown up by British troops on suspicion of aid to the resistance. Consequently, some villages were willing to respond to Fakhri al-Nashshashibi's efforts to organize counterrevolutionary squads which fought the rebels and gave information to the British and the Zionists.[68] During 1938 nearly 1700 Arabs were killed, officially 1138 defined as rebels and 486 considered as civilians. In addition, 292 Jews were killed and over 600 wounded, along with 69 British troops killed and over 200 wounded; British forces "presumably killed a great many more rebels than officially listed."[69] By the end of the year the number of British troops had reached 20,000 once more as divisions were freed from Europe following the Munich agreement between Hitler and Neville Chamberlain in early October in the aftermath of the Nazi invasion of Czechoslovakia. Organized Arab resistance had collapsed by early 1939, reduced to acts of retribution against other Arabs considered to be traitors.

Despite its failure, the Arab Revolt left a lasting imprint on both Palestinian Arabs and British officials. Many of its most devoted participants either had belonged to the Istiqlal party or were followers of the late Shaykh Izz al-Din al-Qassam. Others were led by Abd al-Qadir al-Husayni. All had emerged as leaders during the early 1930s, and many fought during the war of early 1948. Equally important, however, was the lack of central authority over the Arab resistance, a vacuum created by the departure of the mufti that would never be filled. Palestinian Arabs, whether moderates or militants, were essentially leaderless at a time when the Zionists under Ben-Gurion's leadership seemed to be stronger than ever and when Zionist terror squads had established themselves as an independent force with which the British as well as the Arabs would have to contend.

To the British, however, the Arab Revolt signified a rebellion that had to be crushed, not simply to preserve Britain's own position in Palestine as the mandatory power, but consolidate it by appealing for Arab support both within and outside Palestine once the revolt had ended. This stance emerged once a new European war seemed imminent. Nazi and Fascist propaganda encouraging Arabs in other areas of the Middle East to revolt against the British endangered their strategic position in Egypt athwart the Suez Canal. Any such rebellion would require large numbers of troops to be tied down in the Middle East when they would be desperately needed in Europe. These considerations led to the issuing of the 1939 White Paper which, in a stunning reversal of policy, called for severe restrictions on Jewish immigration and seemed to guarantee achievement of an Arab Palestine within ten years.

THE 1939 WHITE PAPER BACKGROUND AND CONSEQUENCES

Throughout the period of the Arab Revolt, 1936 to 1939, British attempts to resolve the crisis in Palestine occurred against a backdrop of developing tensions in Europe and the Mediterranean which ultimately had a major impact on Britain's Palestine policy. Since the Italian invasion of Abyssinia (Ethiopia) in October 1935, British diplomats and military officials had been deeply concerned about the potential Italian threat to Egypt and its naval power in the eastern Mediterranean. The chiefs of staff argued that if war broke out, Britain's eastern Mediterranean fleet would have to proceed to the Far East, essentially conceding the region to the Italians. At best the British could hope to defend

Egypt and the Suez Canal. In such circumstances, British military planners, and diplomats as well, began to view Palestine in light of envisaged wartime needs. They considered that peace in Palestine was essential to British military security, as any troops there would have to be transferred to the canal and Egypt in time of war. Also, assuming Italian control of the Red Sea entrance to Suez by virtue of its Abyssinian position, reinforcements from India would have to be sent overland from Iraq through Palestine to Egypt.

These considerations added to the existing strategic importance of Palestine to the British. In 1933 they had completed construction of a modern harbor at Haifa and in 1935 had finished laying pipe that linked their oil fields in northern Iraq to Haifa, thus bypassing the Suez Canal. France had a similar pipeline that ended at the port of Tripoli in Lebanon. Finally, Palestine was a crucial link in Britain's system of imperial air defense and communications, a major way station, along with Egypt, for flights to Africa, Iraq, India, and the Far East. Given the potential for nationalist unrest in Egypt and Iraq, despite treaties ensuring British use of bases in both countries, Britain's bases in Palestine, under direct control, assumed added significance.[70]

But control of Palestine could not by itself ensure British security in the region. Equally important was British assurance of the tacit, if not open, support of the neighboring Arab countries. To be forced to confront Arab hostility in states such as Syria, Iraq, or Egypt, encouraged by German and Italian propaganda, would place too great a burden on British resources. Here the situation in Palestine was crucial, given the increasing involvement of Arab leaders in Palestinian affairs as the revolt progressed. Resolving the Palestinian crisis in a manner favorable to the Arab population came to be seen as a means of acquiring the cooperation of the Arab world once war began. British strategists on the subcommittee of the Committee of Imperial Defence declared in January 1939,

> we feel it is necessary to point out . . . the strong feeling . . . in all Arab states in connection with British policy in Palestine. . . . We assume that, immediately on the outbreak of war, the necessary measures would be taken . . . in order to bring about a complete appeasement of Arab opinion in Palestine and in neighboring countries. . . . If we fail thus to retain Arab goodwill at the outset of a war, no other measures which we can recommend will serve to influence the Arab States in favor of this country.[71]

These ideas were not new in early 1939, but they served to emphasize that it was only through British retention of its mandatory role in Palestine that Britain could rely on it as a strategic base. This role, set against the partition plan proposed by the Peel Commission in July 1937, raised questions in the Foreign Office: if the Jews were recognized as having national status in part of Palestine, what further justification would there be for Britain's staying there as mandatory authority? Nevertheless, the cabinet approved the Peel recommendations, assuming that the Zionists would also. The government was startled by the force of Zionist opposition to the plan, even though representatives such as Weizmann argued that partition would be acceptable if the borders were renegotiated. Zionist complaints caused opponents of the government, led by Churchill, to call for a new committee to investigate the ramifications of partition and report to Parliament. This tack was adopted, thanks to the feeling of British Gentile Zionists that they were following the wishes of the Zionist leadership. But the recommendation to form a new commission played into the hands of the Foreign Office which, unlike the Colonial Office, strongly opposed partition. Fearing Arab hostility to British policy, the Foreign Office was able to have the new committee, the Woodhead Commission, reopen the question of the practicability of partition, not just its scope. Colonial Office objections were rebuffed as the Foreign Office argued that "the European implications of a hostile Middle East aligned with Britain's enemies must override the arguments in favour of partition."[72]

The Woodhead Commission, formed in January 1938, did not submit its report until November, after a period that had witnessed the more severe aspects of the Arab Revolt that temporarily paralyzed much of Palestine. It concluded that there were no feasible boundaries for "self-supporting Arab and Jewish states."[73] Nevertheless, the four commissioners recommended three different partition plans among them. That supported by two members, Plan C, reduced the proposed Jewish state to about four hundred square miles among the coast, leaving northern Palestine in British hands. The other two plans outlined areas for a Jewish state even smaller than that of Plan C. The Zionists naturally rejected these proposals, enabling the government to issue a White Paper on 9 November 1938 that discarded the entire notion of partition as "impracticable." This left the British with "responsibility for the government of the whole of Palestine" but with the need to confront the fact of Arab-Jewish irreconcilability as portrayed in the Peel Commission Report. The White Paper thus called for a conference of Arabs and Jews in London to discuss "future policy, including the question of immigration into Palestine." The document concluded that if the talks did not end in agreement, the British would "take their own decision in the light of their examination of the problem . . ." an intimation of their willingness to consider the likelihood of a reevaluation of their mandatory obligations.[74]

The new colonial secretary, Malcolm MacDonald, liaison between Weizmann and his father in 1931, opened the St. James Conference in February 1939. He now accepted the rejection of partition, and thence his relations with Zionist leaders deteriorated swiftly. Members of the Higher Arab Committee, other than the mufti, were permitted to attend along with Fakhri al-Nashshashibi. Also present were representatives of Egypt, Iraq, Saudi Arabia, Transjordan, and the Yemen. On the Jewish side were members of the Jewish Agency and leaders of the American and English Jewish communities. The British conducted separate meetings, as the Arabs refused to sit with the Jewish delegates. There was no common ground. Jamal al-Husayni, cousin of the mufti, demanded the creation of an independent Arab state and the dismantling of the Jewish National

Home. Weizmann called for a continuation of the mandate and British sponsorship of unlimited immigration. British officials bowed to al-Husayni's request that the Husayn-McMahon correspondence be reexamined. A joint British-Arab committee could not agree on its findings. The Arabs argued that MacMahon had promised to support Arab independence in Palestine. British members, though concluding that the entire correspondence showed that Palestine was intended to be excluded from Arab territory, admitted that the language was not as precise as formerly assumed and declared it to be evident from the correspondence that "His Majesty's Government were not free to dispose of Palestine without regard for the wishes and interests of the inhabitants of Palestine." This conclusion tacitly backed the Arabs' assertions that they had a right to oppose the establishment of a Jewish state.[75]

The conference quickly reached an impasse. MacDonald presented various proposals to both the Arab and Jewish delegations. For the Arabs he was willing to consider a unitary state, enshrining an Arab majority, if they allowed Jewish immigration to continue on a restricted basis for a limited period. But the Palestinian Arabs rejected this and demanded an independent state immediately, something Britain would not concede. To the Zionists MacDonald proposed that they acknowledge that their presence in Palestine should be based on Arab consent, a matter stated also in the British report on the Husayn–McMahon correspondence but never mentioned in the Balfour Declaration. The Zionists scorned this proposal and demanded continued immigration and a guaranteed position in Palestine, not one subject to Arab veto. The conference fell apart, despite the Arab states' willingness to accept the government proposals. But the negotiations continued with representatives of the Arab states who requested a specific transitional period of ten years after which Palestine could become independent. These discussions took place from mid-March to May 1939, against a backdrop of the German absorption of part of Czechoslovakia, Italy's invasion of Albania, and, on 7 May, the creation of a formal German-Italian military alliance. The British finally agreed to the Arab state overtures and on 17 May published the White Paper that reinterpreted their mandatory obligation and seemed to guarantee an independent Palestine with an Arab majority.

The White Paper declared that "His Majesty's Government believe that the framers of the Mandate in which the Balfour Declaration was embodied could not have intended that Palestine should be converted into a Jewish State against the will of the Arab population of the country."[76] It called therefore for the establishment of a Jewish National Home in an independent Palestinian state. Jewish immigration would be permitted to continue at a maximum pace of 15,000 yearly for five years; after that it could occur only with Arab agreement. In addition, 25,000 refugees would be admitted. Unlimited land transfers to Jews would be restricted to designated coastal areas. The White Paper foresaw an independent Palestine within ten years, at which time the Jews would comprise no more than one-third of the population. The British government would develop self-governing institutions incorporating both Arabs and Jews during this period even if both sides rejected the idea. If there were no cooperation and Palestine seemed unsuitable for independence after ten years, then Great Britain would consult with Palestinian Arabs and Jews, Arab states, and the League of Nations to determine the course it should take.

Both Arabs and Jews rejected the 1939 White Paper. The Jewish Agency declared that the system envisaged was contrary to international law and a violation of the promises made to the Jews in and since the Balfour Declaration. It warned that Jews would resist implementation of the White Paper, and Ben-Gurion declared that although Jews necessarily would "fight with Great Britain in this war as if there was no White Paper," they would subsequently "fight the White Paper as if there was no war." This reflected the Jewish dilemma well recognized by the British. The Zionists had no choice but to fight with the British against the Nazi threat. On the other hand, the Palestinian Arabs, through the Higher Arab Committee, repudiated the White Paper because it did not promise them immediate independence with a halt to Jewish immigration.

GREAT BRITAIN AND PALESTINE ON THE EVE OF WORLD WAR II

In the midst of the abortive St. James Conference in early 1939, British officials, as we have seen, attempted to persuade Zionist leaders to acknowledge the principle of Arab agreement to future Jewish immigration into Palestine, thereby tacitly granting that this was not an absolute right to be undertaken despite Arab opposition. The Zionists objected, not simply because they had always considered Jewish immigration to be a matter for their control, but also because they foresaw the need for increased immigration given the attempts of European Jews to escape persecution in Germany and Eastern Europe. At one point Chaim Weizmann responded angrily to Malcolm MacDonald, "Are the British in Palestine with the consent of the Arabs?"[77] Clearly they were not, and the partnership between British imperialism and the Zionist colonizing effort since World War I had been predicated on the assumption that Arab consent was unnecessary precisely because it was unattainable. Now, however, the circumstances had changed. The Zionists were more willing to consider taking in all Jews who wished to enter, in contrast with their selective immigration quotas of the interwar period that targeted the young and the wealthy. The spread of Fascism confirmed to Jews their original assumptions regarding the irrelevance of Arab consent. But their stance clashed with the increasing British concern for their imperial security that, in the latter's view, required greater interest in Arab than in Jewish goodwill.

In this light, the White Paper of 1939 was even more an act of expediency than was the proclamation of the Balfour Declaration in 1917. Both were motivated by strategic concerns related to war efforts, either existing, as in 1917, or imminent, as in 1939. But the Balfour Declaration did reflect some genuine interest in the future of European Jewry, whereas the White Paper exhibited no corresponding concern for either Palestinian Arabs or Jews. The Balfour Declaration had not provided for a British obligation to take into account Arab opinion regarding Jewish immigration and the building of a national home. Knowing what that opinion was, British officials strove to placate it throughout most of the interwar period while ensuring that no concessions were made that would seriously endanger Zionist efforts. This policy, coupled with an effective Zionist defense of their cause in London as well as Palestine, stymied those few proposals that did seek to respond to Palestinian Arab views, mainly set forth in the 1931 MacDonald letter. In consequence, Britain's newfound regard for Arab objections to Zionism, coming on the heels of a revolt that British forces were suppressing with little restraint toward their opponents, had little to do with morality. Arab opinion in the wider Middle East now seemed more important to British interests than was Jewish opinion in Palestine or Jewish political influence in London. In addition, the abandonment of partition permitted the British to retain control of all of Palestine; the creation of separate entities might have required their abdication of sovereignty over those areas.

For the Arabs and the Jews of Palestine, the White Paper was a disappointment of differing magnitudes. The Arab community in Palestine was essentially leaderless, riven with more factions than ever before. The moderate Arabs of the al-Khalidi and al-Nashshashibi camps found it hopeful, as did the leaders of the Arab governments, but the power of the Higher Arab Committee was still great, even though many of its members had now repudiated Hajj Amin al-Husayni. The example of the Arab Revolt and its presumed success in forcing Britain to deal with the Arabs, whatever its military failure, apparently gave optimism to those who counseled defiance. The Higher Arab Committee's disavowal of the White Paper was based on arguments first presented in 1918 and indicated a consistent refusal to admit that any part of Palestine should be given to the Zionists.

The shock of the White Paper forced the Zionist leadership to reconsider their ties to Great Britain. For Ben-Gurion, the events of the later 1930s and the White Paper proved that the Jews would have to look for the support of another great power and large Jewish community, namely, the United States. Above all, Ben-Gurion insisted on the right of Jews to determine their own course, regardless of British policies. While cooperating with the British militarily to stem the Axis tide in the Middle East in the early years of the war, he oversaw a concerted effort to steal weapons and munitions from them to prepare Jews for a likely armed conflict with Great Britain once the war ended.

The Arab and Jewish communities in Palestine, both greatly expanded since 1919, were much more separate than they had been previously. From approximately 10 percent of the population, Jews had become nearly 30 percent in 1939–1940, about 467,000 out of a total population of about 1.528 million. Nearly 300,000 of these were immigrants who arrived during the 1930s, an increase of 64 percent, not counting the number of illegal immigrants, estimated at between 30,000 and 40,000. From the first census, in 1922, to 1940, the Arab population increased from 660,641 to about 1,060,750, a rate of nearly 27 percent, very little of which was due to illegal immigration. The entrance of Arabs from neighboring countries was principally "casual, temporary, and seasonal. . . . It is not illegal in the sense that the immigrants settle permanently in Palestine," as did Jewish illegal immigrants.[78] The increase in the Arab population was due primarily to a very high birthrate among Arab women, averaging about seven children per mother during the period, and a significant decline in infant mortality.[79]

Yet despite important transformations in Arab patterns of living—the Arab urban population increased 111 percent between 1922 and 1944—there were still major gaps between the traditional Arab and the more modern Jewish economies, with the latter much more closely integrated into the world economic system. The only area in which Arab capital had held its own by means of further development was in citrus cultivation. As of 1943, Arabs (including other non-Jews) held 145,572 dunams in citrus, as opposed to 141,188 held by Jews, with a similar ratio in the valuation of the land. But in industry, for example, although in 1943 Arabs and other non-Jews owned 1558 industrial "establishments," as opposed to 1907 Jewish, there was no comparison in terms of capital invested, slightly over (£P.) 2 million (Arab) versus nearly 12.1 million (Jewish); horsepower, 3625 (Arab) versus 57,410 (Jewish); and persons engaged in, 8804 (Arab) versus 37,773 (Jewish), about 0.7 percent of the Arab population, as opposed to about 8.5 percent of the Jewish.[80] As for land, Jews owned in 1939 nearly 1.3 million dunams, as opposed to 456,000 in 1920, an increase of about 185 percent. This equalled nearly one-seventh of all cultivable land in Palestine, about 9 million dunams, out of a total land area of 26 million. Given the fact that Arabs owned nearly 17 million dunams of uncultivable land, that meant that they owned about 7.75 million dunams of cultivable land in 1939, leaving an Arab-Jewish ratio of six to one.[81] Despite this disparity in favor of the Arabs, they paid £.P. 351,000 in rural and urban property taxes, whereas the Jews paid 448,000, another index of the valuation gap reflecting the divergent natures of both productivity and size of landholdings. Jewish holdings were far more integrated for both political and economic reasons, the result of planning undertaken by the Jewish Agency during the 1930s.

The Arab and Jewish communities in Palestine continued to diverge with respect to both their economic growth and the quality of their leadership. The British entered the maelstrom of World War II aware that their Palestine policy reversal in the 1939 White Paper had outraged the Zionists without satisfying the Arabs. They accepted this as the price for temporarily stabilizing their military and strategic positions in Palestine and the Arab world at large, important in themselves and as a means of securing communications with India and the Far East. It was a short-term strategy of expediency and calculated appeasement designed to serve Britain's immediate wartime and possibly long-range imperial designs that assumed a British presence in Palestine for the foreseeable future.[82]

NOTES

1. Bernard Wasserstein, *The British in Palestine: The Mandatory Government and the Arab-Jewish Conflict, 1917–1929* (London, 1978), pp. 1–2; and Ronald Storrs, *The Memoirs of Sir Ronald Storrs* (New York, 1937), pp. 301–311.
2. Simha Flapan, *Zionism and the Palestinians* (London, 1979) p. 57.
3. Y. Porath, *The Emergence of the Palestinian-Arab National Movement, 1918–1929* (London, 1974), pp. 33–34, and the recent work by Muhammad Y. Muslih, *The Origins of Palestinian Nationalism* (New York, 1988).
4. Wasserstein, *The British in Palestine*, p. 15.
5. Jehuda Reinharz, "Chaim Weizmann As Political Strategist: The Initial Years, 1918–1920," in Frances Malino and Phylis Cohen Albert, eds., *Essays in Modern Jewish History: A Tribute to Ben Halpern* (Rutherford, N.J., 1982), pp. 273–274.
6. The highest British officials in Palestine, Generals Allenby and Bols, supported this idea; see Wasserstein, *British in Palestine*, pp. 60–61. See also Porath, *Emergence*, pp. 69–105, for a detailed treatment of these issues.
7. *British in Palestine*, p. 92.
8. Ibid, pp. 72–73.
9. See the table in ibid, p. 160.
10. Porath, *Emergence*, p. 60.
11. Wasserstein, *British in Palestine*, p. 109.
12. Philip Mattar, "The Role of the Mufti of Jerusalem in the Political Struggle over the Western Wall, 1928–1929," *Middle Eastern Studies*, 19 (January 1983): 113. See also Mattar's book, *The Mufti of Jerusalem: Al-Hajj Amin al-Husayni and the Palestinian National Movement* (New York, 1988), for broader treatment of the mufti's career.
13. Porath, *Emergence*, p. 276.
14. Wasserstein, *British in Palestine*, p. 157.
15. Yonathan Shapiro, *The Formative Years of the Israeli Labour Party: The Organization of Power, 1919–1930*, Sage Studies in 20th Century History, vol. 4 (Beverly Hills, Calif.; Sage Publications, 1976), pp. 12–13. The following draws on Shapiro and Noah Lucas, *The Modern History of Israel* (New York, 1975), pp. 76–93.
16. Ibid., p. 59.
17. Shapiro, *Formative Years*, p. 205.
18. Lucas, *Modern History*, pp. 131–132.
19. Shlomo Avineri, *The Making of Modern Zionism; The Intellectual Origins of the Jewish State* (New York, 1981), pp. 159–186, has a good overview of Jabotinsky's intellectual development, with a brief mention of his attraction to Fascism (pp. 171–176). More detailed treatment of this issue is found in Lenni Brenner, *Zionism in the Age of the Dictators* (London, 1983), pp. 116–134.
20. Howard M. Sachar, *A History of Israel, from the Rise of Zionism to Our Time* (New York, 1976), p. 186.
21. A. Revusky, *Jews in Palestine* (New York, 1936), pp. 200–201.
22. Neil Caplan, *Palestine Jewry and the Arab Question, 1917–1925* (London, 1978), p. 42.
23. Ibid., p. 113.
24. Ibid., p. 13. See also Nathan Weinstock, *Zionism: False Messiah* (London, 1979), p. 152ff.
25. Ben-Gurion could speak of Arab-Jewish cooperation and Arab economic development, but only within the context of absolute Jewish political sovereignty, precisely the issue that the Arab leaders could not accept. The most recent study of these matters is Shabtai Teveth, *Ben-Gurion and the Palestinian Arabs: From Peace to War* (Oxford, England, 1985).
26. Wasserstein, *British in Palestine*, p. 194.
27. Ibid., p. 173.
28. Kenneth Stein, *The Land Question in Palestine, 1917–1939* (Chapel Hill, N.C., 1984), p. 46.

29. Wasserstein, *British in Palestine*, p. 201.
30. Porath, *Emergence*, pp. 67–68.
31. Stein, *Land Question*, p. 38; and Weinstock, *False Messiah*, pp. 65–71. Still a very important source used by modern students of the land issue is A. Granott, *The Land System in Palestine* (London, 1952).
32. Granott, *Land System*, pp. 221–227; and Stein, *Land Question*, pp. 14–15.
33. Ibid., p. 34.
34. Granott, *Land System*, pp. 81–82.
35. Ibid., p. 41.
36. See Stein, *Land Question*, p. 59ff; and Granott, *Land System*, p. 80.
37. Stein, *Land Question*, Chapter 6. A good clear summary discussion of these issues is in Y. Porath, *The Palestinian Arab National Movement, 1929–1939: From Riots to Rebellion* (London, 1977), pp. 80–108.
38. Stein, *Land Question*, p. 48.
39. Ibid., p. 51.
40. A good overview is by John Ruedy, "Dynamics of Land Alienation," in Ibrahim Abu-Lughod, ed., *The Transformation of Palestine: Essays on the Origin and Development of the Arab-Israeli Conflict* (Evanston, Ill., 1971), pp. 119–138. In seeking to redress the balance, Stein seems to err in arguing that comparatively few Arabs were displaced, pp. 56–59.
41. Government of Palestine, *Survey of Palestine: Prepared in December 1945 and January 1946 for the Information of the Anglo-American Committee of Inquiry*, 2 vols. (Jerusalem, 1946), vol. 1, p. 296.
42. Mattar, "The Role of the Mufti," p. 109; Wasserstein, *British in Palestine*, p. 224.
43. Quoted in Mattar, "Role of the Mufti," p. 106.
44. Porath, *Emergence*, p. 266; and Mattar, "Role of the Mufti," p. 107.
45. Wasserstein, *British in Palestine*, p. 227; and Mattar, "Role of the Mufti," p. 113.
46. Stein, *Land Question*, p. 88ff.
47. Quoted in John Marlowe, *The Seat of Pilate: An Account of the Palestine Mandate* (London, 1959), p. 117.
48. Stein, *Land Question*, p. 91.
49. See discussion in ibid., pp. 110–112.
50. The text of the mandate is in Walter Laqueur and Barry Rubin, eds., *The Israel-Arab Reader: A Documentary History of the Middle East Conflict*, 4th rev. ed. (New York, 1984), pp. 34–43.
51. Quoted in Marlowe, *Seat of Pilate*, p. 123.
52. Quoted in Norman Rose, *The Gentile Zionists: A Study in Anglo-Zionist Diplomacy, 1929–1939* (London, 1973), p. 26. Rose, pp. 1–40, has a good treatment of the British-Zionist interactions on this crisis. The text of the MacDonald letter is in Laqueur and Rubin, *Israel-Arab Reader*, pp. 50–55.
53. Revusky, *Jews in Palestine*, p. 224. The 1935 edition does not contain this information. The German laws barring the export of capital predated the Nazi regime, having been passed in 1931 to stem capital outflows during financial panics related to the world Depression. Zionist and Nazi officials reached an accord whereby emigrant German Jews would enter an agreement with the Reichsbank. Their money would be transferred to Palestine in the form of German goods, and they would receive compensatory payment for the value of these goods, minus taxes, in Palestinian pounds. German Jews thus transferred most of their money, and German commerce benefited from the influx of German goods into Palestine.
54. Sachar, *History of Israel*, p. 197. See also Weinstock, *False Messiah*, p. 136ff; and Brenner, *Age of Dictators*, pp. 79–90; Brenner's style is occasionally more condemnatory than analytical.
55. Statistics from Sachar, *History of Israel*, pp. 189–190; compare p. 201 and footnote 94. Immigration figures vary widely. Thus William Polk argues that the Jewish population "quadrupled" between 1933 and 1936. See William R. Polk, David M. Stamler, and Edmund Asfour, *Backdrop to Tragedy: The Struggle for Palestine* (Boston, 1957), p. 91.
56. Stein, *Land Question*, p. 142.
57. Joel S. Migdal, *Palestinian Society and Politics* (Princeton, N.J., 1980), p. 26; and Pamela Ann Smith, *Palestine and the Palestinians, 1876–1983* (London, 1984), p. 54.
58. Said B. Himadeh, "Industry," in Said B. Himadeh, ed., *Economic Organization of Palestine* (Beirut, 1938), p. 297. Text in Laqueur and Rubin, *Israel-Arab Reader*, pp. 39–40.
59. Stein, *Land Question*, pp. 131, 143–144; and Montague Brown, "Agriculture," in Himedeh, ed., *Economic Organization*, pp. 121–133.

60. Porath, *From Riots to Rebellion*, pp. 63–79.
61. See the discussion in Pamela Ann Smith, *Palestine and the Palestinians*, p. 63 and footnote 105, drawing on Nevill Barbour, *Nisi Dominus: A Survey of the Palestine Controversy* (London, 1946, reprinted Beirut, 1969), p. 161.
62. In particular, Nuri Said, the Iraqi prime minister, asked Moshe Shertok (later Sharett), then political officer for the Jewish Agency, to agree to restrict immigration as a sign of willingness to cooperate with the Arabs in seeking to resolve the tensions. Shertok refused, both on the grounds of its being a concession to violence and because immigration was "an absolute Jewish right" and would not be the subject of concessions. Jacob Hurewitz, *The Struggle for Palestine, 1936–48*, 2nd ed. (New York, 1976), p. 70.
63. Ibid., p. 72. See also Porath, *From Riots to Rebellion*, pp. 162–216, for a detailed treatment of this period; and Michael Cohen, *Palestine, Retreat from the Mandate: The Making of British Policy, 1936–1945* (London, 1978), pp. 15–31, for an analysis of the revolt and British policymaking.
64. This discussion is drawn from Hurewitz, *Struggle*, pp. 72–76; Marlowe, *Seat of Pilate*, pp. 140–145; and Cohen, *Retreat*, pp. 32–38.
65. Quoted in Nicholas Bethell, *The Palestine Triangle: The Struggle for the Holy Land, 1935–1948* (New York, 1979), p. 32.
66. Porath, *From Riots to Rebellion*, pp. 237–238; and Cohen, *Retreat*, pp. 52–61.
67. J. Bowyer Bell, *Terror out of Zion: Irgun Zvai Leumi, LEHI, and the Palestinian Underground, 1929–1949* (New York, 1977), pp. 39–42; Porath, *From Riots to Rebellion*, p. 238; Dan Kurzman, *Ben-Gurion, Prophet of Fire* (New York, 1983), p. 218; Yehuda Bauer, *From Diplomacy to Resistance: A History of Jewish Palestine*, 1939–1945 (Philadelphia, 1970), pp. 11–15; and Munya M. Mardor, *Haganah* (New York, 1964), pp. 3–16.
68. Pamela Smith, *Palestinians*, pp. 66–68; and Porath, *From Riots to Rebellion*, pp. 249–256.
69. Bell, *Terror*, p. 46.
70. This material relies on Cohen, *Retreat*, pp. 1–9; and Hurewitz, *Struggle*, pp. 25–26.
71. Quoted in Cohen, *Retreat*, p. 4.
72. Ibid., p. 42. See also Rose, *Gentile Zionists*, pp. 165–173.
73. Cohen, *Retreat*, p. 72.
74. All quotations from Laqueur and Rubin, eds., *Israel-Arab Reader*, pp. 62–63.
75. Quoted in Hurewitz, *Struggle*, p. 99.
76. Laqueur and Rubin, eds., *Israel-Arab Reader*, p. 66. For the European backdrop, see Hurewitz, *Struggle*, p. 101.
77. Bauer, *Diplomacy*, p. 28.
78. Government of Palestine, *Survey of Palestine*, vol. 1, pp. 210–211. Many more immigrants, mostly Jewish women, who entered Palestine legally, were in fact circumventing legal restrictions. They entered marriages of convenience with Palestinian Jews to qualify them to enter as dependents. Once there and awarded citizenship, they divorced their husbands. Indeed, the divorce rate among Jews in Palestine in 1936 was 509 per 1000 marriages: Lister G. Hopkins, "Population," in Himadeh, ed., *Economic Organization*, p. 29. My statistics are extrapolated from Porath, *From Riots to Rebellion*, p. 129; and Rachelle Taqqu, "Peasants into Workmen: Internal Labor Migration and the Arab Village Community Under the Mandate," in Migdal, *Palestinian Society*, p. 266.
79. *Survey of Palestine*, vol. 2, pp. 704–713.
80. Ibid., pp. 566–567. Tables 2 and 3, and p. 719. There is a major discrepancy between this estimate of Jewish industrial enterprises and Sachar's tabulation of 14,000 in 1937; see footnote 55. It may be explained by the fact that the estimate in 1943 excluded small businesses such as printing presses and laundries.
81. *Survey of Palestine*, vol. 2, p. 566, Table 2; and Stein, *Land Question*, p. 226.
82. See the evaluation of Gabriel Sheffer, "Appeasement and the Problems of Palestine," *International Journal of Middle East Studies*, 11 (May, 1980): 377–399.

CHAPTER 5

World War II and the Creation of the State of Israel, 1939–1948

The impact of the Second World War on Palestine and the future of Zionism goes far beyond the military campaigns themselves. In 1941 Adolf Hitler decided to implement his plan for exterminating people designated as inferior according to Nazi ideology and its cult of Aryan supremacy. Although the retarded, insane, and homosexuals were included in this category, Hitler's intent was, first, to exterminate European Jews and, second, European gypsies. It was for them that the crematoria and gas chambers were built in the concentration camps that had originally held German political prisoners. Special attention was paid to the collection of Jews. By war's end approximately 6 million, two-thirds of European Jewry, had been exterminated, along with between 200,000 and 250,000 gypsies. In addition, millions of prisoners who were Slavs, rated just above Jews and gypsies, were exploited as forced labor until they died, when they were not deliberately killed. Though statistics are always approximate, it is known that 3.5 million out of 5.5 million Russian prisoners of war died in German hands. When we add to this thousands of others, we approach, if not exceed, a figure of 10 million dead, either exploited at forced labor until death or, particularly in the case of Jews, rounded up purposefully and with great effort in order to wipe out the Jewish people in Europe.[1]

To Jews in Palestine and elsewhere, especially the United States, knowledge of the Holocaust, available from late 1942 onward, meant that the Allies should undertake all possible efforts to take in refugees. Equally important was their demand that Palestine now be recognized as a Jewish state to house those who survived. To Britain and the United States, these questions were less important than was victory over Germany and Japan, especially because the Zionists often tied the refugee issue to Palestine, creating a political issue that the British in particular sought to evade. By war's end Zionism and the fate of the remnants of European Jewry had become intertwined in the United States, setting the American government in opposition to postwar British policy. For the British, already confronted with Zionist terror in Palestine aimed at driving them out, the burden became too much. The Labour government handed over the issue to the United Nations, setting the stage for war between Jews and Arabs in Palestine and the declaration of the Israeli state on 14 May 1948.

PALESTINE, ZIONISM, AND THE WAR EFFORT, 1939–1945

WORLD WAR II AND THE MIDDLE EAST

As we have noted, the 1939 White Paper appeared on 17 May 1939, following the German invasion of Czechoslovakia on 15 March and Italy's conquest of Albania in April. During the summer Europe moved ever closer to war. On 23 August the Nazi-Soviet Non-Aggression Pact was signed, prompting Great Britain to enter an alliance with Poland, promising aid if it were invaded. Germany attacked Poland on 1 September, leading Britain and France to declare war on Germany on 3 September. Russia entered Poland on 17 September and Polish resistance ended on 27 September when the country was partitioned between Germany and Russia.

The next stage of Germany's offensive began in April 1940 when it absorbed Norway and Denmark. Following the British failure to block Germany's efforts to take Norway, Neville Chamberlain resigned as prime minister and was succeeded by Winston Churchill on 10 May. Germany then invaded the Low Countries and France, overwhelming the combined British-French forces. France sued for peace and signed an armistice on 22 June. Hitler reigned supreme in Western Europe, a fact that led Mussolini to enter the war on his side on 10 June, apparently convinced that the fighting had ended. Great Britain now faced a Nazi-held Europe alone. In the Battle of Britain, fought in August and September 1940, the Royal Air Force beat back the Luftwaffe, but England remained under intensive German air raids well into 1942. In 1940–1941 approximately 43,000 civilians were killed in these attacks.[2] Pressure was relieved somewhat when Hitler ordered the invasion of Russia which began on 22 June 1941, establishing a second front, but the Axis powers, including Japan, continued to score significant victories. The spring of 1942 was especially critical. German forces advanced swiftly through western Russia and drove British forces back to El-Alamein in Egypt, fifty miles from Alexandria; in the Far East the Japanese took Singapore, the largest British naval base in the Eastern Hemisphere. Only in November 1942, with the decisive British victory at El-Alamein (October 23– November 4) did the German threat to Egypt, the Suez Canal, and Palestine recede. This, coupled with the successful Russian defense of Stalingrad in the winter of 1942–1943 and the American naval victories against the Japanese in the Pacific, established a firmer basis for conducting the war.

In the Middle East, the British came under intense military pressure once Italy declared war on 10 June 1940. The Italian position in Libya posed a direct threat to British security in Egypt and Palestine. Additionally, the Italian fleet and air force now continually attacked British convoys through the Mediterranean, supplemented by German air assaults. The Red Sea port of Suez thus became the major supply depot for goods reaching British forces in Egypt. Palestine throughout this period served as a training area for troops. Haifa, once its oil refinery was completed in June 1940, became the major source of fuel for the fleet, refining oil sent by the pipeline from Iraq. This source, plus oil shipped from the Abadan refinery in Iran and stored at Haifa, enabled the war effort in the Mediterranean and North Africa to continue. For the British, the Suez Zone–Persian Gulf connection across Palestine, Transjordan, and Iraq was crucial to its immediate war effort.[3] British military fortunes were at a particularly low ebb in the spring of 1941 once the Germans under Erwin Rommel took command of the desert war. German victories in Libya occurred at a time when their successes in Greece drove out the British and when, in April, the Iraqi prime minister Rashid Ali al-Gaylani ordered his troops to encircle the small British contingents there and called for German military aid. Steadfast British action undermined al-Gaylani's resolve and ultimately forced him and his pro-German retinue, including the mufti, Hajj Amin al-Husayni, to flee. Because German planes sent to Iraq had been given landing rights by the Vichy French in Syria, British forces, aided by Jewish units, invaded Syria and occupied it and Lebanon in a campaign lasting from May into July.

The need for British troops to deal with security in Arab states while confronting the Germans along the Egyptian border raised again the question of Arab loyalty. This led the foreign secretary, Anthony Eden, to issue a declaration, just before the attack on Vichy French forces in Syria, stating British approval of any Arab attempts to achieve unity. This appeal, which included support for Syrian postwar independence—to the fury of the Free French forces under Charles de Gaulle—clearly indicated British wishes to harness Arab nationalism to their own goals after the war. This in turn deeply alarmed the Zionist leaders, who saw it as further evidence of British wishes to restrict the scope of the Jewish National Home and ultimate statehood. But until early 1943 when the danger of a German assault through Egypt into Palestine receded, Zionist officials cooperated militarily with Great Britain while simultaneously striving to undermine the White Paper and ultimately the British position in Palestine. British officials were quite aware of this situation, perhaps best expressed by Ben-Gurion when he told the Zionist Congress in August 1939 that "for us the White Paper neither exists nor can exist. We must behave as if we were the State in Palestine until we actually become the State in Palestine."[4]

PALESTINE: JEWISH IMMIGRATION AND THE BRITISH RESPONSE

Yishuv leaders had decided in 1938, before the 1939 White Paper, to step up the illegal immigration of Jews into Palestine; indeed, the unauthorized immigrants in 1939 totaled 11,156 out of the 27,561 who arrived.[5] With the outbreak of war in September, plans to arrange the transfer of more refugees intensified: thousands were trying to flee Europe, often with Gestapo encouragement. These efforts brought Zionists and British officials into immediate conflict, in London as well as Palestine. British policy was to place illegal immigrants in internment camps in Palestine, which led the Zionists to try to flood the country with immigrants to negate the effectiveness of such tactics. The British then decided to send the refugees who reached Palestine on to the island of Mauritius in the Indian Ocean. At the same time the Foreign Office attempted to stem the flow of refugees from Europe by encouraging countries such as Turkey to deny them transit. An impossible situation arose after September 1939 that created "almost . . . a war within a war."[6] Jews became increasingly bitter at what they saw as British inhumanity. The latter felt the same toward the Zionist leadership, whom they believed to demand special attention and a diversion of war materials at a time when the major theaters of war required all available aid.

Catastrophes occurred as a result. In November 1940, over 1700 refugees from two ships intercepted by British naval patrols were transferred to the SS *Patria* in the port of Haifa for scheduled deportation to Mauritius. The Hagana arranged for a bomb to be placed near the hull to disable the ship, thereby forcing British authorities to permit the Jews to stay. But the plan miscarried, and the ship sank with over two hundred casualties. Zionist outrage and propaganda accusing the British of responsibility led the British cabinet to permit the survivors of the *Patria* to remain in Palestine. One final disaster occurred when the *Struma*, a rickety vessel with 769 Romanian Jews aboard, docked off Istanbul in December 1941 for engine repairs while the British tried to persuade the Turks to forbid its passage through the straits into the Mediterranean toward Palestine. Negotiations and debate went on for over two months. A British concession that children between the ages of eleven and sixteen should be permitted to proceed overland to Palestine was blocked by the Turks, who would permit sea travel only. In the end the Turks sent the ship back into the Black Sea, where it sank on 25 February 1942.[7]

To the Zionists this was proof of British perfidy. Those seen as most responsible for the *Struma's* fate—Harold MacMichael, high commissioner, and Lord Moyne, colonial secretary—were later targeted for assassination attempts; that on Moyne in November 1944 was successful. For British officials, the *Struma* affair, though tragic, was one incident in the midst of a continuing series of crises threatening the survival of the empire and its ability to wage war. Egyptian demonstrations in January 1942 calling for a German victory had forced a showdown in Cairo where on 4 February the British ambassador forced King Faruq to accept the nationalist leader, al-Nahhas, as prime minister, under threat of forced abdication. The Zionist conception of Palestine as a haven for European Jewry conflicted with a British concern for the continuing stability of the region that they deemed crucial to the conduct of the war.

THE JEWISH DIVISION AND THE QUESTION OF JEWISH MILITARY CAPABILITIES

Another issue of contention was the Jewish division that Weizmann proposed should fight as a distinct unit under the Zionist flag alongside British troops against the Nazis. British officials had encouraged both Palestinian Arab and

Jewish enlistments, the latter far outstripping the former, intending to use these troops in British units or as auxiliaries in reserve in Palestine. In addition, Hagana representatives cooperated with British special forces in training Jewish soldiers for secret missions, in both the Middle East and Europe. However, the idea of a separate Jewish division aroused some controversy. The British cabinet approved Weizmann's proposals in principle but resisted his demand that the Jewish Agency be identified with the mobilization of the troops. This was seen as a political move designed to "establish a claim on British gratitude in order that at the end of the war he [Weizmann] may be in a stronger position to induce His Majesty's Government to relax their restrictions on Jewish immigration into Palestine."[8] There was some truth to this assessment in light of other Zionist motives behind the proposal, namely, the hope that the creation of a distinct Jewish fighting force would enhance Zionist claims to Palestine at the Peace Conference after the war. Winston Churchill, prime minister and long sympathetic to Zionism, supported the idea of a Jewish division, but opposition at the highest civil and military levels delayed approval until late 1944 when a Jewish brigade was formed that fought as a separate unit in Europe. In addition, many Jewish soldiers fought as part of British companies.

The dispute over the implications of the Jewish brigade illustrated the complexity of the relationship between the Zionists and the British and the motives behind each one's actions and proposals. The Zionists "still hoped for a peaceful post-war change of British policy which would allow for the creation of a Jewish State. . . . On the other hand, they wished to insure against the possibility of British post-war persistence in the White Paper policy."[9] When Jewish Agency officials argued for Jewish mobilization, they did so knowing that the Hagana could exploit the opportunity to gain greater military experience and, equally important, to have greater access to British arms. In the Hagana's view, Jews "took upon themselves the twofold mission of fighting in the ranks of the British army . . . and at the same time doing whatever they could to ensure the arming of the Yishuv. It was their firm conviction that the one mission did not conflict with the other but that . . . they complemented each other."[10] As a result, many arms operations were carried out at storage depots by Hagana agents in Palestine and the western desert with the cooperation of Jewish soldiers or Jewish guards, not to mention the bedouin. And Jewish units in Europe maintained contact with their Hagana leaders in Palestine and established networks for both the transfer of refugees to Palestine and the stealing of arms that could then be shipped there to build up Hagana strength for war. Estimates of Jewish arms vary, but the Hagana in 1942–1943 had approximately 12,000 pistols, 18,000 rifles, 450 submachine guns and automatic rifles, and 162 machine guns, most in excellent condition and carefully stored. In addition, the Hagana had begun some arms manufacturing and were producing mortars.[11]

The British were aware of these activities and their motives. Foreign Office and Colonial Office officials agreed in 1942 that "there seems little doubt that

. . . the Jews intend to resort to direct action if they fail to secure a post-war settlement compatible with their present aspirations."[12] But during the early years of the war they could do little about such arms acquisitions, as they needed Hagana cooperation in case of a German breakthrough in Egypt. Once the chance of a German onslaught into Egypt and Palestine faded, British officials in Palestine began extensive arms searches, seldom successful, and brought to trial those Jews and British soldiers whom they discovered smuggling arms to the Hagana. Raids on suspected arms caches brought open Jewish resistance and public threats of retaliation by Yishuv leaders. Aware that the British could not cope with such a possibility, the high commissioner advised the military to desist, but he believed that by 1944 the Zionist leadership in Palestine was in effect claiming the right to arm in the face of British authority for the purpose of opposing it.

ZIONISM IN THE UNITED STATES: THE BILTMORE CONFERENCE AND ITS CONSEQUENCES

British fears of a confrontation with Zionism after the war owed much in their view to the growing strength of militant American Zionism and its support of Ben-Gurion's activism against Weizmann's gradualism. This alliance had resulted from developments in the early stages of the war, especially the Biltmore Conference of May 1942.

The conference had been organized by men close to Weizmann. They planned to unite American Jewish organizations behind a program designed to undertake fund-raising and political activity on behalf of Zionism and the probability that thousands, if not millions, of Jewish refugees would seek to go to Palestine after the war. The resolutions passed by the conference called for the opening of Palestine to immigration; the Jewish Agency should be granted control of that immigration and the authority required to develop Palestine; and after the war Palestine should "be established as a Jewish Commonwealth integrated in the structure of the new democratic world."[13] In this regard the Biltmore declarations were designed to mobilize American Jews to action, and they were extraordinarily successful, especially once news of the Holocaust began to spread in the latter half of 1942. Membership in Zionist organizations increased substantially. Publicity for the Zionist cause was pursued, including books published and distributed with Jewish financial aid.[14] In addition, millions of leaflets were sent to members of Congress and to their constituents to send to the members. And Zionists established two Christian organizations to back the call for a Jewish state in Palestine, the American Palestine Committee and the Christian Council on Palestine. Both received Zionist subsidies and proved to be extremely effective in mobilizing support, calling on the United States government to oppose the 1939 White Paper. These efforts resulted in the inclusion of references in both the Republican and Democratic platforms of 1944 that endorsed the creation of a Jewish commonwealth as designated in the Biltmore resolutions.

One area in which the Jewish groups were less successful was in their attempts to galvanize the American government to support refugee operations designed to aid those fleeing Nazi-held Europe. Official American opposition to a concerted attempt to accept Jewish refugees, if available, or to exert efforts to find havens elsewhere lasted into mid-1944. Various studies of the question have either charged responsible officials with blatant anti-Semitism—particularly Breckenridge Long who was in charge of refugee policies in the State Department—or have stressed the general fear of undermining the war effort by diverting material to a specific issue that did not contribute to military victory.[15] It seems clear that administration officials wished to evade the refugee question in general, and the Jewish issue in particular, until after the war. Here the growing support for a postwar Jewish Palestine did not translate into intensive pressure on the American government by non-Jews for either seeking to rescue Jews then or even making public statements condemning the atrocities that were occurring. Only in 1944, with President Franklin D. Roosevelt's backing, was a War Relief Board created that facilitated the flight of several thousand refugees.

What is difficult to ascertain is how many, if any, Jews could have been saved if the British and American governments had opened their doors to them from 1942 onward. The official American response to Jewish calls for action was hindered by divisions within the ranks of American Jewry. Here politics and the question of Palestine intervened. Many American Jews supported the principle of establishing havens for refugees anywhere, even the idea of "free ports" in Palestine where Jews would be permitted to remain throughout the war, with the understanding that their temporary presence did not constitute recognition of their right to stay afterwards as part of the Jewish population. This was proposed so as to avoid the political ramifications of immigration for the war's duration. But the Zionists objected to such plans. They stipulated that any proposed refugee scheme should designate Palestine as the only haven, as part of the creation of a Jewish state and as a means of effectively rescinding the 1939 White Paper. As a result, there arose a situation in which "Zionists were more interested in having the White Paper revoked than in circumventing its effects by means of temporary havens."[16] This state of affairs led to charges that Zionist political considerations blocked efforts that might have saved many Jews. The Zionists' linkage of any proposed rescue of refugees and their right to enter Palestine immediately, thus circumventing the White Paper, has remained a sensitive issue among American Jews to the present.[17]

Despite the impetus the Biltmore Conference gave to American Zionism, it also led to a great rift in the world Zionist leadership. Ben-Gurion, already angered at Weizmann over the latter's handling of the question of the Jewish division, now became infuriated at what he considered to be Weizmann's obsessive reliance on British policymaking and the use of diplomacy as the primary tool to achieve Zionist goals. Ben-Gurion was determined to have the Zionist leadership in Palestine, namely, himself, direct the movement toward statehood which he considered achievable as much by direct action against Great Britain as by cooperation and negotiation with it. The split widened soon after the conference, when Ben-Gurion, as head of the Jewish Agency Executive, challenged the right of Weizmann, as leader of the World Zionist Organization, to suggest any policy without the former's approval. Weizmann responded by accusing Ben-Gurion of "political assassination." Here the matter ended for the time being, but the aftermath of the quarrel saw their increasing estrangement.[18] Behind it lay not only matters of procedure but also fundamental differences in aspirations. Weizmann hoped to persuade the British to revive the 1937 partition plan proposed by the Peel Commission, whereas Ben-Gurion wanted to establish a Jewish state in all of western Palestine, a goal he considered more attainable by direct Jewish action there and lobbying in the United States than through negotiations with London. By the end of 1942, however, the British cabinet was itself reviewing its postwar options for Palestine, a process that with Churchill's encouragement led to a reassessment of the White Paper and a revival of partition as the only feasible option.

THE WHITE PAPER, PARTITION, AND BRITAIN'S PLACE IN THE MIDDLE EAST, 1942–1945

In December 1942, a study of Britain's postwar position in the Middle East was commissioned for the war cabinet. The committee report envisioned the end of the mandates as nations achieved independence. It was vital that Great Britain retain ties with these newly independent regimes through treaty relationships in order to preserve its paramount strategic position in the region. Palestine, in this view, was of great importance. If the mandate were altered, Britain should still retain access to the port of Haifa and be able to secure the Haifa–Baghdad road and the Haifa–Kirkuk oil pipeline; thus military installations to protect these interests would be necessary.[19] In short, the value of Palestine for British imperial planners, including the chiefs of staff, remained essentially what had been outlined in the de Bunsen report of 1915 before the Balfour Declaration, with British strategists anticipating success in fulfilling their basic requirements. Within these parameters, the settling of the question of Palestine called for imposing the clauses of the 1939 White Paper, a matter of increasing importance as the war progressed. The period defined for Jewish immigration up to 75,000 ended in April 1944 (it was extended). Finally, the military and the Foreign Office were increasingly concerned at the apparent success of Zionist propaganda in the United States. They foresaw the need to counter expected American pressure on the matter of the White Paper, a source of potential rivalry, along with the broader question of conflicting oil interests once the war ended.

Nevertheless, a cabinet committee on Palestine was established in July 1943 at Churchill's instigation to examine alternatives to the White Paper. In December 1943 the committee recommended partition. Although intense debate continued on the matter throughout the first half of 1944, led by Anthony Eden, the foreign secretary, backed by the chiefs of staff and British diplomats in the Middle East, Churchill and the committee held firm, though they reduced the area allotted to the Jewish state. In September, final discussions began, and by early November, the war cabinet was ready to examine and approve a partition plan that would be official British policy once the war ended. Weizmann was fully aware of this, as were the leaders of the Agency Executive in Jerusalem. Not only had the White Paper been suspended, though not officially, but London had also rejected an American trusteeship proposal, supported by Eden, that would have placed Palestine under the auspices of the United Nations, a plan that the State Department later revived.[20]

But partition was not officially approved. On 6 November, members of the Jewish terrorist group LEHI (former Stern Gang) assassinated Lord Moyne, now deputy minister of state for Middle East Affairs in Cairo. Moyne was a close personal friend of Churchill's, and the latter reacted by shelving the partition scheme he had seen through, against stiff opposition from his ministers. The prime minister declared to the House of Commons that "if our dreams for Zionism are to end in the smoke of assassins' pistols and our labors for its future to produce only a new set of gangsters worthy of Nazi Germany, many like myself will have to reconsider the position we have maintained so consistently in the past."[21] Partition was not discussed again during Churchill's term as prime minister. When the Labour government took over in July 1945 they had to face the issue. In the meantime Churchill's warning to the Zionist leadership produced action: they stopped underground activities that seemed to threaten the likelihood of any cooperation with a British government after the war.

JEWISH TERRORISM, THE HAGANA, AND THE BRITISH, 1940-1945

Once the British announced the 1939 White Paper in March 1939, the Irgun shifted its focus and began to attack British administrative buildings and police personnel, along with bombing gathering places. But when the war began, Jabotinsky called for the Revisionists to support the British effort against the Nazis. Most of the Irgun in Palestine accepted this directive, and the group's head, David Raziel, later agreed to undertake British-sponsored missions; he was killed on one in Iraq in 1941. But a small faction of the Irgun refused to cease operations during the war. Led by Abraham Stern, they decided to continue their attacks on the White Paper and the British presence in Palestine. Thus the Stern Gang emerged in 1940, willing to rob Jewish concerns, such as a Histadrut bank, with Jewish loss of life, along with its assaults on British officials. At the same time Stern decided that he should establish contact with German and Italian representatives to offer his services to their cause for the duration of the war. The fact that they all were anti-British was sufficient, whatever the anti-Semitic basis of the Nazi regime. As a result the Stern group was condemned by both the Hagana and the Irgun, who gave British police information leading to its temporary destruction; Stern was killed in a British police raid in February 1942.[22]

There was little underground activity from early 1942 to the beginning of 1944. The leaders of the Stern Gang were dead or in prison. The Irgun was also leaderless, with Jabotinsky and Raziel dead, although Menachem Begin began to assume control when he reached Palestine in April 1942. By the end of 1943, however, members of both groups were preparing for anti-British action, inspired by both the receding German threat in the Middle East and the ongoing tensions in Zionist-British relations, exacerbated particularly by the legacy of the refugee ships and the growing awareness of the Holocaust. This led to an accommodation between Begin and members of the Stern Gang who had escaped from prison and who now renewed their actions against the British under the name of LEHI (Fighters for the Freedom of Israel). Among them was Nathan Yellin-Mor, who had been close to Begin as a member of Betar in Poland, and Yitzhak Shamir, who in 1980 became foreign minister in the government led by Begin and prime minister in 1986. Both groups demanded a Jewish state that included all of original Palestine, Transjordan regained, and parts of southern Lebanon and Syria. But at least for the remainder of the war, they disagreed on tactics. LEHI resumed its assassinations of British officials, civilian and military. Begin directed the Irgun to bomb only civilian installations linked to the mandatory authority, not military sites. This, he reasoned, would show that the Irgun was not seeking to impede the war effort, though Irgun operations did lead to the killing of British personnel. Throughout much of 1944, the Hagana objected more strenuously to LEHI than to the Irgun, considering it to be a "'classic' terrorist group," whereas the Irgun was principally a political threat to the program pursued by the Yishuv leadership.[23]

Matters came to a head with the LEHI-sponsored assassination of Lord Moyne. This success followed several failures, Irgun as well as LEHI, to assassinate Sir Harold MacMichael, the high commissioner in Palestine. The Jewish Agency leadership in Palestine had already begun, in October, to move against the Irgun in response to British police requests for aid. But these acts, undertaken against much opposition in Hagana ranks, had been directed at undermining the Irgun extortion rings established to gain funding for their operations. Following the Moyne killing, the Hagana moved swiftly against both the Irgun and LEHI, rounding up operatives, mostly Irgun, interrogating and occasionally beating them, and handing over some Irgun members to the British police; LEHI leaders agreed to suspend operations after negotiations with Hagana envoys. This operation, called "The Season," lasted from November 1944 into the spring of 1945. Its focus on the Irgun, despite LEHI's more active assassination policies, indicated agency concern for the greater appeal that the Irgun might have among the population. But Begin's refusal to retaliate against the Hagana, and the Hagana's inability to destroy the Irgun, strengthened the Irgun and gave it credibility among the populace as loyal to Zionist goals, whatever the extremes of its actions.[24] With the end of the European war on 8 May 1945, terror resumed as part of a new era in British-Jewish relations in Palestine.

PALESTINIAN ARAB LEADERSHIP AND THE QUESTION OF ARAB UNITY, 1939–1945

The Higher Arab Committee had collapsed at the conclusion of the Arab Revolt in early 1939. Many of its leaders were in exile, having fled Palestine to avoid capture by the British.[25] The mufti had been officially banned from the country following his escape in October 1937. With the outbreak of war, British officials in Palestine made overtures to the mufti, by now in Baghdad, to seek his support for the White Paper and implementation of its immigration restrictions. They did so out of fear of his ability to arouse general Arab hostility toward the British position in the Middle East at that time. Al-Husayni rejected these requests and the White Paper itself. Instead, he aligned himself with the Iraqi rebellion against Great Britain in April 1941, and once it failed he made his way, via Iran, to Italy and Germany. There he spent the war supporting the German war effort and German barbarity against the Jews.

Other members of the Higher Committee did respond to British offers of safe return to Palestine in return for promises not to engage in overt political activity. Between February 1940 and November 1942, a number of leading members of the Istiqlal and the Palestine Arab party that represented the Husaynis, along with Husayn al-Khalidi of the Reform party, reestablished themselves in the country. In general they indicated their reserved acceptance of the 1939 White Paper and distanced themselves from the mufti, whom they depicted as only one member of the Higher Arab Committee. Despite the intense Axis propaganda beamed to Palestine during 1941 and 1942, which included the mufti's exhortations to rebel, Arab Palestine remained calm. Though this may be largely attributable to the presence of large numbers of Allied military personnel, the disruption of Arab leadership and the willingness of those former rebels now in Palestine to cooperate, if only cautiously, with the White Paper policy also helped. Finally there was the fact that Palestine, following years of economic deprivation for its Arab population, now entered a period of prosperity that included the Arabs, the result of the great expansion of demand for all goods and services owing to the presence of British military forces. The peasants in particular benefited from the captive market for their crops and the expansion of the labor force which they entered.

With the mufti in Germany and his nephew, Jamal al-Husayni, interned in

Southern Rhodesia for the war, the field was open for rivals to seek to dominate Arab politics. Those in the forefront were the members of the Istiqlal who sought to use the economic boom in Palestine as a means of boosting Arab resistance to Zionism, in particular Ahmad Hilmi, Awni Abd al-Hadi, and Rashid Ibrahim. They had acquired control of the Arab National Bank and through it appealed to a newly emerging Arab bourgeoisie. They also took over the Arab National Fund, which they used as a vehicle to acquire land that otherwise might be bought by Zionists. The fund attracted widespread support. Branches were opened throughout Palestine, with many contributions by peasants who suddenly had spare cash as a result of the new prosperity. In a very real way the fund captured the attention and imagination of the Arab population, but this in itself was seen by the al-Husayni faction as a threat to its anticipated resurgence. Particularly significant about the Istiqlal was its broad base of support, often commercially oriented and not tied to traditional local power affiliations. In this the Istiqlal found itself opposed by all the major clans in Jerusalem who might contend with one another; the al-Nashshashibis as well as the al-Husaynis had rejected the Istiqlal in the late 1930s. The main opposition was still the al-Husayni power base, local leaders and village headmen loyal to their traditional source of authority in Jerusalem. The Palestine Arab party was established once again in April 1944, its real leader being a Greek Orthodox named Emile al-Ghuri, although Jamal al-Husayni's brother was appointed acting president until he returned.

By the end of the European war in May 1945, the Palestine Arab party was once again the most powerful political voice in the Arab community, but its strength was relative. The Istiqlal also commanded widespread respect and had been active in combating Zionism during the war, as opposed to the more propagandistic nature of the al-Husayni appeal. The differences between the two groups were significant, though neither espoused views acceptable to the Zionists. The Istiqlal called for strict implementation of the White Paper which by 1944 the British were avoiding. This stance, though untenable in Zionist eyes, did from the Istiqlal's perspective recognize the existence of a Jewish National Home composed of those Jews then in Palestine. The Zionists wanted unlimited immigration and a Jewish state in which they were a majority. The Palestine Arab party, on the other hand, called for the dissolution of the Jewish National Home and the creation of an Arab government in charge of the entire country. This maximalist position—rejection of any Jewish presence in Palestine beyond that traceable to before 1917—was analogous to the Irgun and Stern calls for a Jewish state on both sides of the Jordan. The difference was that these Jewish groups were minorities within the Jewish community, whereas the Palestine Arab party seemed to reflect the position of a majority of Palestinian Arabs, at least those in positions of local leadership.

Discussion of these factions leaves open the question of Palestinian public opinion which, though opposed to a Jewish state, might have varied on the nature of the society envisioned after the war. It is clear that major structural changes occurred in Arab Palestine between 1939 and 1945, and especially from 1943 onward, following the creation of the Arab National Fund. Muslims began to use the government educational system in increasing numbers, a reflection of the peasant village communities' increased interest. "Between 1943–45 Arab peasants voluntarily contributed [the equivalent of] more than $1,500,000 for educational purposes, as compared with $187,200 for the years 1941–42."[26] New professional groups emerged, a Palestine Arab Medical Association was created, and Palestinian Arab women began to achieve professional status in the medical and legal professions, establishing the nucleus for what later became the Palestinian professional class in the greater Arab world following the Arab exodus and the creation of Israel.

Given the factionalism within Palestine, political leadership devolved once more to heads of neighboring Arab regimes, a process that continued through 1948. Among these Arabs, there was greater consensus on Palestine than on most other issues confronting them. Throughout the war their attention had been directed principally to the question of unity, long an Arab ideal, that had been encouraged by Anthony Eden in May 1941. Whatever the expediency of his declaration, made in concert with British preparations for an invasion of Vichy-held Syria and for recognition of an independent Syrian state after the war, it gained the attention of both Nuri al-Said of Iraq and, once he took office in February 1942, Mustafa al-Nahhas, the Egyptian prime minister and leader of the most popular nationalist party, the Wafd.

Al-Nahhas, recognizing the spirit of Arab nationalism, was determined to include Egypt in any forthcoming discussions to bring Arab states closer together, hoping that Egypt might dominate such a group. On the other hand, there already existed plans for Arab unity in the Levant that specifically excluded Egypt. These were the Fertile Crescent schemes, so named because they applied to Transjordan, Palestine, Lebanon, Syria, and Iraq. But such proposals led to divisiveness. Both the Iraqi and Transjordanian governments, related by Hashemite blood, vied for control over any such Arab government. In turn, Syrian nationalists, as heirs to Faysal's Arab kingdom of 1919–1920, considered themselves the logical leaders of an Arab state. The Saudis and the Egyptians had encouraged the Syrians to resist Iraqi or Transjordanian overtures before the war, because of Saudi hostility to the Hashemites and Egyptian fears of being left out of a large Arab state that might threaten its assumed right to influence Arab politics. They particularly sought to limit Iraq's power, by promoting a more independent Syrian position. These rivalries, and variations on them, dominated Arab politics well into the 1960s and beyond.

Arab heads of state met in Alexandria, Egypt, in October 1944. The Alexandria Protocol issued by this conference called for the formation of a league of Arab states that could further coordinate their political and commercial activities. Palestine was singled out for consideration. A resolution declared that:

Palestine constitutes an important part of the Arab world and that the rights of the Arabs [Palestinian] cannot be touched without prejudice to peace and stability in the Arab world. . . .

The Committee also declares that it is second to none in regretting the woes that have been inflicted upon the Jews of Europe by European dictatorial states. But the question of these Jews should not be confused with Zionism, for there can be no greater injustice and aggression than solving the problem of the Jews of Europe by another injustice, that is, by inflicting injustice on the Palestine Arabs of various religions and denominations.[27]

Herein lay the heart of the Arab argument, whether Palestinian or otherwise, against Zionism, one that has lasted to the present day. With the war's end it confronted a Zionist call for unlimited immigration into Palestine to resolve precisely the injustice that Nazi Germany had imposed on European Jews.

In the meantime, a League of Arab states was formed in March 1945, pursuant to the recommendations of the Alexandria Protocol. The league's charter relaxed the stress on potential Arab unity found in the earlier document. On the other hand, it established more specific provisos for the defense of Palestinian Arabs and created a seat for a Palestinian Arab representative despite Palestine's lack of independence. With this machinery in place the league also undertook to represent the Palestinian Arab case before the Western world and to seek to persuade the powers to deny the achievement of Zionist goals. Certain leaders such as King Ibn Saud had already engaged in such efforts when he met President Franklin D. Roosevelt in early 1945 and gained his promise that no steps would be taken concerning Palestine without consultation with Arab leaders. This informal statement seemed to contradict American policy as declared in party platforms, but it reflected American concern for the stability of the Arab world and its oil, considered vital to the soundness of the Western economies.

In any case, such promises meant little. Roosevelt died in April 1945 and was succeeded by his vice-president, Harry Truman, who had been left uninformed as to American foreign policy. He had his own ideas about resolving the question of Palestine. In England, elections in July led to Churchill's stunning defeat and the rise to power of a Labour government. In 1944 the Labour party platform had called not only for a Jewish state in Palestine but also for the transference of the Arab population to Transjordan. Now its leaders confronted a situation in which Zionist anticipation of Labour's fulfillment of its promises conflicted with the staggering problems of attempting to maintain Britain's imperial position in the world.

THE END OF THE MANDATE AND THE CREATION OF ISRAEL, 1945–1948

The European war ended on 8 May 1945; the war against Japan on 15 August. Prospects for peace soon seemed a mirage, however, especially for Great Britain which faced nationalist demands for independence in the Middle East and Asia while confronting an economic crisis that lasted for years and seriously weakened its capacity to sustain its envisaged imperial role. The United States underwent massive demobilization after the war but soon found itself aligned with the British in a "cold war" with the Soviet Union which was expanding its control and influence in Eastern Europe and beyond. By the end of 1948 the Russians had taken all of Central and Eastern Europe under their wing. The only exception was Yugoslavia which declared its independence as a socialist-communist state in June of that year.

Soviet expansion in Eastern Europe was accompanied by severe pressure on Turkey and Iran, where the Soviet Union sought to acquire territory and influence in a manner reminiscent of tsarist imperial objectives. Turkey had blocked the straits in 1941, fearing German reprisals if it allowed supplies through to Russia. At the war's end Josef Stalin demanded that Turkey permit the Russians to establish military bases in the perimeter around the straits whose governance should become the joint responsibility of the Black Sea powers, not simply Turkey's. Such an arrangement would have placed the Bosphorus and Dardanelles under predominantly Soviet authority, thus achieving a strategic objective that had eluded the Russians throughout the entire history of the Eastern Question. The Turks resisted, with American and British backing, but Russian diplomatic pressures continued throughout 1946, as did Western fears of Soviet military actions in the area.

The situation in Iran seemed equally threatening. Russia, in occupation of northern Iran, encouraged the creation of the autonomous Republic of Azerbaijan in December 1945 under the protection of the Soviet army, and in early 1946 an adjacent Kurdish Soviet Republic was created. These developments, coupled with Soviet ultimatums to Turkey, led President Truman to declare in April 1946 that the Near and Middle East might become an area of international rivalry that could erupt into war. International criticism and ostensible Iranian capitulation to Soviet demands for oil concessions led the Soviets to withdraw from Azerbaijan, but the experience, along with the eruption of an apparently communist-sponsored civil war in Greece, caused Western diplomats deep concern for the fate of the northern rim of the Mediterranean and the Persian Gulf.

These regions had traditionally been the frontiers of British-Russian rivalry, but Great Britain's continuing domestic economic crisis, coupled with its commitments in Palestine, led the Labour government in early 1947 to finally acknowledge that it could no longer sustain its geopolitical commitments in the Mediterranean. On 24 February the British ambassador to Washington told American officials that by early 1948 London would be withdrawing its financial and military assistance to Greece and Turkey and expressed his government's hope that the United States would step into the role the British were abdicating out of financial necessity. The American response was the Truman Doctrine, declared on 12 March 1947 in reply to an official Greek request for aid. It signified an American decision to seek to contain Soviet expansion and the threat of communism. This policy of containment led to a concerted effort by the United States to establish military alliances with the countries on the southern rim of the Soviet Union and to bolster their economies as well as their weaponry in order to counter communist inroads. American statesmen were equally concerned with the weakened condition of the Western European economies, including those of Germany and Italy, as their continued poverty offered greater likelihood of communist electoral success. This led to the Marshall Plan, first broached in late spring 1947 but not approved by Congress until nearly a year later, which committed the United States to the reconstruction of Western Europe while also supplying Greece and Turkey with military aid. Fear of communism and communist infiltration, believed to be fostered by domestic instability, governed the outlook of the State Department and many other officials in Washington.[28]

British and American perceptions of the communist threat and the means to counter it generally coincided in 1946, but their relative capacities to respond differed greatly. Great Britain was becoming financially dependent on American aid at a time when it was still trying to maintain a reduced imperial posture. Finally, a major rift now developed between London and Washington with respect to Palestine and Zionist claims to statehood.

British Foreign Secretary Ernest Bevin's cardinal concern from 1945 to 1948 was the security of British strategic interests in the Middle East and Asia. Though the Labour government was committed to granting independence to India, the route through Suez remained vital because of British oil holdings in the Persian Gulf and its military bases in Aden and Southern Asia. Bevin strove to retain a military presence in the Middle East in the face of anticipated Arab demands for independence. He believed that Arab leaders might accept a continued British imperial role in return for recognition of their calls for total independence. The question was where British troops could be stationed, a matter of particular importance during 1946 when Bevin and Prime Minister Clement Attlee reached a tentative agreement with the Sidqi ministry in Egypt, later aborted, to withdraw all British troops from that country by 1949. For Bevin, the logical place was Palestine. This in turn encouraged Bevin's existing predilection to assure Arab nationalist opinion that Zionism would not achieve an independent Jewish state in Palestine. From the Zionist perspective, the British desire to remain in the country signified their opposition to a separate Jewish entity at a time when the Zionist leadership focused its attention on the plight of Jewish refugees in Europe and the need to bring them to Palestine. Although the Labour government continued the 1939 White Paper quotas of 1500 a month, it ordered British ships to block efforts to land Jews seeking asylum in Palestine, repeating the situation of 1939–1941.

Immigration became the nexus of British-American-Zionist interactions. A cardinal aspect of Zionist ideology during and after the war was that European Jews should be sent only to Palestine; thus Truman was advised by an aide sympathetic to Zionism not to offer haven to Jewish displaced persons in the United States, as this would dilute the argument that an independent Jewish state was required to absorb them.[29] Truman was deeply affected by the plight of European Jews, but his support of Zionism was not simply altruistic. He knew the political implications of his actions and was constantly advised by aides such as David Niles and Clark Clifford of the domestic political impact that his pronouncements on Palestine might have with respect to Jewish voters. At the same time, State Department officials cautioned him to coordinate his policy with the British so as to counter Soviet moves and the likelihood of growing instability in the Middle East.[30]

Though clearly aware of the potential domestic ramifications of his statements on Palestine, Truman was also influenced by his emotional sympathies for the displaced persons. He identified with the underdog, and to him, along with much of the American public, the Jews were the downtrodden who needed refuge. In this he was probably not so much influenced by public opinion as part of it, deeply resentful of organized Jewish pressure on him but moved to making important decisions with far-reaching implications without consulting those responsible for foreign policy, because of emotional appeals made by persons such as Chaim Weizmann. As a rule, Truman issued statements contrary to British designs but refused to commit himself to their implications, namely, support for a Jewish state. Bevin, on the other hand, attempted to create a rationale for the continuing British retention of Palestine while simultaneously consolidating a British-American alliance, crucial to Britain's economic survival, that seemed menaced at times by his Palestine policy.

CONSULTATION AND CONFLICT: GREAT BRITAIN, THE UNITED
STATES, AND ZIONISM, JULY 1945–FEBRUARY 1947

At the end of August 1945 President Truman wrote Clement Attlee requesting that Great Britain sponsor the immediate admission of 100,000 Jewish refugees into Palestine. The request, based on a previous Zionist appeal to the Labour government, signaled the beginning of direct American involvement in the British handling of the question of Palestine. News of Truman's letter was leaked to the press, and Truman soon issued a public statement, in part calculated to help the Democratic party in the forthcoming mayoralty elections in New York.[31] Bevin and Attlee, increasingly concerned over the political ramifications of American statements on Palestine and their potential impact on British-American relations, decided to propose a joint Anglo-American committee to examine the refugee problem in Europe and to suggest means to disperse the refugees to new homes, preferably not in Palestine. Bevin's aim was to make the United States jointly responsible for Palestinian policy, in the hope of muting unilateral statements by its leaders. But his strategy backfired. The British draft of the committee's responsibilities made no reference to Palestine, only "to the possibility of relieving the position [of Jews] in Europe by immigration to other countries outside of Europe." American pressure brought a redrafting of this suggestion so that it read, "to make estimates of those who wish or will be impelled by their conditions to migrate to Palestine or other countries outside of Europe."[32] Having reluctantly accepted this revision, Bevin emphasized that Palestine should not be seen as the solution to the Jewish refugee problem in Europe, and that it was not the committee's responsibility to view the situation in that light. Indeed, Bevin declared that he envisaged a Palestinian state, not a Jewish one, arising under a United Nations trusteeship awarded to Britain.

Bevin's announcement, coupled with British continuance of the immigration quotas of 1500 monthly, infuriated the Zionists, who wanted free immigration and a Jewish state. Bevin's use of the term Palestinian state clearly meant one with an Arab majority. The Palestinian Arabs also objected to Bevin's policies. They saw British willingness to extend the White Paper immigration quotas beyond the five-year transition period as violating promises made to them. Both the Jews and the Arabs thus considered Bevin's actions to be a betrayal of Britain's perceived obligations to their sides, but their responses were quite different. Arab leadership continued to be divided. Though the Higher Arab Committee had been reconstituted, the hoped-for coalition between the Husayni-led Palestine Arab party and the Istiqlal did not last. The Palestine Arab Party thus dominated the Higher Committee, led from February 1946 by Jamal al-Husayni who was permitted to return to Palestine. In May the mufti established himself in Egypt and took over effective, if absentee, control of the committee; the British would not permit him to reenter Palestine.

Whereas Arab differences led to political immobilization and rejection of any option other than an Arab Palestine, Zionist disputes altered but did not impede formulations of policy. Indeed, ideological disputes and disagreements over how to counter British actions often enabled the Jewish Agency, led by Ben-Gurion, to appear moderate and interested in diplomacy while benefiting from the impact of Zionist underground and terrorist activities against British installations and civil as well as military personnel. The Hagana now joined the Irgun and LEHI in their ventures. The only major distinction was that the Hagana did not deliberately assault British servicemen, though their deaths in raids were considered acceptable. The Irgun and LEHI had no such compunctions regarding assassinations.[33]

Ben-Gurion now accepted the idea that military operations would be necessary to force the British from Palestine and had, during the summer of 1945, contacted Jewish millionaires in the United States to arrange for buying and storing weapons to be shipped to the Zionists in Palestine. His willingness to encourage armed resistance was accentuated by his knowledge that some members of the Hagana had rejected any policy of restraint and had joined the Irgun and LEHI. From this time on, efforts were made for the Hagana to be aware of

Irgun–LEHI operations and to approve them beforehand, though this was not always possible.

Clashes with British forces began in October 1945. The British were swift to react, and by year's end 80,000 troops had been sent to Palestine to quell opposition to Labour policies. The British desire to strike back forcibly began to grow, especially after attacks by either the Irgun or LEHI killed 10 British soldiers and policemen and wounded 11 more at the end of December. Ben-Gurion and the Agency Executive were now treading a fine line, seeking to benefit from military resistance against the British but wishing to keep the lines of communication open for potentially rewarding negotiations with the Labour party. British casualties from 1 November 1945 to 30 June 1946 amounted to 18 officers and soldiers of the army killed and 101 wounded, with British police casualties considered about the same. Damage from sabotage amounted to over 4 million British pounds, nearly one-fourth of that caused by an Irgun raid on a British air field and more attributed to railway bombings and derailments. Extensive British searches of settlements for arms were occasionally successful, as when they found a cache of six hundred weapons, half a million rounds of ammunition, and a quarter-ton of explosives spread among thirty-three separate hiding places around one Jewish village.[34]

These activities provided the backdrop in which the Anglo-American Committee of Inquiry began its hearings in Washington and then moved to Europe to interview the displaced persons now in refugee camps. By now they numbered well over 100,000, although they had been only half that when the proposal to grant them passage to Palestine had first been put forward. In response to committee questions, well over 90 percent stated their wish to go to Palestine, even though many hoped to enter the United States.[35] This was a forlorn hope. Americans were concerned at the plight of Jewish refugees, but not to the extent that they would support alterations in immigration laws to permit them entry. Most Americans agreed with the Zionists, though for different reasons, that Palestine should be the haven for Jews who had survived the horrors of war and the camps.

The fact that the Arab population was still double that of the Jews meant little to anyone except the British and the American State Department, who foresaw instability and upheaval in the Arab world with concomitant anti-Western hostility. Arab spokesmen before the Anglo-American Committee in Cairo and Jerusalem stated that the ongoing Jewish immigration would create even more Arab resistance. Albert Hourani, a young representative of the Arab Agency, impressed many committee members when he declared that "no room can be made in Palestine for a second nation except by dislodging or exterminating the first."[36] Chaim Weizmann, to the consternation of Ben-Gurion and the Jewish Agency Executive, admitted the same, though drawing different conclusions. As one committee member wrote, "He is the first witness who has frankly and openly admitted that the issue is not between right and wrong but between the greater and the lesser injustice. Injustice is unavoidable and we have to decide whether it is better to be unjust to the Arabs of Palestine or the Jews.[37] Arabs argued for a Palestinian state based on existing population ratios in which the Arab majority would acknowledge and ensure Jewish rights; they rejected all other solutions. Bevin hoped for a binational state, presumably under British tutelage. Zionist leaders seemed willing to accept partition in lieu of maximalist demands for a Jewish state in all of Palestine, but Arab leaders opposed that. To give up any part of Arab Palestine would be wrong, they believed, constituting recognition of the Jewish right to have it as Ben-Gurion and others argued.

Beset by these conflicting arguments, the report of the Anglo-American Committee of Inquiry struck a compromise between the sentiments of the British and the American members. It called for the immediate issuance of 100,000 immigration certificates to permit entry of Jewish refugees into Palestine. It recommended that land sale restrictions created as part of the 1939 White Paper be removed. But as for the future of Palestine, the report was intentionally vague: "any attempt to establish either an independent Palestinian state or independent Palestinian states would result in civil strife such as might threaten the peace of the world. . . ."[38] Consequently, Palestine should remain under the British mandate "pending the execution of a Trusteeship agreement under the United Nations." The committee seemed to envisage a binational state in which neither Arab nor Jew could dominate the other, but beyond support for admission of 100,000 it made no recommendations for future immigration, thus leaving that matter in British hands. No one was pleased, especially Bevin, who had conceived it as a means to draw the Americans into the problem and compel them to share responsibility for any future actions regarding Palestine. On the day the findings of the Anglo-American Committee were announced, 30 April 1946, Truman, without consultation, declared his support of the recommendation for 100,000 and the relaxation of land sale restrictions but offered no assistance and did not refer to the other portions of the document.

Bevin was outraged at Truman's selective and spontaneous comments, but he needed American financial assistance. On his part, Truman was eager to retain British friendship and cooperation while achieving domestic political objectives; congressional elections were scheduled for November 1946. Thus he was willing to propose a new, cabinet-level committee to discuss the implications of the report of the Anglo-American Committee of Inquiry, to be known after its two chairpersons as the Morrison–Grady Committee. In giving his instructions, Truman emphasized that the United States would make no military commitments to maintain order in Palestine nor accept joint responsibility for overseeing a trusteeship administration. Furthermore, he was prepared to try to gain approval for admission of 50,000 refugees to American soil.

The Morrison–Grady Committee negotiations in July 1946 led to an unexpectedly quick agreement, producing a plan that negated major sections of the

Anglo-American Committee of Inquiry Report. The American delegation accepted a British proposal for provincial autonomy in Palestine, demarcating Arab and Jewish areas with the Negev and Jerusalem under the trustee, namely, Great Britain, for an undefined period. The scheme was very close to that proposed in the 1944 partition plan and was designed so that partition remained possible in the long term. For the moment the proposal served in British eyes to permit them to retain control of Palestine without reference to the United Nations. As the central authority, they would regulate all important administrative matters and the country's infrastructure (police, railways, defense, foreign policy, and so on), and they would gradually cede responsibility for internal affairs while presumably retaining final authority in external matters for an undefined period. The right of 100,000 Jewish refugees to enter Palestine would be conditional on acceptance of the entire plan by both Arabs and Jews. This in particular negated the Committee of Inquiry's call for the immediate admission of the 100,000 which Truman had supported. Despite this, Truman and his foreign policy advisers seemed disposed to accept the plan which they believed to offer stability for the region under British tutelage. This led to intense political pressure on Truman, focusing on the problem of the 100,000 but including references to the abandonment of the report of the Committee of Inquiry. White House aides also stressed the domestic repercussions for the Democrats, as it was known that the Republicans would emphasize the Palestinian question in order to gain Jewish support. Truman thus soon retreated from his tentative acceptance of the Morrison–Grady plan, leaving the British to continue to back it while he moved closer to open support of partition.[39]

Labour party policy had placed the British government in a difficult position. Its need for American financial assistance emphasized to Bevin and Attlee the precariousness of their Palestine initiatives, especially when one American Zionist, Rabbi Hillel Silver, linked them to congressional approval or disapproval of the loan request. In addition, Jewish resistance intensified following the British refusal to admit the 100,000, as advocated by the Committee of Inquiry's report in April. Before the report became public, a LEHI attack on a car park in April achieved its goal of killing many British soldiers. Once Bevin rejected the 100,000, the Hagana and LEHI in June combined forces in consecutive raids on railway installations. On the third night, 18 June, Irgun forces captured British officers and held them hostage under threat of death if two Irgun members were hanged in accordance with their sentencing. In response, Attlee and Bevin decided to attempt to crush the Zionist resistance by raiding the headquarters of the Jewish Agency. This operation, carried out on 29 June, was designed to seize agency files, arrest the Hagana leadership, and thereby disrupt what they believed correctly to be Hagana-coordinated resistance to their presence. But although 2700 people and massive documentation were taken, little of significance was learned, in part because the Zionists had been forewarned.[40]

The Irgun, under Menachem Begin, then decided to blow up the King

David Hotel in Jerusalem which housed the British administrative offices and was a prime symbol of the British presence in Palestine. The Hagana assented initially, but they later withdrew support following an appeal by Weizmann to suspend resistance temporarily. Begin then undertook the operation on his own and scheduled it for the middle of the working day. The resulting explosion, on 22 July, killed ninety-one British, Jewish, and Arab personnel and wounded dozens more.[41] Churchill responded on 1 August by declaring that Palestine was relatively unimportant to British interests; horrified at this loss of life, he questioned the need for future casualties. But many British wished for revenge, especially the military and the Labour party, who were determined not to appear weak in the face of violence. Nevertheless, the logic of Zionist terrorism was bearing fruit. That is, the LEHI and Irgun preferred to kill British soldiers rather than officers in order to bring home to the British public at large the cost of maintaining a hold on Palestine.

Determined to adhere to the idea of provincial autonomy, as outlined in the Morrison–Grady proposals, Bevin called a conference of Arab and Jewish leaders to meet in September 1946. He and Attlee hoped that a resolution holding out the possibility of definitive accord might attract those Zionists opposed to terrorism and that this might persuade Truman to cooperate more fully with them regarding Palestine. But Jewish Agency leaders believed they had compromised by accepting the idea of partition, giving up the plan of a Jewish state in all of Palestine as embodied in the commonwealth declaration endorsed at the Biltmore Conference. They therefore refused to attend the London Conference unless their partition plan was the basis of discussion, a proviso rejected by Bevin. For their part, Palestinian Arabs opposed ceding any part of Palestine and refused to attend when the British denied the mufti entrance to England. With no Palestinian Arabs or Jewish Agency representatives present, British officials conducted a fruitless dialogue with delegates from Arab states who, like the Zionists, found the Morrison–Grady clauses unacceptable. They insisted on an Arab state throughout all of Palestine, with Jews considered a religious minority, a position that reinforced the differences among the parties. Bevin then decided to suspend consultations in mid-September, planning to renew them in early 1947 when he hoped Truman would be more amenable to British proposals.

On the Jewish Day of Atonement, Yom Kippur, which fell on 4 October, Truman issued a statement that seemed to support definitively the Jewish Agency's plan for partition, describing it as likely to create "a viable Jewish State in control of its own immigration and economic policies in an adequate area of Palestine instead of in the whole of Palestine." Truman also reiterated his support of "the immediate issuance of certificates for 100,000 Jewish immigrants" and concluded that "a solution along these lines would command the support of public opinion in the United States."[42] Truman's reasons for issuing the statement at that time were primarily political. He had been advised that a statement helping Democratic chances in the upcoming congressional elections in November was crucial to capturing the Jewish vote. Indeed, soon after his statement, Governor Thomas Dewey of New York issued a call for permitting "several hundred thousand" Jews to enter Palestine. As a political gesture, the statement was totally inadequate, as the Republicans scored a resounding triumph in November, but that itself was seen as significant by American Zionist militants who campaigned for the Republicans. They had succeeded in creating "a Jewish issue in the elections" by threatening to use a "so-called Jewish bloc vote . . . for punitive means." In this manner it could serve as a warning for future campaigns, indicating that Truman would have to be much more explicit in his advocacy of a Jewish state, rather than simply calling for the admission of 100,000 refugees.[43]

Throughout the remainder of 1946, British forces in Palestine encountered harassment and attacks, principally the mining of railways and raids on arms depots, but including in December a car bomb attack by Jews that left several dead and numerous wounded. The Arabs later adopted such tactics. In the same month, the Zionist Congress met in Basel, Switzerland. The congress voted to boycott the upcoming London conference, scheduled to reconvene in February 1947. Activists led by Ben-Gurion engineered the defeat of Weizmann and his call for negotiation; they also won a vote leaving unfilled the post of president of the Zionist organization. Weizmann was thus repudiated, now a man with no position, isolated because he still sought a negotiated agreement with Britain at a time when violence seemed the sole means by which a Jewish state could be achieved.

In London itself, discussions over future policy were inching toward support of partition. The chiefs of staff still favored retention of Palestine, assuming until early January 1947 that the military would be withdrawn from Egypt. Some argued for partition as the only possible solution; a unitary state would only lead to strife. But sentiment was also voiced for submitting the problem to the United Nations, an option that Bevin seemed increasingly to favor. The United Nations was now supervisor of the mandate, and the British would have to report to it sooner or later. To do so and gain U.N. support for a continued British role over a state with an Arab majority would secure British ties with Arab leaders and an ongoing British role in Palestine, still desired by strategic planners. At this point the decision to leave India became a factor, as its loss meant the need to retain bases elsewhere. Palestine, in the face of all odds, seemed a suitable replacement, flanking Egypt which now reemerged as the real bastion in the area once Anglo-Egyptian negotiations collapsed. Finally, U.N. approval would legitimize British activities and, it was hoped, nullify American objections. This seemed preferable to abdication, a choice that not only would threaten Britain's strategic stance in the Middle East but also would "harm her prestige throughout the world," a criterion that found favor in the United States when dealing with Vietnam more than twenty years later. With these considerations in mind, Bevin opened the second stage of the London Conference in February, not expecting success and prepared to resort to the United Nations as the next phase of his efforts to retain British power and prestige in the Middle East.

Bevin and his colleagues hosted an Arab delegation that included Jamal al-Husayni as head of the Palestinian Higher Arab Executive. At the same time he met informally with Ben-Gurion and other agency officials. He sought to strike a balance between the Zionist demand for partition, which he opposed, and the Arab insistence on a unitary state with an immediate halt to Jewish immigration. After consultations with both groups, he proposed on 6 February a five-year trusteeship under British auspices leading to an independent Palestinian state with a Jewish minority. Immigration would be set at 4000 monthly for two years, thus permitting 96,000 to enter by the end of that period. After that, immigration would be allowed only in accordance with the country's economic absorptive capacity. The Zionists would be given immigration, though not nearly what they wished, whereas the Arabs would be given a state with more Jews than they wanted.

After much debate Ben-Gurion offered a compromise, fearing a British resort to the United Nations, but he wished the *status quo ante* before 1939 (unlimited immigration), which to Bevin meant the ultimate achievement of Jewish statehood.[44] The Arabs denounced the proposals, insisting on a declaration of an independent Palestine and an immediate end to immigration. Confronted by this chasm and facing a terrible winter that exacerbated Britain's economic crisis with the costs of maintaining the military in Palestine amounting to nearly £40 million annually, Bevin on 25 February 1947 "hurled Palestine into the arena of the United Nations," in a speech filled with sarcasm for the American position supporting Zionism.[45] He openly denounced the Jewish call for statehood. Bevin and the Foreign Office seem to have hoped that the United Nations would support an independent binational state under U.N. trusteeship, with Britain the responsible party. But Bevin also noted the possibility that the United Nations might reach a decision unacceptable to Britain, in which case it would hand over Palestine to the United Nations for final resolution.[46]

UNSCOP AND UNITED NATIONS RATIFICATION OF PARTITION, FEBRUARY–NOVEMBER 1947

As the Palestinian problem entered the United Nations, Arab leadership was once more firmly in al-Husayni hands, indicating the restoration of control to the traditional authority of the urban notables centered in Jerusalem. Neither the peasantry nor members of the emergent urban bourgeoisie had any real representation.[47] On the Zionist side, the activists led by Ben-Gurion dominated the movement and, at times, had trouble restraining those wishing to focus entirely on violence as the sole means to oust the British. But the Zionists could still rely on allies abroad to apply strong pressures to influence decisions in their favor, something denied Arabs of any political affiliation. This was of immense importance to Zionist success, because in Palestine itself the Jews were still a significant minority.

At the end of 1946 there were an estimated 1.269 million Arabs in Palestine, as opposed to 608,000 Jews, a two-to-one ratio. Jews now owned approximately 1.6 million dunams, about 20 percent of the cultivable land and slightly over 6 percent of the total land area.[48] Whatever the rigidity of the mufti, given such numbers few Palestinians were probably willing to agree to partition. They occupied most of the area and were still a sizable majority in their homeland. For the Jews, their minority status in no way mitigated their assumption of their right to a state in all of Palestine, although Ben-Gurion had reduced Zionist demands in order to accept partition. The Zionists believed more firmly than ever that a state in Palestine was their due, not only on the basis of past heritage, but even more so in light of the Holocaust. Here the need for immigrants became paramount, both as a solution to the refugee problem in Europe and as a means of increasing the minority Jewish population to bolster Zionist arguments that a Jewish state would be viable. Although most Western leaders, including Truman, were not convinced that a Jewish state would advance the region's stability, they were moving toward the conclusion that there was no alternative, if only because the existing situation promised even more violence.

The United Nations formed a special committee on Palestine charged with investigating conditions in the country and recommending action to the General Assembly. The United Nations Special Committee on Palestine (UNSCOP) was composed of eleven members, with representatives from Sweden, the Netherlands, Czechoslovakia, Yugoslavia, Australia, Canada, India, Iran, Guatemala, Mexico, and Peru. They undertook their assignment in an atmosphere of increasing tension and disorder in Palestine. The British had stepped up their efforts to intercept the stream of by now well-organized refugee ship contingents that approached the coast. Once these ships were boarded, often in the face of fierce resistance, the passengers were transshipped to detention camps in Cyprus.[49] These actions spurred the Hagana's efforts to destroy the British patrol boats and free the Jews in temporary holding camps in Palestine. The Irgun and LEHI intensified their attacks on British military personnel and judges considered hostile to Jews.

The committee stayed in Palestine for five weeks, leaving at the end of July. They were feted by the Zionists and boycotted completely by the Palestinian Arab leadership. Such bitterness and defiance could only be characterized as "exceedingly inept diplomacy" guaranteed to arouse more sympathy for the Zionists' open presentation of their case.[50] The committee members were also swayed by the intensity of British-Jewish animosity. On 12 July two British sergeants were kidnapped by the Irgun and held hostage against the death sentence given to three Irgunists. When the latter were executed on 29 July, the Irgun hanged the two sergeants and booby-trapped their bodies. In addition, three committee members witnessed the British handling of a refugee ship, the

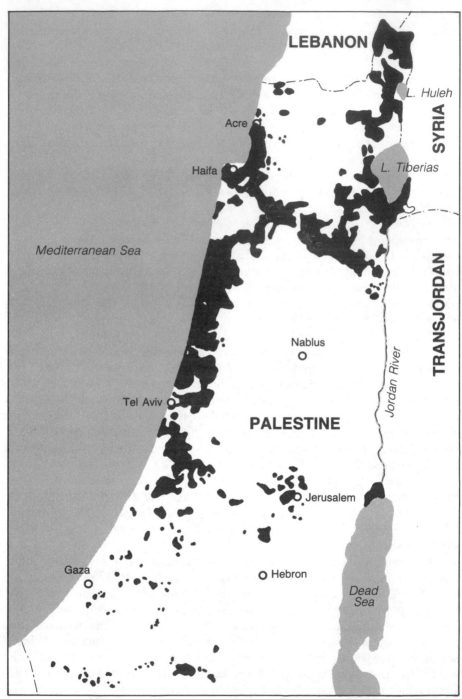

Map 6. PATTERN OF JEWISH LAND HOLDINGS AS OF 1945
(Compare with maps 5 and 7)

President Warfield, renamed the *Exodus* by the Zionists. Crammed with nearly 4500 refugees, the ship was brought into Haifa harbor by the Royal Navy on 18 July, a week after the sergeants had been kidnapped. The next day the passengers were shipped back to southern France, not Cyprus, as a lesson, and one that backfired completely. From Marseilles the ship proceeded to Germany where the refugees from the concentration camps and the war experience were detained in a former camp. The resultant publicity seriously undermined the British position in world eyes at a time when the murders and bombings continued apace in Palestine, including British reprisals against Jews for the hanging of the sergeants.

The UNSCOP report, submitted to the United Nations at the end of August, was unanimous in calling for the end of the British mandate and the creation of procedures leading to the independence of Palestine. But the committee split, eight to three, over what type of state should emerge. The majority called for partition into a Jewish and an Arab state with Jerusalem and its environs internationalized. The minority (India, Iran, and Yugoslavia) advocated "an independent federal state" after a three-year preparatory stage under U.N. trusteeship. This state would in fact comprise two separate entities with local administrative powers, but united central authority would be divided among Arabs and Jews; the minority report allotted more of Palestine to the Arabs than did the majority report.[51] Britain did not wait for the debate in the General Assembly, scheduled for November. On 26 September it declared that the British would withdraw form Palestine, ending the mandate unilaterally and handing the matter over to the United Nations. The Labour government did not recommend a solution. The decision was based on many factors, all of which called attention to Britain's increased inability to meet its obligations abroad.[52]

At the United Nations, many expected that the General Assembly would reject partition because the non-European countries would sympathize with the Arabs, and the Soviets and their allies would presumably oppose the United States, leading to communist rejection of an independent Jewish state. For the Zionists, even United States backing was not considered sure, but David Niles was able to have Truman appoint a pro-Zionist, General John Hilldring, to the United Nations' American delegation to offset the views of the appointees from the State Department. Through Hilldring, Niles established a direct liaison between the United Nations and Truman; indeed, U.S. positions were occasionally relayed directly from the White House without the State Department's having been consulted. Thus, for example, after a private conversation with Chaim Weizmann, Truman phoned the U.N. delegation and told them to reverse American backing for the Arab claim that the Negev (southern Palestine) should be part of an Arab state; the United States would support its inclusion in the Jewish state as recommended in UNSCOP's majority proposal.[53]

As debate over the UNSCOP recommendations continued through November, it seemed clear to Zionists in the United States that extensive lobbying and pressure would have to be brought to bear on certain delegates. Truman remained on the sidelines until the eve of the vote, but he declared in his memoirs that he had never "had as much pressure and propaganda aimed at the White House as I had in this instance."[54] Congressmen and senators along with Supreme Court justices were drafted to send telegrams to heads of states and their representatives either cajoling them or, in some cases, threatening suspension of American aid. On the day the vote was scheduled, 27 November, the partition resolution appeared to be short of the needed two-thirds majority. Filibustering gained a postponement, and Truman approved further pressure on the delegates. Under threat of a Jewish boycott of Firestone rubber and tire products, Harvey Firestone told Liberia that he would recommend suspension of plans for the expansion of development there if Liberia voted against partition.[55] Truman's approval of added lobbying efforts may have saved the day, as until then he and the State Department seemed in accord: the United States would vote for partition but not threaten or lobby other members, leading the Arab officials to assume that they had won. On 29 November the General Assembly voted thirty-three to thirteen, with ten abstentions, to approve partition, with the Soviets backing the Zionists. The right of the Jews to an independent state in part of Palestine had been recognized by the international community, giving legitimacy to Jewish claims for self-rule. Whatever the nature of the Zionist accomplishment in Palestine, the victory at the United Nations was essentially won in the United States where

> the success of the Zionist effort in 1947 represented nearly five years of work, organization, publicity, education, and the careful cultivation of key people in different fields, . . . thus securing the help of influential men and women in the press, the church, the arts, and above all, the government. In the process, the plight of the displaced persons in Europe played an ever-present role.[56]

Amidst the wild celebrations in New York, Tel Aviv, and the Jewish sectors of Jerusalem, both Arabs and Jews prepared for war.

THE BATTLE FOR PALESTINE/ISRAEL, DECEMBER 1947–MAY 1948

Whatever the significance of the U.N. vote in favor of partition, it did not guarantee the creation of a Jewish state. During the six-month period leading up to Ben-Gurion's declaration of statehood on 14 May, the international community was in disarray, with United States policymakers uncertain as to the wisdom of their vote and whether partition should be replaced by a U.N. trusteeship. Truman seems to have fluctuated according to the intensity of the advice given him and the direction from which it came. Much depended on the ability of the Jewish community in Palestine to achieve its goals for itself in the face of Arab resistance and a British policy of "masterly inactivity" designed primarily to lessen the number of its own casualties.

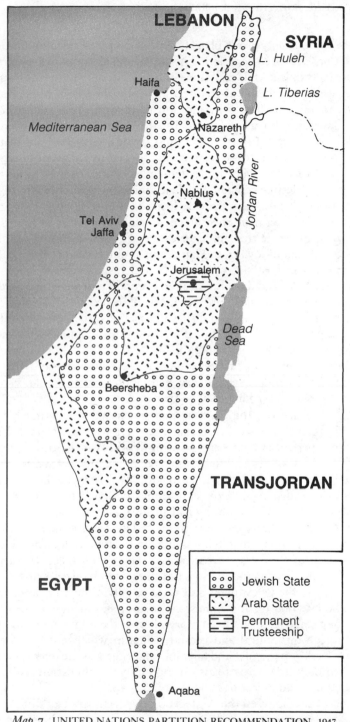

Map 7. UNITED NATIONS PARTITION RECOMMENDATION, 1947

On the Arab side, various plans had been prepared for mobilization if the United Nations approved partition. The mufti, still in Egypt, was determined to control the Palestinian Arab resistance and any aid offered by the Arab states. His forces were led by Abd al-Qadir al-Husayni, the son of Musa Kazim, the former mayor of Jerusalem.[57] In addition there were Arab volunteers led by Fawzi al-Qawuqji who were funded by the Arab League and were mostly non-Palestinians. Both al-Husayni and al-Qawuqji were veterans of the Arab Revolt of 1936–1939, but they were rivals, backed by different groups deeply suspicious of one another. The mufti demanded control over all funds to ensure that the fate of Palestine remained in Palestinian, most specifically his, hands. The Arab League's refusal to provide loans to him to finance resistance or to agree to create a Palestinian government-in-exile confirmed to him that Arab leaders wished to decide the fate of Palestine. Egypt alone came to the mufti's aid, not so much out of loyalty to Hajj Amin as out of suspicion of Abdullah of Jordan's motives in wishing to absorb Jerusalem and central Palestine. The Palestinian resistance and the Arab League's support of it were thus part of a web of rivalries that discouraged any chances of coordinated assaults. Within Palestine, rival al-Husayni–al-Nashshashibi factions, the latter identified with Abdullah, engaged in intercommunal clashes. This, coupled with the lack of preparation for resistance or training in modern military techniques, severely limited the scope of Arab tactics, although their numbers and the strategic locations of their villages gave them excellent opportunities for harassing Jewish communications and attacking their settlements.

On the Jewish side, the Zionists had much superior leadership in both quality and organization, as well as many soldiers who had benefited from the training and experience they received during World War II. Although the Irgun and LEHI were not absorbed into the Hagana, they coordinated activities with it on many occasions, especially in the spring of 1948. In general they specialized in bombings of crowded Arab areas and tactics designed to terrorize the Arab community. The Jewish community had an advantage of roughly 1:5 to 1 among males in the twenty to forty-four age group.[58] The Zionists' problem was one of military communications, maintaining links to isolated settlements and protecting those close to the larger urban areas. They also lacked the armaments sufficient for their people under arms, but their supplies were extensive enough to match those of the Palestinians and were usually of heavier caliber and later models. The question for the Zionist command, and many outside observers, was how they could acquire the territory allotted them by the partition scheme that lay outside the central and coastal plains in which much of the Jewish population lived. A particular and ongoing challenge was the retention of Jerusalem, reached only by narrow roads through hilly terrain extremely convenient for interdicting communications and supplies.

The hostilities between the Arabs and Jews went through different stages. Initially Arab irregulars took the initiative, attacking Jewish settlements and convoys. Hagana tactics, though they fluctuated, remained essentially defensive, protecting settlements and maintaining lines of communication. In this they were successful for the most part, except for the Jerusalem road which was often cut off. From April onward the Hagana took the offensive, establishing control over the area granted to the Jewish state and showing that the lack of coordination of the Arab forces severely impeded their ability to mount a sustained resistance, as opposed to the previous, more opportunistic forays.

Within the major cities, Tel Aviv, Haifa, and Jerusalem, a war of terror reigned which spilled over into the countryside and involved the Hagana as well. Here the major Jewish protagonists were the Irgun and LEHI who specialized in bomb and car-bomb assaults on heavily congregated Arab areas. The Arabs began to use similar tactics. A cycle of attack and retaliation ensued in which each side claimed to be responding to the other's outrage. One series of incidents began with either Irgun or LEHI gunmen throwing bombs at a group of Arab workers at the gates of an oil refinery in Haifa where Jews and Arabs worked together; six Arabs were killed and forty-two wounded. The Arabs inside the plant, a great majority, erupted and killed forty-one Jews and wounded forty-eight before British troops intervened. Two days later the Hagana, in what it called a retaliatory attack to avenge the Arab murder of the Jewish refinery workers, entered a village close to Haifa, dressed as Arabs, and killed approximately sixty persons, including many women and children. For one British military observer, "No better example could be found of the type of incident which from this stage onwards happened commonly in all parts of the country where Jews and Arabs shared the same locality."[59] Terror and atrocities were committed by both sides, with little regard for noncombatants or women and children when avenging an attack. These developments and the city bombings caused approximately 15,000 Arabs to flee during this period, most of them from the major cities, despite the mufti's call for them to stay and his request that Arab states refuse them entry.[60] The British were accused by both sides of favoring the other. They were attacked by both, and their forces intervened on occasion to relieve sieges against either Arab or Jewish communities. But the British also continued to try to intercept ships carrying immigrants who, when landing, were often prepared immediately for combat.

In the midst of this conflict, American policy in Washington and New York underwent shifts in emphasis that alarmed the Zionist leadership and may have influenced their conduct of military operations in Palestine. At the turn of the year the State Department and Truman seemed in agreement that the partition approved by the General Assembly would be impossible to impose except by military force, creating a situation that seemed opportune for the Soviets to exploit. Yet the United States would not and could not commit its own troops to Palestine, nor would the British do anything but continue with their plans for withdrawal. The only recourse seemed to be the United Nations' Security Council and the means it might authorize for implementing the partition vote.

Here the fear of Soviet involvement in any international police force led the State Department, with Truman's blessing, to address the United Nations on 24 February in terms that implied rejection of the Security Council's police powers. The Security Council had the right to restore peace in Palestine but not to impose the partition decision on the unwilling inhabitants of the area, that is, the Arabs. Left unspoken but assumed by observers was the corollary to that argument, that another solution should be found. For American officials, this meant a U.N. trusteeship to oversee Palestine and prepare the respective communities for a possibly different political future, as decided by the United Nations. But such intentions were left unsaid because Truman's domestic political standing in a presidential election year prohibited him from openly endorsing such a stance.[61]

Fear of Soviet penetration of the Middle East and its intentions elsewhere were hardly a mirage at the time these decisions were made. The Soviet-sponsored coup that overthrew the legitimate Czechoslovakian government and installed a communist regime occurred on 25 February. Tension in Berlin led the governor of the American military zone to warn Truman on 5 March that war could erupt at any moment. The Russians began to block Allied convoys to West Berlin at the beginning of April, leading eventually to the Berlin Airlift. Thus Truman went further than approving a redefinition of the Security Council's role in Palestine. He accepted a declaration that rejected partition and supported creation of "a temporary trusteeship for Palestine" under U.N. auspices, a decision duly announced to that body by the American ambassador on 19 March. Nevertheless, Truman immediately repudiated that statement, though not publicly, because on 18 March in a private meeting with Chaim Weizmann he had reiterated his support of partition. He now exploded at the State Department and accused it of betraying him. The real reason for his anger lay in the timing of that announcement, not its contents, but his embarrassment was also largely due to his own brand of policymaking. His private meeting with Weizmann occurred unbeknownst to the State Department and foreign policy specialists, nor did he inform Weizmann of his doubts about partition. The ensuing furor led Truman to back partition even more firmly, influenced both by domestic pressures and by advice from private aides that support of a Jewish state would not threaten peace or American interests in the Middle East: the Arabs were anticommunist and had nowhere to go but to the West, regardless of American support of partition. The pressure from the oil-producing states was minimal. Arab oil was not vital to the American market, though it was crucial to the recovery of Western Europe.[62] Truman's permutations did not inspire confidence in Zionist circles, let alone elsewhere, especially when it was known that official Americn policy still seemed to back a trusteeship proposal. Truman continued to favor partition and in April assured Weizmann privately that he would recognize a Jewish state. The State Department, unaware of such promises, persisted in its efforts to arrange a U.N. peacekeeping force under the guise of a trusteeship before 15 May, when Britain would hand over all powers in Palestine.

The Zionist leadership in Palestine realized that what happened there was crucial to what might be recognized internationally and that they should not rely on the United Nations to enforce partition. They agreed that the Hagana should try to establish control of the zone granted to the Jews by 15 May and additionally to expand the area to include those Jewish settlements outside the partition lines.[63] The Hagana thus went on the offensive at the beginning of April. By 15 May they controlled the area granted them, and a Jewish state had been proclaimed.

It was during these six weeks that the fiercest fighting occurred. Although al-Qawuqji's forces now had some tanks and artillery, the Hagana was arming itself as well. They were receiving major shipments from Czechoslovakia, with Soviet approval; the first consignments arrived on 1 April. Except for Jerusalem, the Hagana offensive achieved success; along the Jerusalem corridor and in the old city, Jewish forces encountered fierce resistance. Throughout the battle for Jerusalem and later struggles for Haifa and Jaffa, the LEHI and the Irgun took part under loose Hagana auspices. In early April Abd al-Qadir al-Husayni was killed, depriving the Palestinian Arab contingents of their most respected leader. Then on 9 April there was a massacre at the Arab village of Dayr Yasin that had a major impact on the fate of the majority of the Arab population in western Palestine.

Dayr Yasin overlooked the Jerusalem road, but it had apparently entered into a nonaggression pact with the Hagana. Nevertheless, a joint Irgun-LEHI force attacked the village, took it after quelling resistance, and slaughtered about 250 men, women, and children whose mutilated bodies were stuffed down wells. The Arabs retaliated on 13 April by killing 70 Jewish doctors and nurses in a medical convoy near Jerusalem. The significance of Dayr Yasin went far beyond its immediate fate. The killings and disposal of the bodies became a staple of Irgun and Hagana propaganda, proclaimed from mobile loudspeaker units that beamed their messages into the Arab areas of major cities such as Haifa and Jaffa; Arab radio also publicized the incident. These broadcasts had a major impact on the Arab will to resist, especially when the population found itself betrayed by its leaders. In Haifa the Arab military command and city officials left on 21–22 April in the face of Irgun assaults coupled with a precipitate British withdrawal of their troops and open Irgun threats of another Dayr Yasin if the Arabs remained. Fifty thousand fled in three days. In short, Zionist psychological warfare and terror tactics, which included the destruction of villages and the ousting of their populations, combined to produce a state of panic that resulted in the flight of over 300,000 Arabs by 15 May.[64]

The matter of the Arab refugees has been in dispute ever since. Israeli officials claim that the Arabs were encouraged to leave by Arab propagandists promising them an easy return once the Arab armies defeated the Zionists. Thus these Arabs should not be considered as refugees having the right to return after the cessation of hostilities, and Israel was justified in permitting Jewish immigrants to take over their lands and homes. This was an ex post facto Israeli stance, taken to sustain an existing situation. At the time, Zionist actions reflected no specific policy but a definite desire to oust as many Arabs as possible. High officials, including the head of land acquisitions for the Jewish National Fund, argued from February onward that the Zionists undertake a policy "promoting measures designed to encourage the Arab flight" and forbidding the return of those who left. Individuals in positions of responsibility, and especially local Hagana leaders, did undertake such measures of encouragement, in addition to the psychological warfare and threats of future Dayr Yasins that were broadcast. These meant more to the Arab civilians than did the pleas of some Jews, such as the mayor of Haifa, for the Haifa Arabs to remain. That a Zionist policy was emerging prior to independence became apparent when some Arabs from Haifa requested permission to return ten days later, with the backing of heads of Arab states. But the Hagana denied the requests and another made in mid-May shortly after independence had been declared. For the Zionists, the opportunity to take advantage of the vacuum created by the fleeing Arabs was too great. Incoming Jews could be moved into the vacant homes in towns and villages, and where the villages were considered primitive, they were razed so that there would be nothing to return to; new Israeli villages were built over or adjacent to them. In this manner a much more cohesive Jewish state with a much smaller Arab population could be built.[65]

All this took place in the midst of ongoing conflict, crisis, and, for the Jews, jubilation. On 14 May 1948 David Ben-Gurion proclaimed the state of Israel to exist within the borders awarded it by the UNSCOP partition plan, minus the Negev where Israeli control was precarious. On 15 May President Truman personally instructed a member of the American United Nations delegation to announce the United States' de facto recognition of Israel, the first country to do so, though the Soviet Union immediately followed suit with de jure recognition. Truman's orders came as a complete surprise to the American U.N. delegation, still trying to arrange for a trusteeship. On the same day, armies from Arab states invaded Arab Palestine and the new Israeli state, sparking a new round of warfare.[66]

THE ARAB-ISRAELI WARS AND THE ARMISTICES, 1948–1949

Plans for a coordinated Arab attack had been made in April under Arab League auspices. The fighting forces included units from Iraq, Syria, Lebanon, Egypt, and Jordan with a token contingent from Saudi Arabia. Nevertheless, the Israelis held a manpower advantage over the Arab armies, backed by much superior military training and commitment compared with that of the Arab troops; the only comparable units were those of Jordan's Arab Legion. In addition, there was no coordination of Arab military movements, as the participants were mutually suspicious of one another's territorial ambitions. All rightly suspected Jordan's Abdullah of seeking to acquire control of the area allotted to the Palestinian Arabs under the partition plan in order to incorporate it into his kingdom, thereby enlarging his country and defeating the mufti in the process. The Israelis were also well aware of Abdullah's aspirations. Zionist representatives had been in contact with him in 1947 and again in 1948 when he expressed his acceptance of partition. Abdullah felt constrained to attack Israeli forces after independence because they were taking over areas within the Arab partition zone, but his Arab Legion, the best of the Arab forces, did not undertake sustained offensives, preferring to establish defensive perimeters around the areas they coveted. Israeli and Jordanian aims generally coincided except with respect to Jerusalem, where the latter were able to retain control of the old, eastern sector, leaving the Israelis the newer, western section.[67]

There were two wars. The first, from mid-May to 11 June, saw the Israelis ultimately stop the Arab invasions after Arab forces penetrated Israeli territory. United Nations peacekeeping efforts then brought about a truce which both sides were glad to accept. In theory an arms blockade was in force, imposed by the British, the Americans, and the French, but its major effect was to block shipment of Western arms to the Arabs. The Israelis stepped up their purchases from Czechoslovakia, eager for Western currency, and began to implement their long-established plans for shipments of arms stockpiled in Europe and the United States. When the truce ended, on 6 July, the Israelis were in a much better military position compared with that of the Arabs, with respect to both weaponry and their unitary command structure.

The truce ended because of Syrian and Egyptian unwillingness to extend it. Beset by internal unrest caused by inflated expectations of victory, they opted for war. This lasted from 6 to 19 July and led to the Israelis' inflicting crushing defeats on all fronts. During this phase they took over much of western Galilee which had been included in the Arab partition zone. By the time the second truce was imposed by the United Nations, the Israelis had greatly expanded the area under their control. The only region left outside it was the Negev, which they wanted but which was partially occupied by Egyptian forces. Nonetheless, in October the Israelis invaded the Negev and incorporated it into Israel, and by the end of 1948 they had driven to the eastern shore of the Gulf of Aqaba, ousting the token Jordanian forces and gaining an outlet to the Red Sea.

Throughout this period, tensions were high. Israel's leaders were determined to gain as much territory as possible, taking advantage of the Arabs' disarray. The U.N. mediator, Count Folke Bernadotte of Sweden, challenged their assumptions. Bernadotte wanted a quick settlement in order to end the hostilities, but he believed that any agreement between the Arabs and the Israelis should achieve a balance in territorial gains to lessen irredentist emotions. With the Israelis already occupying western Galilee, he opposed their desire to have the Negev as well. They could have either one or the other but not both. But the Israelis were not about to cede the Galilee with its rich soil or to acquiesce in the Arab possession of the Negev, which they viewed both in biblical terms as part of ancient Israel and in practical perspective as a potentially fertile area offering access to the Red Sea. The Israelis thus objected strongly to Bernadotte's formulations, accepted by both the British and the Americans. Totally unacceptable also was his idea that Jerusalem be internationalized, a concept equally unsatisfactory to Abdullah. On 18 September, in the midst of a vitriolic Israeli press campaign against him, Bernadotte was assassinated by members of LEHI. His successor, Ralph Bunche of the United States, conducted the armistice negotiations held between Israel and various Arab states on the island of Rhodes, between January and July 1949. The agreed-upon armistice lines defined Israel's boundaries until the 1967 war, but in principle a state of war still existed; only a cessation of hostilities had been achieved.

For the Palestinian Arabs the wars of 1948 had been devastating, those following independence as much as the one before. During the war with the Arab states the Israelis embarked on a deliberate policy of ousting more Arabs from the territories they took over and forcing them across the lines into Arab-held territory; between 400,000 and 450,000 were expelled or fled. Of the approximately 860,000 Arabs who had lived in the area of Palestine now called Israel, 133,000 remained. Of the rest, 470,000 entered camps in Arab Palestine, controlled by Jordan, and the Gaza Strip, held by Egypt. The remainder were dispersed into Lebanon, Syria, and Jordan proper, with Egypt and Iraq taking lesser numbers.[68] With their dispersion, the Palestinian question became one of the refugees, to be handled by the Arab states, until the 1960s when a Palestinian national movement began to emerge, itself often to become the pawn of Arab state rivalries. The mufti's efforts to form an Arab government of all of Palestine, situated in Gaza, was rejected by Abdullah, who saw it as a means of denying him authority over eastern Palestine. In December 1948 he proclaimed the unity of Arab Palestine and Jordan and appointed Raghib al-Nashshashibi as his first military governor of Palestine. This and Abdullah's appointment of other opponents of the mufti to posts in the area signified his defeat of the mufti's forces, now backed by the other Arab states.

In Israel, Ben-Gurion and his dominant Mapai party moved to consolidate the fruits of victory. He had triumphed in a major confrontation with Begin and the Irgun in June, during the first truce, when he challenged Begin's right to control of a shipment of arms that arrived at Tel Aviv on the SS *Altalena*. From Ben-Gurion's viewpoint, those weapons now belonged to the Israeli government and its armed forces, not to a separate unit that he feared might use them to challenge legitimate state authority. After an exchange of gunfire between Hagana and Irgun forces, the Irgun capitulated, and the principal internal threat to the government was removed. With the elections of early 1949, Begin entered the Israeli parliament (Knesset) along with the leaders of LEHI and three Arabs.

By the end of 1949 the Israeli population had jumped to 1 million as a flood of immigrants entered the new state. Approximately half of the newcomers were Jews from Arab lands whose position had become nearly untenable, especially in Iraq, as a result of the creation of Israel. Anti-Jewish prejudice, attacks on Jewish quarters, and loss of Jewish lives became the by-product of Arab frustration connected to Zionism. By 1952, 325,000 Jews from the Arab Middle East had migrated to Israel, ending centuries of existence as minorities under Muslim rule.[69] Only a tentative peace existed between the Arabs and the Israelis, one based on military necessity. The Arabs rejected the legitimacy of the Jewish state, whereas the Israelis were determined to convince the Arabs that they could not threaten their existence. A new phase of the conflict now began, focusing on Arab-Israeli state and military interactions and affected to a much greater degree than previously by great power rivalries and the continuing confrontation between the Soviet bloc and the Western powers.

NOTES

1. Yehuda Bauer, *A History of the Holocaust* (New York, 1982), pp. 200–205, 335.
2. Nicholas Bethell, *The Palestine Triangle: The Struggle for the Holy Land, 1935–1948* (New York, 1979), p. 95.
3. I.S.O. Playfair, *The Mediterranean and the Middle East*, vol. 1, *The Early Success Against Italy (to May 1941)*, in J. R. M. Butler, ed., *The History of the Second World War*, United Kingdom Military Series (London, 1954) pp. 75–79.
4. Quoted in Nevill Barbour, *Nisi Dominus* (London, 1946), p. 206.
5. Bernard Wasserstein, *Britain and the Jews of Europe, 1939–1945* (Oxford, England, 1979), p. 26.
6. Ibid.
7. Ibid., pp. 71ff; and J. C. Hurewitz, *The Struggle for Palestine* (New York, 1976), p. 140.
8. Foreign Office minute in Michael Cohen, *Palestine, Retreat from the Mandate: The Making of British Policy, 1936–1945* (London, 1978), p. 108.
9. John Marlowe, *The Sea of Pilate: An Account of the Palestine Mandate* (London, 1959), p. 173.
10. Munya M. Mardor, *Haganah* (New York, 1964), p. 163.
11. Ronald Zweig, "The Political Uses of Military Intelligence: Evaluating the Threat of a Jewish Revolt Against Britain During the Second World War," in Richard Langhorne, ed., *Diplomacy and Intelligence During the Second World War: Essays in Honor of F. H. Hinsley* (Cambridge, England, 1985), p. 290. The source is an OSS report. Estimates of the quantity of arms varied, but all accounts agree on the superior quality of the Hagana's weaponry. See also Bethell, *Palestine Triangle*, pp. 140–141.
12. Zweig, "Political Uses," p. 119.
13. Cohen, *Retreat*, pp. 130ff; Yehuda Bauer, *From Diplomacy to Resistance: A History of Jewish Palestine, 1939–1945* (Philadelphia, 1970), pp. 224–250; and Melvin I. Urofsky, *We Are One! American Jewry and Israel* (New York, 1978), pp. 10–12.
14. Urofsky, *We Are One!* p.33. Urofsky notes that "Pro-Zionist books, often written by non-Jews, such as Sumner Welles' *Palestine's Rightful Destiny* and Norman MacLean's *His Terrible Swift Sword*, received Zionist subsidies, . . . [and] a number of academic studies were commissioned, all designed to refute the British contention that Palestine could not be further developed to absorb additional immigrants. One of these, Walter Clay Lowdermilk's *Palestine, Land of Promise*, published in 1944, won great popularity as a best seller."

15. Standard works, some more sensationalist than others, are Arthur Morse, *While Six Million Died: A Chronicle of American Apathy* (New York, 1967); Henry L. Feingold, *The Politics of Rescue: The Roosevelt Administration and the Holocaust, 1938–1945* (New Brunswick, N.J., 1970); Saul S. Friedman, *No Haven for the Oppressed: United States Policy Towards Jewish Refugees, 1938–1945* (Detroit, 1973); and two studies by David Wyman, *Paper Walls: America and the Refugee Crisis, 1938–1941* (Amherst, Mass., 1968); and *The Abandonment of the Jews, 1941–1945* (New York, 1984).
16. Feingold, *Politics of Rescue*, p. 265.
17. A commission of American Jews was formed in 1981 to conduct "an objective inquiry into the actions and attitudes of American Jewish leaders and organizations" regarding the Holocaust and efforts to save European Jews. Some members later resigned from the commission which produced a truncated report that noted divisiveness concerning the question. See Seymour M. Finger, ed., *American Jewry During the Holocaust: A Report by the Research Director, His Staff, and Independent Research Scholars Retained by the Director for the American Jewish Commission on the Holocaust* (New York, 1984). The above quotation is from p.i.
18. Cohen, *Retreat*, pp. 131–136.
19. Ibid., p. 157.
20. Ibid., p. 174.
21. Quoted in William R. Polk, David M. Stamler, and Edmund Asfour, *Backdrop to Tragedy: The Struggle for Palestine* (Boston, 1957), p. 108.
22. Bauer, *Diplomacy*, pp. 129–139, 311–333; and J. Bowyer Bell, *Terror out of Zion: Irgun Zvai Leumi, LEHI, and the Palestine Underground, 1929–1949* (New York, 1977), pp. 62–73.
23. Bauer, *Diplomacy*, pp. 320–321.
24. Bell, *Terror*, pp. 121–136. Many of the Hagana opposed these steps and refrained from participating in the campaign.
25. I am relying here principally on Hurewitz, *Struggle*, pp. 146–155, 182–194.
26. Ibid., p. 190.
27. Ibid., p. 192.
28. A standard account of this period, with good bibliography, is Bruce R. Kuniholm, *The Origins of the Cold War in the Near East: Great Power Conflict and Diplomacy in Iran, Turkey, and Greece* (Princeton, N.J., 1980). An important revisionist work that challenges many interpretations of U.S. behavior is Melvyn P. Leffler, *A Preponderance of Power: National Security, The Truman Administration, and the Cold War* (Stanford, 1991).
29. Evan M. Wilson, *Decision on Palestine: How the U.S. Came to Recognize Israel* (Stanford, Calif., 1979), p. 190, n. 15.
30. Michael Cohen, *Palestine and the Great Powers, 1945–1948* (Princeton, N.J., 1982), p.45. In addition to Cohen, another fine study of the question examining British and American positions is W. Roger Louis, *The British Empire in the Middle East, 1945–1951: Arab Nationalism, the United States and Postwar Imperialism* (Oxford, England, 1984). Several books concentrating on Truman and the Palestine issue have appeared in recent years: John Snetsinger, *Truman, the Jewish Vote, and the Creation of Israel* (Stanford, Calif., 1974); Zvi Ganin, *Truman, American Jewry, and Israel, 1945–1948* (New York, 1979); Kenneth Ray Bain, *The March to Zion: United States Policy and the Founding of Israel* (College Station, Tex., 1979). Wilson, *Decision on Palestine*, listed in the preceding footnote, focuses more on the diplomatic aspects of the problem from the perspective of the State Department than do the other sources mentioned. Finally, a recent study of American decision-making regarding the Middle East since 1948 is Steven L. Spiegel, *The Other Arab-Israeli Conflict: Making America's Middle East Policy from Truman to Reagan* (Chicago, 1985).
31. Cohen, *Palestine*, pp. 58–59.
32. Ibid., pp. 62–64.
33. See Bell, *Terror*, p. 104ff; Bauer, *Diplomacy*, pp. 265–345; and Eli Tavin and Yonah Alexander, eds., *Psychological Warfare and Propaganda: Irgun Documentation* (New York, 1982), especially pp. 15–23, which note Irgun anger at the ex post facto Hagana condemnation of operations that Irgun claimed to have been agreed upon beforehand.
34. Major R. D. Wilson, *Cordon and Search: With the 6th Airborne Division in Palestine* (Aldershot, England, 1949), pp. 40–61.

35. Members of the Jewish Agency lobbied the refugees to persuade them to tell committee representatives that they all wanted to go to Palestine. Yehuda Bauer, *Flight and Rescue: BRICHAH* (New York, 1970), pp. 202–203, cites opinions that about 60 percent were actually eager to immigrate there.
36. Louis, *British Empire*, p. 414.
37. Richard Crossman, quoted in ibid., p. 412. Despite Crossman's philosophizing, he also produced wartime photos of Hajj Amin al-Husayni saluting Hitler during the testimony of Arab witnesses before the committee, an obvious attempt to taint the Arab case with the stain of Nazism.
38. Cohen, *Palestine*, p. 105.
39. Ibid., pp. 116–134; Louis, *British Empire*, pp. 434–438; and Hurewitz, *Struggle*, pp. 249–267.
40. Bethell, *Palestine Triangle*, pp. 242–251, states that the British had to rely on the Jews they employed to evaluate the material because so few of them knew Hebrew. But because these Jews were Hagana agents, they destroyed much incriminating evidence.
41. Ibid., pp. 264–265; and Bell, *Terror*, pp. 168–175.
42. Cohen, *Palestine*, p. 163.
43. Ganin observes in *American Jewry*, p. 108, "Toward the end of 1946, the two competitive organs of Zionist diplomacy in America felt for the first time a sense of satisfaction. The Jewish Agency's efforts had secured the Yom Kippur statement, while the political action activities of the AZEC (American Zionist Emergency Council) seemed to have taught Truman and the Democrats the lesson that Jewish allegiance could not be taken for granted."
44. To return to the situation in the late 1930s would mean permitting the Jewish Agency to control immigration and have freedom to purchase land: see Cohen, *Palestine*, p. 220.
45. Louis, *British Empire*, p.463.
46. Ibid., pp. 445–467. Compare Ritchie Ovendale, "The Palestine Policy of the British Labour Government 1947: The Decision to Withdraw," *International Affairs 56* (1980): 73–93, in which he suggests that Bevin was ready to withdraw when he returned from the United States, a position not expressed in his *The Origins of the Arab-Israeli Wars* (London, 1984), p. 99ff.
47. Pamela Ann Smith, *Palestine and the Palestinians, 1876–1983* (London, 1984), pp. 82–84.
48. *Survey of Palestine, Notes Compiled for the Information of the United Nations Special Committee on Palestine, June 1947*, vol. 1 (Jerusalem, 1947), p. 244; and the *Supplement to Survey of Palestine*, pp. 10–11.
49. *Supplement to Survey of Palestine*, pp. 15–16; and R. D. Wilson, *Cordon*, pp. 260–263.
50. Louis, *British Empire*, p. 470, quoting Harold Beely of the British Foreign Office.
51. Cohen, *Palestine*, p. 267; and Hurewitz, *Struggle*, pp. 294–298.
52. Cohen, *Palestine*, p. 269, notes that the Labour government had to impose severe austerity measures on the British public during the summer of 1947, including prohibiting the private use of gasoline.
53. Ganin, *American Jewry*, pp. 139–141.
54. Quoted in Louis, *British Empire*, p. 485. Good summaries of Truman's response to these pressures are Robert J. Donovan, *Conflict and Crisis: The Presidency of Harry S. Truman, 1945–1948* (New York, 1977), pp. 312–331, 369–387; and Spiegel, *Other Arab-Israeli Conflict*, Chapter 2.
55. Robert John and Sami Hadawi, *The Palestine Diary, vol. 2, 1945–1948* (New York, 1971), pp. 260–264; Urofsky, *We Are One!* pp. 143–145; Louis, *British Empire*, pp. 484–486; and Cohen, *Palestine*, pp. 295–300. Ganin, *American Jewry*, pp. 144–145, discounts political factors.
56. Urofsky, *We Are One!* p. 147.
57. I rely here on Smith, *Palestinians, 1876–1983*, pp. 84–86; and Cohen, *Palestine*, p. 305ff.
58. Cohen, *Palestine*, p. 307.
59. R. D. Wilson, *Cordon*, p. 157. His casualty estimates are lower than Cohen's, *Palestine*, p. 308. Cohen's account omits the initial Jewish bomb attack on the Arabs.
60. Cohen, *Palestine*, p. 306.
61. E. Wilson, *Decision on Palestine*, pp. 128–137. Compare Cohen, *Palestine*, pp. 347–354, and Louis, *British Empire*, pp. 495–505.
62. For the oil issue, see Aaron David Miller, *Search for Security: Saudi Arabian Oil and American Foreign Policy, 1939–1949* (Chapel Hill, N.C., 1980).
63. Netaniel Lorch, *Israel's War of Independence, 1947–1949* (Hartford, Conn., 1968), p. 94.

64. Cohen, *Palestine*, p. 337, notes the nonaggression pact between the Hagana and the inhabitants of Dayr Yasin, confirmed indirectly by Christina Jones, *The Untempered Wind: Forty Years in Palestine* (London, 1975), pp. 89, 130–131, who comments on the presumed closeness of the Dayr Yasin residents to the Jews. Jones also refers to the Zionists' use of loudspeakers to terrify Arabs, as does Bell, *Terror*, pp. 295–299, and Arthur Koestler, *Promise and Fulfillment, Palestine, 1917–1949* (New York, 1949), pp. 160–161, 206–207. Begin's account of the propaganda value of Dayr Yasin is in his *The Revolt* (Los Angeles, 1972), pp. 162–165, 363, in which he claims that the Hagana approved the mission and that the British and Arabs, not the Zionists, were the ones who spread the news of Dayr Yasin. An Arab account testifying to the impact of Dayr Yasin and the Zionist tactics used to terrorize village inhabitants to leave, including killing younger individuals, is Nafez Nazzal, *The Palestinian Exodus from Galilee, 1948* (Beirut: Institute for Palestine Studies, 1978). Nazzal's study is based on interviews with Palestinians then in refugee camps. Although some of the testimony might be discounted because of distance in time from the events and the influence of rumors, its consistency and specific identification of individuals by people at widely separated camps suggests the accuracy of many of the stories.

65. The key study of this issue is Benny Morris, *The Birth of the Palestinian Refugee Problem, 1947–1949*, (Cambridge, England, 1987). While an *a priori* Zionist "policy" toward the Arab population did not exist before the major conflicts of the spring 1948, Morris shows how such a policy did develop, fueled by the leadership's desire to rid Palestine of as many Arabs as possible, especially Muslims. Christians and Druse were more likely to be allowed to stay.

66. See the bitter account in Evan Wilson, *Decision on Palestine*, pp. 137–149.

67. Two important studies of Abdullah have appeared recently, one a broader study of his life, the other focusing on Abdullah's contacts with the Jewish leadership between 1947–1949. See Mary C. Wilson, *King Abdullah, Britain, and the Making of Jordan* (New York, 1987) and Avi Shlaim, *Collusion across the Jordan: King Abdullah, the Zionist Movement, and the Partition of Palestine*, (Oxford, 1988).

68. Hurewitz, *Struggle*, pp. 319–321. Yitzhak Rabin, *The Rabin Memoirs*, Hebrew ed., recounts Israeli policies regarding the expulsion of Arabs; the English abbreviated edition (Boston, 1979) does not contain that information. See also Nazzal, *Palestinian Exodus*, pp. 64–110; and Don Peretz, *Israel and the Palestine Arabs* (Washington, D.C., 1958), p. 6.

69. Lucas, *Modern History*, pp. 272–273. There was an assault on the Jewish quarter of Baghdad in the spring, 1941, under the short-lived al-Gailani regime, indicating anti-British as well as anti-Jewish sentiment. Such attacks did not begin to occur with any frequency until after 1945 and the growing awareness of Zionist success in Palestine and in the West. Although governments might intervene quickly, as in Egypt or Lebanon, to protect resident Jews, there was a significant loss of life and extensive damage to Jewish quarters, especially synagogues. In his otherwise admirable book, *The Jews of Islam*, Bernard Lewis attributes Arab anti-Jewish sentiment to their attraction to Nazi ideology, with only passing reference to the impact of the Palestinian question on Arab attitudes toward Jews. He thus discards the concern for historical context and scholarship that pervades his discussion of the subject down to the twentieth century. Contrast with Y. Harkabi, *Arab Attitudes to Israel* (New York, 1971), who documents Arab hatred of Israel and anti-Semitic utterances but qualifies them under the rubric of "political anti-semitism," whose "rise is connected with the tension created as a result of Zionist activity, and especially of the traumatic experience of defeat, the establishment of independent Israel and the struggle against her." (p. 298)

CHAPTER 6

The Beginning of the Arab–Israeli Conflict: The Search for Security, 1949–1957

The conclusion of the armistice agreements between Israel and the Arab states introduced an era of no war–no peace; technically a state of belligerency still existed. Nor did Israel's successful defense of its borders bring official recognition of the status quo either by Arab states or by much of the international community. A major stumbling block was the question of the Palestinian Arab refugees. Western powers called upon Israel to permit at least a portion to return to their homes. The Israelis resisted this pressure or tied its acceptance to the conclusion of peace agreements with Arab governments. The latter insisted on the right of all refugees to return, at least in principle, as a preliminary step signifying Israeli good faith before they would consider peace talks. Some Arab leaders called also for a return to the 1947 partition plan, whose borders they had previously rejected. Israel, which had benefited from that stance by expanding its sovereignty into areas allotted to the Arabs, naturally opposed these claims as being invalid, given the changing circumstances that had resulted from the wars of 1948.

In general, Israel found itself in an almost totally hostile environment. Arab leaders considered it to be the creation of Western imperialism, peopled by Europeans brought in with European and American encouragement at a time when other Arab countries were struggling to gain complete independence from European domination. Furthermore, the armistice lines encouraged border clashes and incidents. Drawn arbitrarily, they frequently cut off Arab villagers from their lands, which were then taken over by Jewish settlers. Palestinian Arab infiltration and Israeli retaliation, especially along the Jordanian line, became a staple of Arab-Israeli tensions. Israel's feeling of encirclement was compounded by Egypt's refusal to permit its ships through the Suez Canal, though Egypt did allow transit to ships of other flags destined for Israel. And from the early 1950s, Egypt frequently blocked traffic through the Straits of Tiran into the Gulf of Aqaba destined for Israel, which cut off the Israeli port of Eilat from access to the Red Sea and Indian Ocean trade. On the other hand, relations along Egypt's border were relatively mild until 1955, compared with the situation existing between Israel and Jordan.

From the Israeli perspective, these Arab attitudes were unwarranted. Arab governments should recognize Israel and absorb the Palestinian Arabs into their own societies. Furthermore, Arab infiltrators should be controlled and the governments be held responsible for any depredations. For Ben-Gurion and his colleagues, the issue of security was paramount, to be met by both military readiness and the encouragement of immigration to bolster the country's strength and effectively undermine the possibility that many Palestinian Arabs might be permitted to return. But Ben-Gurion's conception of security was not merely defensive. He and his chief military advisers undertook a policy of retaliation against the countries from which the infiltrators came, in order to prove to the Arab leaders that Israel could not be defeated and that peace was the only recourse. This activist policy, opposed by Foreign Minister Moshe Sharrett, resulted in serious cleavages within the Israeli cabinet in the early 1950s and led to increased hostilities with the Arab governments, rather than encouraging a receptivity to negotiations.

Arab-Israeli clashes necessarily involved the Western powers, who were eager to draw Arab countries into security pacts ensuring opposition to Soviet overtures in the Middle East. Such efforts, fostered by Great Britain and occasionally encouraged by the United States, seemed to Israel to threaten its security further by aligning the powers with governments opposed to it. The Israelis sought, unsuccessfully, to become the basis of a Western military alliance in the Middle East, isolating the Arabs until they sued for peace with Israel. Though Israel's ambitions did not suit Western strategic interests, neither did the rise to power in Egypt of a young colonel, Gamal Abd al-Nasser, who strove both to reform the Egyptian economy and to oust the British from the Suez Canal zone. Nasser's diplomatic successes and the prestige he gained from them in the Arab world established him in Israeli eyes as a potential threat that should be nullified, a view that gained increasing acceptance in French and eventually British eyes as well. The result was the Suez invasion of October–November 1956, a coordinated attack by Israel, France, and Great Britain that sought to break Nasser's control of the Suez Canal and possibly overthrow his regime.

ISRAEL, THE ARAB STATES, AND THE PALESTINIAN/ISRAELI ARABS

Israel proclaimed itself the true home of all Jews, not simply those within its borders, and called upon those in the Diaspora to return. This doctrine, formally decreed in the Law of Return of 1950, permitted any Jew of good character to enter Israel and receive citizenship. Between 1949 and 1952, Israel's Jewish population more than doubled, as some 666,500 newcomers entered, nearly equally divided between those of European and non-European origin. Among the latter, the largest contingents were from Iraq and Yemen, with nearly 125,000 Iraqi Jews and 45,000 Yemenites arriving. Iran, Algeria, Tunisia, Morocco, and Libya also saw relatively large numbers of Jews leave, many under duress, as were those in Iraq who had become increasingly subject to popular and governmental harassment.[1] Whether from Europe or elsewhere, nearly all these immigrants were poor and needed state assistance. These conditions created massive pressures on the newly established Israeli state and economy, thus stressing the need for aid from abroad, achieved principally in the early years of Israel's existence through private and public contributions funneled through Zionist agencies in the United States, including the sale of Israeli bonds begun in late 1951. During 1951 and 1952, United Jewish Appeal pledges amounted to approximately $150 million and bond sales $99 million.[2] Nevertheless, Israel faced severe economic problems then, as later, in seeking to absorb new citizens. After 1952, as shortages mounted and immigration lessened, the Law of Return was modified in practice to exclude those aged and ailing individuals who had no means of support and who, in practical terms, could not contribute either militarily or financially to the security of the state.[3]

In such circumstances, the fate of the remaining Arab population in Israel, which amounted to about 170,000 by 1950, was subject to Israel's perceived security requirements and the needs of its incoming settlers. Most of these Arabs were considered potential fifth columnists despite their recognition in the constitution as citizens of Israel. Most lived in areas close to the armistice lines, which had been designated military zones, outside the control of civil law and subject to the arbitrary imposition of military edicts. Lawful residents could be banished, properties confiscated, and entire villages moved by military decision.[4] In the military's view, backed by Ben-Gurion though protested by some members of the Knesset, the granting of full civil liberties to Israeli Arabs would endanger the national defense because of the continuing tensions along the armistice lines where frequent incursions by Palestinians occurred.

Equally important in judging the position of Israeli Arabs was the designation of much of their property as "absentee" even if they still lived in Israel. The question of property was crucial to Israel's ability to house its new immigrants. In December 1948 a custodian of absentee property was appointed who had nearly absolute powers for the disposal of lands left vacant as a result of the wars of 1948. The custodian's powers were such that he

> could take over Arab property in Israel on the strength of his own judgment by certifying in writing that any persons or body of persons, and that any property, were "absentee." The burden of proof that any property was not absentee fell upon its owner, but the Custodian could not be questioned concerning the source of information on the grounds of which he had declared a person or property. . . . he could [also] take over all property which might be obtained in the future by an individual whom he certified to be absentee.[5]

The custodian's judgment was wide-ranging and applied to many Palestinian Arabs who had not left the region taken over by Israel. Any Palestinian Arab could be declared absentee if he left his usual place of residence on or after 29 November 1947, the date of the United Nations partition resolution. This applied whether the individual returned to that place of residence the following day or had fled scenes of combat during the war but had not left what became Israeli territory. Tens of thousands of Israeli Arabs were so classified; about 1 percent were able to regain some of their property. Later protests led to a decision by the Israeli government to pay compensation to some claimants and to permit Arabs to lease lands from the custodian.

The nature of the process whereby these decisions were made reflected the conditions existing in Israel after independence. Massive immigration led to the ad hoc occupation of deserted housing in major cities and in villages. Where Arab villages were destroyed, new Jewish villages were constructed, or the land was often absorbed by adjacent Jewish collective settlements. Because the occupied property was then taken over by the Jewish Agency for the use of the new settlers, this property, in the custodian's view, was inalienably Jewish and could not be returned to the Arabs who had left it, even if they remained in what had become Israel. The definition of absentee property served to justify the taking of Arab lands and buildings for the sake of consolidating Israel's hold on the bulk of the land area. Israel's definition of its own needs also served to isolate the Israeli Arab population from consideration for development opportunities or allocation of public services considered normal for the Jewish sector, a practice that has continued to the present.[6]

Palestinian Arabs living outside their former homeland, now refugees, encountered official sympathy and unofficial suspicion that led to their isolation in most of the countries where they settled. The bulk of the Palestinian Arabs in exile, over 500,000 in 1956, resided in Jordan, where they then comprised one-third of the population. Jordan granted them citizenship, the only Arab state to do so, although many Palestinians remained in refugee camps financed by the United Nations through UNRWA, the United Nations Relief and Works Agency created in 1950 when it became clear no resolution of the refugee question was likely. Nearly 200,000 were crammed into the Gaza Strip, under Egyptian rule, where their movement was restricted. The nearly 100,000 refugees in Lebanon in 1956 had not been granted citizenship because the Maronite Christian ruling elite feared the addition of so many Muslims to the population. Of all the states bordering Israel, only Syria at that time had ample land available for the settlement of refugees, though certainly not all. In May 1949 the Syrian ruler, Colonel Husni Zaim, offered to meet Ben-Gurion to discuss arrangements whereby hundreds of thousands of Palestinians might be resettled in Syria. Despite the favorable response of Moshe Sharrett, Ben-Gurion flatly rejected the offer.[7] Ben-Gurion's reaction reflected an insistence on Arab leaders' meeting certain Israeli conditions that precluded preliminary talks that might have resolved outstanding issues.

The refugees remained in camps in most countries, many of them rejecting offers of resettlement that were made. Arab leaders demanded their return to former Palestine, but the government of Israel, from 1950 onward, insisted on their resettlement in Arab lands as part of an equal exchange of populations that, by 1952, included the influx into Israel of over 300,000 Jews from Arab countries. Disorganized and subject to the whims of their hosts, the Palestinians remained an important factor in Arab-Israeli tensions down to 1956 but were then effectively controlled until the emergence of the Palestinian Liberation Organization in 1964, itself created to serve the interests of the Arab states.

THE GREAT POWERS, ISRAEL, AND THE ARAB-ISRAELI CONFLICT, 1949–1954

From the viewpoint of the Western powers—the United States, France, and Great Britain—the Middle East was a source of tension whose causes should be resolved as quickly as possible. The basic issue, that of the Arab refugees, proved intractable and led to the creation of UNRWA. The ongoing border clashes became the responsibility of the Mixed Armistice Commission (MAC), formed by the United Nations General Assembly to resolve disputes. There were separate commissions for Israel and each of its Arab neighbors, including representatives from both sides and U.N. officials. The commission had no independent authority. It could investigate complaints brought by one side or the other, assess responsibility, and report its findings to U.N. headquarters in New York. Its ability to arbitrate depended on both sides permitting the MAC to proceed.

At the same time the West sought to neutralize the military capabilities of the antagonists and align its participants, especially the Arab states, against any possible Soviet incursion. A French-British-American Tripartite Declaration of 25 May 1950 pledged to maintain the existing armistice lines and to limit arms supplies to those required for local security needs; no major arms deal that might alter the balance of power and initiate an arms race would be undertaken. Israel was considered well equipped for its security requirements and superior in its military training and combat readiness to its Arab neighbors. Israel, however, sought more specific guarantees of support from the West. The Ben-Gurion government opposed the Tripartite Declaration and sought acceptance as part of a regional defense system envisaged for the area, an extension of the NATO (North Atlantic Treaty Organization) concept of regional military alliances designed to contain the Russians. But the Allied plans did not include Israel at this time. The containment principle seemed more suitable for Arab participation than Israeli, given the size of the Arab population and its potential for social unrest which could be alleviated by the economic aid that would be part of the assistance granted to any member of such a defense system.

Western interest in Arab participation in regional alliances was resented by Israeli leaders. They wanted to be part of a Western alliance and to have the Arab states excluded. Membership would bring with it needed economic assistance to help provide for the great infusion of immigrants, and arms supplies. The arms supplies, though supposedly preparing Israel to defend itself against the Russians, would ensure its military superiority over the Arab states. Conversely, Arab membership in such a system would bolster its military stockpiles which Israel considered to be aimed at it. But if Ben-Gurion eagerly pursued such an alliance, especially with the United States, he rejected any condition that might restrict his freedom of movement. Thus he refused an American suggestion of a security pact while seeking an arms deal only. The latter would permit him to direct Israeli actions unhindered, a vital factor in Israel's policy toward its Arab neighbors.[8]

Israel's attitude toward the Arabs and its relations with the outside world were predicated on the Jewish experience in Europe, the Holocaust, and the Arab hostility it encountered in the Middle East. Whereas Jews had previously been subject to the will of non-Jews, Israel, as the Jewish state, would never submit to constraints imposed by others. In Ben-Gurion's view, Israel alone was responsible for its existence. Though it might rely on outside help, economically or militarily, that would not signify its willingness to limit its independence in any way. For Ben-Gurion and those allied with him in the Israeli government, the opinions of the outside world meant little, regardless of the aid they might give. He made a nearly absolute distinction between Israel and world Jewry on the one hand, and the *goyim* or non-Jews on the other. If the latter did not fulfill their perceived obligations to Israel, they would at best be ignored, at worst be fought.

This attitude, called "Ben-Gurionism," emerged initially in Zionist perceptions of the British.[9] The British had an obligation to fulfill regarding the creation of the Jewish state. When they drew back, they had to be confronted, militarily and diplomatically, so that Jewish rights could be achieved. As for the Palestinian Arabs, Ben-Gurion assumed that they would understand only armed might. Once they learned that opposition to Zionism was futile, they would ultimately accept it and submit to Jewish rule. Thus he testified before UNSCOP in July 1947 that he would approach the Palestinian Arabs and "tell them, here is a decision in our favour. We are right. We want to sit down with you and settle the question amicably. If your answer is no, then we will use force against you."[10] After independence Ben-Gurion extended to the Arab regimes his perception of Arab hostility and how to confront it. Because the Arabs denied Israel's right to exist, they had to be shown the power of Israel time and again until they were compelled to concede its military superiority and sue for peace.

For the Ben-Gurionists, who included Moshe Dayan, appointed chief of staff in 1953, evidence of Arab hostility should be challenged immediately to remind the particular state that Israel would not tolerate any form of aggressive act that seemed to violate its sovereignty and well-being. This policy of retaliation was implemented with particular harshness on the Israeli-Jordanian frontier, the scene of numerous border transgressions, many involving the theft of crops but, in the early 1950s, increasingly including personal assaults. Most of these forays came from Palestinian Arab villages in the West Bank area that were separated from Israel, and often their former farmlands, by a few hundred yards. From 1952 onward the Israeli government began to sponsor military reprisals against villages assumed, though not known, to be responsible for attacks on

Israelis or Israeli property. In 1953 a special force, led by Colonel Ariel Sharon, was formed to undertake punitive assaults. In October 1953, following the killing of an Israeli mother and two children, this force attacked the Palestinian village of Qibya, dynamiting houses, killing over fifty inhabitants, and wounding fifteen others.[11] The intention was to impose a price on the Arab community disproportionate to the crime committed against Israel in order to encourage deterrence by the host government. To this extent, the practice worked for a while on the Jordanian frontier, though it brought neither side closer to peace, the presumed objective of such retaliatory actions. So far as Dayan and his aides were concerned, any infringement should be punished, even if no threat to life resulted. Thus, when some prize sheep were stolen from an Israeli kibbutz, Dayan wanted a retaliatory attack against an Arab village near the border. He was rebuffed by Moshe Sharrett, then prime minister, who deplored the Ben-Gurionist policy that the majority of Israeli officials supported. The sheep were later returned through U.N. intercession.[12]

Ben-Gurionism combined a sense of being threatened with a belief in Israel's military superiority. In this context Israeli military actions were often intentionally aggressive. Israeli forces frequently engaged in maneuvers close to the borders of Jordan and later Egypt, actions that sparked clashes and that were seen by U.N. officials as deliberately provocative.[13] Although Israeli reprisals were designed initially to force Arab governments to restrain infiltrators into Israel, their success on the Jordanian frontier did not inhibit Israeli military units from undertaking unilateral actions. These tactics were important in Dayan's view, not only to make Arab governments control their borders, but primarily to "make it possible for us to maintain a high level of tension among our population and in the army. Without these actions (assaults) we would have ceased to be a combative people and without the discipline of a combative people we are lost."[14] On occasion that might require provoking an incident to be able to justify a reprisal.

In such an atmosphere, advocates of a more conciliatory approach to the Arabs and the world at large were relatively few, though they predominated in the Foreign Ministry. Moshe Sharrett's conception of Israel's relations with outsiders has been characterized as "Weizmannist" rather than Ben-Gurionist.[15] That is, he was more disposed to rely on outside aid to resolve disputes and to acknowledge it rather than stressing absolute Jewish self-reliance. Though he recognized Arab hostility, he was willing to seek a reconciliation of differences through negotiations and compromise if that were possible. Sharrett did not rule out force as an option, but it remained one choice among several rather than the primary response to problems that arose with Arab neighbors. To react immediately in a military manner prevented any possibility of searching for grounds for discussions with Arab leaders, if only secret or indirect, that might create a more rational atmosphere even if a full peace accord was not achieved. Sharrett decried the militarism that he believed to permeate the Ben-Gurionist camp. To him it meant that Israel

> must . . . invent dangers, and to do this it must adopt the method of provocation-and-revenge. . . . And above all—let us hope for a new war with the Arab countries, so that we may finally get rid of our troubles and acquire our space. (such a slip of the tongue: Ben-Gurion himself said that it would be worthwhile to pay an Arab a million pounds to start a war.)[16]

For their part, Dayan and his contemporaries viewed Sharrett with contempt as a weak man whose views would enfeeble the country. Ben-Gurion agreed, once declaring that "Sharrett is cultivating a generation of cowards."[17]

Israel did make official peace proposals from time to time, based on Arab recognition of the existing borders with minor modifications, and compensation for Arab refugees. But these offers did not meet Arab demands for major border revisions and the right of refugees to return. No Arab state was able to discuss openly the prospect of peace with Israel, often fearing domestic opposition in the midst of increasing social turmoil. Conversely, the Israeli offers were apparently made more with an eye to public consumption abroad than out of expectation of any positive response: "the main impetus for these announcements was pressure from the Western powers for a more conciliatory attitude."[18] And these offers, whatever their motives, drew criticism from sectors of the Israeli public. Some argued that any Israeli overture would only be interpreted as a sign of weakness by the Arabs and encourage a greater steadfastness and designs to destroy Israel. Military preparedness and continual demonstrations of Israel's power were the only means able to bring the Arabs to the peace table. On the other hand, the territorialists such as Menachem Begin denounced the idea of talks because Ben-Gurion seemed willing to accept the existing armistice lines as future boundaries. Begin and his Herut party advocated the immediate Israeli conquest of the West Bank and forcible expulsion of its Arab population to pave the way for Jewish settlement of land linked biblically to ancient Israel. Ben-Gurion shared Begin's aspirations for territorial expansion while rejecting the latter's timing, awaiting a propitious moment when Western backing might be possible, as shown in his proposals during planning for the Suez attack (to be discussed later).

Suez gave Ben-Gurion the opportunity to implement his plans for an attack on Egypt, derived from his long-standing perception that it might pose a threat to Israel's security. With the rise to power of Gamal Abd al-Nasser in mid-1954, these expectations took on the guise of a self-fulfilling prophecy, buttressed by Ben-Gurion's preference for direct military action. In the words of one Israeli analyst,

> The Israeli approach (which granted priority to the attainment of short-range goals even at the expense of the long-range goal) stemmed from the assumption that existence *per se* takes precedence over peaceful existence. . . . From this

stemmed the Israeli tendency to give priority to short and middle-range security considerations over long range political considerations. . . .[19]

As a result, Sharrett's interests in compromise led Ben-Gurion in 1956 to decide that "Sharrett was a serious liability in the preservation of Israel's vital interests."[20] He arranged Sharrett's ouster as foreign minister, thus ensuring that he could plan an invasion of Egypt without strong opposition from the cabinet.

THE GREAT POWERS, THE ARABS, AND THE ARAB-ISRAELI CONFLICT, 1949–1954

For most Arabs the defeat of their armies at the hands of the Israelis was considered a disaster, a shock that seriously undermined the credibility of the regimes that had committed their forces to battle. Many, especially of the younger generation, saw Israel's existence as symbolic of Arab humiliation at the hands of a superior power relying on Western technology that they were denied. Here there existed a desire for revenge coupled with the fear of Israeli military might and possible future expansion.

On the other hand, plans for retaliation played little if any role in Arab political events, whatever the resentment felt at Israel's creation. Attention focused on domestic issues and problems of development in which the defeat at the hands of the Israelis seemed to many a symbol rather than a cause of the corruption and inefficiency they associated with the existing political systems. The Arab states did not develop individually or collectively a policy toward Israel, in contrast with the opposing Ben-Gurionist and Weizmannist policies that could be found influencing Israel's actions toward its Arab opponents. The only course agreed upon by Arab leaders was to refuse recognition to the new state. The exception to this rule was King Abdullah of Jordan, who in private negotiations sought to reach a peace agreement with Israel that would ratify the boundaries created in the 1948 war. To have succeeded would have meant recognition of his control over the West Bank, thus denying any possibility of a Palestinian state, an interest shared by the Israelis as well. These negotiations failed when news of their existence led to severe criticism of Abdullah by other Arab states. His assassination in Jerusalem in 1951 by a Palestinian was a consequence of his efforts to reach that agreement.

Arab rivalries at this time focused primarily on efforts to unite the Fertile Crescent, principally Iraq, Jordan, and Syria, but possibly including Lebanon as well; these plans before World War II had included Palestine. Its chief sponsors were the two Hashemite kingdoms that derived from the descendants of Sharif Husayn, Iraq and Jordan. The chief prize was Syria, considered the heartland of Arab nationalism. Both countries, especially Iraq, intervened in Syrian politics to try to encourage the rise to power of a ruler favorable to such a union. Egypt and Saudi Arabia, drawn together by the proximity of their interests in blocking any merger that excluded them, strove to foster Syrian protégés who would be cool to these schemes. Differing domestic priorities and relations with Western powers also played a part in these disputes. Though nominally independent, both Iraq and Jordan were closely allied to Great Britain and permitted it to use military facilities in their countries, whereas Egypt tried to oust the British.

Syria experienced a serious upheaval following its defeat in the war against Israel. There were three coups in 1949, all bringing colonels to power. Although these changes of government reflected tensions in the military stemming from the war with Israel, they also indicated shifting alliances relating to Fertile Crescent matters. The first of the three colonels, Zaim, was anti-Hashemite; the second, Hinnawai, was pro-Iraqi and approached Baghdad with the idea of uniting the two countries. The third, Adib Shishakli, steered a middle course between the Hashemite and pro-Egyptian factions, ruling Syria with an iron hand until February 1954 when he was overthrown. Although domestic resentment played an important role in his demise, equally significant was the financing of the coup by Iraq in the hope of installing a pro-Hashemite regime, apparently with British support. This in turn led the French to support Shishakli as a means of fostering the restoration of French influence in Syria.[21]

The returns from the free elections held in October 1954 stressed the role of independents in Syrian politics, but the socialist party, the Baath, scored significant gains. Its advocacy of Arab unity and neutrality in great power affairs aroused Western concern, intensified by Syria's hostility toward countries such as Iraq which seemed willing to consider alliances with the West. Throughout this period, tensions flared periodically along the Israeli-Syrian frontier, sparked frequently by disputes over the fate of the demilitarized zones established by the armistice agreements at points along Lake Tiberias at the base of the Golan Heights. The agreements guaranteed the right of these areas' inhabitants to stay, but the issue of sovereignty remained unresolved. Syria argued that the question could be decided only in a final peace accord; Israel claimed sovereignty over the zones and the right to act in them as it wished.

Egypt, with King Faruq still in power until July 1952, experienced great domestic unrest in the later 1940s. Nationalists demanded complete independence from Great Britain and the removal of British personnel from their bases in the Suez Canal Zone. The Muslim Brotherhood called also for drastic socioeconomic reforms based on Islamic principles to redress the inequities that plagued Egyptian society. In the turmoil following the Egyptian defeat in Palestine, the prime minister was assassinated by members of the Muslim Brothers in December 1948; the leader of the Brothers, Hassan al-Banna, was in turn killed by members of the Egyptian police in February 1949. Resultant tensions over the canal zone erupted on 26 January 1952 into the burning of much of Westernized Cairo and led to a bloodless coup on 23 July in which a group of young military officers, led by Gamal Abd al-Nasser, ousted Faruq and took power. Although Egyptian propaganda was often violent in its condemnation of Israel during his first two years in office, Nasser concentrated on domestic reform and securing his own position within the new regime. During this period the Egyptian-Israeli frontier was relatively quiet. A major accomplishment was Nasser's success in reaching an agreement with the British in July 1954 whereby British forces would be withdrawn by June 1956 from their bases in the canal area.

In the eyes of a younger generation of Arabs, Nasser's success in gaining British agreement to withdraw its forces, initialed in July and signed officially in October 1954, aroused a general desire to break military bonds with Western countries at a time when both the British and the United States sought to reinforce such links. The latter were not in total agreement on the matter. The British, with Churchill in office as prime minister and Anthony Eden as foreign minister, viewed Nasser with disdain and distrust and sought to reinforce their bonds with Jordan and especially Iraq. The United States, with Dwight Eisenhower as president and John Foster Dulles as secretary of state after January 1953, shared British desires for military alliances designed to block communist expansion but viewed Nasser more favorably until 1956. They believed that British efforts to retain bases in Egypt aroused nationalist opposition and created conditions more conducive to neutrality and a possible turning to the Soviets. In American eyes it was better to back Nasser and persuade him to join in a military pact if any Arab leader was to be wooed.[22]

Nasser did not consolidate his position as ruler of Egypt until 1954. Although he had led the young officers who overthrew Faruq in July 1952, they had chosen a figurehead leader, General Muhammad Naguib, because of their own obscurity. In principle Nasser dominated policymaking behind the scenes. But Naguib acquired increasing power because of his popularity and by early 1954 seemed to favor the restoration of democracy, which had been suspended following the revolution. A struggle for power in the spring ended with Nasser the victor. He now emerged as the real leader of Egypt but faced challenges, especially from the Muslim Brothers who were embittered by their continued exclusion from the government. A member of the brotherhood attempted to assassinate Nasser in October but failed. Nasser used the incident to crack down on its leadership. They were arrested, brought to trial, and six members identified with the direction of a secret unit formed to instigate violence were executed. It was precisely at this time, the beginning of 1955, that new crises erupted that affected Egypt's relations with the West and its stance toward Israel: the first was the Baghdad Pact, a military alliance between Iraq and Turkey, signed on 24 February, that the British joined a month later; the second resulted from an Israeli attack on an Egyptian post in the Gaza Strip that left heavy Egyptian casualties.

THE BAGHDAD PACT: THE WESTERN SEARCH FOR ALLIES, 1953–1955

The Baghdad Pact was the outgrowth of an Anglo-American search for allies in a Middle Eastern defense system that led them into conflict with each other. Both backed the containment policy aimed at limiting Soviet advances. With respect to the Middle East, both saw merit in the northern tier concept, whereby those countries along Russia's southern borders—Turkey, Iran, and Pakistan—would join alignments backed by the West. Where they diverged was in their prognosis for Arab involvement in such a pact, coupled with British resentment at what they perceived as American attempts to usurp traditional British spheres of influence.

Eisenhower's secretary of state, John Foster Dulles, was a determined backer of containment and an inveterate seeker of regional alliances designed to bolster countries and areas considered strategically important to the West. But Dulles recognized, following a tour of the Middle East in mid-1953, that the Egyptians would not enter into any pact that provided for Western military bases on Egyptian soil. The most they might do would be to back the strengthening of an Arab collective security alliance buttressed by Western arms. That too awaited success in Nasser's negotiations with Eden, stymied by British insistence on a continuing military presence at their bases. Dulles, to encourage Nasser, promised American assistance once an accord was reached. He believed that no Arab security arrangement would succeed without Egypt's participation. In the meantime he placed his hopes on the non-Arab northern tier countries which seemed more willing to accept direct Western ties.

Here Dulles had success. Turkey had become a NATO member in February 1952. During 1953 the United States established closer ties with Pakistan and arranged the coup whereby the Shah of Iran was restored to his throne. With American prodding, a Turkish-Pakistani military accord was reached in April 1954, followed by an announcement of American military aid to Pakistan. This agreement linked the Pakistanis to two regional defense systems, one based on its treaty with Turkey and the other through its membership in SEATO (Southeast Asia Treaty Organization), created to bar Chinese as well as Russian inroads into that region. Dulles and Eisenhower seemed in 1954 to have preferred a northern tier arrangement that excluded all Arab states so as not to draw the ire of nationalists who favored neutrality. Though they appreciated the loyalty of Iraq's Nuri al-Said, they considered him less likely than Nasser to foster Arab acceptance to any collective security pact.[23]

Eden resented the American inroads into Pakistan and Iran, where British interests had once been paramount. Particularly upsetting was what he perceived as American pressure to reach an agreement with Nasser in order to supplant the British in Egypt. He considered Nasser an upstart whose nationalism should be checked. Eden was determined to reassert British prestige in the Arab world, best done, he believed, through open military alliances. Iraq was the most likely candidate, given the pro-Western sympathies of Nuri al-Said and his fear of the younger generation represented by Nasser and the anti-Hashemites in Damascus. Futhermore, Nuri was eager to promote an alliance of Arab states linked to Turkey, Iran, and Pakistan with Western military backing, a framework that presumably would have stiffened the more conservative regimes and furthered Hashemite ambitions.

In January 1955 Nuri announced Iraq's intention to enter a military pact with Turkey, signed on 24 February. Britain, the sponsor, joined a month later, and Iran and Pakistan followed, creating a union officially known as the Central Treaty Organization, more commonly designated as the Baghdad Pact. The pact was Eden's answer to Dulles. He declared in the House of Commons after British entry into the group that "I think . . . we have strengthened our influence and our voice throughout the Middle East."[24] Dulles thought otherwise and refused to commit the United States to full membership, opting for observer status. He believed that open British membership weakened the Western position in the region, especially because the pact's headquarters were in Baghdad. If Iraqi membership were desirable, then the Western powers should have financed the pact behind the scenes rather than being identified openly with one regime in the Arab world.

Nasser vilified Nuri's stance as a betrayal of Arab nationalist interests which called for neutrality; here he identified with India's Jawaharlal Nehru, who had criticized Pakistan's membership, in part because such arrangements brought great infusions of arms that its regional rivals would have to offset. (Israel objected to the Baghdad Pact for the same reason.) Nasser also believed that the pact violated an informal understanding he had with the United States to create an independent Arab military alliance. Nevertheless, he still looked to the West, especially the United States, for military assistance, assuming it to be part of the aid promised by Dulles in 1953; an economic accord had been reached with Washington in November 1954. His search for arms intensified following an Israeli attack on Gaza on 28 February 1955, four days after the Baghdad Pact was announced. The raid highlighted Egyptian military weaknesses and was a catalyst in the increase of Egyptian-Israeli border tensions. Its motives stemmed primarily from Israeli domestic considerations, reflecting the split between Sharrett and Ben-Gurion, and can be considered a turning point in the modern history of the region.

ISRAEL, THE LAVON AFFAIR, AND THE GAZA RAID

Moshe Sharrett had become acting prime minister in July 1953 when Ben-Gurion decided to enter semiretirement at his desert kibbutz, but the latter did not resign his post officially until December. During the interim period, Dayan and other colleagues continued to consult Ben-Gurion without always referring to Sharrett, their nominal superior. Similarly, the new defense minister (Ben-Gurion had occupied both posts), Pinhas Lavon, regarded Sharrett with scorn and sided generally with the school advocating military reprisal. Thus the retaliatory raid against Qibya in October, proposed by Dayan and assigned to Ariel Sharon, was approved by Lavon and tacitly by Ben-Gurion, but Sharrett was informed only in an offhand way, and his objections were ignored.[25] Once Sharrett became prime minister in December, retaining his post as foreign minister, he tried to contain military ventures and apparently established a *sub rosa* dialogue with Nasser that lasted at least until the Gaza raid.[26]

Lavon, however, sought to assert himself as defense minister, thereby incurring the wrath of Dayan and the military because of what they considered to be his meddling in their affairs. His plotting led, in the summer of 1954, to a scheme designed to abort the Anglo-Egyptian agreement for withdrawal of troops from the bases in the canal zone. In alliance with the head of Israeli military intelligence, Lavon decided that the removal of the British troops would open the way for Egyptian military penetration of the Sinai Peninsula, thus creating a potential threat to Israel's existence.[27] He arranged for an Israeli spy ring in Cairo, composed mainly of Egyptian Jews, to plant bombs at the American and British embassy complexes and at buildings that Westerners frequented. The explosions would be attributed to the Muslim Brotherhood and create an atmosphere of distrust and suspicion of Nasser's ability to protect foreigners. As a result, the British would presumably keep their troops in Egypt to protect their citizens. The plan backfired. The conspirators were caught in late July and brought to trial in December. Two members of the spy ring were condemned to death, others to jail sentences; one committed suicide in his cell. Those given the death sentence were hanged on 31 January 1955, despite pleas from abroad and a personal request from Sharrett. Nasser had just executed the leaders of the Muslim Brotherhood for conspiracy, and he could not appear to cater to Israeli requests for leniency in such circumstances.

The impact of what became known as the Lavon Affair on Israeli opinion was immense, especially because the Israeli public was not informed of the actual chain of circumstances until 1960 and believed until then that Nasser had trumped up the charges in order to persecute Jews. Complete censorship was imposed at the time for fear that Israeli confidence in their leadership might be shaken too severely. Sharrett had never known of the planned operation. Once informed, he decided, with the agreement of all concerned, to keep it hidden from the public. An investigation brought about Lavon's resignation after a commission failed to establish guilt or responsibility; there was evidence that the head of military intelligence and others had falsified documents. With the government in disarray and public feeling at Arab persecution approaching hysteria, overtures to Ben-Gurion to return to government intensified. On 17 February he was installed as defense minister, the acknowledged leader of Israel and the symbol of the Israeli will to fight. Eleven days later came the Gaza raid, resulting in over forty Egyptian soldiers dead and scores wounded.

It is generally agreed that the Gaza raid was a turning point for Nasser, radically changing his stance toward Israel and leading to a determined effort to acquire arms, given the potent reminder provided by the Israelis of how inadequate his forces were.[28] Although some incidents, including the killing of an Israeli, had occurred in the two months preceding the attack, there had been no major activity, as suggested by Israel, to justify its assault. Indeed, analysis of

Egyptian documents indicates that "it is difficult to connect the Israeli raid with the activity of infiltration, because the Israeli action came precisely during a period of relative calm in that area and in the wake of major efforts on the part of the Egyptian regime to stop infiltrations in the Gaza Strip."[29] The real reasons seem to have been domestic, the need to reassure Israelis that a firm hand was once more guiding the state, and to impress upon Nasser the risks of confronting Israel in the future. Ben-Gurion already regarded Nasser as a serious potential threat to Israel. Once back in the government, Ben-Gurion "took action to intensify military tension—not with the aim of provoking an overall confrontation, but, on the contrary, in the hope of forestalling it. He believed that if Israel were to strike back hard against Egyptian provocations, Egypt would be frightened off and curb its behavior," behavior that to outside observers did not seem particulary hostile at that time.[30] The attack became a self-fulfilling prophecy, as Nasser's actions following the Gaza incident became much more specifically hostile to Israel. He approved the organization of Palestinian infiltration into Israel and attacks on the population, beginning in the late spring. In addition, he undertook a search for arms that ultimately transformed him into the threat that Ben-Gurion envisioned.

THE ISRAELI-EGYPTIAN ARMS RACE, 1954–1956

Nasser first turned to the United States, but the American government would supply arms only if accompanied by military personnel to oversee their preparation and use, a condition Nasser refused.[31] He then turned to the Soviets who replied in early May, assuring Nasser that they would grant him "any quantity of arms, including tanks and planes of the latest design, against deferred payment in Egyptian cotton and rice," conditions that seemed advantageous set against the payment schedules established by the West.[32] With U.S. officials in Egypt apparently aware of the Soviet offer but Washington unwilling to counter it, Nasser proclaimed the arms deal on 27 September, identifying the Czechs as the partner, a transparent subterfuge given the Russians' role.

The Egyptian arms agreement with the communist bloc undercut Dulles's attempts to isolate the Arab world from Soviet influence. Indeed, British backing for the Baghdad Pact, tacitly but not openly supported by the United States, contributed to this development, along with the Israeli attack in Gaza. The latter jolted Egypt into a search for arms; the former inspired Nasser to intensify his opposition to Iraq and to proclaim his own leadership of an Arab world united in its determination to oust all colonial influence. This vague conception of Arab unity, undefined with respect to specific political arrangements but clearly linked to Third-World neutrality, seemed in Western eyes to encourage Soviet influence and undermine theirs, especially when buttressed by increasingly strident Egyptian propaganda against Arab countries having military alliances with the West during 1955. Nevertheless, Dulles and Eisenhower remained far more reserved in their questioning of Nasser than did the French and British who, for different reasons, came to agree with Ben-Gurion that the Egyptian leader should be attacked and possibly overthrown.

France and Israel had had discussions regarding arms going back to 1953, well before major problems with Egypt arose. Ben-Gurion was determined to maintain Israel's military supremacy. This meant circumventing the Tripartite Declaration of 1950. The United States and Britain generally adhered to that statement, though they had supplied limited quantities of arms to Jordan and Iraq. Israel turned secretly to France which, from 1954 onward, proved a willing accomplice, especially members of the French Defense Ministry who feared continued deterioration of France's colonial strength. Indochina was slipping away, symbolized by the North Vietnamese victory at Dien Bien Phu. Then the Algerian revolution began in October, striking at what many French people believed to be French national territory, not simply an imperial possession.[33] To the French military, the Algerian resistance was sparked by Arab nationalism, epitomized by Nasser's call for liberation from foreign bonds. Worse, they became convinced, wrongly as it happened, that Nasser was giving the Algerian rebels crucial military and financial assistance without which the rebellion would collapse. Israel thus became an anti-Arab ally to be bolstered, a perception encouraged by Shimon Peres, Ben-Gurion's envoy from the Israeli Defense Ministry.[34] One arms agreement reached in August 1954 provided jets, tanks, and radar equipment, shipped under great secrecy, although the Egyptians apparently became aware of the developments. Peres's rapport with French officials expanded in 1955, buttressed by French opposition to the Baghdad Pact which cemented the Israeli-French bond. France saw the pact through World War I glasses as a move designed to expand British influence against the French in Syria. The French military approved a major arms transaction early in 1955, but final agreement was delayed until after Nasser's announcement of the Czech arms deal because of French Foreign Office objections, backed by American pressure; Dulles withdrew his opposition in late 1955. The November arms pact included the latest Mystère 4 jets and tanks. They did not approach the quantity of weapons the Russians had begun to supply to the Egyptians, but Dayan was confident that the Israelis could absorb their deliveries into the military far more quickly than could the Egyptians.

Not the least of the ironies of the Suez crisis was that France and Israel ultimately joined with Great Britain, the author of the Baghdad Pact whose creation had consolidated their own relationship. These developments took place amidst increasing tensions along the Egyptian-Israeli frontier, most specifically that defined by the Gaza Strip. Raids organized by Palestinians (*fedayeen*) under Egyptian sponsorship became more numerous and destructive from August onward. Israeli retaliatory assaults against Egyptian installations and Palestinian civilian areas resulted. Additional acrimony erupted over strategic demilitarized zones where, contrary to armistice agreements, Israel established a military settlement disguised as a civilian kibbutz. Egyptian countermoves led to frequent exchanges of fire and more casualties. Israel was provocative—not simply responding to border incursions—in part to show Egypt its weakness in circumstances that seemed increasingly intolerable to the Ben-Gurion government. Since that September the Egyptians had fully blockaded the Straits of Tiran, forcing ships going to Israel to request permission in advance and prohibiting also transit of the air space above the area.

This full blockade and the accompanying hostilities led Dayan to propose an attack on Egypt to Ben-Gurion, who became prime minister once more in November; he retained the defense ministry while Sharrett remained foreign minister. Ben-Gurion backed it, but it was defeated by the cabinet in early December. Nevertheless, the option of a military initiative remained open. The Israeli military wanted it not simply to remove the blockade but also to destroy the Egyptians' military arsenal before they had fully absorbed their new Russian equipment. Egypt had sought these armaments to defend itself against future Israeli attacks; Israel now intended to wreck the Egyptian supplies which it saw as a potential offensive threat.

Israel embarked on a campaign to seek more weapons, emphasizing publicly its feeling of military weakness, although Dayan felt his troops could defeat the Egyptians with little difficulty. What Ben-Gurion really wanted was an alliance to offset the Egyptian-Russian alignment, preferably with the United States. Yet here too Ben-Gurionism neutralized the search for American arms. While Sharrett was in Washington in December negotiating for an agreement, Ben-Gurion ordered an Israeli assault on Syrian positions that inflicted heavy casualties. Though his justification was a supposed Syrian provocation, the planning of the operation suggested otherwise. It was one more lesson to be delivered to the Egyptians as well as the Syrians, intended to show them that they were no match for Israel; the two countries had formed a military alliance in October. Here too the interaction of factors and their interpretation reflected different preoccupations. The Egyptian-Syrian defense pact was a move designed essentially to enhance Nasser's position as an Arab leader by blocking Hashemite plans to undermine the Syrian regime. Though lip service was paid to the protection of the Arabs against Israel, Nasser did not pursue implementation of the agreement's military provisions.[35] But the pact was viewed by Ben-Gurion as designed to encircle Israel, and an editorial in the *Jerusalem Post* expressed the hope that "the Israeli raid has convinced many Syrians that the military pact with Egypt has increased the dangers to Syria instead of guaranteeing Syria's defense."[36] The opposite occurred. As with the Gaza raid, the Israeli action encouraged further militarization. Syria intensified its own purchase of Soviet arms and moved closer to Egypt. In addition, the attack undercut any chance that Sharrett had of convincing the United States that Israel was in serious danger and needed not only more arms but possibly even a military alliance. Dulles and Eisenhower believed that Israel was at least as aggressive as the Arabs and militarily superior to them, not the weak, beleaguered nation portrayed to outsiders.

Israel wanted the United States and, if possible, all the Western powers to "go on with Israel alone. If the Arabs have no alternatives and enough pressure is put on them . . . they may acquiesce and make peace as they did once before when they signed the armistice agreements."[37] Washington officials considered the Israeli arguments to be logical but narrow and shortsighted. Dulles disliked Nasser's neutralism and viewed Egyptian propaganda as potentially destabilizing, but to reject Nasser would be to ensure Soviet paramountcy as no alternative would be left, something much worse than neutrality. But the risk of confrontation was not unthinkable to Ben-Gurion or, increasingly, to the French, as their difficulties in Algeria mounted in early 1956. And although Great Britain retained ties to Egypt, Anthony Eden, prime minister since April 1955, was growing more eager to blunt Nasser's appeal. The catalyst for an alliance among the three was Nasser's nationalization of the Suez Canal following the Western withdrawal of an offer to build the Aswan Dam.

THE ASWAN DAM PROJECT, THE ANDERSON MISSION, AND
NASSER'S NATIONALIZATION OF THE SUEZ CANAL,
JANUARY–JULY, 1956

The Aswan Dam symbolized to Nasser and many Egyptians the key to their progress and agricultural and industrial stability. The regime had considered the idea since late 1952 and their eagerness to build it was well known. Serious discussions did not arise until the fall of 1955, and then with the United States and Great Britain. American willingness to entertain financing the project was related to political considerations. The Eisenhower administration was alarmed at the ramifications of the Soviet arms deal. To establish bonds to Egypt through such a project would presumably reinforce its ties to the West. Furthermore, Dulles and Eisenhower hoped that an American offer to back the project could be linked to efforts to achieve peace between Egypt and Israel, indirect leverage to pressure Nasser to enter negotiations. In December 1955 an agreement was reached in principle, whereby the United States, Great Britain, and the International Bank for Reconstruction and Development (IBRD) would commit themselves to funding a large portion of the expenses, with a major share coming from the Egyptians.[38] The stage was set for negotiations to arrange the nature of the payments and Egypt's obligations to its Western creditors. At the same time Robert Anderson, later secretary of the treasury, was entrusted with a highly secret mission to see whether Nasser and Ben-Gurion would consent to negotiate.

Anderson's talks with the two leaders lasted from January to March 1956. Nasser professed interest in continuing secret discussions but set as his terms the creation of a route through the Negev linking Egypt to Jordan and the right of Palestinian refugees to return to live in their former homeland with compensation if they desired. Ben-Gurion rejected consideration of the refugees. He stressed that there should be direct public negotiations between him and Nasser if peace were to be discussed. Nasser refused. He would not agree to direct talks, especially because Ben-Gurion insisted on recognition of Israel's existing frontiers and acceptance of compensation for refugees.[39] The effort to create a basis for talks had failed, as had the possibility to use them as pressure to bring Nasser to agree to terms for funding the Aswan Dam project.

From February 1956 onward, difficulties increased between the Egyptians and their Western partners. The IBRD had approved its share of the funding, but Nasser still had to reach an accord with Dulles and Eden who had pledged $70 million to initiate the project. Nasser wanted a commitment for the full amount to see it through, without having to seek annual approval of financial commitments. Such a process would create in his view the possibility of political pressures being imposed, something he had recognized in the timing of the Anderson visits. But the suspicion of Nasser as a threat to Western interests was increasing in London and Washington. On 1 March King Husayn of Jordan had dismissed General John Glubb, head of the Arab Legion for twenty-five years. This came at a time when Nasser had led a campaign to replace the ongoing British financial subsidy to Jordan with an Arab grant and after a propaganda campaign aimed at Husayn's defensive alliance with the British. Husayn's step was interpreted in the West as a great victory for Nasser and an intended insult to Britain. Eden now believed that "Nasser was the incarnation of all the evils of Arabia who would destroy every British interest in the Middle East unless he himself were speedily destroyed."[40] Eden was moving closer to the perception of Nasser held by Guy Mollet, French premier since January, who believed that Nasser was another Hitler, aiming to disturb world peace.

Dulles did not share these views, but he too was increasingly distrustful of Nasser; the United States had approved French arms shipments to Israel in late 1955. The promise to assist the Aswan Dam project was becoming a political liability in an election year, with various factions opposing the grant. Southern senators lobbied heavily against it. They feared increased competition from Egyptian cotton if the dam were built and more land placed under cultivation. Pro-Israel supporters argued that Nasser posed the only threat to peace. Cold-war activists opposed to aiding those with ties to the Russians were equally outraged. The lineup was impressive but not crucial. What mattered was the commitment of the administration, and to them Nasser's actions were offensive. His objections to conditions attached to the loan annoyed Dulles. Far worse, Dulles suspected Nasser of seeking better terms from the Russians, a possibility that led him to consider withdrawing American aid, if only to punish the Egyptian. The catalyst seems to have been Nasser's recognition of Communist China in May, a step that to Dulles was an insult that had to be repaid.

A cardinal point of Dulles's foreign policy was not simply the containment but also the denial of the existence of Communist China, a point the United States made annually by mobilizing support to block it from membership in the United Nations. Hence Dulles's response to Nasser's step, leading him to believe that such disloyalty should not be rewarded by American assistance. He was encouraged in this view by the China lobby which threatened to block the entire foreign aid bill in Congress. The question was how to evade the American promise to support the dam project. Dulles appears to have hoped that Nasser's bargaining over terms would prolong the issue so that it might ultimately die of its own accord, a process Eden seems to have agreed with, both out of his own dislike of Nasser and his increasing concern at Britain's financial stability. But the Egyptians decided instead to accept the American conditions. Their ambassador returned from Cairo in July to declare, on the eighteenth, that "all decisions now are up to Washington and London."[41]

Dulles's hand had been called, but in his meeting with the ambassador the following day he told him that the United States was withdrawing from its commitment to fund the dam. He implied that the Egyptians were seeking to blackmail the Americans by threatening to go to the Russians. If they wished to, they should. In this Dulles believed that he was teaching Nasser a lesson as he doubted the Soviets would fund the dam, thus leaving Nasser adrift. The secretary of state's actions "mystified" many Western diplomats who believed that he had rebuffed Nasser just when the latter was moving closer to the United States. It infuriated the American head of the IBRD, Eugene Black, who later stated that "it was the greatest disappointment of my professional life. . . . It was a classic case where long-term policy was sacrificed because of short-term problems and irritations. And war came shortly after."[42] Dulles, acting almost entirely alone, had decided to show Nasser that neutralists should not dally with the United States. He chose to punish him publicly, knowing that Eden agreed and apparently convinced that the Russians would not step in.[43]

Nasser had told his ambassador to accept the American offer but expect rejection. What he did not anticipate was Dulles's pique and his apparent intent to humiliate the Egyptian leader. Confirmed in his suspicion of American and British hostility, he then decided to teach Dulles and Eden a lesson while asserting Egyptian independence. On 26 July he nationalized the Suez Canal to great popular acclaim.

FROM NATIONALIZATION TO INVASION, JULY–NOVEMBER 1956

Nasser's nationalization of the Suez Canal set in motion a series of events leading to a joint Israeli-French-British attack on Egypt. His action was not so much the cause of their aggression as the excuse for it. All had expressed, separately or jointly, the desire to invade Egypt before Nasser took over the canal. In June the French and the Israelis reached agreement on a massive arms sale, including two hundred tanks and seventy-two Mystère 4 jets; they began arriving secretly in late July. Ben-Gurion was by now determined to attack Egypt, preferably in alliance with France but alone if necessary. He forced Sharrett's resignation as foreign minister in June to ensure that the latter would not lead opposition to his plans in future cabinet meetings. Ben-Gurion replaced Sharrett with Golda Meir who could be counted on to follow his lead.

Nevertheless, Israel was left out of discussions in the immediate aftermath of the nationalization. Eden and Mollet led Anglo-French talks aimed at coordinating an attack, only to be checked by Dulles. There arose a muted confrontation between Dulles and Eden, the latter eager, as were the French, to exploit the Suez issue to serve their political interests in the Middle East which they believed to be best served by either humiliating Nasser or creating "a pretext for the use of force to unseat him."[44] Dulles, on the other hand, hoped to resolve the dispute peacefully by gaining Nasser's acceptance of arrangements backed by the international community designed to guarantee the canal's secure operation. In this he was aided somewhat by Egypt's assurances of compensation to shareholders of the canal company, gestures that exasperated Eden, Mollet, and Ben-Gurion. Egypt's promise to live up to all international obligations pertaining to the canal's operation was for them an obstacle to be refuted rather than a sign of conciliation.

While Eden continued to try to gain American backing for more forceful action, the French began consultations with the Israelis in early September regarding a joint attack, keeping them informed of their separate discussions with the British. It was only in late September that the British entered the French-Israeli scheme for an assault. By then Eden was convinced that Dulles had betrayed him by seeming privately to approve a forceful response but publicly undercutting him. American officials believed that Eden misled himself. Beset by ill health and increasingly obsessed by Nasser, he viewed the crisis as the replication of the Nazi assault on international order in the later 1930s.[45] In this, his view of Nasser coincided with Mollet's mistaken belief that without Nasser the Algerian rebellion would collapse, permitting France to retain what seemed a vital colonial possession.

There was general agreement that any operation should be undertaken by the end of October, in order to take advantage of still-favorable weather conditions and, equally importantly, to invade toward the end of the American election campaign. The participants assumed that Eisenhower would not oppose Israel and risk the Jewish vote so near to election day. Representatives of Israel, France, and Great Britain met secretly in France on 21 October. At the initial meeting, Ben-Gurion proposed settling all outstanding issues. First priority went to "the elimination of Nasser," but beyond that he called for

> the partition of Jordan, with the West Bank going to Israel and the East Bank to Iraq. Lebanon's boundaries would also be moved, with part going to Syria, and another part, up to the Litani River, to Israel; the remaining territory would become a Christian state. In newly expanded Syria, the regime would be stabilized by being under a pro-Western ruler. Finally, the Suez Canal would enjoy international status and the Straits of Tiran would be under Israeli control.[46]

Ben-Gurion may have had little hope for acceptance of his scheme, but he did apparently envisage Israel's taking over the Sinai Peninsula, which he refused to believe was part of Egypt. His plan indicated an Israeli hope of fulfilling the initial Zionist conception of Israel's borders (minus eastern Palestine) presented in 1919.[47] The French demurred, stressing the need to concentrate on Nasser. Final agreement was achieved on 23 October. Israel would invade the Sinai on the twenty-ninth. With their forces already sailing for Egypt from Malta, the British and French governments would call for a truce on 31 October, demanding that both sides withdraw to ten miles from the banks of the canal. In effect, this would give the Israelis the right to continue their attack until they reached that boundary, while the Egyptians should withdraw all their forces from the Sinai. Because Nasser would presumably not agree to this, Eden and Mollet could then blame him for continuing hostilities and thus justify their scheduled attack.

The Israeli forces entered the Sinai and the Gaza Strip as scheduled. Once Nasser refused the Anglo-French ultimatum on the thirty-first, British planes from Cyprus attacked Egyptian air fields. This caused Nasser to withdraw his forces from the Sinai, precipitating a rout by the Israelis after some initial stiff defense by certain Egyptian units. As the crisis deepened, British radio called for the Egyptian people to arise and overthrow their leader. Still, no Anglo-French assault took place until 5 November, and landings were not made until the sixth. Although successful in military terms, the operation was by now thoroughly compromised, as the fiction of Anglo-French neutrality and goodwill had been exposed. Eisenhower and Dulles were infuriated at what they considered to be allied deception and stupidity. Although they disliked Nasser, they did not believe that armed force would resolve the matter. In this they were correct. Dulles had resisted Eden and Mollet primarily in order to ensure that the canal remained open; after the attack, the Egyptians scuttled ships in the channel, blocking passage for months. To his chagrin, Dulles found himself leading the opposition to the Suez attack at the United Nations in unwitting tandem with the Russians. It was particularly galling because the Hungarian rebellion had occurred at the same time as the Suez crisis. After some hesitation, the Soviets had invaded and crushed the uprising, but the allied action against Egypt prevented Dulles from using the Hungarian crisis to prove the immorality of communism and the need for all nations to rely on the West.

Eisenhower and Dulles now pressured Eden to agree to end the operation. They refused to help relieve financial pressure on the beleaguered pound or release oil supplies until he acquiesced. Under great strain Eden capitulated, deserted by those colleagues, especially Harold Macmillan, who had most firmly advocated the Suez venture. The United States voted with a large majority in the United Nations to censure the aggressors. British and French forces withdrew from Port Said by 23 December. Eden resigned on 9 January after stating to the House of Commons in late December that Great Britain had not conspired with Israel in the attack, a denial that further damaged his reputation.

There remained Israel to deal with. Ben-Gurion was determined to remain in the Gaza Strip and at Sharm al-Shaykh. Extensive discussions and pressure from the United States finally led to his agreement to withdraw, but only on the condition that United Nations Emergency Forces assigned to the area occupy Sharm al-Shaykh and patrol the Gaza Strip to prevent fedayeen infiltrations. If Egyptian forces once again occupied Sharm al-Shaykh and blockaded the entrance to the Gulf of Aqaba, Israel would consider this a *casus belli*, a condition it imposed in June 1967.

THE SUEZ CRISIS AND ITS RAMIFICATIONS:
THE EISENHOWER DOCTRINE

The Suez invasion and its failure signaled the end of Britain's tenure as the dominant imperial nation in the Middle East; it also scuttled Eden's career. An obituary in the *London Times* in 1977 declared that "he was the last prime minister to believe Britain was a great power and the first to confront a crisis which proved she was not."[48] Britain's collapse weakened its allies in the area, Iraq and Jordan, and left them more vulnerable to Nasser's propaganda, especially because Britain had conspired with Israel. For the French, the invasion was a fiasco for which they blamed Eden's caution, not the goals themselves. The Israelis considered Suez to be a major success. They achieved a significant military victory with relatively few casualties. They opened the Straits of Tiran, freeing Israeli shipping from the Gulf of Aqaba to the east. Finally, they secured for the next ten years a de facto, if not an official, peace along the Israeli-Egyptian frontier which remained quiet, patrolled by U.N. forces. Ben-Gurionism had not brought Nasser to the peace table, but it seemed to have brought security.

An added benefit for Israel was greater sympathy in the United States government, facilitated by effective lobbying by Jewish groups in early 1957 when Ben-Gurion sought to retain control of Sharm al-Shaykh. Many American congressmen and the public began to look at the Middle East in terms of a Soviet threat in which Israel appeared to be a potential bulwark against Russian influence because it had attacked Nasser. This view was encouraged by the fact that the Soviets had escaped their repression of the Hungarian revolt relatively unscathed, whereas Israel was being pushed to withdraw from a portion of the Sinai.[49]

Nasser emerged a victor, despite the military defeat his forces had suffered. The Israeli-French-British attack provided to many Arabs clear evidence of continuing Western imperial collusion with Israel to seek to impose outside control on developments within the Arab world. It seemed to prove Nasser's contention that opposition to Western arms alignments and support for neutrality were the best means to retain Arab freedom. The Suez crisis and Nasser's defiance made him far more an Arab hero than he had been previously and weakened those who argued for continued reliance on Western pacts. Ironically, Egyptians looked to Washington more hopefully after Suez, believing that American opposition to the attack and pressure on Israel to withdraw from

Sharm al-Shaykh would lead to improved relations. This did not occur. The United States government refused to grant shipments of food and grain under programs that had previously provided such assistance. Throughout 1957, Washington froze Egyptian funds under its control. Nasser thus turned to Moscow which supplied the needed food and other goods blocked by Washington. This gave more proof to Nasser's critics in Washington that he favored Soviet to American aid.

Eisenhower and Dulles were determined to back the more moderate, pro-Western Arab states against Nasser. Their antagonism toward the joint attack on Egypt did not lessen their wish to punish and isolate the Egyptian leader. Thus they undertook in the aftermath of Suez to strengthen regimes such as Iraq against the spread of Egyptian influence. Because the regional pact idea had proved futile, they decided to establish conditions whereby the United States could intervene openly to combat communist infiltration or aggression. Eisenhower developed the strategy in what became known as the Eisenhower Doctrine, first proposed by him in early January 1957 but not approved by Congress until March. The doctrine provided for military and economic assistance to be granted "to any nation or group of nations which desires such aid." In addition, Eisenhower was authorized to commit American military forces "to secure and protect the territorial integrity and political independence of such nations, requesting such aid, against overt armed aggression from any nation controlled by International Communism."[50] That such an overture was aimed against Nasser was clear from the promise of economic aid given in the declaration following Washington's refusal of Nasser's request for such assistance.

Eisenhower's rationale for the doctrine was that "the existing vacuum in the Middle East must be filled by the United States before it was filled by the Russians."[51] The vacuum was the loss of British and French prestige after Suez which prevented them from intervening openly to back allies. Having castigated them for colluding with Israel to seek to overthrow Nasser, the United States now encouraged friendly Arab states to invite its own intervention; it also sought to overthrow regimes considered hostile to American interests, leading to even closer relations between these governments and the Russians. Cold-war containment triumphed over concern for regional rivalries and rapidly changing sociopolitical conditions in the Arab Middle East. No member of the State Department concerned with the region was consulted before Eisenhower proposed his plan.[52] The United States now embarked on a period of active intervention in Arab regional politics that in the long run led it closer to Israel.

NOTES

1. See the statistical tables in Bernard Reich, *Israel, Land of Tradition and Change* (Boulder, Colo., 1985), p. 15.
2. Melvin Urofsky, *We Are One! American Jewry and Israel* (New York, 1978), p. 203.

3. Ernest Stock, *Israel on the Road to Sinai, 1949–1956* (Ithaca, N.Y., 1967), p. 11.
4. Don Peretz, *Israel and the Palestine Arabs* (Washington, D.C., 1958), p. 94ff. A recent work that concentrates on the period since 1955 is Ian Lustick, *Arabs in the Jewish State: Israel's Control of a National Minority* (Austin, Tex., 1980).
5. Peretz, *Israel*, p. 151.
6. For Israeli Arabs, see Lustick, *Arabs in the Jewish State*, especially Chapter 4; and Fouzi el-Asmar, *To Be an Arab in Israel* (London, 1975).
7. See the review by Yoram Nimrod of Yehoshua Freundlich, ed., *Documents on the Foreign Policy of Israel*, vol. 3 (Jerusalem, 1983), in *Studies in Zionism* 5 (1984): 154–156.
8. Livia Rokach, *Israel's Sacred Terrorism: A Study Based on Moshe Sharrett's Personal Diary and Other Documents* (Belmont, Mass., 1980), p. 44, quoting Sharrett's account of a meeting with Dayan and Ben-Gurion. Sharrett also favored an alliance with the United States, but as a defensive alliance designed to prevent hostilities. See the diary entry quoted in Itamar Rabinovich and Jehuda Reinharz, eds., *Israel in the Middle East, Documents and Readings on Society, Politics and Foreign Relations, 1948–Present* (New York, 1984), pp. 95–96.
9. Michael Brecher, *The Foreign Policy System of Israel* (New Haven, Conn., 1972), pp. 282–290, 378–391, includes an extensive discussion of differences between Ben-Gurion and Sharrett.
10. United Nations Special Committee on Palestine, *Report to the General Assembly*, vol. 3, annex A (Official Records of the 2nd session of the General Assembly, supplement 2, 1947), p. 56, quoted in George Kirk, *The Middle East in the War, Survey of International Affairs, 1939–1946* (London, 1953), p. 243.
11. Ibid., pp. 390–391; Elmo Hutchison, *Violent Truce* (New York, 1956), pp. 43–45.
12. E. L. M. Burns, *Between Arab and Israeli* (New York, 1962), pp. 41–44; Brecher, *System*, p. 261.
13. Burns, *Arab and Israeli*, pp. 66–67.
14. Quoted in Sharrett's diary, Rokach, *Sacred Terrorism*, p. 44.
15. Brecher, *System*, pp. 282–290, 378–391.
16. Rokach, *Sacred Terrorism*, p. 44.
17. Michael Bar-Zohar, *Ben-Gurion* (London, 1978), pp. 217–218. This study contains much new material not found in the author's earlier biography, *Ben-Gurion, the Armed Prophet* (Englewood Cliffs, N.J., 1968). Sharrett did see the value of some reprisals, as noted in Rokach, *Sacred Terrorism*, pp. 95–97.
18. Stock, *Road to Sinai*, p. 104.
19. Dan Horowitz, quoted in Baruch Kimmerling, *Zionism and Territory: The Socio-Territorial Dimensions of Zionist Politics* (Berkeley and Los Angeles, 1983), p. 153.
20. Ibid., p. 390.
21. Patrick Seale, *The Struggle for Syria: A Study of Post-War Arab Politics, 1945–1958* (Oxford, England, 1966), pp. 132–147.
22. For the British perspective, see Anthony Nutting, *Nasser* (New York, 1972); Anthony Nutting, *No End of a Lesson: The Story of the Suez Crisis* (London, 1967); and the critical study of Eden by David Carlton, *Anthony Eden, a Biography* (London, 1981). The American viewpoint is well summarized in Townsend Hoopes, *The Devil and John Foster Dulles* (Boston, 1973); Stephen Ambrose, *Eisenhower*, vol. 2, *The President* (New York, 1984); Wilbur Crane Eveland, *Ropes of Sand: America's Failure in the Middle East* (London, 1980); and Miles Copeland, *The Game of Nations: The Amorality of Power Politics* (New York, 1969). Both Eveland and Copeland served in the Central Intelligence Agency, occasionally as rivals, according to Eveland. His book covers a broader scope in space and time than does Copeland's which focuses on U.S. relations with Nasser, especially during the period down to Suez.
23. Seale, *Syria*, pp. 200–201, and sources in note 22.
24. Quoted in Keith Wheelock, *Nasser's New Egypt, a Critical Analysis* (New York, 1960), p. 221.
25. Brecher, *System*, pp. 390–391; and Bar-Zohar, *Ben-Gurion*, pp. 202–206.
26. Nutting, *Nasser*, pp. 92–96. Sharrett also tried to initiate substantive peace talks with Nasser through American auspices in late 1955, though strongly opposed by Ben-Gurion; see Eveland, *Ropes of Sand*, pp. 155–157.
27. Bar-Zohar, *Ben-Gurion*, pp. 209–216.
28. For example, Burns, *Arab and Israeli*, pp. 17–21, 75ff; Nutting, *Nasser*, pp. 92–96; Seale, *Syria*, pp. 235–236; and Bar-Zohar, *Armed Prophet*, p. 185.

29. Ehud Yaari, *Egypt and the Fedayeen*, 1953–1956 (in Hebrew) (Givat Havivah, Israel, 1955), pp. 18–23, quoted in Rabinovich and Reinharz, eds., *Documents*, p. 78; a statement backed by Wheelock, *New Egypt*, p. 222; and Burns, *Arab and Israeli*, p. 21. Compare Stock, *Road to Sinai*, p. 67ff, who talks of "almost nightly violence."

30. Bar-Zohar, *Ben-Gurion*, p. 219.

31. Testimony of Admiral Radford before the Senate Committees on Foreign Relations and Armed Services, quoted in Wheelock, *New Egypt*, p. 229.

32. Seale, *Syria*, p. 235, quoting a confidant of Nasser's.

33. Algeria was considered a part of metropolitan France rather than a colonial possession. A superb study of the Algerian revolution and the French response is Alistair Horne, *A Savage War of Peace: Algeria, 1954–1962* (New York, 1978).

34. The most detailed account of Israeli-French contacts is that of the major Israeli emissary, Shimon Peres, *David's Sling* (New York, 1970), pp. 47–65. See also Bar-Zohar, *Armed Prophet*, pp. 188–189; and Anthony Moncrieff, ed., with an introduction by Peter Calvocoressi, *Suez, Ten Years After* (New York, 1967), pp. 38–39, 61–66.

35. Seale, *Syria*, p. 254.

36. Quoted in ibid.

37. Stock, *Road to Sinai*, p. 144. See also Eveland, *Ropes of Sand*, pp. 150–151; and Chester L. Cooper, *The Lion's Last Roar; Suez, 1956* (New York, 1978), pp. 91–92.

38. Robert Bowie, *International Crises and the Role of Law: Suez 1956* (New York, 1974), p. 11.

39. Donald Neff, *Warriors at Suez: Eisenhower Takes America into the Middle East* (New York, 1981), pp. 130–131ff; Michael Brecher, *Decisions in Israel's Foreign Policy* (New Haven, Conn., 1975), p. 259ff; and Kennett Love, *Suez, the Twice-Fought War* (New York, 1969) have differing views of whose hard-line policies undermined the possibility of further talks. As noted, Ben-Gurion had already tried to gain approval for an attack on Egypt.

40. Quoted in Nutting, *Nasser*, pp. 122–123. See also Evelyn Shuckburgh, *Descent to Suez: Diaries, 1951–56*, Selected for Publication by John Charmley (London, 1986), p. 346. Shuckburgh was Eden's private secretary from 1951 to 1954 and then under-secretary in charge of Middle East affairs at the Foreign Office from May 1954 to June 1956.

41. Quoted in Cooper, *Lion's Last Roar*, p. 97.

42. Quoted in Love, *Twice-Fought War*, p. 297. Love has an extensive discussion of this matter, pp. 297–327.

43. Cooper, *Lion's Last Roar*, pp. 98–99; Hoopes, *Devil*, pp. 338–340. Compare Charles C. Alexander, *Holding the Line: The Eisenhower Era, 1952–1961* (Bloomington, Ind., 1975), p. 175, who has Eisenhower primarily responsible for the decision at a National Security Council meeting. In fact, the president was recuperating from illness and had little input.

44. Bowie, *Suez*, p. 15.

45. Carlton, *Eden*, pp. 298–309, 327–330, 428ff.

46. Bar-Zohar, *Ben-Gurion*, p. 236.

47. Ibid., p. 242. See also Moncrieff, ed., *Suez, Ten Years After*, p. 71, for Ben-Gurion's discussion in which he denies he hoped to annex the Sinai. For Lebanon, see Rokach, *Sacred Terrorism*, pp. 24–25.

48. Quoted in Neff, *Warriors at Suez*, p. 437.

49. Stephen L. Spiegel, *The Other Arab-Israeli Conflict: Making America's Middle East Policy from Truman to Reagan* (Chicago, 1985), pp. 77–81.

50. Ambrose, *Eisenhower*, p. 382. See also Spiegel, *Middle East Policy*, pp. 83–86.

51. Quoted in Hoopes, *Devil*, p. 406.

52. Copeland, *Game of Nations*, p. 216.

CHAPTER 7

From Suez to the Six-Day War, 1957–1967

The decade between 1957 and 1967 was, in the final analysis, dominated by inter-Arab rivalries that centered on the personality and prestige of Gamal Abd al-Nasser. Though not always in control of events, he was usually in their forefront, seeking to maintain his stature as leader of an increasingly hostile Arab world in which rivals began to challenge his dominance of Arab politics. From 1964–1965 onward, those ruling in Damascus were his principal antagonists, seeking to exploit Palestinian grievances against Israel to establish themselves as the true representatives of the Arab nationalist cause. As a result, Arab-Israeli hostilities, dormant during much of the period, once again intensified. The ensuing war stemmed finally from Nasser's attempt to use anti-Israeli sentiment to reassert his prominence. His brinkmanship failed, though his tactics were recognized by Israeli and American leaders. The United States seemed willing to permit Nasser to resolve the crisis peacefully, but the Israelis were not so amenable. They decided to seize the opportunity to destroy the Egyptian forces then massed in the Sinai. Whereas the Suez affair had greatly enhanced Nasser's prestige, the 1967 war nearly toppled him. It introduced a new era in which the Palestinians emerged as an independent force in Arab politics.

THE STRUGGLE FOR SYRIA AND THE CREATION OF THE UNITED ARAB REPUBLIC, 1957–1958

Syria had long been the focus of attention for Arab states trying to dominate Arab politics, especially Iraq and Egypt. As early as June 1956 the socialist Baath party in the Syrian government called for union with Egypt as the first step toward the goal of one Arab nation. This, combined with increasing Soviet aid to Damascus, inspired an Iraqi plot, backed by Great Britain, to instigate a rebellion designed to install a pro-Western government that might join Nuri al-Said's Fertile Crescent scheme. During the summer, the Central Intelligence Agency (CIA) also became involved in planning a coup, not necessarily coordinated with the British; they may have been rivals, played off against each other by Syrian politicians.[1] The revolt, planned for the end of October, never occurred, however, canceled because of friction among the Syrian participants and because the timing of the Suez invasion compromised Iraqi participation. In the words of an American agent, "it was a totally unprofessional CIA operation,"[2] one whose traces had already been recognized by Syrian intelligence. On 23 November, Damascus announced its discovery of plans to overthrow the government. Amidst the publicity, "the failure of the conspiracy powerfully reinforced the radical pro-Egyptian factions in Syria by eliminating from the scene their most dangerous opponents."[3] The Syrian government, reshuffled to include more Baathists, now joined Cairo in attacking Nuri al-Said's government in Baghdad, accusing him of treachery and of sacrificing Iraq's independence to Western interests.

This was the context in which the Eisenhower Doctrine was proclaimed in January 1957 and in which the United States openly joined the Baghdad Pact in March. The Lebanese government of Camille Chamoun accepted the doctrine. Nuri al-Said and King Husayn of Jordan indicated their approval though they declined to embrace it officially. These developments led to more intense propaganda attacks from Radios Cairo and Damascus calling for the overthrow of their regimes. This in turn further convinced officials in Washington that Damascus was the principal conduit for Soviet propaganda designed to undermine Western influence in the Arab world.

In the aftermath of a new Syrian-Russian economic and military aid agreement announced in June 1957, the CIA decided to finance another coup attempt. The plans were immediately exposed to Syrian officials, who expelled three members of the American embassy involved in arranging their overthrow. The United States responded by mobilizing pro-Western forces in the region and announcing that Syria was about to become communist. Plans to airlift arms to Iraq, Jordan, and Lebanon were discussed publicly, and Turkish army units were encouraged to undertake maneuvers along the Syrian border, accompanied by threats of an invasion and calls for a popular uprising against the government. These developments did not lead Syrian rulers to become more pro-Western. Realizing the folly of the American approach, the Saudis decided to mediate the crisis, distancing themselves from the United States but also trying to isolate Nasser from their resolution of the problem. He in turn sent troops to Syria on 13 October, declaring that they were prepared to defend the country. Though essentially a publicity move, it served to link Syria's security to Egypt's and furthered Baathist ambitions for union, precisely what Washington hoped to avoid.

Baathist calls for Arab unity were both ideological and practical in motivation. Michel Aflaq, the leading theoretician of the Baath, believed it to be the destiny of the Arab people, with Syria playing the principal role in its achievement because, in his eyes, it was the heartland of Arab nationalism. But Aflaq also realized that Egypt's exclusion—given Nasser's prestige—could guarantee its failure. The Baath seemed to dominate the governments of 1956–1957, but its leaders feared that the continuing crises and attempted coups could only strengthen the hand of the Syrian communists, however few they were, at Baathist expense. This, plus rampant factionalism in the military, led to the decision to seek union with Egypt. Nasser opposed the idea; whatever mileage he gained from calling for Arab unity, "he had sought to control Syria's foreign policy . . . not to assume responsibility for her government."[4] But Syria's continuing internal disarray and repeated Baath overtures finally convinced him to accept the invitation, if only to forestall any further increase in the popularity of Syria's communists.[5] The United Arab Republic (UAR) was proclaimed on 1 February 1958.

The Syrian-Egyptian union lasted three and a half years, ending with Syria's abrupt secession in September 1961. By then most Syrians had had enough of Egyptian protection. Nasser had refused to share power with the Baath, alloting key positions to Egyptians who dominated the Syrian administration. The final straw came when Nasser imposed nationalization decrees on the Syrian economy in the summer of 1961, following those he had declared for Egypt. Despite the apparent strength of Baathist socialism, the Syrian economy had remained essentially private. Most Syrians backed their country's withdrawal from the United Arab Republic and the formation of a new government from which the Baath was excluded.

The Syrian-Egyptian rift left a legacy of distrust and resentment that contributed to the outbreak of the 1967 war. Equally important, however, were events elsewhere in the Arab world that had been affected by the formation of the UAR, in particular its impact on Lebanon and Iraq. Subsequent developments led the United States to invoke the Eisenhower Doctrine and land forces in Lebanon in July 1958.

LEBANON, THE LEBANESE CIVIL WAR, AND THE IRAQI REVOLT, 1957–1958

The underlying causes of the Lebanese civil war lay in the nature of the political arrangements created to balance the interests of competing religious communities. Lebanese political representation has been characterized by the principle of confessionalism since the resolution of the crisis of 1860. Confessionalism meant that political representation was based on religious affiliation and the size of one's religious community, initially applied to Mount Lebanon, as outlined in Chapter 2. The creation of Mount Lebanon as a separate administrative unit governed by an Ottoman Christian from outside the area served to stabilize the region to the end of World War I. Nevertheless, France never lost sight of Mount Lebanon and its environs as the basis of its influence in the Middle East. In their turn, most Maronite Catholics still looked to France as a European protector to guarantee their continued separateness from the predominantly Arab Muslim world of the interior.

French acquisition of Lebanon and Syria after World War I was a mixed blessing for the Maronites. French officials, though eager to guarantee Maronite ascendancy in the new Lebanon, also strove to ensure their imperial presence in the region. They expanded the area to be known as Lebanon, thereby reducing what would be defined as Syria. They did this because "Lebanon" would be under their direct control, "Syria" under their indirect rule according to the clauses of the Sykes–Picot accord. They consequently added to Mount Lebanon the interior Biqa' Valley and second range of mountains known as the anti-Lebanon, along with the coastal plain. This extension of French rule more than doubled the territory and greatly altered the population ratios according to religious affiliation.[6] The Sunni Muslim population leaped nearly eightfold, the Shi'i Muslims nearly fourfold, and the Maronites by about one-third. The Maronite Catholics thereby lost the overwhelming majority they had held in Mount Lebanon which had justified their claim to preserve a "Christian Lebanon," although they still tried to accomplish precisely that in order to ensure their control of Lebanese politics. Conversely, the Sunni Muslims looked to Syria and, in the early period, accepted the legitimacy of Faysal's short-lived government in Damascus. The split between total isolation from Arab nationalist currents and great sympathy for them has been a staple of Lebanese politics since that time.

As a result of the French creation of Greater Lebanon, the Christian majority was reduced to slightly over 50 percent of the population. Within this segment, Maronite Catholics clearly predominated; the next largest group was the Greek Orthodox, with smaller numbers belonging to various Catholic and Orthodox denominations (Syrian Orthodox and Catholic, Armenian Orthodox and Catholic). On the Muslim side, Sunnis held a slight but definite majority over the Shi'is, with the Druze about one-third of the Shi'i population.[7] The French sought to establish political institutions that would formalize these ratios and ensure Christian rule, particularly that of the Maronites with whom they were most closely allied. The constitution drawn up in 1926 established that the president would always be a Christian; practice made him a Maronite. Likewise, the prime minister was a Sunni Muslim, and the principle became rooted that other offices and representations in the chamber of deputies would reflect the size of one's religious community. Percentages came to be based on the 1932 census which established that Christians outnumbered Muslims by a six-to-five ratio; this became the basis of parliamentary representation. Within this framework, seats were to be allotted according to the population of specific communities. The same procedure was followed for administrative posts once Lebanese independence was achieved in 1943. Thus the president was a Maronite, the prime minister a Sunni Muslim, the speaker of the chamber of deputies a Shi'i, and the deputy prime minister and deputy speaker Greek Orthodox. Similarly, the foreign minister was generally a Maronite, the interior minister a Sunni, and the defense minister a Druze.[8] Nevertheless, the ratification of these arrangements in 1943 was itself ambiguous, comprising part of an unwritten "National Pact" that sought to guarantee the status of Lebanon as a separate nation and to calm the fears of the major religious communities. The pact enshrined the principle that Lebanese Christians would not seek foreign protection, alluding to the wish of many Maronites to retain a French mandate, if under a different guise. On the other hand, the Muslims agreed to support Lebanese independence, meaning that they would forgo union with Syria or any other Arab state.

Despite the "national" aura surrounding this agreement, its success depended on preserving traditional rights held by the major communities, usually identified with specific regions of the country. The Maronites were strongest in Mount Lebanon and the northern areas of the country where there was also significant Sunni representation. Shi'i strength lay in the south and in the Biqa', but the Shi'is were the poorest community. Political power often belonged to local lords who held nearly feudal authority over the surrounding villages. In these circumstances, Sunni leaders found it worthwhile to align themselves with Maronites because as the two largest sects they divided many perquisites of influence. In general the arrangement preserved in enlarged form the system found under the Ottomans, to the extent that the highest religious officials of various sects, such as the Maronite patriarch, retained great prestige and did not hesitate to challenge political officials from their own community. Indeed, lines of allegiance did not always follow religious identities. Serious clan cleavages arose frequently among the Maronites. Other Christian sects, particularly the Greek Orthodox, often sympathized with the Arab orientation of the Muslim population against the Francophile outlook that many Maronites retained.

These factors and their potential for divisiveness became increasingly significant during the 1950s. There were sectors within both the Maronite and the Muslim communities that still longed for more specific ties to either Europe and the West or, for the latter, the Arab world, especially as Arab nationalism came to the fore under the banner of the Baath or Nasser. Each tendency fed the other. At the same time, many groups in Lebanon felt increasingly resentful at the continuing power of the Maronites, particularly as their role and general Christian dominance rested on the 1932 census, which the Maronite president and Christian-controlled chamber refused to update. Indeed, the president could veto any legislation approved by the chamber and could be overridden only by a majority of that body, a virtual impossibility.[9] The president thus had the power as well as the inclination to block any initiative to revise the proportional system based on the 1932 census, which most observers agreed was out of date: by the later 1950s, the Muslims were believed to be a majority of the population.

Most Arab states viewed Lebanon as a useful anomaly in the Arab world. Its links to the West served various interests and opened the way for profits that might not be realized within one's own country. It served as a port of entry for goods going on to Syria, Iraq, Jordan, and the Persian Gulf principalities. Of vital importance was Lebanon's lack of foreign exchange controls and the creation of the Beirut port as a free-trade zone. This led to Beirut's becoming a freewheeling center for world commerce and finance. The conditions were so favorable for banking and exchange that in the early 1960s there were twenty-one branches of foreign banks in Lebanon plus thirty-six local banks. These institutions serviced the funds generated by the oil boom in the Persian Gulf and Saudi Arabia as well as Iran. Lebanon appeared to be an island of stability, despite the fragility of its political framework, in a sea of political coups and revolutions from which it profited. The country became a haven for people fleeing failed plots, bringing with them money put to good use.[10] These circumstances also attracted foreign intelligence services who could finance payments to agents and conspirators without fear of accountability.

Yet if Lebanese independence was accepted by most if not all Arab leaders, the composition of its government became subject to scrutiny in the latter half of the 1950s. The president at that time was Camille Chamoun, a Maronite whose support rested more on the burgeoning middle class than on traditional clan patronage. His foreign minister was Charles Malik, a distinguished scholar of Greek Orthodox persuasion totally committed to close ties to the West, especially the United States. These views were known and aroused controversy during and after Suez, when Chamoun and Malik refused to sever diplomatic relations with England and France, and following the declaration of the Eisenhower Doctrine which they accepted openly. Consequently, both Egypt and Syria launched propaganda campaigns against the Chamoun–Malik tandem. Within Lebanon, various groups accused the government of subverting Lebanon's traditional neutrality by seeking to bind itself to the West; a significant critic was the Maronite patriarch.

These disputes over international alignments became intertwined with domestic politics. Chamoun appeared to hope to manipulate elections to the chamber of deputies, scheduled for June 1957, so that he could amend the constitution and run for reelection when his term expired in September 1958. Throughout the crisis of 1957–1958 he did not openly declare his intent to do so, but his supporters did and Chamoun himself intimated that he was awaiting the right moment to take that step.[11] There is little doubt that the 1957 elections were engineered to bring in Chamoun supporters, even at the expense of alienating other Maronite families and the Maronite patriarch, who joined the opposition.[12]

By now external forces were involved. The Egyptians were funding the opposition, and the United States was openly backing Chamoun.[13] The results of the 1957 elections, which stacked the chamber of deputies with Chamoun adherents, inaugurated a fierce round of fighting in the mountains above Beirut that continued sporadically for nearly a year. The formation of the UAR in February 1958 exacerbated the tensions. Muslim delegations went to Damascus to greet Nasser, as did representatives of the Maronite patriarch. In the meantime, the opposition front, made up of Druze and Muslim leaders primarily but including Maronites and other Christians opposed to Chamoun, received arms smuggled across the Syrian border. These developments, and Chamoun's continued refusal to deny his intention of amending the constitution, prolonged the crisis, which then erupted into open civil war in May following the assassination of a Maronite journalist critical of Chamoun's policies. Beirut itself became divided between competing Maronite and opposition factions.

The Lebanese civil war of 1958 reflected various strands of allegiance beyond religious loyalties.[14] Some Sunni dignitaries sided with Chamoun, whereas several prominent Maronites backed the United Front opposing him. Nevertheless, Chamoun defined the struggle in terms of a Muslim assault on Christian Lebanese in order to arouse more support for his cause and to appeal to public opinion abroad. At the same time he found he could not rely on the Lebanese army whose Maronite commander, Fuad Shihab, refused to commit his forces to resolve an internal dispute. Shihab himself was considered a candidate for the presidency once Chamoun's term ended in September. Chamoun asked the United States for support, hoping to invoke the Eisenhower Doctrine and use the appearance of American troops to bolster his position. Eisenhower hesitated, although he and his advisers shared a "deep-seated conviction that the Communists were principally responsible for the trouble and that President Chamoun was motivated only by a strong feeling of patriotism."[15]

The crisis might have ended quietly once it became clear in early July that Chamoun wished only to serve out his allotted term. But then, on 14 July, the Iraqi revolution occurred, in which the Hashemite monarchy and the government of Nuri al-Said were overthrown and most of their members killed. Chamoun immediately demanded American military intervention, claiming that he was threatened by the Iraqi coup. Though not necessarily agreeing with the logic behind his request, Eisenhower decided to accede to it. American marines thus landed on the beaches of Beirut on 15 July, to be met by bikini-clad bathers and ice-cream vendors who recognized immediately the opportunity for increased sales. But the troops were also confronted by the small Lebanese army led by General Shihab, now arrayed to confront the invading force. Swift intervention by the American ambassador resolved a potentially dangerous situation. Agreement was reached that General Shihab would succeed Chamoun in September, an orderly transition effected under the protective guise of the American military which left the country by 25 October.

The final resolution of the Lebanese crisis had followed closely Nasser's proposals to the United States made in June, that Shihab replace Chamoun.[16] But to Washington, its action in sending troops to Lebanon helped stabilize countries friendly to the West and was thus a defeat for Nasser and the Soviets. Eisenhower and Dulles believed that the Soviets had been "stirring up trouble" in various parts of the world and that the "United States had for one reason or another often been unable to lend a hand."[17] By requesting aid, Lebanon offered the opportunity to show the Soviets that the United States could and would act. From this perspective, the operation was a success. Not only had "the Communists come to be aware of our attitude," but "the peoples of the Middle East, inscrutable as always to the West, have nevertheless remained outside the Communist orbit."[18] Indeed, the new Iraqi regime of Colonel Abd al-Karim Qasim, whose nationalism and apparent pro-Nasserite sympathies had provoked the American action, soon seemed to be independent of the Egyptian leader. When the American special envoy, Robert Murphy, finished his mediation efforts in Beirut, he flew to Baghdad to meet Qasim. The United States recognized his government on 2 August.

In October the Russians and Egyptians reached an agreement for the construction of the Aswan Dam. Surprisingly, this did not worsen American-Egyptian relations, which took a turn for the better. Economic aid resumed in 1959, shortly after a series of American actions directed against Nasser and Nasserism, whereas Dulles had refused to grant such assistance after Suez. The change may have been due to Dulles's fatal illness which forced his retirement. Equally important was the perception that "Eisenhower was comforted by having finally acted decisively towards the Egyptian leader." Lebanon was a "catharsis" whose resolution—relieving frustrations stemming from the fear that America had not responded to apparently communist-provoked agitation—permitted the president to focus his attention elsewhere.[19] In this the Lebanese crisis is particularly instructive as an example of how a local problem, fanned by regional rivalries, is evaluated by a great power in light of the message it can send to its principal adversary. Nevertheless, "the 1957–1958 tensions between the Chamoun regime and the Syro-Egyptian partnership, though eased after Shihab's advent, was more than just an episode. It was a dramatic symptom of Lebanon's endemic schizophrenia in the presence of pan-Arab nationalism."[20] These tensions exploded into a much more brutal civil war in the 1970s.

INTER-ARAB RIVALRIES, 1958–1964

The events of July 1958 and their resolution seemed to portend even greater scope for Gamal Abd al-Nasser's influence within the Arab world. His union with Syria had been expanded to include Yemen, and the conclusion of the Lebanese crisis had ensured a government less closely identified with the West. Finally, the Iraqi revolution of 14 July had overthrown his chief rival, Nuri al-Said, and apparently signified the further extension of Nasser's pan-Arab nationalism, creating a unified bloc that could wield great influence as a neutral force balancing Western and Soviet interests to its advantage. But this vision soon proved ephemeral. The new Iraqi leader, Abd al-Karim Qasim, proved to be unimpressed with Nasser and his ideology. He reasserted Iraqi independence of regional alignments while attacking and even mocking both Nasser and the Baath, supporters of which were brought to trial after an apparent coup to oust Qasim failed in early 1959. Iraq was still the strongest opponent of Egypt's Arab aspirations, all the more upsetting because it too now espoused a neutralist, independent policy. Having called Nuri al-Said a lackey of Western imperialism, Nasser now accused Qasim of being "a stooge of international Communism" who compromised the goal of true Arab nationalism, separation from all power blocs.[21]

Egyptian-Iraqi relations remained strained until Qasim's overthrow and death in February 1963 at the hands of Iraqi Baathist officers who seemed eager to establish closer ties with Nasser. A month later there was a similar coup in Damascus, ousting those who had led the secession from the UAR. The Syrian

Baath returned to office. They and their Iraqi counterparts immediately called for talks designed to create a new union, but negotiations with Nasser during March and April proved fruitless.[22] None of the participants was eager to subordinate his country's sovereignty to that of another, whatever their rhetoric about one Arab nation. Nasser used the talks to humiliate his visitors, proposing terms he knew were unacceptable to them.

Hostile propaganda resumed once negotiations failed. As Egyptian-Syrian invective escalated, Syria drew closer to Iraq, and an agreement uniting the military commands of the two countries was signed on 8 October. But no union resulted, not because of Egyptian opposition so much as because of Baathist rivalries with unaligned officers in the Iraqi military. By the end of 1963, General Abd al-Salam Arif, an admirer of Nasser, had removed the Baath from office in Baghdad. Egyptian-Iraqi relations were once again amicable if not close, and Syrian-Iraqi contacts had degenerated into open hostility. Baathist authority in Damascus now rested in military hands, acknowledged openly when General Amin al-Hafiz assumed the post of prime minister in November.

Nasser still appeared to hold the high ground amidst these coups and countercoups, in the vanguard of progressive Arab nationalism set against the "feudalistic reactionary" monarchies of Saudi Arabia and Jordan allied with the West, especially to the United States. He believed that he had reinforced that image through his involvement in support of the Yemen revolution that had erupted in September 1962, pitting young colonels against the Islamic rule of the Zaydi Imamate. Saudi Arabia backed the forces of the imam which managed to hold the countryside and mountain ranges while the colonels retained the cities and adjacent areas. For the moment it was one more area where Nasser appeared to encourage modernization and reform, providing an arena for a productive clash with Riyadh and Amman that enhanced his stature in the Arab world to the detriment of aspiring leftist challengers in Damascus and Baghdad. But in the long run Nasser found himself in a quagmire, committing 40,000 troops to bolster the regime of Colonel Abdullah al-Sallal.

Immersed in these Arab rivalries, Nasser strove to avoid direct confrontation with Israel. He thus found himself in early 1964 seeking to moderate a new flare-up of Arab-Israeli friction in order to guarantee that he would not be drawn into clashes for which he and his military were unprepared. This led him to seek a rapprochement with other Arab leaders, including King Husayn of Jordan and King Faysal of Saudi Arabia, in hope of softening Syria's demands for military action against Israel because of the latter's plans to divert water from the Jordan River.

Arab-Israeli animosity over exploitation of the Jordan River waters had existed since 1950. The river was crucial to the agricultural plans of Jordan and Israel, but its headwaters originated in Lebanon, Syria, and Israel from whence it dropped down into Lake Tiberias and flowed southward to end in the Dead Sea; more water flowed into it from the Yarmuk River, originating in Jordan, south of Lake Tiberias. Israel had previously tried to divert waters unilaterally from the Jordan at a point within the Syrian-Israeli demilitarized zone to which it claimed sovereignty. Armed clashes led to U.N. condemnation of Israeli plans but also resulted from 1953–1955 in American-sponsored efforts to reach an agreement on sharing the waters among the riparian states. When these failed, the United States decided to back separate Israeli and Jordanian projects in 1958 aimed at diverting Yarmuk River waters for irrigation purposes. Israel undertook to channel waters out of Lake Tiberias, thereby avoiding further confrontation with Syria in the demilitarized zone.[23]

Israel's pending completion of this diversion in late 1963 aroused renewed Arab concern. Nasser called for a meeting of Arab heads of state under Arab League auspices to determine an appropriate but muted Arab response. Collaboration denied the Syrian Baath the opportunity to accuse him of evading his responsibilities as the dominant Arab figure. In this he was successful. The summit approved the diversion of those tributaries of the Jordan River lying in Arab territories. This project, which could endanger Israeli water resources both qualitatively and quantitatively, led to Israeli attacks on Syrian construction sites in 1965 and 1966, but for the moment it served to postpone consideration of a military response. In keeping with this spirit of compromise, Nasser restored his ties with Jordan and Saudi Arabia, hoping particularly to reach agreement with the latter so that the Yemen conflict could be settled and he could withdraw his troops. For the time being a mood of conciliation seemed to dominate inter-Arab relations, but this was soon broken, in part out of Syrian obduracy and in part because of another decision taken at the Cairo summit, to create the Palestine Liberation Organization.

THE FORMATION OF THE PALESTINE LIBERATION ORGANIZATION (PLO), AL-FATAH, AND INTER-ARAB POLITICS, 1964–1966

The decision of the Arab League to sponsor the formation of an organization that would represent Palestinians and strive toward "the liberation of Palestine," in the words of the Cairo summit, presumably indicated a new Arab commitment to the Palestinian cause. In fact, in the view of various Arab leaders, its significance differed considerably. Nasser apparently backed the idea in order to integrate the new group within the league under his control. This in turn would prevent Palestinians from undertaking actions against Israel that might draw him into a confrontation with it. His purpose was consistent with his motives in calling for the summit meeting, to deflect Syrian demands for a military challenge to Israel's water diversion plans. Such tactics also placed him once more in the forefront of the Arab cause, as one deeply concerned about the Palestinian issue. Syrian-Egyptian tensions in 1962, stemming from the breakup of the UAR, had led to Syrian charges that Nasser hoped to shelve the Palestinian issue, accusations that Cairo denied vehemently.[24]

Arab leaders chose as head of the Palestinian Liberation Organization (PLO) Ahmad al-Shuqayri, an aging Palestinian lawyer who had served for years as Saudi Arabia's representative at the United Nations. Known principally for his bombast, he was considered Nasser's man. Similarly, the Palestinian Liberation Army that was subsequently formed was placed under the Arab unified command headed by an Egyptian. Once the PLO held its inaugural conference in May 1964, Shuqayri began to tour Arab capitals and Palestinian refugee camps to rouse both support and recruits. It soon became clear that Shuqayri's efforts seemed designed to create an activist facade behind which nothing would occur; he specifically foreswore organizing raids against Israel. Nevertheless, the formation of the PLO aroused consternation in the almost forgotten offices of the Higher Arab Committee of Hajj Amin al-Husayni, still existing in Beirut; he denounced the PLO as "a colonialist, Zionist conspiracy aiming at the liquidation of the Palestinian cause."[25] At the other extreme was Jordan, where King Husayn viewed Shuqayri and the idea of the PLO with deep misgiving.

Husayn ruled over a population of which nearly 60 percent were Palestinians. He also controlled the West Bank, deemed essential to the Jordanian economy. Two months after the PLO's founding, Shuqayri declared, in Amman, that all of Jordan, both east and west banks, was part of Palestine, as was Israel, and should be recovered for Palestinians. Jordanian-PLO animosity intensified to the point that Husayn barred the organization from all activities, including recruitment, in his country. But if Shuqayri's efforts appeared ominous to Husayn, they seemed far too tame to the Syrians, who realized that Nasser had outmaneuvered them at the Cairo summit of July 1964 and muffled their demands for militant action. They began during 1965 to try to coopt Shuqayri for their own purposes, to acquire credit for support of the Palestinians at Nasser's expense. More significantly, they turned to a smaller Palestinian organization, al-Fatah, that was prepared to undertake operations into Israel. The Syrian backing of Fatah molded the pattern of Arab-Israeli and inter-Arab interaction essential to the outbreak of the 1967 war.

Fatah was formed in either 1959 or 1962, depending on one's choice of recollections of the original members.[26] The core group was composed of young Palestinians who had fled to Gaza when Israel was created. Several had lived in Cairo during the mid-1950s where they dominated the Palestinian Students Union while attending classes at Cairo University. Among them were Salah Khalaf, Khalil al-Wazir, and Yasir Arafat, related on his mother's side to Hajj Amin al-Husayni. All left Cairo following the Suez war, in part because of Egypt's close surveillance of Palestinians and in part to search for better-paying jobs. They settled in Kuwait, as many other Palestinians previously had done. Among those who became members of Fatah's nucleus were Faruq al-Qaddumi and Khalid al-Hassan. All remain today prominent members of the organization. They began to publish a journal called *Our Palestine* that was issued from time to time in Beirut. Several factions emerged that later evolved into small but significant entities, most identified with the current trends of Arabism and Arab unity. Within this framework the liberation of Palestine could occur only after Arab unity had been achieved, a process that delayed the encouragement of military activities. For the leaders of Fatah, however, the proper procedure was precisely the opposite. The liberation of Palestine had to precede Arab unity, meaning also that militancy and military action were the preludes to politics. These sentiments reflected the recent success of the Algerian revolt against the French and the belief propounded by Franz Fanon, deeply influenced by the Algerian experience, that violence was the only way to purge oneself of the stigma of defeat and dependence.

What is unclear is how representative this messianic faith in history was among Fatah's leadership. Later writings suggest that the group's philosophy of action changed according to its circumstances, especially its dependence on Arab state aid or its dedication to self-reliance. By mid-1965, when Fatah had begun to attack Israeli installations and to develop plans for terrorizing the population, its pamphlets argued that these activities would help establish a desirable state of tension between Israel and its Arab neighbors. Israeli military threats would necessarily bring about Arab unity to confront them, resulting ultimately in Arab victory and the liberation of Palestine from Israeli control. This view assumed Arab military superiority over Israel in conventional weapons. Finally, war seemed necessary because Israel was rumored to have developed a nuclear capability. This therefore might be the last opportunity to engage Israel in conventional warfare in which Arab numbers should prevail.[27]

Although these justifications seemed to accord with Fatah's precepts, they also indicated Syrian sponsorship of acts aimed at reestablishing its primacy in the Arab revolutionary struggle, stymied since 1964. In addition, Syria hoped to prevent the Israelis from using its water diversion projects and avenge the latter's raids on its own. Accordingly, the first Fatah raid was aimed at Israeli water installations. That these activities would eclipse Shuqayri and the PLO was in the mutual interests of both the Baathists and Fatah. Nevertheless, the Baathist leadership in Damascus did not necessarily envisage open war with Israel, precisely what Fatah hoped to provoke. By the end of the year, at least thirty-nine operations seemed to have been carried out, most of them harassments consisting of random bombings that inflicted relatively few casualties but aroused intense Israeli concern about this new threat to its security. What was less clear initially was the state backing the raids, as they were undertaken from Jordan rather than Syria. This naturally aroused the Jordanians' fears of Israeli retaliation against them despite their lack of involvement in the operations, fears that later proved justified: Fatah's first casualty was due to Jordanian efforts to stop its infiltrations. Equally prescient in light of later developments was Egypt's negative reaction to news of these early raids.[28] Both Husayn and Nasser feared an outbreak of hostilities, but their caution served Syrian interests, which were to paint each with the brush of being soft on Israel. At a meeting of the Palestinian

National Conference in Cairo in May 1965, Syrian Baathists accused Nasser of hiding behind the United Nations Emergency Forces (UNEF) stationed in Sinai since 1957. Nevertheless, Nasser held his ground, scorning Syrian criticism and seeking to retain good ties with both Jordan and Saudi Arabia, as he still hoped to gain an agreement whereby he could withdraw his troops from the Yemen.

The catalyst for the collapse of the Cairo summit and the ties created between Nasser and the monarchs, Husayn and Faysal, was the coup that took place in Damascus in February 1966. It installed a more radical Baathist regime under the guidance of the chief of staff, Salah Jadid, who took over as head of the Syrian Baath party. Also important was Britain's declaration in the same month that it planned to withdraw in two years from the Aden Protectorate, contiguous to Yemen's southern border. This announcement, coupled with the breakdown of Egyptian-Saudi efforts to mediate between opposing Yemeni factions, led Nasser to decide to keep his forces in Yemen, not so much to gain control over that country as to influence events in Aden and establish his ascendancy there through nationalist protégés once the British left. Nasser's eagerness to embellish his Arab nationalist credentials led him closer to Syria as the revolutionary-conservative split once more emerged in Arab politics. Now, however, it was exacerbated by the Syrian backing of Fatah, as one of the aims of the new Baathist regime was to arouse Palestinian opposition against King Husayn, with the aim of toppling him. This goal was aided by the growth of Israeli retaliation raids aimed primarily at Palestinian towns on the West Bank. At the same time, clashes erupted with Syrian forces on Israel's frontier, more intense than at any time since 1955–1956.

To a great degree the crisis was being managed by the Syrian Baathist regime, hoping to radicalize Arab society under its leadership and bring Nasser within its orbit in the process. Israeli reprisals, aimed principally against Jordan, helped the Syrian cause, as it proved Husayn's weakness and the futility of his reliance on the United States, which armed Israel also. The fact that Husayn had barred the PLO and Fatah from Jordan and forbidden them to recruit in the refugee camps there bolstered Syrian propaganda attacks against him. In Israel, however, Husayn's inability to block all access to its borders made little impression. A policy of retaliation against Jordan, a fellow ally of the West, was more convenient and would draw a less drastic response than would one against a more hostile and unpredictable government such as the Syrian Baath.

Husayn became increasingly isolated in his alliance with Saudi Arabia as Nasser moved toward the radical camp in the summer of 1966. Israel bombed the Syrian water diversion project on 14 July. Nasser declared at the end of the month that he now rejected collaboration with the "reactionary forces" and would seek to "liberate Palestine in a revolutionary manner and not in a traditional way."[29] Such rhetoric sought to enhance his reputation in radical eyes while being vague enough to enable him to control events and avoid a major confrontation with Israel. On 7 November 1966 he signed a mutual defense treaty with Damascus, and diplomatic relations were restored after a prolonged rupture, establishing a joint military command that should give Egypt a deciding voice in any future confrontation. Nearly a week later, 13 November, Israeli forces undertook a major retaliatory raid against the town of Samua on the West Bank, evicting the population and blowing up 125 homes. The responding Jordanian forces were ambushed and suffered extensive casualties. Husayn was caught between the Syrians and the Israelis, unable to stop all raids by Fatah, counter Israeli attacks, or maintain his credibility among his Palestinian subjects. Massive Palestinian demonstrations followed the Samua raid, protesting their exposure to Israeli attacks and the lack of adequate Jordanian protection. Husayn's only recourse was to meet Syrian and Egyptian propaganda charges with his own. If according to Radio Cairo, he was now the "harlot of Amman," Nasser was to Radio Amman the coward who hid behind UNEF forces in the Sinai and refused to protect fellow Arabs from Israeli assaults, the same charge leveled against him for years by the Syrians.

As 1966 ended, the world of Arab politics remained as fragmented as before. Nasser now faced the challenge of restraining Damascus while indicating simultaneously that he was the true leader of the Arab front against Israel, all the while avoiding a real conflict with that country. He did so amidst mounting Israeli determination to punish the Arab raiders more severely.

ISRAELI POLITICS AND GREAT POWER RIVALRIES IN THE MIDDLE EAST TO 1967

Israeli political alignments had experienced severe tremors in the decade since 1957, resulting in the decline of Ben-Gurion's prestige and his resignation from the Mapai party that he had led for many years. In 1965 he had formed the Rafi party, joined by his younger colleagues Moshe Dayan and Shimon Peres, to confront a Mapai-led government run by his rivals. Ben-Gurion's departure from the Mapai resulted from a long-standing confrontation between different branches of government that spilled over into a generational conflict as well. It was complicated by the role played by Pinhas Lavon, former defense minister and apparent architect of the abortive espionage operation of 1954 that led Ben-Gurion to return to office in early 1955.

At the heart of the problem was the question of military involvement in politics and the role of the defense ministry in matters considered by diplomats subject to their own expertise. Ben-Gurion had long admired and nurtured young men who shared his concern for Israel's military preparedness and who were personally loyal to him. Loyalty rather than merit often motivated his selection of high military personnel, notably in his choice of Moshe Dayan over Yigael Allon to become chief of staff.[30] In general, key positions in the military and those related to military matters were unavailable to those outside the Mapai and were awarded to men who shared Ben-Gurion's militancy, such as Dayan, or Shimon Peres in the ministry of defense.

The process of rupture began when a new secretary of Mapai, identified with the younger group, was appointed in 1956. At the same time a new general secretary of the Histadrut was named, Pinhas Lavon. Whereas the Mapai executive secretary, Giora Josephtal, encouraged the rise of new faces, Lavon, still a power in Mapai circles, defended the old guard, in part because of his continuing animosity toward Moshe Dayan and Shimon Peres, the two Ben-Gurion protégés who had opposed him in 1954–1955. Here Lavon had support from other quarters, including the foreign minister, Golda Meir. Meir herself was of a younger generation than Ben-Gurion and was an ardent Zionist who had proved her loyalty to him; Ben-Gurion had appointed her to replace Moshe Sharrett whom he removed from office in June 1956. But although Meir generally supported Ben-Gurion's Arab policy, she shared one bias with Sharrett. She too resented bitterly the continued interference of the military and the defense ministry in matters considered the prerogative of her office, personified in Shimon Peres and Moshe Dayan. Thus she and other long-time Mapai members such as Levi Eshkol sided with Lavon in his feud with younger party members pushed by Ben-Gurion.[31]

In 1960, the Lavon affair, heretofore secret, returned to undermine Ben-Gurion. Lavon asked him, as prime minister, to clear the former of responsibility for the events of 1954. Ben-Gurion, mistrustful of Lavon, refused to do so and instead ordered that a commission of inquiry be formed to investigate the entire matter. Lavon, angered by this procedure, brought the question into the open. In doing so he impugned the integrity of Peres and Dayan by suggesting that they were involved, thereby infuriating Ben-Gurion because the military's reputation had been challenged. Ben-Gurion, prime minister and head of the Mapai, was now determined to pursue the matter to its final outcome, but many Mapai officials wanted only to resolve the matter as quickly as possible to save the party from further embarrassment. With Ben-Gurion absent, the cabinet, led by the finance minister, Levi Eshkol, established a committee that swiftly exonerated Lavon, foiling the prime minister, who wanted a full judicial investigation. The Lavon crisis of 1960 thus symbolized the rift within the Mapai. Eshkol, Meir, and others sought to spare the party, whereas Ben-Gurion was principally concerned with freeing the military, especially Peres and Dayan, of any blame, regardless of the harm done to the Mapai.[32]

Ultimately the conflict over Lavon caused Ben-Gurion to leave the Mapai. He had resigned as prime minister in 1963, to be succeeded by Eshkol. In 1965 the new Mapai heads began considering a coalition with their main rival for labor support, the Ahdut Ha'Avodah. Ben-Gurion objected and challenged Eshkol in a bitter public debate that focused more on their handling of Lavon than on the question of coalition. The new leadership, centered on Eshkol and Meir, defeated Ben-Gurion who resigned and established the Rafi (Israeli workers') party. Peres and Dayan joined, but the Rafi failed to prevent the Mapai from returning to office after the 1965 elections. Nevertheless, the heroes of the 1950s were in the Rafi, their public image that of the victors at Suez. This led in 1967 to public suspicion that the new Mapai leaders were not equal to the task of defending Israel. And following the war, when the Mapai and the Ahdut Ha'Avodah decided to expand their alignment into a full merger, they included the Rafi, whose justification for existence had been its opposition to such a union. The amalgamation of these three groups in 1968 became the Israeli Labor party.[33]

On the right, another symbol of Zionist militancy began to gain greater credibility during the 1960s. Menachem Begin's Herut party insisted on its vision of an Israel controlling all territory considered Palestine in World War I, namely, that east and west of the Jordan River. Herut had become the second-largest party in Israel as of the 1955 elections, but Begin remained discredited in Ben-Gurion's eyes; he even refused to use his name when addressing him in the Knesset.[34] The Eshkol government initiated a public rehabilitation of the Irgun, bringing back the remains of Vladimir Jabotinsky to Israel and adding to the image of national legitimacy to be granted to Begin and the Irgun as well.

In 1965 the Herut merged with the Liberal party to become the Gahal party. This did not help the party in new elections, but it furthered the process of acceptance. Also helpful was the growing outspokenness of members of a younger generation who agreed with Begin's call for Israeli expansion. Among them was Ezer Weizmann, nephew of Chaim Weizmann and chief of operations for the Israeli Defense Forces. He and others in command positions were eager to acquire more of what had been ancient Eretz Israel.[35]

Domestic political turmoil did not affect a growing closeness between Israel and the United States during the 1960s, especially once Lyndon Johnson became president following John F. Kennedy's assassination in November 1963. President Kennedy had balanced many different strands of policy during his brief tenure as president. He owed much to Jewish backing for his extremely narrow margin of victory in 1960, apparently based on his proclamations of American support for Israel.[36] In the Middle East he pursued a two-pronged policy of seeking closer ties with Israel while at the same time establishing better relations with the Arab neutralist camp, led by Nasser. Economic aid agreements with Egypt were increased, especially regarding grain shipments, but at the same time greater economic assistance was given to Israel. And in a major move, the Kennedy administration decided to enter the Middle East arms race by providing military aid to Israel, in this case, Hawk antiaircraft missiles, which were deemed necessary to balance the Soviet military shipments to Iraq and Egypt.

The United States thus began a process of ever deeper involvement in supplying its allies in the Middle East, often with apparently contradictory purposes in mind. As radical-conservative Arab rivalries intensified from 1963 onward, the United States found itself determined to send military assistance to regimes such as Jordan and Saudi Arabia to bolster them against threats from their Arab enemies. This in turn made it impossible to refuse the demands of Israel's supporters that it needed more arms to counter shipments to conservative Arab states, as they could be used against Israel. The apparent fragility of the conservative Arab governments led many Washington officials to see a strong Israel as all the more important to American hopes of combating Soviet influence in the region, a view naturally encouraged by the Israelis who profited from the continuance of American-Soviet rivalries. Israeli views were well known in Washington because of the close links established between Israeli intelligence (Mossad) and the CIA, with the CIA receiving from Mossad during 1966 increasingly alarmist reports about Soviet intentions. Such assessments, accepted more readily in the Pentagon and the CIA than in the State Department, bolstered Israel's image as an ally of the United States againt the Soviets, all the more important as America became increasingly involved militarily in Southeast Asia.

At the time of Kennedy's death in November 1963 there still were certain outstanding issues between Israel and the United States. One was Kennedy's effort to resolve the question of the Palestinian refugees, an inquiry that failed owing to uncertainty on both sides as to the number of refugees they would have to accept. Another was Israel's development of a nuclear reactor, initially denied by Ben-Gurion following its chance discovery by American intelligence in 1960. The American agreement to sell Hawk missiles to Israel was conditioned on the latter's willingness to permit on-site inspection of the reactor by the United States.[37] But these matters became of relatively minor importance once Lyndon Johnson assumed office at a time when Syrian-Israeli tensions were mounting. Although Nasser initiated his summit policy at the beginning of 1964, failure to resolve his dispute with Saudi Arabia over Yemen led the Johnson administration to support an Islamic alliance of the Saudis and Jordanians against Nasser's apparent control of the radical Arab states. In addition, clashes over American policy in Africa seriously strained American-Egyptian relations at the end of 1964. American aid to Egypt declined and was finally suspended in early 1967. The State Department had an increasingly minor role in decision making during this period and "during late 1966 and early 1967 the State Department Policy Planning Council did not have a member assigned to the Middle East."[38]

Here emotions and world views blended easily. Johnson's perceptions harked back to those of Dulles, but in cruder fashion given his lack of experience in foreign affairs. Johnson's judgments were often visceral, based on his sense of loyalties and his and his aides' increasing obsession with Vietnam where they saw themselves confronted by world communism. Johnson personally felt great affinity with Israel and Israelis, based in part on his religious upbringing and reading of the Old Testament and in part on his identification with Israelis as a frontier people, "a modern-day version of the Texans fighting the Mexicans."[39] Americans and Israelis were similar in his eyes, a feeling shared and encouraged by most of his domestic advisers who were themselves strong supporters of Israel. These associations became particularly important following the intensification of Syrian-Jordanian hostility in 1965. Though backing military assistance to King Husayn, the Johnson administration also decided to grant Israel's request for tanks, a major step in that these were the first truly offensive weapons that the United States had authorized for that country. Johnson's willingness to accelerate an American commitment to arm Israel proved most important when France, the latter's traditional arms supplier, refused to continue in that role on the eve of the 1967 war.[40]

From the Soviet perspective, continuing military and economic assistance to Egypt, Syria, and Iraq provided a wedge for gaining access to the Arab world through governments opposed to Western efforts to maintain their dominance. Growing American identification with Israel in the 1960s provided more opportunities for Soviet inroads into the region. Ideology played a minor role. The Soviets were quite willing to have local communist parties suppressed for the sake of geopolitical strategy during the Khrushchev era (1955–1964); mere support of neutralism worked to Russian advantage, given its condemnation by the Eisenhower administration. From the Soviet perspective, Egypt became all the more important as the 1960s progressed. Once the United States began bombing North Vietnam in 1965, Soviet aid to that country increased drastically. The Suez Canal and its security were crucial to the swift transit of Soviet arms and oil to its ally, achieving an importance analogous to what it once had had for the British.[41]

The Soviet Union's close ties with Egypt and other Arab states were also spurred by competition from its main communist rival, China, which sought to acquire paramountcy in "progressive" Third World countries at Russia's expense. Here the Soviets found themselves forced to defend their credibility against a communist challenger while striving to unite the radical Arab states— Syria, Iraq, and Egypt—in order to form an "anti-imperialist camp" that would counter American interests in the region. They seemed to have tried to gain a more forceful image as a defender of Syria particularly. Israeli complaints against Syrian sponsorship of guerrilla attacks were blocked by Soviet vetoes in the U.N. Security Council, and Soviet diplomats accused Israel on several occasions in 1966 of fomenting disturbances and massing troops on its Syrian frontier. At the same time, the Brezhnev government paid little attention to the rise of Fatah and condemned the PLO, reiterating its concern for the legal status of Palestinian refugees in terms close to those used by the United States.[42] Throughout this period, American emphasis on combating communism, reinforced by its perceptions of the struggle it had now intensified in Vietnam, led to increased military aid to Jordan and Saudi Arabia as well as Israel. This in turn seems to have encouraged the Soviets to back their clients more emphatically.

Soviet supplies to Egypt, Syria, and Iraq clearly outweighed Israel's in quantity and probably contributed to Nasser's confidence during the initial stages of the 1967 crisis. Qualitatively, however, the Israelis had a clear edge. Each Soviet weapons system had been balanced by a Western one, and the offensive capability of the Israelis' weapons, especially aircraft, far outdistanced that of the Arabs'. It seems likely, given the increasing potential for American-Soviet involvement in the region, that once the United States became an arms supplier of Israel, the Soviets wished to avoid a direct confrontation. Moscow provided weapons designed for defensive or limited offensive purposes, but not sufficient "to allow contemplation of successful first strike or total victory."[43] In contrast, the Israeli arsenal possessed significant offensive capabilities, including long-range attack bombers, and its personnel were capable of handling advanced weapons technology, a characteristic that the Arab military, especially the air force, lacked in abundance. Once the possibility of war developed in May 1967, the Israeli military leadership had little doubt they could demolish the Egyptians in the Sinai. The question was whether the Eshkol government would permit them to do so.

THE 1967 WAR: ITS CAUSES AND CONSEQUENCES

As the year began, Fatah increased its infiltrations and left explosives designed to kill civilians and create an atmosphere of terror in Israel. This presumably would instigate their hoped-for crisis that would unite the Arab governments against Israel and lead to war. The Syrian military was now much more openly involved. Border clashes along the Golan Heights escalated quickly in January to include tank and artillery exchanges, creating an atmosphere of tension that lasted throughout the spring. The Syrian president, Nureddin al-Attassi, declared his country's support for a Palestinian war of liberation modeled after that of Algeria's against the French and of the Vietnamese against the United States. In response, Prime Minister Eshkol warned of Israeli retaliation amidst increasing pressure from his military commanders to undertake major reprisals against Syria. Jordan remained under intense criticism from Cairo and Damascus, now for refusing to accept Egyptian, Syrian, and Iraqi forces as part of an Arab defense system against future Israeli attacks. The Arab propaganda war continued, with Amman mocking Nasser for hiding behind the UNEF in Sinai.[44]

Then, on 7 April, Syrian-Israeli exchanges of fire over the demilitarized zone beneath the Golan Heights, long a bone of contention, led to Syrian air support and an Israeli reply in which six Syrian fighters were shot down and the Israeli planes mockingly buzzed Damascus. President al-Attassi might refer to that clash as "very useful to us" in furthering the liberation cause, but Cairo was clearly alarmed, and high Egyptian officials went to Damascus for consultations. Syrian spokesmen became more vocal about a joint CIA-Israeli scheme to threaten them, whereas in Israel, experiencing more attacks by Fatah, tensions mounted.

During the weekend of May 12–13, a prelude to Israeli independence day ceremonies, speeches were made by various officials that seemed to indicate plans for a major retaliatory raid against Syria if attacks from there continued. A press report stated that "a highly placed Israeli source said here today (12 May) that if Syria continued the campaign of sabotage in Israel, it would immediately provoke military action aimed at overthrowing the Syrian regime."[45] This news aroused concern in the United Nations and elsewhere. On 13 May, a secret

Soviet message to Nasser informed him that Israel had massed forces on the Syrian frontier. Nasser accepted this information at face value, although doubts about its accuracy and the likelihood of Soviet encouragement of a crisis to enhance its stature in the Arab world predominated. Israel had sent some tank units there following the 7 April clash, but no "large forces."[46]

Having had this information reaffirmed by other Soviet messages, however, Nasser mobilized his army and sent troops into the Sinai. He took this decision on 14 May. On the sixteenth he had emissaries in the Sinai request that the United Nations Emergency Forces withdraw from their positions, thus removing the international buffer between him and Israel. Controversy still exists as to whether Nasser intended a partial ouster of UNEF forces that would leave Sharm al-Shaykh still in U.N. hands. What is clear is that U Thant, secretary general of the United Nations, believed that a partial withdrawal was impossible. It had to be full or not at all, and he accepted Egypt's right to make that request. Egypt formally demanded a full withdrawal on 18 May, and its troops began occupying U.N. posts along the frontier. U Thant then asked Israel to accept U.N. forces to act as a buffer, but Israel refused. Yet as tensions mounted, Nasser refused to occupy Sharm al-Shaykh overlooking the Straits of Tiran until 21 May, under the taunts of the Saudis and Jordanians that he was afraid to do so. On the next day he closed the Straits of Tiran to all shipping destined for Israel, recreating the circumstances Israel had stipulated as justifying war in 1957.[47]

Despite these actions, Nasser apparently believed that establishing a threat to Israel would not lead to war. Rather, he would gain a clear political victory in the cause of Arabism that would deflate Syrian pretensions and send news of his own militancy "to the chanceries and streets of the Arab world."[48] He thus occupied Sharm al-Shaykh to blunt Arab criticism rather than with a clear expectation of what Israel might do. He seemed to have accepted the assurances of his chief of staff and old crony, Abd al-Hakim Amr, that his forces could withstand an Israeli assault, while growing more confident as the days passed that no such attack would occur. He thus stressed defensive preparations and insisted that Egyptian forces in the Sinai adopt a defensive posture, albeit in forward, offensive positions.[49] This confusion probably reflected the desire of his military chiefs for war. His war minister, Shams al-Din Badran, returned from Moscow on 25 May and lied to Nasser, telling him he had Soveit backing for war when in fact Moscow was desperately urging restraint. Badran and Amr both hoped for the opportunity to attack Israel, in contrast with the political goals of their president.

Nevertheless, at times Nasser lent his voice to the war hysteria. Although he insisted that any conflict would be initiated by Israel, he also stated that such an act would result in the restoration of the situation existing in 1948, presumably referring to the abolition of Israel. Others were not so circumspect. Ahmad al-Shuqayri was quoted as stating that Israel was about to be destroyed and few if any Jews would survive.[50] Ironically, Shuqayri's speech was delivered in Amman. On 30 May King Husayn had signed a joint defense pact with Nasser, placing his forces under the command of an Egyptian general. Husayn had just previously broken off relations with Syria after a car filled with explosives exploded at a Jordanian border post. Egypt now had defense pacts with two nations who were sworn enemies of each other. Militant rhetoric notwithstanding, the Arab military was hardly united.

Yet if Nasser seemed to be moving from expectation of Israeli attack to cautious optimism that he would achieve a diplomatic triumph, Israel was progressing in the opposite direction, from consideration of his actions as a bluff to belief that war was necessary and probably imminent, if only to achieve Israel's own objectives. The Eshkol cabinet had countered Egypt's placement of troops in the Sinai by mobilizing its own forces; all reserves had been called up following the closure of the Straits of Tiran. For most of the Israeli public, the strident Arab propaganda and increasingly specific threats of destruction established an atmosphere of encirclement that became increasingly oppressive as the crisis wore on. Eshkol hesitated, apparently fearing that Israel might be forced to attack but seeking guarantees of American support. Officials in the Johnson administration strove to avoid war, assuring Israeli emissaries, including the foreign minister, Abba Eban, that they would do everything possible to open the Straits of Tiran. With this backing, but denied a public American commitment to support Israel that Eban had sought, the Eshkol cabinet voted on the evening of 27–28 May not to go to war but to accede to Johnson's request to delay such a decision for two weeks while his administration attempted to mobilize international support to open the straits.

Now Eshkol faced the wrath of his generals, backed by reserve officers prominent under Ben-Gurion who "saw his efforts to solve the crisis by diplomatic means as hesitancy, vacillation and lack of authority; . . . they wanted a minister who would unleash a war" which they were convinced they would win and which for some would signal the hoped-for expansion of Israel's borders to include Jerusalem and the West Bank.[51] Recognizing Eshkol's weakness, the military now demanded that he include the Rafi and Gahal parties, the latter led by Begin, in a national cabinet in order to add to the cabinet's militancy. On 1 June Eshkol succumbed to the pressures building about him; he appointed Moshe Dayan, symbol of the Suez campaign, as minister of defense, and he installed Menachem Begin as minister without portfolio.[52] These additions, along with Husayn's joining a defense pact with Nasser, seemed to many to ensure that war was inevitable. The question was when.

Immediate attack seemed advisable for several reasons: the element of surprise; the ongoing mobilization of troops that might create economic problems; and the increasing unease among the public given the barrage of Arab propaganda threatening to destroy Israel. But for the leadership, a decisive factor was the news on 2 June that in response to American requests, Nasser had agreed to send his vice-president, Zakariya Mohieddine, to Washington on the seventh to discuss measures to defuse the potential for confrontation over the Tiran blockade. This was totally unacceptable, even to Eban who had resisted the military option until 1 June: "It was probable that this initiative would aim at a face-saving compromise—and that the face to be saved would be Nasser's not Israel's. For us the importance of denying Nasser political and psychological victory had become no less important than the concrete interest involved in the issue of navigation."[53] Egyptian occupation of Sharm al-Shaykh and the blockade might be the *casus belli* justifying attack, but Israel was also determined to deny Nasser his political triumph in the Arab world.

In this context the Eshkol government received reports that Washington might condone such a move. Meir Amit, the head of Mossad, whose reports to the CIA about Soviet penetration of the Middle East helped align Israel and Washington, had gone to the United States incognito to ascertain American opinions about a possible Israeli strike. He consulted only with CIA and Pentagon officials and apparently received encouragement for an Israeli assault intended to destroy Nasser's Soviet-supplied arsenal and severely damage his and Moscow's prestige. Amit did not consult with State Department officials, whose diplomatic efforts were aimed in the opposite direction.[54] With increased confidence in American approval, determined to punish Nasser and thwart the intent of Mohieddine's forthcoming visit to Washington, the cabinet on 4 June approved Dayan's plan to attack Egypt the next morning.

Within three hours of the initial Israeli air strikes on Egyptian air fields in the Sinai, the Egyptian air force was nearly obliterated, its planes destroyed on the ground. Although the Israeli forces did not achieve all their objectives—occupation of Sharm al-Shaykh and reaching the Suez Canal—until 9 June, the Sinai war had, for all practical purposes, been decided. Egyptian troops had no air cover in the desert to shield them from Israeli air and ground attacks. The Eshkol cabinet appealed to Husayn to stay out of the fighting, but once it became clear that Jordanian shelling would continue, the cabinet decided to fulfill the "historic opportunity" afforded them, namely, the taking of the old city of Jerusalem. In keeping with Dayan's plans, Israeli forces also moved into the West Bank toward the Jordan River. Fierce fighting ensued, especially in and around East Jerusalem. As the conflict continued, Israeli diplomats in Washington and New York tried to gain American support to delay pressing for a cease-fire until "the opportunity for a permanent settlement was created. Israel needed time to finish the job."[55] The Security Council of the United Nations had called for a cease-fire, but Israel was able to delay acceptance because the Arab states refused. Nevertheless, Israel, fearing implementation of the Security Council resolution, hastened to take old Jerusalem beforehand, securing the area by midday, 7 June.

Israel then pressed on toward the Jordan River, declaring its support for a cease-fire but moving swiftly before Husayn announced his acceptance, as he did later in the day. On 8 June Egypt accepted the cease-fire. Shortly after midnight on the ninth, Syria, which had contributed so much to the crisis and nothing to the conflict, did also. But this was unacceptable to Dayan, as there had not yet been a major confrontation with Syria. He now ordered an all-out assault without informing either Eshkol or Yitzhak Rabin, chief of staff, of his decision; it was an act reminiscent of Ben-Gurion's style as minister of defense, anticipating civilian objections.[56] But Eshkol, though angered at Dayan's *modus operandi*, pushed for deeper advances into the Golan than Dayan had envisaged. If possible he wanted to gain control of the headwaters of the Jordan River. Israel finally stopped after occupying the key town of Qunaitra on 10 June after it had been abandoned by the retreating Syrians. The Six-Day War had ended.

American intelligence estimates had predicted a clear-cut Israeli victory in case of war, whether against Egypt alone or on all three fronts. Yet despite apparent Pentagon and CIA support for an Israeli attack, especially into the Sinai, Israeli planes and torpedo boats staged a deliberate assault on an American intelligence-gathering ship, the U.S.S. *Liberty*, on 8 June, causing thirty-four deaths and over seventy wounded. The ship was stationed off the Sinai near Israel to monitor radio signals from all sources. The Israelis attacked probably in order to sink the *Liberty* and forestall American awareness of their plans to expand to the Jordan River on the West Bank or, more likely, to move against Syria.[57] Johnson and his aides accepted Israeli apologies for the "accident," relieved that the attackers had not been the Russians.

There may well have been conflicting motives behind the United States' search for a diplomatic resolution to the crisis. Whereas the State Department pursued it with hope of success, predicated on the Mohieddine visit, Johnson encouraged it out of fear that the United States might be forced to intercede on behalf of Israel if war erupted; this in turn stemmed from apprehensions that the Russians would intervene on behalf of the Arabs, inducing a great power conflict while the bulk of American forces were committed to Vietnam. Once it became clear that the Soviets were sincere in seeking an immediate cease-fire and would not act aggressively, the Johnson administration felt able to back Israel while relieved that it had not openly associated the United States with its effort. White House support for Israel also reflected the assumption that there now was an opportunity for peace as a result of the attack. Johnson accepted the Israeli arguments presented when seeking American support for war and for its conditions for returning the territories it would occupy. Israel would withdraw only in return for peace agreements with Arab states, thus ending the state of belligerency that had existed since 1949. Here the United States believed it had Israeli assurances, given on 5 June, that Israel did not intend to expand its borders as a result of the conflict. Even before the war's end, a special committee in the White House began investigating proposals for possible peace settlements.[58]

Nevertheless, it is unlikely that anyone, including the Israelis themselves, anticipated the scope of their victory, including Jerusalem, the West Bank, and the Golan Heights, in addition to the Sinai. Certain areas, especially East

Jerusalem, were now incorporated into Israel, regardless of past promises. As soon as the area was secured, Israeli officials ordered the demolition of the Moghrabi quarter opposite the Wailing Wall and the eviction of its over 600 Muslim residents so that Jews coming to worship the next Sabbath at the holiest site in Judaism would be secure and have ample room to pray. This was done swiftly to create new facts and preempt any U.N. resolution regarding their administration of East Jerusalem.[59] In the meantime, over 100,000 new refugees from within Israel as well as the West Bank crossed into East Bank Jordan, many forcibly evicted from their homes; villages were bulldozed to ensure they would not return. Given these circumstances, Eshkol declared in a report to the Israeli people that "there should be no illusion that Israel is prepared to return to the conditions that existed a week ago. . . . We have fought alone for our existence and our security, and are therefore justified in deciding for ourselves what are the genuine and indispensable interests of our state and how to guarantee our future. We shall never return to the conditions prevailing before."[60] With this and other statements, Israel's assurances that it would not expand its borders became moot, overrun by euphoria and a sense of having broken the noose of encirclement that seemed to threaten it and recalled, especially for European Jews, the Nazi experience. Here Arab propaganda, feeding on itself and aimed at self-inflation, provided to many in the West more than adequate justification for the Israeli attack.

In Washington, Johnson seemed unconcerned with the new Israeli position as stated by Eshkol. His domestic advisers had already suggested that he not insist on restoration of the territorial status quo. Such circumspection "could lead to a great domestic bonus—and not only from the Jews. Generally speaking it would seem that the Mid-East crisis can turn around a lot of anti-Vietnam, anti-Johnson feeling, particularly if you use it as an opportunity to your advantage."[61] The question remaining was how all parties would deal with a radically new situation. The United States would try to assure both sides of its good offices while not appearing to place excessive pressure on Israel, because of domestic political considerations. For its part, Israel was determined to establish itself in a new territorial framework whose boundaries, still undefined, would be quite different from those existing previously. The Arab governments would strive to restore the pre-1967 borders. As for Fatah, its leaders viewed the debacle as justification for their increased independence of Arab state constraints in confronting Israel now that their initial hypothesis of an Arab victory had been invalidated.

NOTES

1. Patrick Seale, *The Struggle for Syria: A Study of Post-War Arab Politics, 1945–1958* (London, 1966), pp. 270–282; and Wilbur Crane Eveland, *Ropes of Sand: America's Failure in the Middle East* (New York, 1980), pp. 158–230, discuss these events extensively. Eveland was active as a CIA representative in the area during the period.

2. Eveland, *Ropes of Sand*, p. 220.
3. Seale, *Syria*, p. 281.
4. Ibid., p. 321.
5. Two reliable studies of Nasser, with different emphases, are Robert Stephens, *Nasser, A Political Biography*, Penguin Series, Political Leaders of the Twentieth Century (London, 1973); and Anthony Nutting, *Nasser* (New York, 1972).
6. Fahim I. Qubain, *Crisis in Lebanon* (Washington, D.C., 1961), p. 16ff.
7. Albert Hourani, *Syria and Lebanon, a Political Essay* (London, 1954), p. 121, relying on 1938 French estimates.
8. Michael C. Hudson, *The Precarious Republic: Political Modernization in Lebanon* (New York, 1968), p. 23.
9. Qubain, *Crisis*, p. 19.
10. Charles Issawi, "Economic Development and Political Liberalism in Lebanon," in Leonard Binder, ed., *Politics in Lebanon* (New York, 1966), pp. 74–78.
11. See the speeches quoted in Hudson, *Precarious Republic*, p. 108.
12. Qubain, *Crisis*, pp. 56–57.
13. Eveland, *Ropes of Sand*, pp. 246–255.
14. See Hudson's detailed analysis, *Precarious Republic*, pp. 109–117.
15. Dwight D. Eisenhower, *The White House Years: Waging Peace, 1956–1961* (New York, 1965), p. 266. Eisenhower's account is a bit muddled in that he admits that Chamoun was wrong to try to amend the constitution.
16. Ibid., p 268.
17. Ibid., p. 266.
18. Ibid., pp. 289, 291.
19. Steven L. Spiegel, *The Other Arab-Israeli Conflict: Making America's Middle East Policy, from Truman to Reagan* (Chicago, 1985), p. 89.
20. Malcom H. Kerr, "Political Decision Making in a Confessional Democracy," in Binder, ed., *Politics in Lebanon*, p. 209.
21. Malcolm H. Kerr, *The Arab Cold War: Gamal 'Abd al-Nasir and His Rivals, 1958–1970*, 3rd ed. (London, 1971), p. 17. Kerr's study remains the best discussion of this period.
22. See the excellent survey of these talks in ibid., pp. 44–78.
23. Fred J. Khouri, *The Arab-Israeli Dilemma*, 3rd ed. (Syracuse, N.Y., 1985), pp. 225–229.
24. Kerr, *Arab Cold War*, p. 39.
25. Quoted in Helena Cobban, *The Palestinian Liberation Organization: People, Power, and Politics*, (Cambridge, England, 1984), p. 31.
26. Ibid., p. 23. See also Ehud Yaari, *Strike Terror, the Story of Fatah* (New York, 1970). Khouri, *Arab-Israeli Dilemma*, p. 229, is in error when he states that Fatah was founded with Syrian help in 1964.
27. Fuad Jabber, "The Palestinian Resistance and Inter-Arab Politics," in William Quandt, ed., *The Politics of Palestinian Nationalism* (Berkeley and Los Angeles, 1973), p. 160.
28. Yaari, *Fatah*, pp. 61–62.
29. Stephens, *Nasser*, p. 461.
30. Yoram Peri, *Between Battles and Ballots: Israeli Military in Politics* (Cambridge, England, 1983), pp. 51–69; and Tom Segev, *1949, The First Israelis* (New York, 1986), p. 11.
31. I rely here on Peri, *Battles and Ballots*, pp. 70–80; Noah Lucas, *The Modern History of Israel* (New York, 1975), pp. 391–407; and Michael Bar-Zohar, *Ben-Gurion* (London, 1978), pp. 282–297.
32. Bar-Zohar, *Ben-Gurion*, pp. 294–295; and Lucas, *Modern History*, pp. 397–398.
33. The reappearance of the Ahdut Ha'Avodah requires explanation. Led by Ben-Gurion, the party had merged with the Hapoel Hatzair in 1930 to become the Mapai. The Hapoel Hatzair at that time represented those with a much stronger ideological commitment to socialism than Ben-Gurion and his colleagues had. As Ben-Gurion concentrated on leadership of the Jewish community and called for Jewish statehood, leftist members of the Mapai formed a block of opposition. They believed that socialism should triumph within the Jewish community in Palestine before statehood. They took the name, Ahdut Ha'Avodah, when they split with Ben-Gurion and the Mapai in the mid-1940s over the issue of the Biltmore Declaration. They later merged with another leftist party, the Hashomer Hatzair, to form the Mapam in 1948, subsequently seceded from that party and then reunited with the Mapai and the Rafi to become the Labor party in 1968. See Lucas, *Modern History*, pp. 128–130, 190–192, 282, 311–312, 399–406.

34. Rael Jean Isaac, *Party and Politics in Israel: Three Visions of a Jewish State* (New York, 1981), pp. 139, 149.
35. Donald Neff, *Warriors for Jerusalem: The Six Days That Changed the Middle East* (New York, 1984), pp. 46–47. For Begin, see Eric Silver, *Begin, a Biography* (London, 1984), pp. 124–129; and Isaac, *Three Visions*, pp. 135–151.
36. Spiegel, *America's Middle East Policy*, p. 97: "Unlike Eisenhower, Kennedy could please his domestic constituency—labor, liberals, Democratic party officials—with strong support for Israel."
37. Ibid., p. 113; and Stephen Green, *Taking Sides: America's Secret Relations with a Militant Israel* (New York, 1984), pp. 148–179, where he discusses the probability that Israeli agents arranged to steal uranium from a nuclear plant created in Pennsylvania for that purpose, with the acquiescence if not the collusion of some American officials.
38. Spiegel, *America's Middle East Policy*, pp. 119–120. For the question of American aid to Egypt and its underlying political rationale, see William J. Burns, *Economic Aid and American Policy Towards Egypt, 1955–1981* (Albany, 1985).
39. Spiegel, *America's Middle East Policy*, p. 123.
40. Unbeknownst to the Israelis, America was supplying tanks to Jordan also. De Gaulle had initiated a chill in French-Israeli relations following revelations that Israeli intelligence, under the direction of Meir Amit, had collaborated with French and Moroccan security forces in kidnapping a Moroccan opposition figure, Mehdi Ben Barka, in Paris and transporting him to Morocco where he was put to death. The French officers involved had objected to de Gaulle's decision to withdraw from Algeria and acted on their own as it seemed Amit did also, without Eshkol's approval. See Peri, *Battles and Ballots*, pp. 240–244.
41. Karen Dawisha, *Soviet Foreign Policy Towards Egypt* (New York, 1979), p. 27ff; and Galia Golan, *Yom Kippur and After, the Soviet Union and the Middle East Crisis* (Cambridge, England, 1977), pp. 1–18. An excellent overview of Soviet foreign policy is Robin Edmonds, *Soviet Foreign Policy, the Brezhnev Years* (Oxford, England, 1984).
42. Galia Golan, *The Soviet Union and the Palestine Liberation Organization: An Uneasy Alliance* (New York, 1980), p. 7; and Theodore Draper, *Israel and World Politics: Roots of the Arab-Israeli War* (New York, 1968), pp. 34–39.
43. Jon D. Glassman, *Arms for the Arabs: The Soviet Union and War in the Middle East* (Baltimore, 1975), p. 36.
44. Draper, *World Politics*, pp. 41–43; Stephens, *Nasser*, pp. 462–465; and Neff, *Warriors*, pp. 56–58.
45. Quoted in Walter Laqueur, *The Road to War: The Origin and the Aftermath of the Arab-Israeli Conflict 1967–8* (Baltimore, 1968), p. 89. Laqueur's discussion of this report is somewhat convoluted, as he seeks to absolve Israel of any responsibility for such a statement.
46. Michael Brecher, with Benjamin Geist, *Decisions in Crisis: Israel, 1967 and 1973* (Berkeley and Los Angeles, 1980), p. 45. On the veracity of Soviet reports of Israeli troop movements, compare Draper, *World Politics*, pp. 54–58, and Laqueur, *Road to War*, pp. 86–97, who discount them, with Stephens, *Nasser*, pp. 469–470, and Nutting, *Nasser*, pp. 397–399, who give them more weight.
47. Compare Laqueur, *Road to War*, pp. 100–104, and Nutting, *Nasser*, pp. 309–404, for differing interpretations of Egypt's demands and intentions. The most detailed accounts are those of the commander of the UNEF forces in the Sinai, Indar Jit Rikhye, *Sinai Blunder* (London, 1980); and the texts and commentary in Rosalyn Higgins, *United Nations Peacekeeping, 1946–1967: Documents and Commentary*, 4 vols. (New York, 1969), vol. 1, *The Middle East*, pp. 271, 326, 338–339, and especially pp. 345–349, where the official and oral Egyptian requests are given verbatim. It appears that the written request for withdrawal mentioned observation posts along the Egyptian-Israeli border which could exclude Sharm al-Shaykh. On the other hand, Rikhye was told orally to remove UNEF troops from Sharm al-Shaykh also. The Egyptian military may have upped Nasser's ante without his knowledge. Higgins argues that U Thant could have stalled and did not have to accede to the Egyptian demand. For a good overview that also makes these points, see Michael Brecher, *Decisions in Israel's Foreign Policy* (New Haven, Conn., 1975), pp. 318–453, especially pp. 363–364 and notes.
48. Kerr, *Arab Cold War*, p. 127.
49. Nutting, *Nasser*, p. 411; Rikhye, *Sinai Blunder*, pp. 96–97, who inspected the positions; and Draper, *World Politics*, p. 95, who notes the "contradiction" between Egypt's strategic intentions and the appearance of their troop movements.

50. Stephens, *Nasser*, p. 480.
51. Peri, *Battles and Ballots*, p. 250. See also Brecher, *Decisions*, pp. 99–100.
52. Peri, *Battles and Ballots*, pp. 244–251, who notes how the direct involvement of military leaders in these decisions was concealed from the public by the censor; and Brecher, *Decisions*, p. 150.
53. Quoted in Neff, *Warriors*, p. 181.
54. See ibid., pp. 176, 181; Brecher, *Decisions*, p. 164; and Dennis Eisenberg, Uri Dan, and Eli Landau, *The Mossad, Israel's Secret Intelligence Service: Inside Stories* (New York, 1978), pp. 160–164, who state that Robert McNamara, secretary of defense, intimated strongly to Amit that Israel should go ahead with its plans.
55. Brecher, *Decisions*, p. 273.
56. Peri, *Battles and Ballots*, p. 80; Brecher, *Decisions*, pp. 278–280. It should be noted that Chief of Staff Rabin also favored attacking Syria. The Israelis benefited from the enormous confusion caused by Egyptian leadership of the joint command overseeing Jordanian operations as detailed by Samir A. Mutawi, *Jordan in the 1967 War* (Cambridge, England, 1987).
57. Green, *Taking Sides*, pp. 212–242; Neff, *Warriors*, pp. 246–266; and an account by a survivor of the attack, James M. Ennes, Jr., *Assault on the Liberty: The True Story of the Israeli Attack on an American Intelligence Ship* (New York, 1979); but Lyndon Baines Johnson, *The Vantage Point: Perspective of the Presidency, 1963–1969* (New York, 1971), p. 301, states that he and his staff knew of Israeli military "intentions" regarding Syria.
58. William B. Quandt, *Decade of Decisions: American Policy Towards the Arab–Israeli Conflict, 1967–1976* (Berkeley and Los Angeles, 1977), pp. 63–64; and Green, *Taking Sides*, pp. 202–203, referring to a memo from McGeorge Bundy to Johnson.
59. Brecher, *Decisions*, pp. 273–274, 328–329; and Neff, *Warriors*, pp. 289–290.
60. Quoted in Neff, *Warriors*, p. 299.
61. Green, *Taking Sides*, pp. 219–220, quoting from a memo to Johnson from Ben Wattenberg and Larry Levinson, drafted after a visit to them the same day by David Brody, head of the Jewish Anti-Defamation League.

CHAPTER 8

War and the Search for Peace in the Middle East, 1967–1976

For its citizens and Jews everywhere, Israel's victory in the Six-Day War was an unprecedented triumph, interpreted by many as an almost mystical deliverance from the Arab foe. The victory gave the Jewish state a new set of frontiers that promised greater security by distancing Arab armies from the nation's heartland. Israel now considered the borders established by the 1949 armistice agreements to be invalid, and its leaders declared that they would not withdraw from any territory except in return for full peace agreements negotiated directly with Arab states. Here the Eshkol cabinet pointed to the experience of the 1956 Suez invasion when Ben-Gurion finally withdrew from Sharm al-Shaykh under assurances it would not be reoccupied by Egyptian troops.

For the Arabs the 1967 war was a shocking debacle. Nasser resigned from office, only to be swept back in by a massive public outcry of support. But his policies and those of his allies were in disarray. At the Khartoum Conference in August 1967 the Arab states took the position that the territories should be returned immediately, as they had been acquired through Israeli aggression, without any corresponding concessions such as peace agreements on their part. They expected that the United States as well as Russia would demand Israel's withdrawal, as had occurred a decade earlier.

The United States backed Israel's position of no withdrawal without peace agreements during the period following the war. However, both the Johnson administration and later the Nixon administration expected that Israel would ultimately withdraw from nearly all the lands it occupied in 1967 and that any border changes would be minor. The United States supported the United Nations resolution condemning Israel for unilaterally annexing East Jerusalem. Nevertheless, Johnson and his aides were determined not to pressure Israel, treading cautiously out of sympathy and because of the tremendous outburst of American public support. American Jews were mobilized as never before, both monetarily and politically. Consequently the United States expressed in public full support for Israel but at the same time sought in private to moderate its position. Indeed, U.S. diplomatic initiatives, undertaken unilaterally but also in tandem with the Soviet Union, achieved terms that were usually closer to the Arab position than the Israeli, leading to major Israeli efforts to undermine them. Israeli governments tried to "forge a de facto if not formal alliance" with the United States to ensure that the United States did not try to balance Israeli and Arab interests, as Israel hoped to force the Arabs to meet its terms, which were not Washington's.[1]

Diplomatic initiatives between 1967 and 1975 were seriously affected by governmental and organizational factionalism. Israeli cabinets were often paralyzed by differences over what territories should be retained and what offered in return for peace. Nasser attempted to balance his hope for negotiations with the desires of his military command for renewed hostilities, all the while facing increasing domestic unrest. Although the Arab heads of state and the Israelis differed markedly on peace terms, the PLO opposed all efforts to attain peace, as it feared its political objectives would be ignored. Soviet policy was divided. Diplomats and communist party heads apparently backed the negotiations, whereas military officials opposed them out of fear that they would lose access to the Egyptian bases they had recently acquired. Finally, the Nixon administration's approaches to the Arab-Israeli conflict were severely hampered by the rivalry between National Security Adviser Henry Kissinger and Secretary of State William Rogers. Rogers and the State Department viewed the issue principally as a regional problem that should be resolved through negotiations as soon as possible, in concert with the Soviet Union if necessary. Kissinger, a globalist, wanted to oust the Soviets from the region before undertaking such talks, in order to establish total American dominance of the negotiating process. The State Department thus backed joint Soviet-American efforts to bring Israel and Egypt together while Kissinger worked to frustrate them.

Regional developments helped the Israeli cause in the short run. Jordanian-Palestinian strife in September 1970 seemed to confirm Israel's value as an arm of American policy in the region, eager to counter Soviet objectives. From that point onward, American aid to Israel increased measurably, with the Nixon administration deciding that no efforts would be made to push further peace talks until the Egyptians rid themselves of the Russians and turned to the United States. This policy, conceived and controlled by Kissinger, who became secretary of state in 1973, remained in force until the Egyptians and the Syrians attacked Israel in October 1973. Their goal was to force American diplomatic involvement in the area and set in motion the process whereby they might regain territory in return for some form of peace. The new Egyptian president, Anwar al-Sadat, who assumed office following Nasser's death in September 1970, had tried to involve the United States and ousted the Soviet advisers in his country in July 1972. But the American response never materialized, in part owing to efforts to resolve the question of Vietnam and in part because the Watergate scandal was beginning to absorb much of Nixon's and then Kissinger's attention. With the outbreak of war, however, Kissinger reversed himself and exploited the changed situation to force talks between Egypt and Israel. These discussions and later negotiations with Syria led to agreements in 1974–1975 to disengage forces on the Golan Heights and in the Sinai that resulted, on the Egyptian side, in the Camp David accords of 1978.

LIMITED WARS AND THE SEARCH FOR NEGOTIATING LEVERAGE, 1967–1971

ISRAELI-ARAB NEGOTIATING POSITIONS AND THEIR BACKGROUNDS

Officially Israel called for direct negotiations without preconditions, presenting a public image of conciliation that enabled it, with Arab rejection of these terms, to avoid defining what it itself might seek to absorb. This was the only way the cabinet could survive, but it indicated a "paralysis in decision making" that served the interests of those advocating settlements in all the lands, not simply the West Bank.[2] With respect to that area, different ministers spelled out conflicting visions of its future status. Menachem Begin, minister without portfolio, seemed to support de facto annexation. He demanded full government approval of Jewish settlements there, a position espoused also by a new movement, the Greater Land of Israel, that arose immediately following the war. The Greater Land of Israel Movement included many who belonged to the Labor camp, indicating a spectrum of support beyond that of Begin's Herut ideology. Moshe Dayan likewise favored settlements on the West Bank, intending to "create facts" through a Jewish presence there, as the Zionist movement had done during the mandate period. He was therefore very close to Begin and the Greater Land of Israel in his goals, but his inspiration remained elusive. He justified his position principally on grounds of security and did not rule out autonomy for the Arab population or a possible restoration of Jordanian sovereignty over the Arab residents while the region remained part of Israel. On the other hand, he assumed that the creation of settlements would guarantee Jordanian rejection of that option, leaving the area open to full Israeli control. The labor minister, Yigael Allon, drafted a plan in July 1967 that would provide for an Israeli security belt along the Jordan River valley, strategically situated to block any Arab invasion route. But he otherwise seemed more amenable to recognizing Jordanian sovereignty over the Arab inhabitants of the West Bank and most of the land.[3]

This ongoing debate occurred despite an official government statement to the United States three weeks after the war's end that Israel would return the Golan Heights to Syria and the Sinai Peninsula to Egypt, provided that they were demilitarized and that Israel was granted riparian rights to the headwaters of the Jordan River in the Golan. Israel would retain control of the Gaza Strip and Sharm al-Shaykh under this plan, with the status of the West Bank left open. It seemed clear that various Israeli groups were trying to coopt government policy, at times with the collusion of cabinet members. Citizens began to establish settlements in the conquered territories during the summer of 1967. Some were in the West Bank, but two others were in the Golan Heights and the Sinai, areas that the government had told the United States were open to return to Syria and Egypt. Indeed, the Golan settlement was approved in mid-July and supported

Beirut

LEBANON

Sidon

Tyre

GOLAN HTS.

Haifa

SYRIA

ISRAEL · Nablus

Jordan R.

Tel Aviv · **JORDAN**

Jaffa

Amman

Jerusalem

Gaza · Hebron · Dead Sea

GAZA STRIP

Mediterranean Sea

Nile Delta

Port Said

El Arish

Suez Canal

Qantara

Auja

NEGEV

Ismailiya

Great Bitter Lake

Cairo

Suez

SINAI PENINSULA

Eilat

Taba · Aqaba

E G Y P T

UNITED ARAB REPUBLIC

Gulf of Suez

Gulf of Aqaba

SAUDI ARABIA

Mt. Sinai

El Tor

Tiran Is.

Str. of Tiran

Sharm el Sheikh

0 Miles 50

Map 8. ISRAEL AND ADJACENT ARAB STATES, 1947, 1949, 1967, 1982

by the military commanders in the region. It was then backed by Allon who, as labor minister, granted to the settlers unemployment funds to finance their efforts and lobbied to gain cabinet approval which was given in late September when the new kibbutz was awarded 6000 dunams in the Qunaitra region. The government thus sanctioned after the fact actions taken to undermine its official policy and force it to retain the Golan, setting a precedent that was repeated in the future.[4] By mid-1968 the initial Israeli proposals to the United States were quietly dropped as a consensus to keep the Golan Heights emerged, but no Israeli government stated this openly until the elections of 1969 when the Labor party was forced to present its platform for the lands taken in 1967.

Arab reactions to the defeat in the June war reflected the stances that various leaders had assumed before the conflict. Husayn of Jordan sought the United States' assurances that it would seek to restore the West Bank to him and to rebuild his armed forces. Syria, backed by Iraq and Algeria, refused to consider a diplomatic resolution to the crisis. Nasser intended to combine military threats of retaliation with diplomatic overtures. He decided to seek greater Soviet assistance and granted them additional military facilities, especially in the port of Alexandria where a Soviet naval presence might offset the power of the American Sixth Fleet. Rebuilding his forces was a major priority to counter the Israeli troops on the east bank of the Suez Canal, which remained closed. But Nasser also drew closer to Husayn and King Faysal of Saudi Arabia, hoping to use them to create contacts with the United States, with whom he had broken diplomatic relations. At the same time Nasser was determined to maintain his prominence in the Arab world, where he was still challenged by the Syrian Baathist regime led by Salah Jadid which hoped to draw him away from the conservative monarchs into a "progressive front."[5] Although Nasser strove to balance opposing constituencies in the Arab world, his interests lay principally with the Arab moderates. Both he and Husayn hoped to receive subsidies from the oil states of Saudi Arabia, Kuwait, and Libya to replace the revenues lost through the war. He also wished to resolve the Yemen imbroglio, cutting costs and again improving relations with the Saudis. But he preferred to accomplish these tasks within the framework of a unified Arab position, which meant that no public response to Israeli or Western overtures was possible until an Arab summit was held.

This meeting took place in Khartoum, Sudan, at the end of August, with most heads of state in attendance, although the Syrians decided to boycott the sessions. Nasser and King Faysal resolved their differences over Yemen, and subsidies to Egypt and Jordan were approved. The key resolution stated that

> the Arab heads of state have agreed to unite their political efforts at the international and diplomatic level to eliminate the effects of the aggression and to ensure the withdrawal of the aggressive Israeli forces from the Arab lands which have been occupied since the aggression of 5 June. This will be done within the framework of the main principles by which the Arab states abide, namely no peace with Israel, no recognition of Israel, no negotiations with it, and insistence on the rights of the Palestinian people in their own country.[6]

The text was a compromise. The first sentence reflected the policy backed by Nasser and Husayn stressing political resolution of the problem. The second sentence effectively negated the first, at least outwardly, by rejecting negotiations. Nasser and Husayn apparently believed that they had gained agreement for pursuing diplomatic options with a nod to the intransigence demanded by the Syrian regime and the Palestinians, who feared any agreement that might isolate them. They recognized the need to give Israel de facto, though not de jure, recognition through negotiations conducted by third parties, specifically the United Nations, if Israel would return to its prewar frontiers. They could discard the Palestinians at the proper moment.

Israel and the Arab states interpreted the stalemate in ways that to them vindicated their stances. The Israelis refused intermediaries, fearing outside attempts to compromise their position. They demanded withdrawal only in return for full peace agreements signed through direct negotiations with individual Arab states. Israeli leaders were determined to keep some territory and to have Arab states acknowledge their right to do so. If the Arabs rejected these terms, then the Israelis would benefit from a continuing status quo that gave them great military advantages which they would not cede in exchange for promises that might recreate the conditions that led to the 1967 war. But this position, reinforced in the Israeli perspective by Arab calls for armed struggle to regain the territories, justified to many Arabs their rejection of Israeli terms. They viewed the call for direct negotiations as intended to humiliate them and as a pretext for progressive annexation, regardless of Israeli statements that no conditions existed. The proof was in Israel's immediate incorporation of East Jerusalem and its declaration that its status was nonnegotiable, as well as in the various statements by ministers indicating that regions such as the West Bank should not be returned. Nasser and Husayn preferred indirect negotiations, through third parties such as the United Nations, leading to Israeli withdrawal from the territories, as a precondition for the tacit recognition of Israel's right to exist; this would be given by agreements to enter into a state of nonbelligerency with Israel.

DELIBERATE AMBIGUITY: SECURITY COUNCIL RESOLUTION 242

Despite the apparent chasm between the Arab and Israeli negotiating platforms, the Soviet Union and the United States attempted during 1967 to reach an agreement on a suitable framework within which peace talks might be held. Russia was willing to rearm Egypt but also encouraged Nasser to be open to diplomatic overtures. Similarly, the United States, while committed to ensuring Israel's military parity, if not superiority, over its Arab opponents, also hoped that discussions would begin as soon as possible. And if, in the words of Moshe Dayan and Golda Meir, Israel sat by the phone waiting for the Arabs to call, the Americans occasionally tried to lend the Arabs a phone booth and an area code that might satisfy some of their demands as well.

In July 1967 the United States and the Soviet Union negotiated a draft agreement that they were prepared to present to the U.N. General Assembly as a basis for resolving the questions raised by the Israeli occupation of Arab lands. The draft declared that the assembly

> affirms the principle that conquest of territory by war is inadmissible under the United Nations Charter and calls on all parties to the conflict to withdraw without delay their forces from the territories occupied by them after June 4, 1967.
>
> Affirms likewise the principle of acknowledgment without delay by all member states in the area that each of them enjoys the right to maintain an independent national state of its own and live in peace and security, as well as the renunciation of all claims and acts inconsistent therewith are expected.[7]

This draft ignored the idea of direct negotiations or Arab recognition of Israel through peace agreements as the basis of the latter's withdrawal to prewar lines, but concerted Israeli opposition was unnecessary. Egypt, pressured by Syria and Algeria, refused to accept this formula, despite Soviet pleas that it do so. Great power discussions continued. The result was the passage of Security Council Resolution 242 on 22 November 1967. It has remained the official basis of negotiating efforts to the present.

Approval of the resolution reflected great power efforts to establish a set of principles whereby the United Nations could seek to achieve both peace and withdrawal. Lord Caradon, British representative on the council, drafted the final version. As he saw it,

> the Arab countries insist that we must direct our special attention to the recovery of their territories. The Israelis tell us that withdrawal must never be to the old precarious peace but to secure boundaries. Both are right. The aims of the two sides do not conflict. To imagine that one can be secured without the other is a delusion. They are of equal validity and equal necessity. . . .[8]

The resolution stressed the "inadmissibility of the acquistion of territory by war and the need to work for a just and lasting peace in which every state in the area can live in security." It called for "withdrawal of Israel from territories occupied in the recent conflict" and for "termination of all claims or states of belligerency and respect for and acknowledgment of the sovereignty, territorial integrity, and political independence of every state in the area and their right to live in peace within secure and recognized boundaries free from threats and acts of force." Another clause referred to "a just settlement of the refugee problem" and the resolution concluded by requesting the appointment of a special U.N. representative to initiate negotiations based on the principles espoused in the document.[9]

Resolution 242 incorporated language from the Soviet-American draft of July, specifically the reference to the inadmissibility to acquire territory by war. But whereas that draft called for Israel's withdrawal from "the territories" occupied, Resolution 242 deliberately omitted "the" from the clause. This was done to meet Israel's refusal to agree to withdraw from all the territories it had taken. Nevertheless, the Arab states were assured that the omission was insignificant and that only minor border changes were envisaged; the operative statement was the initial reference to "the inadmissibility of the acquisition of territory by war." Jordan agreed to sign the document only after assurances from the United States' U.N. delegate, Arthur Goldberg, that his country would strive to return the West Bank to Jordan, and the United States continued to tell Israel in private that it expected a "virtually complete withdrawal."[10] Nevertheless, Israel immediately offered a different interpretation, namely, that secure boundaries were the key to any peace and that this would require significant rather than minor revisions of the 1949 armistice lines. This position was later supported by Goldberg who argued that "the resolution does not insist on only 'minor border rectifications,' " a statement that is legally correct but that differs in its assumptions from the American position he defended at the time and that was held also by Great Britain, France, and the Soviet Union.[11] Finally, Eshkol issued a statement shortly after the approval of Resolution 242 insisting on direct negotiations, a stance that rejected the negotiating framework established by the document. The role of the U.N. negotiator, Gunnar Jarring of Sweden, was to be confined to attaining the Arabs' agreement to such talks.

The negotiating climate was hardly propitious. Egypt reacted to Eshkol's statement by arguing that Jarring should focus solely on Israeli withdrawal. Syria, which had refused to sign the resolution, openly supported raids by Palestinians who were themselves determined to thwart Jarring's efforts. The reference to "a just settlement of the refugee problem" threatened to establish the Palestinian question as a nonpolitical issue, denying the PLO the sovereignty it claimed over its former homeland. These Arab positions in turn reinforced the arguments of those Israelis who called for the retention of the territory as security buffers because the Arabs would never agree to peace. The stage was set for further confrontation as the United States began to withdraw from active involvement in the region. Lyndon Johnson's last major act was to promise Eshkol in January 1968 that the United States would furnish Israel with Phantom jets, adding to the grant of Skyhawk aircraft promised in October 1967, thus giving Israel clear air superiority in the area.[12] The Tet offensive in Vietnam in February 1968 led to Johnson's decision in March not to run for reelection. The presidential election campaign, in which both candidates declared full support for Israel, precluded any likelihood of diplomacy in the Middle East.[13] American initiatives now awaited the installation of the new president, Richard Nixon, in January 1969.

WARS OF ATTRITION AND THEIR INTERNAL REPERCUSSIONS: JORDAN, LEBANON, THE PALESTINIANS, AND ISRAEL

In the midst of Arab and Israeli efforts to define their terms of diplomatic engagement, Palestinian groups reevaluated the means by which they could overcome Israel and regain control of Palestine. Yasir Arafat advocated the inauguration of a war of liberation from within the newly occupied West Bank, assuming that Fatah could mobilize great support among the million Palestinians now suddenly brought under Israeli rule. He entered the West Bank in July 1967 to direct the effort which failed to arouse mass response, due to effective Israeli retaliation and intelligence efforts and the unwillingness of most Palestinians there to adopt such tactics.[14]

Fatah's failure in the West Bank led to a marriage of convenience between Arafat and King Husayn. Both feared that Israel was about to annex the area. Husayn preferred diplomacy. He pursued a peace accord through the United States and through private contacts with Israeli leaders, but he could not accept the direct negotiations that the Israelis demanded in light of existing political tensions. Husayn therefore decided to tolerate Fatah's assaults on Israeli positions on the West Bank and into Israel itself when possible, seeing it as a means of discouraging Israel from retaining the land. This course helped him in Jordan, where many of his Palestinian subjects sympathized with the guerrillas much more than did their brethren on the West Bank. The problem was that Husayn intended to use Arafat but to control Fatah, assuming he could discard the group if he reached an agreement with Israel. Conversely, Arafat and Fatah hoped to use Jordan as a springboard for continued raids into Israel and Israeli-held territory, expanding the scope of their acts and the violence of the confrontation. Once started, Husayn found it increasingly difficult to restrict Fatah's activities or those of other groups that began to emerge.

Israeli reprisals into the Jordanian East Bank began in February 1968, seeking, as in the 1950s, to force Husayn to quell the resistance. But now the situation was different, because this time there were organized groups to rally the Palestinians from the camps to their cause. A massive Israeli response against the Jordanian town of al-Karamah in February met with stiff Palestinian opposition, staffed mainly by Fatah and aided by Jordanian artillery. Though technically a defeat for the Palestinians, they stood their ground and inflicted numerous casualties on the Israelis. Karamah became a great propaganda victory for Fatah. Recruits flocked to join, just as they did following further Israeli raids which often resulted in civilian casualties, as in the towns of Irbid and Salt. As time went on, Fatah and rival groups began to take over control of the refugee camps in Jordan, removing them from Husayn's authority.

Fatah's numerical preeminence seldom enabled it to control the resistance, as the movement became increasingly fragmented. A major rival had emerged in December 1967 with the creation of the Popular Front for the Liberation of Palestine (PFLP) under Dr. George Habash.[15] Sympathetic to the Pan-Arab nationalism of the 1950s, Habash had directed a Palestinian-dominated group called the Arab National Movement during much of the 1960s. He now formed the PFLP with Ahmad Jibril who, unlike Habash, had good relations with the Syrian Baathist leadership. Habash was imprisoned by the Syrians for much of 1968 while seeking Damascus's approval for raids from Syrian territory. During the year three factions split from the PFLP. Jibril formed his own group, backed by Syria, and another faction received Egyptian assistance. Finally, many of the younger members of the PFLP broke with Habash in early 1969 to follow Nayif Hawatmah in creating the Popular Democratic Front for the Liberation of Palestine (PDFLP).

The differences among these groups were both ideological and tactical. Fatah, led by Arafat, was composed primarily of Sunni Muslims who focused their attention on the recovery of Palestine. Arafat stressed that the Palestinians should not become involved in Arab state rivalries. Habash and Hawatmah were Christians. Habash sought to form a broad Arab revolutionary front that would radicalize the regimes of the Arab world as the first step toward the liberation of Palestine. Hawatmah agreed but saw himself as more truly imbued with Marxist-Leninist principles than Habash was. Factionalism became endemic in the Palestinian movement, with intra-Palestinian rivalries manipulated by Arab states. Because the Syrians backed Hawatmah as well as Jibril, and Nasser helped another, Ali Zarur, Habash turned to Iraq for financial assistance, a pattern that has continued, although the specific alliances have often changed; Fatah has consistently sought to maintain contacts with all regimes.

These disputes became implanted in the structure of the Palestine Liberation Organization itself. Ahmad al-Shuqayri had been forced to resign as its head at the end of 1967. During a year of interim leadership, the PLO decided to absorb the commando groups by giving them membership on the Palestine National Council. Fatah gained the most seats, and at the National Congress held in February 1969, Arafat was elected head of the PLO. Fatah held 33 of the 57 seats allotted to the commandos, out of a total of 105. Fatah's strength reflected its size relative to smaller units and its ability to gain the support of other members, but Arafat's ability to dominate the organization was and has been severely circumscribed.[16] A particular problem was the hostility of Habash's PFLP to Arafat and Fatah. The former was determined to pursue his course of overthrowing conservative Arab monarchs, regardless of the opposition of the majority of the PLO. In the view of a colleague of Arafat's,

> it wasn't that we didn't want to [get rid of the PFLP]. But it was practically impossible to unify the commando organizations when each one of them was supported and subsidized by one or another Arab country whose causes and quarrels they espoused. That is why the Central Committee of the Palestinian Resistance, instead of being a coordinating and decision-making body, turned out to be a sort of parliament where all the conflicts and intrigues of the Arab world were reflected. Yasir Arafat, speaking for more than half the Fidayin members, had to deal as an equal with the delegate of a tiny group just because the latter was the protégé of one of the richest Arab states [Iraq]. That's how difficult, if not impossible, it was to enforce even a minimum of discipline at the very heart of the movement.[17]

Coordination of activities within the PLO seemed impossible despite the call in the revised charter, issued in 1968, that different groups submerge their identities to unite in a common struggle to liberate Palestine. What often mattered most was the nature of Palestinian militancy, stressed in the 1968 charter which declared that "armed struggle was the only means to liberate Palestine," to be accomplished through commando actions. Armed struggle was a strategy not a tactic to be discarded if diplomacy seemed preferable. This emphasis on conflict, along with a deemphasis on the Palestinian question as part of the search for Arab unity, marked the change between the 1964 and 1968 charters, along with a refusal to grant citizenship to any Jew who had lived in Palestine (or descendants) after the Balfour Declaration.[18] This uncoordinated militancy by groups seeking to vie with one another for prestige within the movement placed greater pressure on Israel to respond not only against Jordan but also against Lebanon where Palestinian groups were seeking to expand their activities.

The Lebanese had long avoided involvement in the Arab-Israeli conflict, but from 1968 onward, various groups inside and outside the PLO tried to establish a new front in southern Lebanon for attacks on Israel or rocket barrages from Lebanese territory. At the same time, rival factions within the PFLP began to use Lebanon as a base for hijacking operations. Jibril oversaw the hijacking of an El Al plane (Israeli) to Algiers in July, perhaps seeking to acquire prestige against both Arafat and his supposed ally, Habash, who was still in prison. In December, Habash ordered an attack on an El Al plane in Athens in which two were killed. In response, Israeli forces landed at the Beirut airport the same month and destroyed thirteen planes belonging to Arab airlines. Israel announced that it held the Lebanese government responsible for tolerating PFLP activities.[19] But Israel's action, a classic Ben-Gurionist response of massive if selective retaliation designed to teach the Lebanese government a lesson, again had the opposite effect. It aroused an uproar sufficient to force the collapse of the government and cause civil strife as differing Lebanese groups either backed or opposed support for the Palestinians. From this point onward, the question of the Palestinians became part of the question of Lebanese society with all its confessional splits and rivalries.

Most Maronite Catholics opposed Palestinian activities. Lebanon had had correct relations with Israel until then. But most Muslims sympathized with the Palestinians, who numbered 14 percent of the total population in 1968 and who had never been permitted to become incorporated into Lebanese society. This sympathy reflected the general Muslim feeling that they too were deprived of rights due them by their numbers but continually unrecognized by the Maronite hierarchy which sought to preserve its long-standing dominance.[20] Throughout much of 1969, Lebanese military and security forces confronted Palestinian groups and sought to restrict their actions in the midst of growing domestic strife, the onset of tensions that remained unresolved until they exploded into true civil war in 1975. The immediate crisis was overcome only after intervention by Nasser and the signing of the "Cairo Agreement" between Arafat and the Lebanese government, marking significant concessions granted to the PLO.

While the Palestinian leader recognized Lebanese sovereignty and promised to respect it, the government granted the PLO autonomy in controlling the refugee camps that had previously been supervised by Lebanese security forces. Lebanon also gave the PLO specific routes of access to the Israeli frontier, attempting thereby to limit its actions but being unable to block them totally. Syrian supply lines to the groups in southern Lebanon were also accepted. In return for a *modus vivendi*, Lebanon decided to look the other way, but the result was intensified Maronite opposition accompanied by the expansion of paramilitary groups outside government control that prepared to confront the Palestinians.[21]

By the end of 1969, Israel faced greatly increased PLO activity on both the Jordanian and Lebanese borders in circumstances in which its clear military superiority and ability to retaliate in force sparked increased support for the Palestinians and seemed to undermine rather than strengthen both governments' ability to control the attacks. At the same time, the Meir cabinet was deciding to try to destroy Nasser, a tack that resulted in a massive infusion of Soviet personnel into Egypt that served to neutralize the Egyptian-Israeli frontier along the Suez Canal.

DIPLOMACY AND THE WARS OF ATTRITION: EGYPT AND ISRAEL, 1968–1970

The degree of intensity of the Egyptian-Israeli confrontation along the Suez Canal often indicated the combatants' desires to influence the actions of their sponsors, the Soviet Union and the United States. In turn, each great power experienced internal rivalries as different branches of government tried to determine the nature of the support that should be offered to its client. Israel was resolved to maintain its vaunted military superiority in the region, not just over Egypt, through continuing arms sales from the United States. Skyhawk jets had begun arriving in 1968, and Phantom jets, promised that summer, became available in September 1969. American officials tried to control the flow of weapons, hoping to pressure Israel to be more flexible in its negotiating stance in return for arms grants. Israel attempted to reverse the nature of the exchange, demanding arms before professing to agree to any diplomatic initiatives, which it interpreted in terms that differed substantially from those of the Nixon administration, which took office in January 1969. A fundamental contradiction thus emerged in the American-Israeli relationship, in that Israel sought arms to secure the territorial status quo it had achieved until the Arab states submitted to its conditions which entailed substantial border revisions. The United States hoped to use these promises of arms to gain Israeli concessions that far exceeded what Israel was willing to consider. In these circumstances, Israel's ability to use its supporters in Congress and pressure groups to modify or preempt administration policies often proved successful.

Egypt, on the other hand, refused to negotiate from weakness, precisely those terms that Israel strove to impose. Nasser restored and upgraded Egypt's military forces. By October 1968, Egypt's military supplies were superior in quality and quantity to those it had possessed on the eve of the 1967 war.[22] The Egyptians were determined to establish a military standoff so costly that Israel would find it preferable to withdraw and settle on Egypt's terms. Nasser, under intense Soviet pressure, had agreed to Resolution 242. He responded to Jarring's overtures in early 1968 by proposing that in return for an Israeli withdrawal to the prewar armistice lines, both sides would "deposit with the U.N. a declaration concerning an end to the state of war, respect for and recognition of sovereignty, territorial integrity, and the independence of each government in the given territory and their right to live in peace in secure and recognized borders; concomitantly, other measures would be discussed for resolving disputed questions."[23] This offer gave Israel indirect rather than formal recognition through third-party rather than direct negotiations. Israel rejected it. It sought full peace negotiated by the two governments while keeping some land; Egypt offered a peace sponsored by the United Nations in return for all the land. The promise of a continuing stalemate led Nasser and his advisers to see military confrontation as the best means to achieve political goals, namely, better negotiating terms through American or great power intervention to stop the fighting.

Although the term *war of attrition* has usually been applied to the period between March 1969 and August 1970, intermittent clashes had begun much earlier. In September 1968 the Egyptians initiated a new round of artillery duels with Israeli forces, hoping to arouse renewed diplomatic interest at the United Nations. These tactics failed politically and militarily. No U.N. response ensued, and Israel reacted by raiding deeper into Egypt and by accelerating the construction of a massive fortification along its side of the canal, the Bar-Lev line. This in turn led the Egyptians to undertake a more extended war of attrition. They hoped to weaken the Israeli defenses through intensive artillery barrages, creating conditions conducive to an attack across the canal that would establish a limited bridgehead. The war and Egyptian gains would compel the great powers to intercede to stop the fighting, thus opening the way for diplomacy to deal with the newly created circumstances, precisely what happened in 1973. Egypt inaugurated this policy in March 1969. By July, Egypt's protective air defense missile systems as well as its heavy weapons had been wiped out. Israel then moved at will from July to December with full air superiority, apparently placing Egypt at its mercy. But it was precisely at this moment, in response to diplomatic initiatives, that Israel undertook more extensive military measures that finally negated its advantage.[24]

Throughout 1969, Egyptian-Israeli hostilities had been accompanied by ongoing talks between the Soviet Union and the United States. They were intended to create agreement on conditions for an Egyptian-Israeli cease-fire and subsequent negotiations that might attain a full peace accord. These efforts resulted in a proposal by Secretary of State William Rogers, announced on 9 December, that was rejected immediately by Israel and later by Russia; the Egyptians indicated their displeasure but refrained from outright repudiation.[25]

Roger's terms reflected assumptions found in the majority interpretation of Resolution 242: nearly full Israeli withdrawal in return for an indirectly negotiated mutual recognition of sovereignty. This infuriated the Israelis. The cabinet of Golda Meir decided immediately to escalate the war with Egypt by inaugurating deep penetration bombing raids far beyond the limits imposed until then. They were designed to humiliate Nasser and to force him either to capitulate on Israel's terms or to resign in disgrace because he had been proved incapable of conducting Egypt's affairs. These tactics were also intended to forestall further American initiatives by getting rid of the Egyptian leader with whom the Americans intended to negotiate. Meir and the majority of her cabinet chose this course with the encouragement of the Israeli ambassador in Washington, Yitzhak Rabin, who reported that American officials had made it known to him they would not oppose Israeli efforts on their behalf to eradicate the Egyptian military machine and indirectly humiliate the Soviets.[26] These raids, which sometimes caused extensive civilian casualties, produced results contrary to Israel's expectations. In desperation Nasser went to Moscow, asking not only for weapons but also for Soviet combat personnel and technicians. After some hesitation, the Soviets complied, gaining in return new rights regarding control of air fields and other installations. By mid-March 1970, new and extensive emplacements of advanced SAM missiles were operational, and Soviet pilots were flying missions. The Israelis' policy had backfired. Their forces were once more restricted to the canal zone area where their air force suffered significant losses during the summer.

This sudden infusion of Soviet military forces into Egypt sparked new diplomatic initiatives by Rogers, though with more limited objectives than his initial proposals for a package settlement had had. He suggested a cease-fire that included a memorandum of understanding that both parties agreed to Security Council Resolution 242 as the basis of negotiations, with a specific reference to "Israeli withdrawal from territories occupied in the 1967 conflict." Egypt and Jordan accepted the Rogers note, but the Israelis rejected it outright, only to have Ambassador Rabin refuse to deliver the message.[27] The Meir cabinet objected to an open acceptance of Resolution 242 and feared that a cease-fire might lead to an American decision to scale back its arms shipments. Israel accepted the Rogers offer only under duress and after Nixon had assured Meir that American military support would continue and that the United States would not back calls for Israel's withdrawal to the prewar lines of 4 June 1967, a stance that meant very different boundaries as conceived by the Americans and the Israelis. Even then, Israel's acceptance was costly. Members of the Gahal party, led by Menachem Begin, resigned from the Meir cabinet in protest at Israeli acknowledgment of the principle of its withdrawal from territory before peace terms had been established with the Arab states. Israeli acceptance of the cease-fire marked the first time the government had publicly declared its willingness to withdraw from any territory taken in 1967.

Military assertiveness had resulted in an Israeli political setback, whereas

Nasser had gained a respite that enabled him to consolidate his missile defense systems. In addition, American intervention gave him room for maneuver, opening lines of communication with the United States that might free him from total reliance on Soviet diplomatic efforts. But his intentions were misinterpreted by Washington, as most officials viewed the Middle East conflict more in terms of an American-Soviet rivalry than as a series of disputes stemming from regional antagonisms.

INTERNATIONAL DIPLOMACY AND DOMESTIC INTRIGUE: THE NIXON ADMINISTRATION AND THE ROGERS PLANS, 1968–1970

Richard Nixon's accession to the presidency in January 1969 brought a renewed intensity to the pursuit of diplomatic objectives throughout the world. Nixon, and his national security adviser, Henry Kissinger, were deeply troubled by Soviet power and decided to challenge, whenever possible, Moscow's position in strategically sensitive areas. Yet although determined to confront Russia, their stance was part of a broader policy designed to offer the Soviets advantages and closer relations if they were persuaded, in the administrations's view, to abandon their hostile behavior. The Nixon–Kissinger approach sought therefore to balance areas of détente and confrontation, using the latter to promote the former in areas of trade and general diplomatic cooperation.[28]

With regard to the Middle East, détente seemed circumscribed by competing views within the administration. Rogers and the State Department believed that cooperation with the Soviets had merit if each could bring its satellite to the bargaining table. Rogers pursued this concept with particular vigor because it was the only region where he and the State Department had been permitted to initiate policy, Nixon and Kissinger reserving other areas for themselves. Kissinger was not one to remove himself from any policymaking sphere, however. He believed that Rogers's suppositions were badly flawed. Serious efforts to achieve an accord in the Middle East should await a time when the United States could dominate the negotiating process and exclude the Soviets, a scenario that assumed that Egypt would turn away totally from the latter when it realized that it could achieve an Israeli pullback only by relying on the Americans.[29] Beyond this question of policy was another issue, Kissinger's desire to amass control of all aspects of diplomacy, which led him automatically to denigrate approaches he had not proposed. This was a matter principally of Kissinger's ego, attested to by his slightly contemptuous references to Rogers and by the accounts of others who had contact with both at the time.[30]

Given the circumstances, the prospects for success seemed slight, with many opportunities for foes of Rogers's efforts to undermine him. The United States undertook discussions on two levels during 1969. One was a four-way dialogue that included France and Great Britain along with the Soviet Union. The other and more important framework was a series of meetings held between the

Americans and the Soviets to seek to reach accord on a proposal that each would present to its ally. These talks were conducted by Joseph Sisco, assistant secretary of state for Near East and South Asian affairs, and Anatoly Dobrynin, the Soviet ambassador in Washington, with the Israelis informed of developments and becoming increasingly alarmed in the process. Rogers had already referred positively to Resolution 242 and had stressed that border alterations in any peace settlement should "not reflect the weight of conquest," meaning that they should be minor. Equally unsettling was an American proposal for talks between Israel and Jordan in addition to the envisaged Egyptian-Israeli negotiations that would occur under U.N. auspices. Here the American position foresaw nearly total Israeli withdrawal from the West Bank and joint Jordanian-Israeli administration of Jerusalem.

The Israelis saw it differently. Israel held an election campaign during the fall of 1969, and the Labor Party was forced to present its terms for settlement to the people. The Meir-led party committed itself to retain the Golan Heights, Sharm al-Shaykh, and Gaza along with undisclosed areas of the West Bank, a stance that reflected the divisions within the party as to how much of that area should be returned to Jordan. Jerusalem was declared nonnegotiable.[31] With that platform in the open, Israel began a campaign to undercut the American-Soviet talks whose assumptions contradicted its declared intentions to keep Arab lands. Ambassador Rabin and Foreign Minister Abba Eban learned quickly to deal with Kissinger rather than Rogers while also mobilizing backers in Congress. Their impression that they could discount the secretary of state was reinforced when Nixon established "a special channel between Kissinger and Rabin to sidestep the State Department" in September.[32] Kissinger himself downplayed the significance of the negotiations while working to establish his own relationship with Israeli officials, intending to maneuver them toward talks in the future on his own terms.

Why, then, did Rogers announce the draft publicly on 9 December and as an American initiative, given the known opposition to it, including by now the Soviet Union?[33] He did so apparently to preempt a National Security Council meeting headed by Kissinger that was scheduled for 10 December and that might well have proposed scrapping the negotiations. His decision indicated the nature of intraadministration rivalries more than diplomatic calculations.[34] Once Rogers presented the American terms for an Egyptian-Israeli agreement on 9 December, Israel rejected them on the tenth. American U.N. representative Charles Yost announced the draft of a Jordanian-Israeli agreement, approved by Nixon, on 18 December, and Israel rejected that on the twenty-second, followed closely at this point by the Soviet Union which declared the terms unacceptable. Nixon, anticipating domestic pressure from Israel's supporters, had sent word to Golda Meir that he would not push the policy outlined by Rogers, even before the Jordanian-Israeli formula, which he approved, had been announced.[35] This fiasco culminated in Rabin's pressing Meir to embark on the deep penetration raids into Egypt that in turn brought about a massive Soviet presence in Egypt that led to renewed American pressure for the cease-fire achieved in August. Rabin had assumed U.S. acquiescence in the raids because of conversations he had with various officials, especially Joseph Sisco, the very person who was conducting the parleys with the Soviets but whose eagerness to please various patrons seemed to outweigh his diplomatic talents.[36]

The lessons to be learned from American diplomatic efforts between 1968 and 1970 lasted, along with the contradictions inherent in the United States' approach to the Middle East. Attempts to gain a packaged settlement including Jordan and Egypt along with Israel had failed. This suggested that attainment of limited agreements made between Israel and individual Arab states might prove more successful. Israel and the United States continued on different tracks, each trying to bring the other into line. The Americans, especially Kissinger, who remained in charge of foreign policy until 1976, were determined to seek Israeli concessions, but only after those Arab leaders with ties to Russia, such as Nasser, realized they should abandon the Soviets and rely solely on the United States. In Kissinger's view, "Arab leaders would, I thought, have to come to us in the end."[37] From its perspective, Israel hoped to prevent any great power intervention, including that of the United States, so that it could force Arab capitulation in circumstances in which its territorial gains could be maximized. By the time the cease-fire came in August 1970, most American officials, including Kissinger, believed that Israel had been unnecessarily obstructive, but developments elsewhere in the region soon changed that view. By October Nixon and his chief adviser considered Israel to be a full ally, a development that encouraged Kissinger to ignore Egyptian actions that met the terms he had supposedly defined.

JORDAN AND THE PALESTINIANS, AUGUST–SEPTEMBER 1970

If the Israeli government was upset at the cease-fire established by the United States, the groups that comprised the PLO were horrified that Nasser and Husayn had signed the agreement. Here there arose a symbiotic relationship between Israel and the Palestinians that has lasted, each refusing to recognize the other and each bent on denying the other control over at the least the West Bank, at most Israel. Both dreaded peace plans that might undermine their positions, but from differing vantage points. Israel feared outside intervention that might force it to give up territory that it felt essential, either for security reasons or, for many, because the West Bank was part of ancient Israel, the provinces of Judea and Samaria. The Palestinians watched for signs of any willingness to reach a peace agreement on the part of their Arab sponsors, as that accord would probably refer to the refugee problem and not to rights of Palestinian self-government. From this perspective, Husayn and even Nasser were caught, at times, between the Israeli hammer and the Palestinian anvil, apparently willing to abandon the latter but presenting conditions that continued to be unacceptable to the former. For many Palestinians, however, the message was clear. The cease-fire should be destroyed if possible, and the means to do so existed in Jordan. Habash and Hawatmah now decided to overthrow King Husayn.

Palestinian-Jordanian tensions had long been strained. PLO forays into the Israeli-held West Bank had accomplished little and had resulted in Israeli retaliations that caused many civilian casualties and damaged Jordan's economic infrastructure. What Arafat ultimately hoped for, the destruction of Israel, was to Husayn a fantasy, and what Arafat might conceivably settle for, the West Bank, was unacceptable to the king. Husayn wanted the West Bank for himself and at most would permit Palestinian autonomy under the cloak of Jordanian sovereignty. Likewise, the PLO demanded a degree of tolerance in Jordan that Husayn found increasingly untenable. The PLO sought a secure base of operations, "a place where the revolutionaries [had] complete control and authority," which naturally meant a corresponding decrease of government legitimacy.[38] Quarrels had erupted on several occasions, most notably in June 1970 when animosity between Palestinian groups and Husayn's Arab Legion led to armed clashes and the PFLP's taking of many Westerners as hostages in tourist hotels that the group commandeered. They were released only after Husayn agreed to realign his cabinet in accordance with Habash's demands, a humiliation not likely to be forgotten. This encounter was part of a larger context in which most Palestinian fedayeen acted as the rulers in Jordan, flouting Jordanian laws and intimidating the citizenry at will.

With the cease-fire declared in August, Arafat and a majority of the PLO prevaricated, unwilling to confront Husayn directly but equally unwilling to challenge the PFLP and the PDFLP, who called for Husayn's overthrow. Matters came to a head when the PFLP hijacked four airliners between 6 and 9 September, forcing three of them to land at an air field twenty miles from Husayn's palace. Husayn once more capitulated to ensure the safey of the hostages, but once they were released and the planes were blown up, he turned against the Palestinians. The civil war began on 16 September. It included pitched battles between Jordanian troops and most Palestinian groups, and Jordanian shelling of the refugee camps where the various organizations had their offices. Over three thousand were killed and over eleven thousand wounded, the majority Palestinians and many of them civilians, before the conflict finally ended on 25 September in a clear military victory for the Jordanians.

Husayn's triumph had not come easily. He had faced a Syrian tank invasion in support of the Palestinians that had early successes before his forces repulsed it. And he had borne the censure of other Arab leaders who strove to preserve the Palestinian resistance without causing Husayn's overthrow in the bargain. Intense negotiations ensued among Arab heads of state as Nasser attempted to contain the struggle. As a result of Arab-sponsored compromises, Husayn was forced to accept the principle of PLO leadership of the Palestinians, presumably denying him the right of sovereignty over most of his subjects, an agreement he shied away from observing. And in the process, exhausted by the strain of negotiations, Gamal Abd al-Nasser collapsed and died on 28 September 1970.

Sparked by ongoing factional disputes and regional tensions, the Jordanian crisis instigated considerations of great power competition that redounded to Israel's benefit. Once the fighting erupted, Nixon declared that American intervention might be required and called for a show of force by the Sixth Fleet in the Eastern Mediterranean. But the Syrian tank strike called Nixon's hand with troubling implications: "U.S. military maneuvers were designed primarily to convey signals to the USSR, . . .not to intervene directly in the fighting." American face was saved by Israeli promises of intervention on Husayn's behalf. He committed his air force to attacks against the tank column only after assurances of supporting Israeli air strikes if requested. Israeli compliance "helped protect the United States from having its bluff exposed as a rather empty one."[39] In the end a regional confrontation had been resolved satisfactorily for Husayn, Israel, and the United States, whose leaders were pleased at what they believed to be the defeat of Soviet-sponsored unrest. Israel's offer of cooperation enhanced its image as an anticommunist ally, pushing into the background its obstructionist reputation regarding regional peace proposals. Nixon and Kissinger now pushed for arms shipments to Israel which could be used to counter envisioned Soviet-encouraged machinations while the United States committed most of its resources to Vietnam.

THE JORDANIAN CRISIS: REGIONAL AND
INTERNATIONAL REPERCUSSIONS

For those directly involved in Arab-Israeli hostilities, the significance of the Jordanian civil war went far beyond the cessation of combat. The PLO had suffered a major setback that finally forced all Palestinian organizations to withdraw from Jordan after a renewed flare-up of fighting in July 1971. They moved to Lebanon where their appearance in force further destabilized that country's domestic politics while embroiling it ever more directly in the conflict. Fatah–PFLP antagonisms over tactics continued, but even elements of Fatah now embarked on terrorist missions against Israelis abroad. The most famous was that undertaken by the Black September group, named after the September 1970 Jordanian affair, in which it took eleven Israeli athletes hostage at the 1972 Olympic games in Munich. All, along with many of their Palestinian captors, were killed, most during an abortive attempt by German forces to kill the Palestinians and rescue the Israelis. But Black September operations during the Olympics were only the most visible signs of a continuing war in which Palestinian groups sought to assassinate Israelis abroad and Israeli agents and commandos retaliated in kind. Here Lebanon again became the focal point of Israeli punitive raids. Air strikes and armed incursions into southern Lebanon against PLO positions began to occur more frequently, resulting in many civilian as well as guerrilla dead and wounded. During 1973, Israeli squads landed near Beirut and assassinated three Fatah officials in their apartments. Other PLO officials were killed and wounded by car and letter bombs, indicating that Israeli agents could operate in Beirut with relative impunity. At the same time, PLO rocket attacks into northern Israel from Lebanon continued, with occasional casualties among the population of the northern settlements.

Not the least among the ironies related to the concentration of the PLO in Lebanon was the appearance in November 1970 of a new head of state in Syria, Hafiz al-Assad. Assad had sponsored the Syrian backing of Fatah and Arafat in 1965, but as president he sought to control Arafat, using the Syrian-supported Palestinian militia, al-Saiqa, against Fatah and other groups when necessary and refusing to allow PLO operations from Syria against Israel. Assad's attempts to regulate PLO actions out of fear that the Palestinians might draw the Syrians into an unplanned conflict with Israel greatly exacerbated Syrian-Palestinian tensions. Conversely, Assad tried to restore relations between Syria and its former rivals, Egypt, Jordan, and Saudi Arabia, eschewing the confrontational style of his predecessor, Salah Jadid.[40]

For Egypt, Nasser's sudden death inaugurated a series of changes that gradually led his successor, Anwar al-Sadat, to seek an accommodation with the United States regarding Israel. Much of Sadat's motivation was economic. Nasser's state capitalism had become mired in inefficiency in the mid-1960s. The 1967 conflict and the subsequent war of attrition undermined Egypt's economic health still further.[41] Sadat hoped to break both the diplomatic deadlock and Egypt's economic stagnation by appearing more forthcoming in negotiations and seeking American financial assistance in the process.

American policymakers remained divided, however. Most considered Sadat a neophyte whose tenure as head of Egypt might be short. Rogers and the State Department continued to prod U.N. Ambassador Gunnar Jarring's attempt to implement Resolution 242 through mid-1971, at which point Jarring abandoned his efforts. Kissinger continued to criticize Rogers and Jarring to Nixon and to the Israelis through Ambassador Rabin. American initiatives were often uncoordinated, the State Department and Kissinger undertaking inquiries without informing the other.[42]

Jarring withdrew from the negotiating process following his failure to get Israel to agree with Egypt to "parallel and simultaneous commitments" that might settle their differences. He asked Israel in February 1971 to agree to withdraw to the pre-1967 borders in return for security arrangements that included extensive demilitarization of the Sinai and U.N. forces at Sharm al-Shaykh; Israel would also receive freedom of navigation through the Suez Canal. He asked Egypt to enter a peace agreement with Israel that included an end of belligerency and respect for Israel's independence and right to exist in secure boundaries. Sadat responded quickly, agreeing to all terms and adding others, which included settlement of the refugee problem in accordance with U.N. resolutions, a position indicating that he had broken with the stances taken by the PLO and at the Khartoum Conference. Israel then rejected Sadat's terms, refusing to withdraw to prewar lines and insisting on direct negotiations without prior conditions; the Meir cabinet was determined to retain at least Sharm al-Shaykh and a strip of land connecting it to Israel. Suspicious of Rogers, who backed the Jarring initiative, the Meir cabinet attempted to undermine him in favor of Kissinger and refused to accept a negotiating process mediated by a third party.[43]

At year's end, American-Israeli relations were closer than ever. Kissinger had gradually taken over control of Middle East policy, at Nixon's behest, to create a positive climate conducive to the latter's reelection campaign. Part of Nixon's campaign strategy was to divert Jewish votes from the Democrats by appearing supportive of Israel. Kissinger "assured Rabin that plane deliveries would continue and that State Department pressure would stop."[44] Rabin, in turn, openly backed Nixon's candidacy. At the same time the Nixon administration took advantage of Israel's popularity in Congress to place funding requests for recipients such as South Korea, Taiwan, and Cambodia on Israeli assistance bills.[45] The White House had no intention of concerning itself with the Middle East until after the 1972 elections.

THE 1973 WAR AND ITS CONSEQUENCES

THE ARABS AND THE 1973 WAR: SEEKING RESPONSES TO SIGNALS

Kissinger's assumption of Middle East policy in early 1972 did not signify total disinterest in that arena. Rather, he decided to incorporate it within his concept of linkage, seeking Soviet agreement on principles for future approaches to the region but forgoing specific overtures until after Nixon's reelection in November. He and the Soviets reached a private agreement on principles in the spring of 1972 that closely resembled the Jarring package that Sadat had accepted and the Israelis rebuffed in February 1971. But these talks remained private, save for a joint communiqué in May that proclaimed support for the pursuit of peaceful coexistence and, regarding the Middle East, for Resolution 242 and the Jarring mission. Though ostensibly threatening to Israeli positions, it was Egypt that reacted angrily. Sadat did not know of the Soviet talks with Kissinger. Already frustrated with delays in receiving arms supplies from Moscow, in contrast with American shipments to Israel, Sadat and his advisers believed that the Soviets were allying themselves with the United States to maintain the status quo in the region. From the Egyptian perspective, this put them at a disadvantage, given ongoing American aid to Israel. And it was particularly embarrassing to Sadat, who had been proclaiming since 1971 that the "year of decision" was at hand, threatening a new war in order to compel new diplomatic efforts that moved the situation off center. Sadat's military command had already complained about the Soviet refusal to give the Egyptians more leeway. And Sadat knew from various

American channels that the United States demanded the expulsion of the Soviets before moving to attain peace in the Middle East.

On 8 July Sadat ordered that Russian advisers and military personnel leave Egypt within one week, a move that caught Washington as well as Moscow totally by surprise. Sadat acted for domestic as well as diplomatic reasons, seeking to mollify his military while still sending a message to Washington that its terms had been met. The timing, amidst an American election campaign, meant that Egypt did not expect an immediate response but that Cairo antici-pated an American iniative once the elections were over. Sadat received assur-ances of this from Kissinger through private channels. But no such undertaking occurred, although Kissinger did meet privately twice in early 1973 with Sadat's security adviser, Hafiz Ismail, arousing expectations that were not fulfilled. By this time Kissinger was on the verge of running the entire government, not simply its foreign policy. The scandal of the Watergate break-in was beginning to isolate Nixon from other matters, leaving in limbo most diplomacy other than Vietnam.

Kissinger assumed that the Middle East stalemate would last. His com-placency increased the Egyptians' determination to force the issue and finally convinced the Soviets to give Sadat the arms he desired. From February 1973 onward, the Soviets began supplying Egypt with offensive weaponry and the means of countering Israeli air strikes that they had withheld previously out of fear of encouraging an Egyptian attack. Moscow's decision to reverse its course apparently stemmed from the realization that the United States would not undertake any corrective diplomacy following the elections. This undercut the faction that supported détente and provided justification for those, notably in the Soviet military, who called for renewed arms supplies as a means of establishing a more militant posture toward the United States.[46]

Kissinger misjudged also the circumstances in which other Arab leaders, not only Sadat, found themselves regarding the impasse existing in the region. Of particular importance was the role of Saudi Arabia, long close to the United States and seeking its protection against any threat of communist subversion. The Saudis agreed with Kissinger that the Soviets should be excluded totally from the region, but they disagreed as to the role that American support of Israel contributed to the success of that policy. Here also Saudi leaders became increasingly agitated about the continuing Israeli dominance of Jerusalem, a holy city to Islam and one that the Saudis, as the declared true practitioners of the faith, were determined to have returned to Muslim control. Once it became clear during 1973 that the United States might not act to break the Arab-Israeli deadlock, representatives of King Faysal began to warn American officials, as did Sadat, that war might erupt. The Saudis were also willing to consider, if reluctantly, the threat of another weapon to use against the United States, namely, a cutback in oil production that could seriously affect America's energy supplies.

American policymakers did not believe that Egypt and the Saudis could achieve a rapprochment and considered the likelihood of an energy pinch improbable. But here a conjunction of factors created an unforeseen crisis. The Organization of Petroleum Exporting Countries (OPEC) had been formed in 1960 to create a common front to achieve higher prices and a greater share of the profits for the producing countries, but OPEC had little success until the end of the decade. Then increasing demand and radical politics led gradually to greater assertiveness by the oil states and greater willingness by the oil companies to reach agreements more beneficial to the former. Libya's Muammar al-Qadhdhafi, who took power in a coup in 1969, led the way in demanding at least 50 percent of the profits and a rise in price per barrel. He was supported in this by his ideological opposite, the shah of Iran, who, as America's ally, needed additional funds to buy the arms America wanted to sell him. Here the Saudis found themselves in the middle, seeking to moderate oil price increases but to gain a greater share in the running of ARAMCO, the oil consortium that controlled production in Arabia.[47]

From 1970 onward, experts began to recognize that the United States was increasingly vulnerable in that its energy consumption and demand far outstripped its domestic production.[48] Unaware of the implications of this and distracted by Nixon's problems, Kissinger viewed Sadat's threat of war and Faysal's linking of oil prices to the Arab-Israeli issue as so much rhetoric. But Sadat was now joined by Syria. Assad also felt that Arab willingness to negotiate had been rebuffed. He had announced his acceptance of Resolution 242 in 1972, with no response. Eager to regain control of the Golan Heights, he now joined Sadat in a concerted effort to create an Arab *fait accompli* and force new diplomatic probes that would achieve terms more favorable to the Arabs.

THE 1973 WAR: ISRAEL AND THE POLITICS OF EXPANSION

Arab frustration was matched by Israeli confidence on the eve of the 1973 war. Dayan declared repeatedly during 1972 and 1973 that he did not envisage a war for the next decade, asserting that the influx of new weapons to Israel would enable it to ensure its qualitative advantage over its Arab neighbors. American support seemed assured, meaning that Israel could reject Arab overtures it did not consider totally acceptable. This in turn enabled the Meir cabinet to avoid a political storm by being forced to commit itself fully to defining the concessions that Israel might make. When Meir had stated in 1971 that Israel would retain the Golan Heights, Sharm al-Shaykh and a connecting road to Israel, and parts of the West Bank with the Sinai demilitarized once returned to Egypt, Begin attacked her for being too lenient.[49] Now there were significant developments as new elections approached, scheduled for November 1973. The Labor Party found itself making a major shift toward annexation of territories it had previously defined as subject to negotiation and at least partial return.

As noted earlier, Israel's continued retention of the territories captured in the 1967 war fostered calls for their absorption into Israel. Groups such as the Greater Land of Israel Movement, cabinet ministers eager to hold certain regions for strategic purposes, and opposition parties such as Menachem Begin's Gahal coalition advocated permanent control of all lands once included in ancient Israel. With such pressure from below and within the cabinet, the Meir government found itself "implementing a policy which a majority of its members opposed" and that the cabinet was on record as rejecting if peace were accessible, especially regarding the Sinai and the West Bank. At the beginning of 1973, forty-four settlements had been installed on the West Bank, the Golan, and in the northern Sinai, and fifty more were scheduled to be created by year's end. Most of these were planned for the Sinai and the West Bank where paramilitary camps (Nahal) supposedly intended as defense outposts would gradually turn into civilian sites. In this way the Allon Plan, envisioning only defense perimeters on the West Bank, was being manipulated to further create facts on the ground for retention of the area.[50] The implications for responses to peace overtures had already emerged in 1972 when King Husayn proposed that the West Bank enter a federation with Jordan following Israel's withdrawal. Allon called it promising, but the Knesset (Israel's parliament) went on record that it "reaffirms and confirms the historic right of the Jewish people over the Land of Israel."[51]

As the 1973 election campaign continued, the Meir cabinet was forced further toward Land of Israel ideology by its minister of defense, Moshe Dayan, who was in charge of the conquered territories. Until this point, no land had been sold to private individuals. Rather, land had been appropriated by the military government of the territories, acting as it had after the 1948 war. It could declare land "abandoned" and did in order to make it available to settlements, especially when Arab owners refused to sell desirable property even under considerable pressure. Now, however, the prospect of private investment in the West Bank arose, encouraged by Dayan to ensure a Jewish presence.[52] Domestic debate, plus an international outcry over policies applied to land supposedly to be returned in case of peace, led Meir finally to back away from Dayan and reject his proposals.

But Dayan was not finished. Still highly popular, he threatened to withdraw from the Labor party in the midst of the election campaign unless it included in its platform recognition of the right of individuals to buy land in the occupied territories with provisions for tax concessions and to provide for the development of industrial centers in heavily settled Arab areas of the West Bank. This plan was also intended to expand Israeli settlements around Jerusalem where a belt suitable for occupation by 100,000 Israelis had already been mapped out, in addition to facilitating extensive acquisition of land by the Israeli Land Authority. In the Sinai, Dayan called for the creation of a new city to be called Yamit in the northeast sector of the peninsula, significantly expanding Israeli control there. Finally, he proposed a partitioning of the Sinai from Eilat west to the Gulf of Suez, a slicing of the peninsula along the eastern coast and its southern third that would have also given Israel permanent control of the oil fields captured from Egypt in 1967.

After much debate and resistance in the cabinet, opposition faded owing to the "political common sense" of the moderates, recognizing that Labor might be threatened if it opposed calls for absorption of Arab lands that seemed to have great popular support.[53] Meir's approval came in the form of the Galili Document, written by her minister without portfolio, which was accepted as the Labor party's program for the occupied areas. Dayan and Galili envisioned these new regions to be settled primarily by incoming Russian Jewish emigrés, which explains in part Israeli eagerness to pressure the Soviet Union on this matter and to seek American political support for this cause.[54] Labor's adoption of this platform effectively nullified its previous declarations regarding Resolution 242 and the territories it would be willing to return in exchange for peace. It angered Sadat and probably encouraged him to attack when he did so as to forestall its ratification by the electorate.[55]

THE 1973 WAR: THE CHANCE FOR DIPLOMACY

The details of the 1973 war can be quickly summarized. Egyptian and Syrian forces attacked Israeli units on 6 October, the Jewish holy day of Yom Kippur and the Muslim anniversary of the Prophet Muhammad's first victory over his Meccan adversaries at the battle of Badr. The war officially ended on 22 October following a second cease-fire agreed upon by all parties, but Israeli efforts to prevent Egypt from realizing its gains led to continued attacks that brought the United States and the Soviet Union to the brink of a nuclear confrontation.[56]

The war itself moved through several stages, from initial Arab victories that shocked and in places overwhelmed Israeli defenders to what amounted to a total Israeli military victory on the Syrian front and a partial triumph along the Suez Canal. On the Golan Heights, Syrian forces were pushed back and more territory added to that taken in 1967. On the Egyptian front, Israeli forces under Ariel Sharon's command crossed the canal and destroyed much Egyptian armor. At war's end Israeli troops were engaged in bitter fighting trying futilely to take the city of Suez. But Egyptian forces still held out in two major pockets along the east bank of the canal, establishing an Egyptian presence in Israeli-held territory. It was this new fact that Kissinger strove to exploit, determined to establish a framework for negotiations that took into account these circumstances and forced Israel to bargain under conditions that denied it the status quo it had maintained for over six years.

Kissinger showed great agility during the war in seeking to establish agreement for diplomacy once the hostilities ended. The Nixon administration assumed a quick Israeli victory once Israel recovered from its opening setbacks, and tried to achieve a cease-fire on 12 October that would preserve some Egyptian gains and set the stage for talks. Israel accepted, but Sadat refused the offer, believing that Egyptian forces could gain the strategic Giddi and Mitla passes. This plan failed as Israeli retaliatory strikes began to drive back Egyptian divisions, leading to the crossing of the canal. Here the Nixon administration decided to release major arms supplies to Israel that it had been withholding deliberately in order to force Israel's acceptance of the 12 October cease-fire. These supplies, and the announcement of a $2.2 billion appropriation for Israel on 19 October, caused Faysal to apply an oil embargo and cut back production. It also encouraged the Israelis to seek a total victory, driving Egyptian forces out of the Sinai. Kissinger, though angered by Sadat's rejection of the first cease-fire offer, still intended to preserve at least a minor Egyptian foothold on the east bank of the canal to create new facts suitable for bargaining and a potential withdrawal of Israeli forces. Kissinger's efforts led to increased American-Israeli and American-Soviet tensions before the 22 October cease-fire was finally implemented with U.N. peacekeeping contingents established in place.[57]

Henry Kissinger, secretary of state since August while also remaining national security adviser, was now in full control of American foreign policy. He believed, in the aftermath of the war, that reliance on Israel's military might to maintain peace in the Middle East had been wrong and that Israeli unwillingness to make concessions had contributed to the outbreak of hostilities. Though appreciating Israel's security concerns, he thought that compromise rather than insistence on unattainable terms better served peace and American interests as well; prolonged stalemate could only aid the Soviets. Kissinger thus strove to establish his and the United States' dominance of the negotiations, through which he hoped to move the Arab-Israeli question toward some resolution.

This meant balancing several issues and considerations at once. Kissinger agreed to a Soviet request that a Geneva Conference be called. He backed the meeting, held for one day in December, in order to give the Soviets the impression he would pursue peace in tandem with them. He then undertook direct talks with Sadat and the Meir cabinet, newly reelected in December, to seek an interim or step-by-step accord that he preferred. Sadat encouraged this strategy. He had decided to seek American support in negotiations and to sever his ties with the Soviets if necessary. Kissinger thus began his renowned shuttle diplomacy that in the end produced two withdrawal agreements between Egypt and Israel and one between Israel and Syria. His initial successes caused Faysal to end his oil embargo and also alleviated tensions between the United States and its European allies; they and Japan were nearly totally dependent on Arab oil and had been seriously affected by the oil cutbacks.

In principle Kissinger was operating according to the framework established in Security Council Resolution 338, passed on 22 October. It called on all parties to begin "implementation of SC Resolution 242 in all its parts" through negotiations "under appropriate auspices aimed at establishing a just and durable peace in the Middle East."[58] In practice Kissinger bypassed the United Nations as well as the Russians, hoping to achieve partial agreements that could establish trust between the signatories and create momentum that might lead to final peace accords. But Kissinger's methods in seeking success often undermined his supposed final goal, as he promised the parties different results. He told the Israelis that achieving accords would relieve international pressure and condemnation directed at them and the United States and would reduce demands for further concessions. By giving up a little, Israel might be able to retain more in the end. He told the Arabs the opposite, that moving toward partial peace agreements with Israel would create an impetus for future pacts leading to a final peace with, he intimated, nearly full Israeli withdrawal from the Sinai and the Golan Heights.[59]

After extremely hard bargaining, Kissinger gained two partial withdrawal agreements in the first six months of 1974. On 18 January, Egypt and Israel signed a "Disengagement of Forces Agreement" providing for the final withdrawal of Israeli troops from the west side of the Suez Canal and delineation of the zones in which Egyptian forces could be stationed on the east bank. Syria and Israel signed a disengagement pact on 31 May 1974, whereby Israel withdrew just beyond the key town of Qunaitra in the Golan Heights. Assad agreed in a private memorandum to prevent Palestinian groups from undertaking attacks and terrorist activities from Syria.[60]

Attainment of these pacts had been difficult. The Labor party, led by Golda Meir and Moshe Dayan, had won delayed elections held in December 1973 but with a reduced plurality; it acquired 39.6 percent of the vote and fifty-one seats, as opposed to 46.2 percent and fifty-six seats in the 1969 elections. Much of this loss had been the gain of a new party, formed by General Ariel Sharon in September, before the war. Sharon, angered at being passed over for a command assignment, had resigned from the military. He then engineered the formation of a new coalition, combining Menechem Begin's Herut and the Liberal party, already linked together as the Gahal, with smaller parties on the right. The result was the Likud, still led by Begin, who deeply admired Sharon. The latter emerged from the war as a hero following his crossing of the Suez Canal. His prestige and Begin's warnings about surrendering territory led the Likud party to acquire 30.2 percent of the vote and a significant thirty-nine seats in the Knesset.[61]

Worn out by the war and political infighting, Meir resigned in April 1974, along with Dayan, who had been severely criticized by the public for the army's state of unreadiness. She was succeeded by Yitzhak Rabin, former chief of staff of the army and ambassador to Washington, who won the post within the Labor party conclave by a narrow margin over Shimon Peres, formerly of the Rafi, who was an archrival. The Rabin–Peres antagonisms and competition for prestige within and outside Israel have lasted to the present.[62] Peres became defense minister, with Yigael Allon deputy prime minister; the three disagreed frequently, with Peres and Rabin trying to undercut the other. Rabin did sign the second disengagement accord with Egypt in September 1975, removing Israeli forces beyond the strategic passes and giving Egypt access to some oil fields in the Gulf of Suez. It was agreed that any future pact between Israel and Egypt would be a final peace agreement, but the United States also gave Israel assurance that it would push for only minor territorial concessions in any forthcoming negotiations with Syria and would not press Israel toward any partial treaty with Jordan. Only a full peace treaty would be acceptable there. Finally, Kissinger assured Israel that the United States would not talk to the PLO unless it specifically recognized the former's right to exist under Resolution 242, something he assumed unlikely if not impossible.

These latter stipulations indicated the direction Israel's policies would take in regularizing its relations with its Arab neighbors and how it hoped to retain U.S. backing in the process. Israel was determined to remain in the Golan Heights, regardless of the Syrian agreement to abide by Resolution 242. Israel also insisted on a full pact with Jordan mainly because it knew this would be unacceptable to Husayn, given Israeli terms. This enabled the cabinet to retain the West Bank and avoid a crisis over disposition of the territory. It was also clear that Israel hoped to isolate Egypt from the rest of the Arab world, especially Syria. Success in this tack would give Israel a free hand to dispose of the territories other than the Sinai through direct dialogues or confrontation, without fear of an Egyptian military threat, a strategy admitted openly by Rabin in December 1974.[63] Here Sadat's willingness to sign a second disengagement agreement with Israel in September 1975 was interpreted by Assad and others as revealing Egypt's willingness to abandon a general Arab position and to follow an Israeli-designed plan intended to further its own military and territorial aims. Finally, Kissinger's assurance regarding the PLO came at a time when that organization was redefining its own objectives with a view to political as well as military strategies, a shift Israel was determined to block with American cooperation if at all possible.

TACTICS AND ULTIMATE INTENTIONS: THE PLO AND ISRAEL, 1973–1977

Israel's stance toward the West Bank following the 1973 war greatly helped Arafat and the PLO and undermined Husayn's position in Arab decision making. Husayn had hoped for a partial pullback of Israeli forces on the West Bank, analogous to what had occurred in the Sinai and in the Golan Heights. Such a move would have restored at least partial Jordanian sovereignty over the region, giving Husayn greater authority to speak for the Palestinians there against the claims of the PLO. Husayn's failure correlated with a general willingness among Arab leaders to give the Palestinians a greater prominence in international gatherings, itself reflecting what seemed to be a move toward a negotiating posture by the Palestinian leadership. In October 1974 an Arab summit meeting in Rabat, Morocco, recognized "the right of the Palestinian people to establish an independent national authority under the command of the Palestinian Liberation Organization, the sole legitimate representative of the Palestinian people, in any Palestinian territory that is liberated."[64] A month later Arafat and the PLO received international recognition when he spoke before the U.N. General Assembly, which granted the organization observer status.

The Rabat Declaration stripped Husayn of any power to negotiate for the West Bank and its Arab inhabitants, a decision he accepted. It seemed a disaster to Kissinger, who believed that Israel should have dealt with Husayn, if only to deny the PLO the appearance of legitimacy it derived at Husayn's expense. In Kissinger's view, Husayn's survival was in America's interests, but his credibility in the Arab world, based on his ties to the United States, had been weakened in part by America's chief ally, Israel. Kissinger sought to neutralize the PLO. He had agreed to a meeting between an aide and a leading member of Fatah in November 1973 as a pretext to suggest an interest in a dialogue in order to keep the PLO quiet while he undertook diplomacy designed to exclude it from the peace equation. But it was at precisely this moment that Arafat was eager to pursue further contacts based on changes in positions that were beginning to emerge within the Palestinian leadership.[65]

The official stance of the PLO, based on its 1968 charter, called for the liberation of Palestine through "armed struggle" and the establishment of a secular democratic society in the place of Israel. No clear distinction was made between pre- and post-1967 Israel. And for leftist groups such as George Habash's Popular Front for the Liberation of Palestine (PFLP) and Nayif Hawatmah's Popular Democratic Front for the Liberation of Palestine (PDFLP), the way to victory required revolutionary change in the wider Arab world, specifically the overthrow of King Husayn, as the precondition to undertaking the struggle against Israel. By late 1972, Hawatmah and the PDFLP had begun to modify this vision, affected both by their conclusion that Husayn would remain in power and by the reality of the expansion of Israeli settlements in the West Bank. This led to the introduction of the term *national authority*, intended to apply to the West Bank and Gaza and signifying a willingness to accept sovereignty over what had been part of Palestine rather than stressing conquest of what was now Israel. The PDFLP proposal was designed to create conditions that might block Israeli retention of the occupied lands while also establishing an alternative to Husayn's plans for them. Hawatmah's stance, which was encouraged by the Soviet Union, was strongly opposed by what became known as the Rejection Front, Habash's PFLP and Ahmad Jibril's PFLP General Command. Both argued that to accept openly the limited objectives offered Israel the chance to reject them while conceding abdication of the ultimate goal, control of all of former Palestine. Furthermore, this tack tacitly abandoned the Arab revolutionary struggle to change the Jordanian government.[66]

The debate over the idea of Palestinian national authority in any lands taken from Israel lasted for years, but its basic terms were accepted in the Rabat

Declaration of October 1974. This meant that such lands, though directly "liberated" from Israel, were also being indirectly liberated from Jordan, given Husayn's own ambitions. The question remaining was the exact position of Arafat and the PLO central leadership, an issue that remained in doubt for some time.

It seems clear that Arafat personally was attracted to the idea of a negotiated settlement that might regain the West Bank and Gaza from 1973 onward—hence his overture to Kissinger. But he hesitated to declare himself openly in favor of this option for fear of losing control of the PLO. Despite his influence, he still had to take into account the attitudes of various factions; to splinter the organization over such a debate could cause him and the PLO to lose credibility as representing the Palestinian cause. The problem became more complex after 1973 because West Bank Palestinians increasingly favored a limited settlement, whereas the Palestinian refugees in the camps who made up the fighting cadres were mostly from what was now Israel. They resisted suggestions to abandon their hopes of achieving their former homeland, whereas the West Bankers sought to retain what they had.[67]

Arafat's strategy seems to have been to float suggestions of settlements through aides close to him, though not committing himself or the organization to them. What he sought was a positive response to such ideas from Arab states, the Soviet Union, and especially the United States. Explicit American solicitude could permit him to present the peace options more directly to the PLO National Council for approval. Here Arafat did permit himself to support openly the idea of a Geneva Conference following the 1973 War in hopes of gaining an American response. But Kissinger opposed a conference. In addition, the United States demanded a specific PLO overture accepting Resolution 242 and recognizing Israel as a precondition of official discussions, whereas Arafat wanted the opposite, open American willingness to deal with the PLO on terms less than those officially stated. The principal obstacle here was Resolution 242, which referred only to the Palestinian refugee problem. Arafat suggested in 1974 that the resolution be amended to refer to Palestinian rights of self-determination, permitting him to bring this concession to the National Council.

A further obstacle was PLO obtuseness in defining what national authority really meant. Did it mean a state? If it did, this might signify open acceptance of limited goals, a Palestinian state in the West Bank and Gaza that accepted an Israeli state. The PLO shied away from the term for several years, despite Soviet encouragement to present the idea in order to open the way for possible acceptance into the diplomatic arena. In addition, PLO definitions of national authority stipulated that this was only the first step toward a final goal, namely, the liberation of all of Palestine. Differing factions might disagree as to what that meant—future armed struggle or peaceful contacts leading to an integration of Palestinian and Israeli societies—but no one would speak clearly on the subject to oppose the rejectionist viewpoint.[68]

The PLO's vacillation served Israel's interests, as it could point quite logically to these proposals as smokescreens rather than serious questions. In addition, Arafat's inability or unwillingness to control various Palestinian groups also bolstered Israel's position. In April 1974, a PFLP squad infiltrated Kiryat Shimona, took hostages, and was wiped out along with several of their captives. A month later a PDFLP unit undertook a suicide attack on Maalot, holding hostage Israeli schoolchildren; twenty-four were killed along with the Palestinians and sixty-three wounded in the ensuing shoot-out when Israeli troops stormed the school. The fact that two forces ideologically opposed to each other should undertake these assaults highlighted the tension among the factions and the need of various groups to prove that they were still committed to armed struggle if necessary. In this particular context, the raids were also designed to foil Kissinger's shuttle diplomacy between Tel Aviv and Damascus, tactics recognized by the Israeli leaders and Kissinger who continued the talks.[69] Nevertheless, the terrorist raids gave further weight to the Israeli refusal to deal with the PLO as a whole, attributing responsibility to its leader. As a result, the PLO's jockeying for position, caught between various strands of allegiances, discredited even further its efforts toward moderation, leaving the way open for Israel to increase its settlements on the West Bank without much fear of American protest.

The Labor government's support of new settlements was based on various factors. The signing of the second disengagement pact with Egypt in September 1975, coupled with the upcoming American presidential election campaign in 1976, meant there would be little official criticism of Israel. In fact, President Gerald Ford suspended American diplomatic efforts in the Middle East during the year to avoid offending American Jewish voters.[70] In addition, the Labor party, under Prime Minister Yitzhak Rabin, was weakened by the "endemic personal rivalry between [him] and Shimon Peres, the Minister of Defense."[71] The leadership thus submitted to pressures imposed by its coalition partner, the National Religious party, and a new organization that emerged in 1974, Gush Emunim. Once opposed to annexation of the conquered territories, the National Religious party had been taken over by a militant wing that called openly for the absorption of the West Bank, thus incorporating the ideology of the Greater Land of Israel Movement into the Labor coalition. At the same time, Gush Emunim committed itself to creating illegal settlements in the heart of Arab populations and forcing the government to accept them. Their goal was to shift the focus of Israeli settlement activity from a strategic perspective to one that insisted on the right of Jews to colonize all areas of the region as part of what had been Eretz Israel. In this, Gush Emunim had the behind-the-scenes backing of Peres and military leaders responsible for the area, leaving Rabin helpless to oppose *faits accomplis* that brought the Labor party much closer to the posture of annexation called for by Menachem Begin. The founding of new settlements approved by the Labor party thus rose by 45 percent between mid-1975 and 1977.[72]

Political events brought new faces to power in the United States and Israel in early 1977. Jimmy Carter became president of the United States in January, and Menachem Begin was elected prime minister of Israel in March, assuming office in June. At the same time, the PLO National Council, meeting in March, declared for the first time its willingness to seek an "independent national state" as part of the Palestinian right to self-determination. This was part of a series of clauses that also called for PLO participation in a Geneva Conference, the clearest expression yet of a PLO wish to engage in international diplomacy. Yet even here, concessions to the rejectionists mitigated the declaration's impact. The West Bank and Gaza were not mentioned, nor was there any recognition of Israel as part of this stance.[73]

Although perhaps an opening gambit that served to appease the PFLP, these clauses helped Israel harden its position in the face of new challenges from the United States. Carter tried to reverse American strategy, dumping the step-by-step process for diplomacy aimed at a general peace accord; Begin was determined to consolidate and expand on the settlement process encouraged by his Labor predecessors. Likewise, Carter at first seemed amenable to some form of Palestinian participation in international talks, something Begin opposed implacably. The collision of these approaches resulted in the Camp David Agreement of 1978, a limited agreement rather than a general peace and thus a major victory for the Israeli strategy of seeking to isolate Egypt, as expounded by Rabin in 1974.

NOTES

1. Michael Brecher, *Decisions in Israel's Foreign Policy* (New Haven, Conn., 1975), p. 444.
2. Ibid., p. 462.
3. Rael Jean Isaac, *Israel Divided: Ideological Politics in the Jewish State* (Baltimore, 1976), pp. 115–126; and Shlomo Aronson, *Conflict and Bargaining in the Middle East: An Israeli Perspective* (Baltimore, 1978), p. 87ff, discuss the different approaches to the problems. For statements made in 1967, see Daniel Dishon, ed., *Middle East Record, 1967* (Jerusalem, 1971), pp. 276–277.
4. William Wilson Harris, *Taking Root: Israeli Settlement in the West Bank, the Golan and Gaza-Sinai, 1967–1980* (New York, 1980), pp. 34–44. Harris's study is the most detailed on the subject.
5. Dishon, *Middle East Record, 1967*, pp. 134–141, 262–266; Robert Stephens, *Nasser, a Political Biography* (Middlesex, England, 1973), pp. 520–524; Malcolm Kerr, *The Arab Cold War: Gamal 'Abd al-Nasir and His Rivals, 1958–1970* (London, 1971), pp. 137–140; and Mohamed Haykal, *The Road to Ramadan* (London, 1971), p. 52.
6. Quoted in Dishon, *Middle East Record, 1967*, p. 264.
7. Quoted in Abba Eban, *Abba Eban, an Autobiography* (New York, 1977), p. 443.
8. Institute for the Study of Diplomacy, Georgetown University, *U.N. Security Council Resolution 242: A Case Study in Diplomatic Ambiguity* (Washington, D.C., 1984), p. 5. Compare Dishon, *Middle East Record, 1967*, p. 88, for a slightly different version.
9. The text is in Walter Laqueur and Barry Rubin, eds., *The Israel-Arab Reader: A Documentary History of the Middle East Conflict* (New York, 1984), pp. 365–366.
10. See Lord Caradon in *Resolution 242*, pp. 13–15; and William B. Quandt, *Decade of Decisions: American Policy Toward the Arab-Israeli Conflict, 1967–1976* (Berkeley and Los Angeles, 1977), p. 65.
11. Goldberg in *Resolution 242*, p. 23. To add to the confusion, the French and Russian translations of the document refer to "the territories," adding the article omitted in the English original.
12. Quandt, *Decade*, p. 66. The deal also included tanks for Jordan.

13. For a discussion of American domestic politics and the timing of Middle East diplomacy, see William B. Quandt, *Camp David, Peacemaking and Politics* (Washington, D.C., 1986), pp. 6–29.
14. Ehud Yaari, *Strike Terror: The Story of Fatah* (New York, 1970), pp. 123–150.
15. Ibid., pp. 198–255; Helena Cobban, *The Palestinian Liberation Organization: People, Power and Politics* (Cambridge, England, 1984), pp. 141–147; and William Quandt, Fuad Jabber, and Ann Mosely Lesch, *The Politics of Palestinian Nationalism* (Berkeley and Los Angeles, 1973), pp. 57–78.
16. Quandt, Jabber, and Lesch, *The Politics*, p. 69ff; Cobban, *Palestinian Liberation Organization*, pp. 43–45; and Kerr, *The Arab Cold War*, pp. 136–137. The remaining 48 of the 105 seats were held by representatives of student and labor groups, the Palestinian Liberation Army, and so on.
17. Eric Rouleau, "Les Palestiniens face au trône jordanien, IV: Le dilemme," *Le Monde*, 4 December 1970, quoted in Kerr, *The Arab Cold War*, p. 145.
18. The text of the 1968 charter is in Laqueur and Rubin, *Israel-Arab Reader*, pp. 366–372. An analysis of the 1964 and 1968 charters is Y. Harkabi, *The Palestinian Covenant and Its Meaning* (London, 1979).
19. John Cooley, *Green March, Black September: The Story of the Palestinian Arabs* (London, 1973), pp. 146–148. Cobban, *Palestinian Liberation Organization*, p. 47, wrongly dates the hijacking of the plane to Algiers in December. PFLP spokesmen justified these attacks as being aimed at Israel's lifeline to the outside world, but one cannot discount the element of rivalry within the PLO, different groups seeking to outdo others to gain prestige and more recruits.
20. Fuad Jabber, in Quandt, Jabber, and Lesch, *Palestinian Nationalism*, p. 193.
21. Kamal S. Salibi, *Crossroads to Civil War: Lebanon, 1958–1976* (New York, 1976), pp. 32–51.
22. Alvin Z. Rubenstein, *Red Star on the Nile: The Soviet-Egyptian Relationship since the June War* (Princeton, N.J., 1977), p. 68; and Jon D. Glassman, *Arms for the Arabs: The Soviet Union and War in the Middle East* (Baltimore, 1975), pp. 66–69.
23. Rubenstein, *Red Star*, pp. 54–55.
24. I rely on the following sources for the war of attrition and accompanying diplomatic efforts to resolve it: Yaacov Bar-Siman-Tov, *The Israeli-Egyptian War of Attrition, 1969–1970* (New York, 1980); Yaacov Bar-Siman-Tov, "The Myth of Strategic Bombing: Israeli Deep-Penetration Air Raids in the War of Attrition, 1969–70," *Journal of Contemporary History* 19 (1984): 549–570; Rubenstein, *Red Star*, pp. 66–117; Edgar O'Ballance, *The Electronic War in the Middle East, 1968–70* (New York, 1974); Yair Evron, *The Middle East, Nations, Superpowers, and Wars* (New York, 1973), especially pp. 78–128; and Lawrence L. Whetten, *The Canal War: Four-Power Conflict in the Middle East, 1967–1974* (Cambridge, Mass., 1974) which covers a broader period, 1967 to 1974. A good military history of this period and the 1973 war is Trevor N. Dupuy, *Elusive Victory: The Arab-Israeli Wars, 1947–1974* (New York, 1978), pp. 343–383.
25. Haykal, *Road to Ramadan*, p. 91. Most Western sources are vague as to whether Egypt actually rejected the Rogers Plan. Compare Rubenstein, *Red Star*, p. 97ff, and Whetten, *Canal War*, pp. 78–82.
26. Yitzhak Rabin, *Rabin Memoirs* (New York, 1979), pp. 157–165. See also Bar-Siman-Tov, "Myth of Strategic Bombing," p. 553; Rubenstein, *Red Star*, p. 106ff; and Nadav Safran, *Israel, the Embattled Ally* (Cambridge, Mass., 1978), p. 436.
27. Brecher, *Decisions*, pp. 488–495; and Rabin, *Memoirs*, p. 177.
28. I rely principally on Steven L. Spiegel, *The Other Arab-Israeli Conflict: Making America's Middle East Policy, from Truman to Reagan* (Chicago, 1985); Raymond L. Garthoff, *Detente and Confrontation: American-Soviet Relations from Nixon to Reagan* (Washington, D.C., 1985); Seymour M. Hersh, *The Price of Power: Kissinger in the Nixon White House* (New York, 1983); Tad Szulc, *The Illusion of Peace: Foreign Policy in the Nixon Years* (New York, 1978); Richard M. Nixon, *RN, The Memoirs of Richard Nixon* (New York, 1978); Henry Kissinger, *White House Years* (Boston, 1979); and Quandt, *Decade*, pp. 72–104.
29. Kissinger, *White House Years*, p. 351.
30. Spiegel, *America's Middle East Policy*, pp. 173–176; Kissinger, *White House Years*, p. 357; Hersh, *Price of Power*, pp. 213–233; Quandt, *Decade*, pp. 72–81; Roger Morris, *Uncertain Greatness: Henry Kissinger and American Foreign Policy* (New York, 1977), a bitter account of Kissinger's handling of policy and his staff; and Barry Rubin, *Secrets of State: The State Department and the Struggle over U.S. Foreign Policy* (Oxford, England, 1985), who notes, p. 146, that Kissinger would not tolerate questions from his staff regarding the substance of the policy he and Nixon had decided on.
31. Brecher, *Decisions*, pp. 454–478.

32. Spiegel, *America's Middle East Policy*, p. 185.
33. Ilana Kass, *Soviet Involvement in the Middle East: Policy Formulation, 1966–1973* (Boulder, Colo., 1978), pp. 58–97. According to Kass, Moscow's switch to calls for renewing the four-power talks resulted from deep divisions within the ruling establishment over the wisdom of pursuing the diplomatic option. The military strongly opposed negotiations, as they might lead to a settlement whereby Egypt lessened its reliance on the Soviets and abrogated its agreements to grant them control of bases there. Those supporting negotiations, the foreign office and the party leadership, found their stances weakened by the American delivery of Phantom jets to Israel in November, though their arrival had been announced much earlier.
34. Spiegel, *America's Middle East Policy*, pp. 186–187; and Hersh, *Price of Power*, pp. 218–221.
35. Kissinger, *White House Years*, pp. 375–376. Nixon states that he believed Rogers's efforts would fail but that they would send a message to the Arabs indicating American interest in its proposals. He omits mention of the specific messages he sent the Israelis: *RN*, pp. 478–479.
36. For comments on Sisco, see Rabin, *Memoirs*, p. 165; Bar-Siman-Tov, "Myth of Strategic Bombing," p. 533; Rubenstein, *Red Star*, p. 96, who is relying on Henry Brandon's critical account, *The Retreat of American Power* (London, 1973), pp. 115–116; Quandt, *Decade*, pp. 74–75, who refers to Sisco as the "consummate bureaucratic politician"; and Morris, *Uncertain Greatness*, pp. 218–219, who states that "with practiced instincts, Sisco dutifully staffed the futile negotiations for Rogers, while quietly nurturing close relations with Kissinger."
37. *White House Years*, p. 379. It is difficult to know how much of Kissinger's attribution of foresight to himself is the product of hindsight.
38. *Fatah*, 17 April 1970, quoted by Jabber in Quandt, Jabber, and Lesch, *Palestinian Nationalism*, pp. 196–197. Jabber's discussion of these developments remains an excellent source. See also Kerr, *Arab Cold War*, pp. 140–145.
39. William B. Quandt, "Lebanon, 1958, and Jordan, 1970," in Barry M. Blechman, Stephen S. Kaplan, et al., *Force without War: U.S. Armed Forces as a Political Instrument* (Washington, D.C., 1978), pp. 278–279.
40. For rivalries within the Syrian political elite, civilian and military, see Nikolaos Van Dam, *The Struggle for Power in Syria: Sectarianism, Regionalism and Tribalism in Politics, 1961–1978* (New York, 1979), especially pp. 83–97 which treat the Assad-Jadid feud; and Moshe Ma'oz and Avner Yaniv, "On a Short Leash: Syria and the PLO," in Moshe Ma'oz and Avner Yaniv, eds., *Syria under Assad: Domestic Constraints and Regional Risks* (London, 1986), pp. 191–208. Most sources state that Assad, as defense minister, had refused to commit the Syrian air force to the Syrian-backed invasion of Jordan encouraged by Salah Jadid, thereby exposing the rift in the Baath leadership and permitting Jordanian aircraft to dominate the battlefield, leading to a Syrian defeat. Patrick Seale, *Asad: The Struggle for the Middle East* (Berkeley and Los Angeles, 1988), pp. 158–160, argues that the Assad-Jadid rivalry was not a factor, relying on Assad's version of the events.
41. John Waterbury, *The Egypt of Nasser and Sadat: The Political Economy of Two Regimes* (Princeton, N.J., 1983), p. 112ff. See also the overview by William J. Burns, *Economic Aid and American Policy Towards Egypt, 1955–1981* (Albany, N.Y., 1985), pp. 173–177.
42. As Kissinger acknowledges, *White House Years*, pp. 1276–1300.
43. Quandt, *Decade*, pp. 130–143; Whetten, *Canal War*, pp. 139–195, who has a very detailed treatment of the issues; and Aronson, *Conflict and Bargaining*, pp. 139–154.
44. Marvin Kalb and Bernard Kalb, *Kissinger* (New York, 1975), p. 208.
45. Spiegel, *America's Middle East Policy*, p. 203. During the early 1970s, Congress increased aid to Israel by nearly 9 percent over the White House's requests while reducing total foreign aid expenditures by 25 percent. See Marvin C. Feurwerger, *Congress and Israel: Foreign Aid Decision-Making in the House of Representatives, 1969–1976* (Westport, Conn., 1979), p. 40 and passim.
46. See the incisive analysis by Dina Rome Spechler, "Soviet Policy in the Middle East: The Crucial Change," in Paul Marantz and Blema S. Steinberg, eds., *Superpower Involvement in the Middle East: Dynamics of Foreign Policy* (Boulder, Colo., 1985), pp. 133–171.
47. A good overview of these matters is Anthony Sampson, *The Seven Sisters: The Great Oil Companies and the World They Shaped* (New York, 1976), especially pp. 186–310. A survey of the growing dependency of developed and developing nations on oil is Peter R. Odell, *Oil and World Power* (New York, 1979). For Libya, see relevant portions of Sampson and Ruth First, *Libya, The Elusive Revolution* (Baltimore, 1974).

48. See the articles in Raymond Vernon, ed., *The Oil Crisis* (New York, 1976), especially those by Joel Darmstadter and Hans H. Landsberg, "The Economic Background," pp. 15–38; and Edith Penrose, "The Development of the Crisis," pp. 39–58.
49. Aronson, *Conflict and Bargaining*, p. 162; and Quandt, *Decade*, pp. 138–139.
50. Isaac, *Israel Divided*, p. 128–129; and Harris, *Taking Root*, pp. 42–57.
51. Quoted in Isaac, *Israel Divided* p. 128.
52. Baruch Kimmerling, *Zionism and Territory: The Socio-Territorial Dimensions of Zionist Politics* (Berkeley and Los Angeles, 1983), pp. 164–165, who notes that in at least one case the military approved the destruction of crops to force an Arab landholder to sell his property. Dayan's mercurial nature is well treated in Conor Cruise O'Brien, *The Siege: The Saga of Israel and Zionism* (London, 1986), pp. 507–508.
53. *Jerusalem Post Overseas Edition*, 21 August 1973.
54. Ibid., 11 September and 2 October 1973. Aronson, *Conflict and Bargaining*, pp. 408–409, lists the provisions of the Galili plan. American Jewish efforts to gain greater Soviet Jewish emigration were backed by Senator Henry Jackson who tied the issue to American trade policy with the Soviets, in part out of sympathy but also through eagerness to exploit the matter for a possible presidential candidacy in 1976. A book on the subject is Paula Stern, *Water's Edge: Domestic Politics and the Making of American Foreign Policy* (Westport, Conn., 1979). See also the second volume of Kissinger's memoirs, *Years of Upheaval* (Boston, 1982), pp. 250–256, 986–997.
55. Haykal, *Road to Ramadan*, pp. 22, 205.
56. Capable summaries of the war can be found in Frank Aker, *October 1973: The Arab-Israeli War* (Hamden, Conn., 1985); and Dupuy, *Elusive Victory*, pp. 387–617.
57. Aronson, *Conflict and Bargaining*, pp. 168–211; and Quandt, *Decade*, pp. 165–206. Two books that treat Kissinger's negotiating tactics from October 1973 onward are Edward R. F. Sheehan, *The Arabs, Israelis, and Kissinger: A Secret History of American Diplomacy in the Middle East* (New York, 1976); and Matti Golan, *The Secret Conversations of Henry Kissinger: Step-by-Step Diplomacy in the Middle East* (New York, 1976). Compare Sheehan's comments on Matti Golan, *Secret History*, p. 81.
58. The text is in Quandt, *Decade*, p. 200.
59. Ibid., p. 251; Sheehan, *Secret History*, p. 83; and Golan, *Secret Conversations*, p. 152ff.
60. Texts in Sheehan, *Secret History*, pp. 238–244.
61. The statistics are in Itamar Rabinovich and Jehuda Reinharz, eds., *Israel in the Middle East: Documents and Readings on Society, Politics, and Foreign Relations, 1948–Present* (New York, 1984), appendices (unpaginated). See also Eric Silver, *Begin, a Biography* (London, 1984), pp. 144–146.
62. See *The Rabin Memoirs*, in which every indexed reference to Peres is critical, sarcastic, or both. For a reaction to these memoirs, see Matti Golan, *Shimon Peres, a Biography* (New York, 1982), pp. 232–235.
63. Matti Golan, *Secret Conversations*, p. 229; and Quandt, *Decade*, p. 261.
64. Quoted in Cobban, *Palestine Liberation Organization*, p. 60.
65. Ibid., pp. 208, 236–237; and Kissinger, *Years of Upheaval*, pp. 624–629, 976–978, cover these matters, including an overture for talks from Arafat to Kissinger.
66. My discussion of PLO debates and positions relies mostly on Alain Gresh, *The PLO, the Struggle Within: Towards an Independent Palestinian State*, trans. A. M. Berrett (London, 1985), especially pp. 118–210, which provide a detailed treatment of the issues. Also useful are Shaul Mishal, *The PLO under Arafat: Between Gun and Olive Branch* (New Haven, Conn., 1986), pp. 32–64; and Galia Golan, *The Soviet Union and the Palestine Liberation Organization: An Uneasy Alliance* (New York, 1980), pp. 56–58, where she treats the question of a state.
67. Gresh, *Struggle Within*, pp. 133–138.
68. *Years of Upheaval*, p. 626; Cobban, *Palestine Liberation Organization*, pp. 61–62, 154–156; Gresh, *Struggle Within*, pp. 143–149.
69. Matti Golan, *Secret Conversations*, pp. 202–203. Israeli policy is not to bargain with terrorists but to attack and kill them, even if this risks the loss of hostage lives.
70. William B. Quandt, *Camp David: Peacemaking and Politics* (Washington, D.C., 1986), p.33.
71. Meron Benvenisti, *The West Bank Data Project: A Survey of Israel's Policies* (Washington, D.C., 1984), p. 52.

72. Ibid.; and Harris, *Taking Root*, p. 126ff. For Gush Emunim, see the following sources in addition to Benvenisti: Lily Weisbrod, "Gush Emunim Ideology—From Religious Doctrine to Political Action," *Middle Eastern Studies* 18 (1982): 264–275; the various chapters in David Newman, ed., *The Impact of Gush Emunim: Politics and Settlement in the West Bank* (London, 1985); David J. Schnall, *Radical Dissent in Contemporary Israeli Politics: Cracks in the Wall* (New York, 1979), pp. 139–155; David J. Schnall, *Beyond the Green Line: Israeli Settlements West of the Jordan* (New York, 1984), which includes interviews with leaders of Gush Emunim and with West Bank Arabs; and Myron J. Aronoff, "Gush Emunim: The Institutionalization of a Charismatic, Messianic, Religious-Political Revitalization Movement in Israel," in Myron J. Aronoff, ed., *Religion and Politics*, Political Anthropology Series, vol. 3 (New Brunswick, N.J., 1984), pp. 63–84. I will give a detailed treatment of the West Bank under Jordanian and Israeli rule at the beginning of the next chapter.
73. Ibid., pp. 203–207; Mishal, *PLO Under Arafat*, pp. 56–64; and Cobban, *Palestine Liberation Organization*, pp. 78–87, 156–157.

Lebanon, the West Bank, and the Camp David Accords, 1977–1984: *The Palestinian Equation in the Arab-Israeli Conflict*

The Carter White House staff and advisers "achieved a rare degree of consensus" regarding the approach to be taken toward the Arab-Israeli conflict.[1] Unlike the Rogers–Kissinger rivalry during Nixon's first term in office, Secretary of State Cyrus Vance and National Security Adviser Zbigniew Brzezinski generally agreed on terms of an ideal settlement and the importance of that settlement to American interests and those of its allies. All concurred that an inclusive agreement was preferable to Kissinger's step-by-step procedures, though they realized that Sadat might prefer that course, hoping to reach an accord that would accelerate the infusion of American economic assistance to his beleaguered economy. In January 1977 there were serious outbreaks of unrest in Egypt as a result of government efforts to raise prices on staples and thus reduce its subsidies on those goods. Full peace with Israel, if achieved separately, would strengthen Egypt's ties with the United States, in Sadat's view, and stabilize his country as well as his own rule.

Administration officials also agreed that the Palestinian question had to be addressed and resolved. The Carter administration was willing to invite the PLO to an international conference if it accepted Resolution 242. This scenario demanded that Israel make substantial concessions regarding territory and acceptance of the PLO and that the PLO and Arab states in general give Israel full recognition. The Carter administration was committed to Israel but defined its security more in terms of treaties than retention of territories, believing that Israel's settlement policies were counterproductive to peace efforts.

Carter's efforts were undermined by several factors. Menachem Begin was determined to retain the Golan Heights and the West Bank and to resist inclusion of the PLO, regardless of American hopes to the contrary. On the Arab side, various states, especially Syria, viewed with deep suspicion Sadat's eagerness for an accord. Assad had little interest in negotiations unless the Arabs formed a united front, although he accepted Resolution 242.

The period of diplomacy that culminated in Camp David was marked by major developments elsewhere, on the West Bank and in Lebanon. Under Begin, settlement projects in the West Bank were increased, at times in apparent violation of commitments given to the Carter administration. In Lebanon, the aftermath of a vicious civil war saw the south caught up in a struggle among

Palestinian groups, Israeli proxies, and Israel itself, acting at times in direct alliance with Maronite politicians and paramilitary forces. This struggle, and increased PLO terrorist activity in Israel designed to forestall progress in American diplomacy, led to an Israeli invasion of south Lebanon in mid-March 1978. But the Israeli attack did not solve the question of the PLO in Lebanon, which became increasingly tied to the sentiments of the Palestinian population of the West Bank following Camp David.

For West Bank Palestinians, the Egyptian-Israeli agreement seemed to confirm continued Israeli rule over them, declared openly by Begin himself, whatever the expectations of Carter and Sadat. This in turn bolstered Arafat's prestige, as he seemed the only leader able to achieve recognition of Palestinian rights. PLO strength in southern Lebanon and continued unrest in the West Bank, often spawned by Israeli attempts to destroy nationalist sentiments there, led finally to a long-planned Israeli attack into Lebanon in June 1982. It was designed both to eradicate the Palestinian presence in Lebanon, in collaboration with Maronite allies, and by doing so to erase any hopes among West Bank Arabs that they had an alternative to Israeli rule. A corollary of the invasion was a plan, held principally by Ariel Sharon, to drive the Syrians from Lebanon and establish a Maronite-controlled government headed by the leaders of the Gemayel family in alliance with Israel.

Throughout this period, the fate of Lebanon and of the West Bank became increasingly intertwined, especially in light of Israel's consideration of its vital interests under the Begin government. These interests played a major role in Begin's willingness to sign a separate peace treaty with Sadat. We shall first discuss the nature of the West Bank and then the problems deriving from the Lebanese civil war to establish the backdrop for Camp David. The results of Camp David in turn provided incentives for the PLO to oppose the agreement and for Israel to decide to reinvade Lebanon in order to secure a stable border under a client Christian regime and a docile West Bank Arab population no longer willing to resist Israel's hegemony.

WEST BANK AND ISRAELI ARABS BETWEEN JORDAN AND ISRAEL, 1948–1977

Since 1948 the West Bank, inhabited by Palestinian Arabs, has experienced the determined efforts of Jordanians and Israelis to erase its affiliation with mandatory Palestine. The term refers to the area taken by Jordan's King Abdullah in the 1948 war with Israel, comprising most of the region in eastern Palestine allotted to the Arabs in the 1947 partition plan. Abdullah officially annexed the West Bank to his kingdom to create the Hashemite Kingdom of Jordan, deliberately expunging the word *Palestine* from all sources referring to it. It would be known as the West Bank, as opposed to the East Bank, which had made up Abdullah's former principality of Transjordan, developed under British patronage. He set about cementing ties with West Bank notables who had opposed the mufti, many of whom were rewarded with prominent posts in government and in administrative positions dealing with West Bank affairs, among them the al-Nashshashibis, Abd al-Hadis and the Tuqans. Husayn continued his grandfather's policy of maintaining ties with prominent Palestinian families from the West Bank, at times playing them off against one another, while keeping close surveillance over political activity among the general populace which identified more closely with Arab nationalist currents prevalent in Cairo or Damascus.

Economically, the West Bank saw its relative prosperity vis-à-vis the East Bank decline owing to Hashemite concentration of investment in the latter. Agriculture remained the predominant occupation on the West Bank, with industrial development concentrated in the East Bank. Those few with fairly large landholdings benefited from a market for export of their produce to East Jordan and to the Arab shaykhdoms of the Persian Gulf, but the bulk of the population continued to be small landholders, with a sizable tenant farmer component. Circumstances were complicated by a greater concentration of refugees situated in the West than in the East Bank, 360,000 added to the 400,000 West Bank Palestinians already there. The small properties and lack of opportunity for growth meant that many West Bankers emigrated, most initially to the East Bank but later into the wider Arab world and abroad. This outward flow stabilized the population at about 900,000, despite a birthrate of nearly 3 percent.[2] The aggregate of these factors suited Hashemite interests. The monarchy pursued a policy of political fragmentation buttressed by economic backwardness that aimed to prevent the formation of large political parties or newly wealthy groups independent of its control who might challenge Husayn's rule.

Israel's assumption of control over the West Bank did not signal a change of political direction for the region. Israel, like the Hashemites, maintained the practice of political and social fragmentation, dealing with village leaders on an individual basis and seeking to prevent any growth of a collective identity as Palestinians. This was not accidental. It reflected the Israelis' perception that they were "the only legitimate collective in the land of Israel [including the West Bank] and therefore all Palestinian claims to communal (economic and political) rights are illegitimate and, by definition, subversive."[3] Economic practices developed whose aim was to subvert West Bank Palestinian interests to those of Israel, but their impact also reflected the government's political tactics.

By any standards, the material prosperity of the West Bank Palestinians increased enormously under Israeli domination, particularly from 1967 to 1973 when the Israeli economy experienced a boom. Agricultural production rose, as did rural income. However, the latter was not directly tied to the former: increased prosperity through agriculture alone redounded again to a relatively few families. The tremendous increase in income per se, from a per-capita rural revenue of $133 in 1966 to $930 in 1975, was principally the product of West Bank labor working in Israel, a development of great significance. The result was the subordination of the West Bank economy and labor force to Israeli needs, leading to increased individual well-being coupled with dependence on Israel's economic fortunes for continued prosperity.

In agriculture, many crops grown by West Bankers in 1967 competed with those cultivated by Israeli farmers. The Israeli government forbade the sale of some West Bank crops in Israel and placed quotas on others so as not to compete with Israeli products. In addition the latter received extensive subsidies from the government not available to the West Bankers; they were considered outside the Israeli system politically, not being citizens, while being integrated into the economic system to benefit Israeli producers. Israeli farmers could dump excess produce into the West Bank at lower prices than those considered viable by Palestinians, and the Israeli government reserved the region as a special zone for its industrial goods, to the exclusion of those from other countries.[4] Little relief was found in Jordan. Israel permitted West Bankers to retain economic ties to the East Bank, meaning that much of the surplus agricultural crops traditionally farmed went there, but Jordanian quotas to protect East Bank agriculture left West Bank sales at the 1967 level. As a result, increased agricultural productivity did not greatly increase prosperity in the agricultural sector for those traditionally identified with landed wealth, namely, the old-time leaders that the Israelis sought to cultivate. Instead, these larger farmers lost laborers to the Israeli economy, undermining their prestige and weakening them financially. This in turn led to the rise in status and wealth of those members of the lower classes formerly dependent on the largesse of the landed class.[5]

It was here that the West Bank became integrated into the Israeli economic network. From the early 1970s, total employment among the West Bank labor force averaged about 98 percent. Although the Palestinians (including the Gaza Strip workers) amounted to no more than 5 percent of the total Israeli work force, their representation in low-wage sectors and menial labor was very important, "constituting almost one-third of the total labor force in the construction branch, and . . . a majority of unskilled laborers on actual construction sites."[6] These workers were the major contributors to West Bank income, rural particularly, as they came from that sector. Their presence enabled the Israeli economy to experience a major economic boom in the mid-1970s, aided by a comparative decrease in collateral costs. This availability of labor allowed the Israeli economy to postpone mechanization in many areas, reducing costs, along with paying low wages unacceptable to most Israeli workers but comparatively high to many Arabs. Although by law these Arab workers are required to return to their homes at night, violations were tolerated until recently.[7]

The net result has been that Israeli control of the West Bank and the Gaza Strip has been economically beneficial to both parties, but on different levels. Although the Arab laborers in Israel receive social security, they also pay income taxes. Non-Israeli goods entering the territories are subject to customs duties, whereas Israeli-owned industries in the West Bank are permitted to "export" their products to Israel duty-free, in comparison with the procedures applied to Arab-produced agricultural goods. In many ways the regions paid for themselves until the 1987 uprising, leading one student of the process to conclude that "two-thirds of military government expenditure on the local population has been covered by revenues collected from the population. . . . There are indications that the territories place no fiscal and monetary burden . . . [and] it may well be that the territories are a net source of revenue to the Israeli Treasury. . . ."[8]

But if the government perceived economic as well as militarily strategic advantages to retaining the territories, especially the West Bank, so also did a sector of Israeli society that considered itself deprived in Israel, the Jews from Arab lands. These oriental Jews, now a majority of the Jewish population in Israel, have long considered themselves, with justification, as having been discriminated against by the dominant European Jewish (Ashkenazi) elite. Great differences in cultural background were reinforced by perceived state needs following independence and by a disinclination on the part of the elite to associate itself too closely with a group it considered inferior to itself. The oriental Jews' upward mobility, though impressive over the years, has not erased the gap between their overall economic level and that of the Ashkenazi, occasionally arousing great bitterness.

This situation, especially the influx of Arab laborers from the territories after 1967, has proved a boon to the oriental Jews' upward mobility, pushing them up the ladder out of jobs with which they had been traditionally associated.[9] Oriental Jews are well aware of these circumstances and the benefits they have accrued from Israel's retention of the territories and the Arab labor force. Many fear that if these lands were returned for peace, they would be forced back by the Ashkenazi into the menial positions they have escaped. It is no accident that a majority of oriental Jews supported Menachem Begin and his call for holding the West Bank (Judea and Samaria) in perpetuity. Not only did they identify with him as outsiders in a Labor party–Ashkenazi-controlled Israel until 1977, but his desire to retain the West Bank for historical and religious reasons blended perfectly with their conceptions of their ability to preserve their economic gains. Oriental Jews backed Begin by nearly a three-to-one ratio in the 1977 elections, and he received the vote of over 50 percent of a younger generation that had grown up in an Israel that included the area.[10]

In light of these circumstances, Menachem Begin could feel that he had great popular support for his already determined plan to retain the West Bank, a course he had always backed on grounds of emotional and historic identity. And he strove to facilitate the efforts of the Gush Emunim to establish settlements in heavily populated Arab sectors, tactics that the Labor party had opposed. Here he identified with the Gush Emunim's combination of mystical attachment to areas of ancient Israel and practical steps taken to ensure continuity of a Jewish presence in the region. Religiosity and land went together, a connection fostered by Ariel Sharon who, as minister of agriculture, tried to establish a greater Jewish presence so as to preempt any idea of concessions in the area.[11]

Israel's expansion of settlements into high-density Arab areas on the West Bank coincided with its renewed attention to the place of those Arabs who had remained in Israel since 1948. Here, as on the West Bank, the Likud party's policies reflected an intensification of past Labor practices rather than a radical shift of emphasis.

As noted previously, the status of Israeli Arabs loomed as a threat to the integrity of the Jewish state of Israel soon after the state's founding in 1948. Technically citizens of that state, these Arabs were seen as part of the enemy, fifth columnists whose possession of land obstructed the settlement of incoming Jews. Under the absentee laws, land could be expropriated from individual Arabs or Arab villages. When the legal clauses did not apply, forcible expulsion could be used. These practices, initiated during the 1948 war, lasted until 1953. During this period nearly one million dunams of Arab land was taken to be "redeemed" for Jewish ownership by transference to the Jewish National Fund so that it became inalienably Jewish. In 1953 the Israeli law of compensation for lands taken or to be taken in the future based the value of a dunam on rates current in 1950, regardless of inflation of Israeli currency or increases in land values.[12]

An additional motive for expelling entire villages rested on the fact that the majority of Arab settlements were clustered in the upper Galilee near the Lebanese border, creating a region with very little Jewish settlement. From the early 1950s, efforts were made to "Judaize the Galilee," albeit with little success. However, when settlements such as Maalot or Kiryat Shimona were founded, they were often situated where Arab villages had once stood; the Arab inhabitants had been ousted from Israel across the Jordanian border to make room for Jewish towns that would break up the Arabness of the region. When wholesale villages were not destroyed, a frequent practice was to take valuable land from these towns, restricting the potential for any Arab expansion and opening the way for either Jewish settlement or development of the land. The frequency of these occurrences decreased dramatically after 1956, but principally because government attention was focused elsewhere. Once the Likud entered office in 1977, it called attention to the still-existing concentration of Arab settlements in northern Israel, and Ariel Sharon declared that he had undertaken an "offensive" to "stem the hold of foreigners on state lands," to be achieved in part through Judaizing the Galilee.[13] Sharon's militaristic terminology and his reference to foreigners, namely, Arabs in Israel, coincided with his attitude toward West Bank Arabs, living in what had been Israel; he identified them all as alien to a Jewish state. His assumptions resemble those of Meir Kahane, former head of the right-wing party, Kach, who in the 1980s called for the expulsion of all Israeli Arabs in order to purify Israel by ridding it of alien blood.[14]

As a rule, Israeli policy toward the Arabs sought to "reinforce the internal fragmentation of the Arab population and its isolation from the Jewish majority."[15] This could be done through land expropriation or the imposition of Jewish settlements among the Arabs, but it could be furthered only by fostering the development of Jewish sectors at a pace unavailable to the Arab inhabitants. Technically this did not reflect deliberate governmental decision making but, rather, the process of state development aided by the Jewish National Fund. Thus, most Arab villages still do not have basic amenities because they must pay for their purchase out of taxes they must levy on their inhabitants. Because most are farmers and poor, little money is available for such services, whereas the Jewish settlements received nearly free electricity, paved roads, sewage systems, and the like.[16] The same policy has been carried out on the West Bank.

Nevertheless, the government has fostered the isolation of Arab regions from the national economy by encouraging development plans that seek to keep them agricultural and dependent on a Jewish industrial and larger agricultural base, unless they can finance it themselves, which they cannot do.[17] This, plus encouraging educated Israeli Arabs either to leave or not to return from education abroad for advanced degrees, serves the same purpose. Arab resentment has exploded at times, as following the demonstrations in May 1976 to protest Israeli expropriation of land. The communist-sponsored Land Day rally attracted large crowds and drew Israeli military retaliation; soldiers fired on the protesters, of whom six were killed and scores wounded, establishing a legacy that remains. Israeli policies have created a greater sense of kinship between Israeli and West Bank Arabs since 1977 than might have otherwise existed.

THE LEBANESE CIVIL WAR AND ITS AFTERMATH, 1975–1978

Scholars date the period of the Lebanese Civil War from April 1975 to October 1976, when an Arab summit led to the formation of a peacekeeping force to maintain order in central Lebanon. These dates are technically correct, but the existence of tensions between the Maronites and the Palestinians, on the one hand, and between the Maronites and the Lebanese Muslim and leftist forces, on the other, long predated the war. These dual antagonisms suggest the interaction of domestic and external factors in spurring the further disintegration of the Lebanese polity.

Domestically, the major issue remained that of Christian, and especially Maronite Catholic, control of the government and the patronage system related to it. This system was increasingly challenged by a coalition of Muslim and leftist groups that coalesced around the Druze patriarch, Kamal Jumblat, to form the National Movement in 1969. Its aim was dismantling the National Pact of 1943 and recasting the political structure of Lebanon, best depicted in its program announced in 1975 that called for the "deconfessionalization" of the government. If realized, this would have meant the complete breakdown of the basis of Maronite ascendancy, the taking of a new census, and the subsequent allocation of governmental and electoral posts on the basis of a majority rule.[18] This program threatened not only Maronite power but also the authority of those Muslim and other Christian politicians (mainly Sunni and Greek Orthodox) who benefited from the plums of office. Given that the majority of those excluded from the existing system were Muslim, the opposition seemed to have a totally religious cast. In fact, it was a radical front that included Christians along with Muslims, often opposing their own leaders who acquiesced in denial of their rights. A purely religious delineation of the conflict could overlook the complexity of allegiances. For example, the parliamentary elections of 1972 witnessed "the overwhelming victory of a young neo-Nasserist candidate against an established conservative rival in Beirut," an event that showed the "crystallizing Moslem radical mood." Both candidates were Greek Orthodox Christians, but the district was composed primarily of Sunni Muslims. And the Greek Orthodox victor, by being a "neo-Nasserist," belonged to a faction financed by Libya's Muammar al-Qadhdhafi.[19]

For the Maronite leadership, however, the question remained one of Muslim-Christian relations, all the better to depict the issue as such to the outside world, as they had done since 1958. Here the matter was complicated by the growing alliances between the National Movement and elements of the PLO, especially the Marxist-oriented PFLP and PDFLP controlled by George Habash and Nayif Hawatmah. Finally, there was the matter of the PLO attacks on Israel that brought Israeli retaliation and greater sympathy for the Palestinian cause on the part of many Muslims and leftists. As a result of the Cairo Accords of 1969, the PLO controlled the refugee camps, most of which were concentrated in poorer suburbs of Beirut or in the south, and gradually created a ministate within Lebanon.[20] One consequence of these developments was to spur the growth of private Maronite militias under the control of individual politicians but outside governmental authority: the Phalange, under the Gemayels, and the paramilitary organizations linked to the family of Camille Chamoun and that of Sulayman Franjiyah. These paramilitary groups often vied with one another for dominance.[21]

A final element in the Lebanese equation was the alignment of states and factions either supporting or rejecting American diplomacy and the disengagement accords, especially Sadat's agreement to sign the second pact in September 1975. Within the PLO, the "Rejection Front," backed by Libya and Iraq, joined with Jumblat's National Movement to seek to redress the political balance in Lebanon.[22] Arafat and Fatah hedged, seeking to avoid total immersion in Arab communal strife but striving also to retain independence of action because Arafat hoped to be included in any forthcoming Geneva Conference, ultimately never held. His later commitment to the radical alignment in the civil war was in part motivated by realization that the PLO would gain no benefits from great power diplomacy. Likewise, Syria joined Iraq and Libya in condemning the Sinaii II accord of September 1975, but Syria's general role in the Lebanese maelstrom illustrated its attempt to balance competing demands related to international diplomacy and its regional security.

In principle Syria backed the Rejection Front. Assad felt that Sinai II indicated Sadat's willingness to break with other Arab states to seek an independent treaty with Israel that would leave Damascus isolated and at Israel's mercy.

Forming an alliance with radical PLO groups and Lebanese militants could help establish a new political situation that served Syria's interests. But this could occur only as long as Damascus controlled Lebanese political developments and the PLO to ensure that the latter did not act unilaterally and provoke an Israeli response that could embroil Syria. Consequently, once the civil war erupted in April 1975, when Phalangist gunmen strafed a bus carrying Rejection Front Palestinians, Syria sided cautiously with the latter and subsequently intervened diplomatically to seek to restore the status quo, with some concessions to leftist demands. Later, however, when it seemed that Palestinian-leftist forces might overrun Maronite positions and communities, the Syrians switched sides during 1976 and backed the Maronites, stopping what seemed like the potential defeat of the major Christian groups. In June Assad ordered his troops to enter Lebanon in force because he preferred a balance of power in which the Maronites preserved their political and military role. But this also meant that Assad permitted the ongoing Maronite blockade of a major refugee camp, Tal al-Zaatar, which finally succumbed in August 1976 with many of its inhabitants being killed outright by Maronite militiamen after they surrendered, adding to the atrocities committed by both sides during the conflict.

Syria's actions illustrate in microcosm the manner in which allegiances could shift as the war continued. Equally complex were the sources of armaments for the combatants, with manifest contradictions in their implications for state policies. Although the Saudi rulers seem to have discreetly backed the Maronites in the beginning, other princes continued to fund the Palestinians. The Maronites used money from the Saudis and conservative Arab states such as Kuwait to buy arms from Czechoslovakia and Bulgaria, communist regimes whose master, the Soviet Union, was arming Syria and, through it, the PLO. Once the communist supplies to the Maronites ended, the Maronites bought weapons on the open market and ultimately found their new supplier in Israel. Beginning in May 1976 Israel began funneling arms and tanks to the Maronites in the north while building up Maronite enclaves in the south. Israeli advisers also were sent to Maronite territory north of Beirut, and vehicles with Israeli markings took part in the final siege of Tal al-Zaatar.[23] Thus during the summer of 1976 both Israel and Syria were, either directly or indirectly, backing the Maronites against the Palestinians.

In the end, following an Arab summit in Riyadh in October, a deterrent force composed primarily of Syrians remained in central Lebanon to try to restore peace. But Lebanese politics had now become even more splintered as many small factions emerged seeking to control urban neighborhoods, unanswerable to any recognized political authority. As a final irony, the Riyadh accords called for the PLO to withdraw its forces from central Lebanon, removing them from contact with the main Maronite militias. The Palestinians returned in force to the south where their presence contributed to the tensions that finally caused the Israeli invasion of southern Lebanon in March 1978.

Israel had its own priorities. Initially the Israelis backed the Maronites out of sympathy but primarily to block any extension of Syrian power over Lebanon. In addition, strengthening the Maronite militias meant the possible destruction of the Palestinian camps and their inhabitants. Finally, the Israelis began an open fence policy along their northern border, seeking to establish relations with the Lebanese in the vicinity, especially the Maronites, who made up about 5 percent of the population. From 1976 onward, the Israelis also facilitated the transfer of Maronite militiamen through Israel into the south to bolster the Maronite position there. Here the Israelis linked their efforts with those of a dissident Lebanese army officer, Saad Haddad, a Greek Catholic who decided to opt for close relations with Israel as a means to combat the Palestinians in the region and enhance his own prestige. Throughout this period Israeli policy focused on supplying Haddad's forces and helping them expand their control, meaning that they would take over the numerous Shi'i villages to establish a security belt along Israel's northern boundaries. This support increased once Begin took office. He likened the Maronites, and Christians in general, to Jews who had been threatened and finally exterminated by the Nazis in World War II. By extension, the Arabs, and especially the Palestinians, were the incarnations of Nazis and should be given no quarter, an analogy he developed more specifically as time passed.

Haddad's efforts to expand the range of his territory led to increased tensions with Palestinian forces, who had begun to return to the south following agreements that they withdraw from the north around Beirut. In the midst of these clashes, both Syria and Israel strove to define their areas of interest from which the other was excluded. Israel notified Syria that its forces could not extend beyond a "red line" that remained undefined but was assumed to be the Litani River. Accepting this the Syrians tried to restrict the PLO's activities to lessen the potential for a massive Israeli intervention. At the same time Damascus backed Lebanese government efforts to insert newly formed army units into the south to establish the principle of Lebanese authority throughout the whole country. In July 1977 Syria, the PLO (Arafat), and President Elias Sarkis reached an agreement at Shtaura whereby the Palestinians would withdraw their forces from the border regions adjacent to Israel and permit Lebanese army units to enter. Haddad and Begin rejected this idea. They opposed restoration of any central authority that might limit their freedom of action against the PLO.

These activities took place during a period of intense American diplomacy (to be discussed in detail later) that aimed during most of 1977 to establish conditions suitable for a Geneva conference of all parties to the conflict, including at one point the PLO. The abandonment of these goals resulted in American support for Sadat's initiative of November 1977. These developments made the PLO, including Fatah, more determined to undertake raids into Israel to try to defeat any progress toward a peace that would enshrine recognition of non-Palestinian control over the West Bank. Terrorist activities could thus be seen as designed to strengthen Begin's resolve not to capitulate to American pressures.

This might lead to increased settlements, but it might also block a treaty accepted by all that decided the fate of the West Bank. The interrelationship of these factors emerges clearly in the events leading up to the Israeli invasion of south Lebanon in March 1978.

On 11 March 1978, eight Palestinian commandos belonging to Fatah landed on an Israeli beach along the coastal highway between Haifa and Tel Aviv, commandeered a passenger bus, and headed for Tel Aviv. A lengthy shoot-out followed, causing the deaths of six of the Palestinians and thirty-four Israelis, with seventy-eight more wounded. The raid was timed to interrupt a planned visit of Menachem Begin to Washington, scheduled for 14 March, and presumably to enable Begin to resist American pressure to soften the Israeli position on the future of the Palestinians on the West Bank.[24] The immediate result of the raid was the Israeli invasion of south Lebanon on 15 March, leading to an occupation that ended in June only after staged withdrawals designed to permit Haddad's forces to strengthen their positions. The invasion was ostensibly a retaliatory raid designed to punish the PLO. But it was in actuality an attack of approximately 20,000 troops that had long been planned and whose objective seems to have been the ousting of many Lebanese civilians, other than Maronites, from the area in order to give freer rein to Israeli and Maronite military actions. Various accounts note that the intensive shelling took mostly civilian casualties and caused an evacuation of over 100,000 Lebanese, many of them Shi'ites who had returned only after fleeing the strife in that region in the mid-1970s.[25]

Once the attack was under way, Israeli officials contacted Sadat to gain his tacit acceptance of the move, something he gave. The Egyptians did not want to derail the momentum toward peace talks and were not averse to punishing the Palestinians for seeking just that. In the short run the Fatah strategy seemed to work. PLO casualties in south Lebanon were slight, and "the terrorist attack greatly strengthened Begin's position," encouraging many in the United States to shift from criticism of his hard-line stand on West Bank settlements, which seemed to block progress in talks, to stressing the need for bolstering Israel's security.[26]

But if Sadat was willing to acquiesce in Israeli actions against the PLO, he still hoped to achieve recognition of Palestinian rights on the West Bank and possibly the Gaza Strip, both out of sympathy and in order to protect himself against charges that he sold out the Palestinians. Here the discrepancies between his and Begin's approaches emerged clearly. They were on the same track in their eagerness to sign a separate peace, but with differing objectives in mind where the West Bank was concerned. President Jimmy Carter and his advisers recognized the dilemma. They had hoped to bring in the PLO to attain a lasting peace. Unable to accomplish that goal, owing to developments in the Middle East and domestic limits to the terms the United States could offer, Carter was surprised to encounter resistance on that score from Sadat as well as Begin. By mid-1978 he and his aides realized that their initial objectives were impossible to achieve and that their best course was to salvage an Egyptian-Israeli pact that could serve as a model for future negotiations with other states, an upgraded version of the Kissinger model. In doing so, however, they seemingly, if unwittingly, ensured Israel's control over the West Bank, leading to increased Israeli-PLO hostilities, intensified Arab resistance to an escalation of Israeli repressive measures on the West Bank, and the decision by the Begin government to invade Lebanon in June 1982.

THE CARTER ADMINISTRATION AND CAMP DAVID: THE INITIAL STAGES, JANUARY–NOVEMBER 1977

The first efforts to define the parameters within which agreement might be reached indicated the difficulties ahead. Prime Minister Rabin, facing elections in March 1977, told the United States that Israel could give up most of the Sinai and none of the Golan Heights; the West Bank was the most delicate, but he left room for compromise. Regarding inclusion of the PLO in any talks, he remained noncommittal by stating that if the PLO accepted Resolution 242, the basis of negotiations, it would no longer be the PLO.[27] But once Begin took office in June, matters changed. Israeli officials had continually reminded Washington that Kissinger's 1975 promise still held; no contacts with the PLO were possible until it accepted Resolution 242, to which Israel presumably adhered. But Begin sought to change the applicability of 242, insisting that it did not apply to the West Bank, in keeping with his campaign promises never to return any portion of Judea and Samaria, as he called the region. In addition, Begin declared emotionally that the PLO was a Nazi organization; even if the PLO accepted 242 and recognized Israel, he would never deal with them, a statement that had widespread approval in Israel.[28]

These assertions clarified the forthcoming confrontation. Husayn of Jordan, eager to be included in a Geneva summit, supported inclusion of the PLO because he could not afford to oppose it. But he could not countenance the supposed goal of such participation, namely, the creation of an independent Palestinian state in the West Bank and Gaza, because he wanted the West Bank to be returned to Jordan. He therefore proposed that Palestinians outside the PLO be permitted to attend a Geneva meeting as part of his delegation, hoping to counter the latter's demands for a state and gain international recognition of his own title to the land. Begin might agree with him on the need to defeat the PLO, but he refused to consider Jordanian recovery of the region. The PLO's various groups considered the possibility of attending a summit in light of the Lebanese crisis they had just undergone. They had faced both Syria and Israel, directly and through each other's proxies, and were aware that Assad's support of the Maronites had had American approval.[29] They refused to accept Resolution 242 because of its reference to Palestinians only as refugees; the matter of statehood had to be considered. But the question of a state was itself fraught with difficulties, as noted in Chapter 8, and it was only in March 1977 that Arafat had gained PLO approval of a call for a Palestinian state to be created in "the territories from which Israel withdraws," an apparent though indirect acceptance of Israel's existence in its pre-1967 form.[30] This amounted to a signal marking Arafat's eagerness to be included in any international conference that convened.

Henry Kissinger had never considered the PLO a factor in the peace process, but Jimmy Carter thought otherwise, although his remarks often seemed contradictory, and he was occasionally forced to qualify them in such a manner as to negate their original implications. He was eager to instill new life into the Middle East conflict. In March 1977 he mentioned during a talk in Clinton, Massachusetts, that the Palestinians should be given a "homeland" as part of an overall resolution of the Arab-Israeli stalemate. This remark was part of a context in which he also called upon the Arab states to come to terms with Israel, but the code word *homeland* seemed to suggest a separate state, something his aides denied and he later repudiated.[31] Carter wanted to resolve the Palestinian problem and genuinely believed that the PLO should be involved in the discourse, conditional upon the organization's acceptance of Resolution 242. He was willing to have it add a reservation disclaiming acceptance of the resolution's reference to the Palestinian issue as solely one of refugees, something Arafat had proposed. In Carter's view this would indicate the PLO's acceptance of Israel and would enable its inclusion in the Geneva conference in which a separate Palestinian entity might be accepted, though linked to Jordanian sovereignty over the West Bank.

The effort failed, despite various American overtures encouraging a positive response. Sadat and Assad vied to control the PLO against the other while determined it should not act totally independently.[32] Another problem concerned events in Lebanon. In September 1977, in the midst of PLO deliberations as to how to respond to Carter's invitation, Israel had encouraged Saad Haddad to attack Palestinian positions in south Lebanon. The attack occurred on 14 September, with the Palestinian National Council scheduled to resume discussions on the twentieth. As the Israelis were aware of this meeting and the topics to be discussed, it is unlikely that the timing was coincidental; it was probably designed to encourage a hardening of positions and undermine American diplomacy, just as PLO terrorism sought to stiffen Israeli postures at times. Nevertheless, Arafat argued strongly for accepting the invitation, responding not only to private American inquiries but also to a State Department announcement on 12 September that "the Palestinians must be involved in the peace-making process. Their representatives will have to be at Geneva for the question to be solved," assuming these delegates had accepted Resolution 242. Arafat failed, apparently defeated by rejectionist arguments that the United States would not be able to force Israel to withdraw from the West Bank and Gaza, given its inability to gain

Israeli agreement to let Lebanese peace-keeping forces into the six-mile strip north of Israel's border.[33] The initiative ended after further developments provided evidence of the gap between Carter's vision and the Palestinians' hopes. The president had been forced to respond to strong criticism of the State Department's announcement of 12 September, and on the sixteenth he denied in a meeting with journalists that he had ever committed himself to the PLO or that he envisioned a separate Palestinian state; he was only calling for Palestinians to be represented at the conference.[34]

Defeat did not mean the end of American efforts, however. The Carter administration reached agreement with the Soviet Union on a joint declaration of principles that could guide the forthcoming Geneva summit. This announcement represented another significant departure from Kissinger's strategy, reflecting the belief that the Soviets could contribute to the process by pressuring Assad and the PLO. Moscow agreed to omit references to the "national rights" of the Palestinians and to Israel's withdrawal to "the" 1967 borders; the communiqué referred to Israeli withdrawal from territories and to the "legitimate rights" of the Palestinians, placing the statement more squarely within the context of Resolution 242.[35] Informed beforehand of the announcement, Sadat welcomed it, but for Israel and its American supporters, it signified a major setback that should be neutralized if possible. The task fell to Foreign Minister Moshe Dayan who succeeded, during a tense meeting with Carter and his chief aides on 4 October, in gaining a declaration including the sentence that "acceptance of the Joint U.S.–U.S.S.R. Statement of October 1, 1977 is not a prerequisite for the reconvening and conduct of the Geneva Conference."

Ostensibly a compromise, this American-Israeli announcement undermined the set of procedures agreed upon by the United States and the Soviet Union.[36] Israel would not be bound by them, regardless of the Arab states' position, and it would be supported in its position by the Americans. Dayan had bargained for the statement, ceding ground on the nature of Palestinian participation—to Begin's horror—but he had gained his ultimate objective. Israel opposed Soviet involvement principally out of fear that the Russians might persuade the Syrians and the Palestinians to reduce their demands, thereby placing greater international pressure on Israel to withdraw from the Golan Heights and the West Bank in return for peace, something Dayan made clear was unacceptable.[37] Either course would interfere with what Dayan stressed as Israel's real objectives, those Rabin had outlined as Israel's strategy in 1974: a separate peace with Egypt, to be achieved preferably through separate negotiations that eschewed the wrangling that would inevitably occur if a Geneva conference were held.

Carter's retreat from the Soviet-American declaration convinced Sadat that direct negotiations with Israel were preferable to an international forum in which discussions over procedures would greatly lengthen the negotiating process. Aware of Israeli interest in a direct dialogue, he had sent an emissary to meet Dayan in Morocco in September; Dayan left the session with the impression that

Sadat would sign a separate peace in return for the Sinai. Now Sadat took the initiative. On 9 November he announced to a stunned Egyptian National Assembly, with Arafat in the audience, that he was willing to go to Jerusalem.[38] Exchanges with Begin led to his historic visit on the nineteenth, setting in motion the contacts that, after several false starts, led to Camp David and a subsequent Egyptian-Israeli peace accord.

THE ROAD TO CAMP DAVID: NOVEMBER 1977–SEPTEMBER 1978

Both Sadat and Begin wanted any separate peace agreement to justify their diametrically opposed stances on the fate of the West Bank Palestinians. Sadat demanded references to Israeli recognition of Palestinian rights to self-rule; Begin sought clauses that would permit continued Israeli control of the West Bank to ensure denial of any semblance of an independent Palestinian entity. The potential for stalemate emerged soon after Sadat's visit to Jerusalem. On 18 January 1978 he summarily recalled his delegation from that city, suspending talks because of Israeli actions that seemed to justify the barbs of his Arab critics.

Amidst these exchanges the Begin cabinet had approved a proposal by Agricultural Minister Ariel Sharon to create dummy settlements in the Sinai beyond those in the Rafa salient west of Gaza. Sharon's aim, accepted by Begin and Dayan, was either to gain more land in the Sinai or to bargain with Sadat by openly abandoning these fake encampments in order to keep the established Jewish communities there. These actions angered Washington as well as Cairo, already unhappy with Begin's proposals to retain rights to the oil fields in the Sinai and the air bases built there and to permit Israelis who might wish to remain in the settlements under Egyptian sovereignty to keep arms for self-defense. These latter proposals could be seen as bargaining tactics, but the new settlements appeared to be a breach of faith, arousing intense Egyptian hostility which in turn angered the Israelis.[39]

A six-month hiatus set in during which the Carter administration initially sought an alliance with Sadat to place pressure on Begin to relax his stand regarding the West Bank, especially his refusals to apply Resolution 242 to the area or to agree to some future Israeli withdrawal of armed forces. This strategy failed because several corollary factors proved unattainable. Carter had hoped that leading members of the American Jewish community would encourage Begin to be more forthcoming. They did not, especially after the terrorist raid into Israel in mid-March 1978 which stiffened Begin's resolve to hold fast to his position and led American Jews to back him against any concessions. Damaging also was Carter's decision during this period to push for sales of F-15 jets to Saudi Arabia, a move that challenged the Jewish lobby and aroused great opposition within the American Jewish community.

Given Begin's determination to stand fast on the West Bank, Carter finally decided to work through him, if not with him. Here Carter was also influenced by Sadat's apparent disinterest in the specifics of a plan for West Bank autonomy. The president and his advisers concluded that the Egyptian leader would settle for a vague formula regarding the Palestinians, whereas they had hoped for a more specific proposal tying the future of the area to Jordan. This approach now seemed futile, as Jordan could not be brought into the talks, Sadat would not demand guarantees, and Begin would not provide them even if he did. With such an impasse Carter decided in July to call a summit to resolve the discord between Begin and Sadat, conceding as he did that his hopes of a broader peace in any form had been dashed. All that seemed possible was a separate agreement, precisely what the Israelis had been hoping for and what they believed, as now did Carter, Sadat would accept.[40]

The Camp David talks lasted from 5 to 17 September. Two sets of agreements resulted. One established arrangements for determining the future of the West Bank and the Gaza Strip. The other comprised principles whereby an Egyptian-Israeli peace treaty would be formulated ratifying the conclusion of hostilities and the establishment of normal relations between the two countries. Success came only at the very end, with most of the participants near exhaustion and several crucial details left open to interpretation. Begin refused throughout to agree to withdraw the Sinai settlements; he compromised finally by declaring he would accept the vote of the Knesset on the matter, meaning that he could not be accused of abandoning Jewish territory. As a result, Israel did undertake a staged pullback from the Sinai that was completed in April 1982. But in return Begin and his aides gained much. They were able to delete references to Resolution 242 as applying to the West Bank, and its clause noting the "inadmissibility of territories acquired by war," implying by omission the acceptability of retaining some territory by such means. No reference to Jerusalem appeared, again suggesting Sadat's acceptance of a united Jerusalem under Israeli rule, although official positions remained the contrary. And finally from Begin's perspective, "the Sinai had been sacrificed, but Eretz Israel had been won," referring to the manner in which understandings pertaining to the West Bank had been left open deliberately.[41]

Here there emerged differences of opinion that have remained at the heart of Arab opposition to Camp David and that have seriously weakened American credibility in the Arab world. In seeking an accord on the fate of the West Bank and Gaza, Begin had accepted inclusion of the term "the legitimate rights of the Palestinian people," because he considered it meaningless in light of guaranteed Israeli occupation of the region. But he later informed Carter that by "people" he meant the inhabitants of the areas, whereas Carter and Sadat assumed this meant other Palestinians as well and theoretically did not rule out PLO participation. Though left unresolved, Begin's qualification was later accepted by the Reagan administration with major implications for American policy in the region.[42]

In addition there arose the question of Israeli settlements in these areas. Carter wanted an Israeli commitment to freeze implantation of new settlements during the period required to negotiate the autonomy of the areas. That process, drafted to include Jordan also, although Husayn had never been consulted, would presumably take a long time. Carter and other officials believed they had Begin's oral acceptance of this proposal, but the latter then informed Carter in writing that he would accept only a three-month moratorium; this suspension applied to the period envisaged as necessary to conclude the details of the Israeli-Egyptian peace treaty, not the autonomy talks regarding the West Bank and Gaza, a significant distinction. This gap in interpretation arose on the final day. Carter decided to leave the matter open to conclude the talks successfully. But this enabled Israel to argue that it had never agreed to anything more than the three-month period with no written verification other than Begin's memorandum. Carter and his aides were and remain convinced that the context of the original discussion clearly tied Begin's oral agreement to the autonomy negotiations and that he later reneged. With no written document, however, the point remained moot, with Israel in full control over the territories and intending to expand settlements once its self-defined period of abstention ended.[43]

Subsequent developments permitted the Begin interpretation to be implemented. The Egyptian-Israeli peace treaty, signed in March 1979, remained separate from any linkage to the autonomy scheme for the West Bank, despite Sadat's belated efforts to connect the two and defend himself against charges he had abandoned the Palestinians. Negotiations leading to the final treaty were acrimonious and exhausting, but compromises were made on both sides. Sadat agreed to an exchange of ambassadors and full diplomatic relations before Israel had completed its withdrawal from the Sinai; the latter reduced the period of its departure from five to three years. Negotiations over the format of autonomy for the West Bank, begun in May 1979, dragged on for over a year with no agreement. The Begin government reasserted its claim to the West Bank and its interpretation of autonomy as personal, not applying to land and water rights which would continue to belong to Israel. This came during accelerated efforts to extend Jewish settlements in the area (to be discussed later). Sadat called for full governing autonomy for the territory, not simply its inhabitants, within a Jordanian entity, a stance that had American backing but little will to support it forcefully.

Already looking ahead to the 1980 Democratic primary and reelection campaign, Carter found himself confronted by crises elsewhere that eroded his leadership image. The departure of the shah of Iran from that country in January 1979 and the arrival of the Ayatollah Khomeini in February signaled a new era for that country, culminating in the taking of American hostages in the U.S. embassy in Teheran in November. This, coupled with the Soviet invasion of Afghanistan in December, left the president little room for maneuver in the Arab-Israeli forum, especially given a renewed upward spiral of oil prices that called his overtures to the Saudis into question in the public eye despite their relative moderation on price matters. The official American position remained as before, that Israeli settlements in occupied territory were illegal and that East Jerusalem was considered to be occupied territory despite its incorporation into Israel, but Carter preferred not to argue this openly in the midst of politicking.[44] Carter had achieved the Camp David accords and the Egyptian-Israeli peace treaty, but at personal cost, holding to established American positions that, when declared openly, harmed his chances for a second term.

THE REAGAN ADMINISTRATION AND THE ARAB-ISRAELI CONFLICT: AN OVERVIEW

Ronald Reagan assumed the presidency in January 1981 at a time of increased regional strife in the Middle East. In addition to the Soviet occupation of Afghanistan and a hostile regime in Iran, Iraq had attacked Iran in September 1980, seeking to overthrow the regime of the Ayatollah Khomeini. The Ayatollah's pronouncements regarding the advent of a Shi'ite revolution under Iranian auspices had struck fear throughout the Persian Gulf region where Arab oil-producing states, including Saudi Arabia, had significant Shi'i minorities.

The Reagan administration viewed these events in a global perspective dominated by the apparent Soviet ability to exploit them to their advantage. Reagan believed that the Soviets were an evil presence on earth whose machinations if not their very existence should be ended. This vision affected most other perceptions he held. His lack of knowledge of foreign affairs was equaled by his disinterest in rectifying that situation. The new president "was well-known for lack of mastery over finite material," responding mainly to information that confirmed his preconceptions.[45] With regard to the Middle East, Reagan saw Israel, following the shah's departure from Iran, "as perhaps the only remaining strategic asset in the region on which the United States can truly rely. . . . Only by full appreciation of the critical role the State of Israel plays in our strategic calculus can we build the foundation for thwarting Moscow's design on territories vital to our security and our national well-being."[46] Reagan also identified with Israel in light of Old Testament prophecies as proclaimed by fundamentalist Christian groups who have called for staunch support of Israel.[47]

Unconcerned with detail, the president left policy formulation to his advisers, who hoped to align Israel and the conservative Arab states, especially Egypt and Saudi Arabia, in an anti-Soviet military defense system. This search for a "strategic consensus" ignored the underlying reality of continuing Arab-Israeli hostility which made such an initiative impossible to achieve, though this did not deter its proponents, especially the secretary of state, Alexander Haig, from occasionally assuming that its realization was at hand. Additionally, the Reagan administration's support for this policy aroused strong opposition in Washington when funding was requested for arms packages to Arab states as well as Israel in the spring of 1981. Congress approved aid to Israel, but a major furor erupted over proposed assistance to Saudi Arabia as part of the same strategic approach, especially the offer to sell five AWACS planes (Airborne Warning and Command Systems). These aircraft were intended to buttress Saudi defense systems in the Persian Gulf against either Soviet or Iranian aggression, but Israel's supporters viewed it as a major threat to its security. The proposed package, with modifications, finally passed, but only after Reagan's direct intervention. The fray left both sides angered, the Israelis that they had lost the battle and the Saudis that they had been forced to justify their need for such weapons in what they deemed a humiliating manner. In early June, in the midst of the controversy, Israeli planes had bombed an Iraqi nuclear reactor. The planes had crossed Saudi airspace to reach their target.

In such less-than-amicable circumstances, the chances for any strategic consensus regarding Middle Eastern affairs seemed slight, but the Reagan administration tried to apply the concept elsewhere, namely, regarding Nicaragua and supplying the contras. President Reagan's willingness to personally back the AWACS sale to Saudi Arabia was apparently tied to a private agreement that the Saudis would fund anticommunist movements. Although this included Afghanistan, it probably included the contras as well.[48] Rumors of Israel's aiding the contras have surfaced frequently, but with no apparent evidence of direct ties. However, Israel may have aided the contras by providing heavy military assistance through a third party, possibly Argentina which the Reagan administration had "convinced . . . to spend many millions of dollars in secret to train and equip the fledgling Nicaraguan rebel army" in 1981. The source of this equipment and funds was obviously not Argentina itself.[49]

In general, the contrast with the Carter administration could not have been greater. Where there had existed a consensus concerning Middle East policy, now there was none, with major rifts appearing within the Reagan administration. Whereas Carter had immersed himself in details, perhaps overly so, Reagan ignored both the details and the need to coordinate policy, creating a situation in which officials fought among themselves while forced to respond to events, often instigated by the logic of Israel's policies that helped intensify hostilities in the region. The search for a strategic consensus among anticommunist Middle Eastern countries was justified only in exploiting Saudi and Israeli resources to fund resistance to leftist regimes outside the region, not to establish a common front in the area of direct confrontation.

In the Middle East, 1981 was characterized by increasing violence in Lebanon as tensions escalated between Syria and Israel, sparked by Maronite militias, PLO factions, and the units under Saad Haddad, as well as by Israel's continuing policy of preemptive air strikes on Palestinian positions. By the end of the year Menachem Begin and Ariel Sharon, the latter appointed defense minister in August, had drafted plans for a massive invasion of Lebanon up to Beirut designed to wipe out the PLO at the least and possibly force most Palestinians from the country. An important by-product of this accomplishment would be consolidation of Israel's control over the West Bank. Destruction of the PLO would presumably demoralize Arafat's supporters in the area and compel them to acquiesce in Israeli rule.

The West Bank factor became more significant following the assassination of Anwar al-Sadat on 6 October 1981, the eighth anniversary of the Egyptian crossing of the Suez Canal opening the 1973 War. Sadat had been playing for time, planning to become more forceful in his criticism of Israel's West Bank policies once he had regained the Sinai. But his tactics had opened him to severe criticism in Egypt. He had visited Israel before the June elections, a clear gesture of support for Begin designed to ensure progress toward recovery of the Sinai. Three days after his departure, Israel had bombed the Iraqi nuclear reactor, associating him by default with the plan. In September Sadat had ordered massive arrests of critics of his policies, both on the left and the right, an act that intensified hostility toward him in his own country. Egyptian disillusionment with his course of action showed itself in the nearly total absence of public remorse at his death. His successor, Husni Mubarak, indicated his adherence to the Camp David Agreement, but it was clear that Begin could not afford to pressure him for further concessions before proceeding with the final withdrawal from the northeast corner of the Sinai, scheduled for April 1982. The Begin government thus turned to imposing new administrative measures to seek to consolidate its control over the West Bank.

ISRAEL AND THE WEST BANK, 1977–1982

Since taking office in 1977, the Begin administration, led by its then minister of agriculture, Ariel Sharon, had exerted great efforts to expand Jewish settlements on the West Bank and in Gaza, especially the former. Sharon had close ties to the Gush Emunim and backed the group's efforts to settle in areas adjacent to large Arab centers of population, a strategy he believed necessary both to ensure enlargement of the Jewish population of the West Bank and to intimidate the Arab inhabitants. Sharon was aided by the fact that the West Bank was governed by an Israeli military administration whose acquisition of private land for supposed military purposes traditionally went unchallenged by Israeli courts; in many cases this land was then handed over to the agriculture ministry for Jewish settlement. When unilateral acts by the Gush Emunim brought this policy into question, however, Sharon found avenues open to circumvent the decree and to make much more West Bank land inalienably Jewish.[50] He had close personal ties with and financial backing from the Jewish National Fund, part of the World Zionist Organization. Using these sources enabled Sharon's Ministry of Agriculture and officials from the Jewish National Fund to concentrate on acquiring sectors considered public or state land rather than privately owned. But the process was time-consuming and seemed to indicate that much land might be considered private property. In 1980, therefore, the government decided to declare arbitrarily as "state land" large tracts regardless of title, with the stipulation that the land could be turned over to Israeli settlers in three weeks if Arab claimants could not prove ownership during that period, an unlikely prospect in the Begin government's view. Judgment over the status of ownership would be made by military tribunals within the territory with no further recourse for a plaintiff.

Done hastily, this "process of declaration and seizure [was] not the outcome of a long, multistage judicial process but was intended specifically to preempt it."[51] Authorities designated over two million dunams (500,000 acres) to be acquired, or 40 percent of the total land area. At the same time the World Zionist Organization, overseer of the Jewish National Fund, authorized plans to purchase extensive private property where the Arabs were willing to sell. Whereas this had been the primary form of land acquisition during the mandatory period, the proportion of land acquired through buying and selling, as opposed to state requisition, was now less, perhaps 25 percent of the total by 1983, although at a relatively high cost, as land values had risen enormously.[52]

With Begin's narrow electoral victory in June 1981 behind him and Sharon now his minister of defense, he looked for other means of establishing Israeli dominance over the West Bank in the face of increasing Palestinian hostility. Unable to gain Egyptian agreement to any autonomy scheme following Sadat's assassination, the government decided to implement its own version of Palestinian autonomy while claiming that it fulfilled the intent of the Camp David Agreement. On 8 November 1981, the Begin cabinet announced that it had created a separate civilian administration designed to handle all local concerns except military and security matters on the West Bank; the military government established after the 1967 War was abolished. This was in effect a subterfuge, as the Israeli military remained in control of affairs on the West Bank with civilian officials subordinate to them. The only difference was that the military authority was now situated in Israel rather than centered in the West Bank. This enabled the Begin government to claim that it was fulfilling the Camp David clauses stating that the military government and "its civilian administration" be removed "as soon as a self-governing authority has been freely elected."[53]

Having "removed" the military government by transferring its headquarters, Israeli officials set about trying to constitute a Palestinian self-governing authority staffed by individuals who would accept their directives. Here they focused on an arrangement of local village leagues created in 1978 around Hebron and decided to use this structure as a basis for developing an areawide system run by Palestinians. These leagues would be given legislative powers, excluding elected mayors and village officials who rejected the Israeli initiative. By controlling patronage and the power to issue permits and by being given the right to carry arms, the Israeli administration hoped that the village league heads would win support either by their control of purse strings or through intimidation. The immediate result was to arouse strong West Bank Palestinian resistance to these moves, which were accompanied by an "iron fist" policy of retaliation and harassment encouraged by the chief of staff, Rafael Eitan. As a result, the West Bank became a scene of intensified repression during the first six months of 1982, with military officials tolerating if not encouraging settler violence toward Arab residents.[54]

LEBANON: THE STRUGGLE TO ESTABLISH HEGEMONY

As noted, Israel's West Bank strategy paralleled plans to undertake a massive invasion of Lebanon designed to destroy the PLO and facilitate the recreation of a united Lebanon under the leadership of Bashir Gemayel, the head of the Maronite paramilitary Phalange. By the end of 1980, Bashir Gemayel, younger son of Pierre, the patriarch of the Gemayel clan, had established his dominance over all the Maronite military forces. Gemayel had long been in contact with Israeli leaders, hoping to use them to realize his ambitions. Many of his assistants had received extensive training in Israel during and following Israeli intervention on the side of the Maronites in 1976. In Lebanon, Bashir Gemayel was backed by the Maronite religious establishment, now centered in the monastic orders which themselves contributed fighters to paramilitary groups. They agreed that their choice was either to regain total Maronite control of the country, regardless of the size of the Muslim communities relative to their own, or to establish a separate state north of Beirut, an alternative that would lead to the cantonization of Lebanon into separate and autonomous communities defined by religious affiliation. They preferred the former course, one that was also more attractive to Israeli leaders, as it would ensure a friendly power on their northern frontier governed by a religious minority in the Middle East, just as they were. A central concern of both was the removal of the PLO from Lebanon, as its existence threatened any chance of Maronite success and, from Israel's perspective, any assurance that their northern frontiers would be spared the possibility of raids and rocket attacks. But Gemayel went further. He and his Maronite advisers spoke openly of the removal of most if not all Palestinians from Lebanon, the methods to be left to their discretion.[55]

The first half of 1981 saw the increasing interrelationship of Israeli-Maronite activities vis-à-vis Syria and the PLO. Some Israeli operations were apparently influenced also by domestic political considerations, namely Prime Minister Begin's desire to enhance his reelection chances which had seemed threatened by a faltering Israeli economy.[56] Throughout the period Israel continued to conduct raids against PLO positions in southern Lebanon, not so much in retaliation for specific attacks, but as part of a preemptive strategy designed to destroy the Palestinians' ability to take initiatives. As these raids often caused civilian and non-Palestinian casualties, a by-product was the development of intense opposition to the PLO in southern Lebanon among the majority community, the Shi'ites, who suffered their own dead and wounded from Israeli raids. The largest Shi'ite paramilitary group, Amal, engaged in clashes with Palestinian militias, occasionally backed by Syria with which Amal established close ties and from which it received arms.[57] One of the paradoxes of this situation was that PLO groups were arming themselves with heavier weapons, including tanks, that were transferred often through Syria in order that they might be able to withstand an Israeli assault reminiscent of the 1978 invasion of south Lebanon. But in light of the Syrian-Amal relationship, it appears that Arafat and Fatah also wanted these arms to use to ensure their independence from Syria.

Although Syria tried to balance Palestinian power in south Lebanon by building its own client military organization, Amal, it also sought to preserve its freedom of action in central Lebanon, including access to Beirut. The Lebanese presidential elections were slated for September 1982. It was no secret that Hafiz al-Assad hoped to install Sulayman Franjiyah as president, the one Maronite with whom he had close ties. This in itself challenged Bashir Gemayel's determination to be elected president, an ambition shared by Ariel Sharon. As a result, Gemayel sought to broaden his patronage as 1981 began, seeking to show himself to be the protector of all Lebanese Christians, not simply the Maronites. He thus decided to gain control of Zahle, an important city located adjacent to the Beirut–Damascus highway in central Lebanon with a population composed principally of Greek Orthodox and Greek Catholic Lebanese. Gaining their allegiance would give his cause greater legitimacy. Moreover, establishing the Phalange there would challenge the Syrians directly, as their main forces were situated behind Zahle, and might instigate an encounter that would bring Israel in on Gemayel's side, something he apparently hoped would happen. Begin had promised him in 1978 that if Syrian planes attacked Christian forces, Israeli planes would intervene on their behalf.[58]

At the beginning of April 1981, clashes erupted between Phalangist and Syrian forces in and around Zahle. Syrian troops shelled the city, causing heavy civilian casualties, and took strategic high ground overlooking the city from Phalangist units. Gemayel called for Israeli aid and received it in the form of planes that downed two Syrian helicopters.[59] Assad responded by installing ground-to-air missiles in the hills overlooking Zahle, a significant escalation in that these weapons covered air space heretofore open to Israeli reconnaissance and to their attacks on Palestinian positions. A "missile crisis" ensued with the United States' sending a veteran diplomat, Philip Habib, to restrain both sides from further escalation, a task he concluded successfully in May.

Despite its accomplishments, the Habib mission pointed out the contradictions in American policy. Secretary of State Alexander Haig had visited the Middle East in late March and early April. He had pointedly omitted Syria from his itinerary and, during his stay in Israel, equally pointedly had referred to Assad's regime as Soviet dominated and a threat to peace. Such remarks could have scarcely deterred either Gemayal or Begin from assuming that the United States would approve escalation of tensions with Damascus. On the other hand, Habib found it necessary to work with Assad. He seems to have encouraged him to believe that further progress on an overall peace agreement might develop with

American approval and, he hoped, with Saudi backing in the near future. The disparity between the Haig and the Habib visits, one a junket and the other a specific effort to dampen hostilities, highlighted the disparity between Washington's search for a strategic consensus against the Soviets that encouraged confrontation with Soviet "clients," and efforts to resolve regional disputes that necessarily had to include countries such as Syria whose truculence was inspired in part by their determination not to be omitted from any peacekeeping efforts. This disparity in interpretations arose again, with bloody ramifications for American forces, after the 1982 Israeli invasion of Lebanon.

The PLO found itself in a precarious position in the spring of 1981. It feared that it would be caught in a vise between the Maronite militias to the north and an Israeli invasion from the south, but those factions supporting Arafat also found that they were facing increasing Syrian hostility as well. Under Arafat's guidance the PLO had pursued peace initiatives with the United States and European countries since 1977. Unable to accept Resolution 242 in a manner acceptable to Washington, Arafat nevertheless scored impressive gains. In June 1980 the nine-member European Economic Community issued the Venice Declaration, which called for recognition of the Palestinians' right to self-determination and the PLO's right to be linked with any peace initiative. Though not stipulating whether such self-determination should result in an independent state or one linked to Jordan, the declaration did call for dismantling Israeli settlements in territories occupied since the 1967 war in preparation for the return of these territories as a prerequisite for peace.[60] This statement and subsequent pronouncements indicated the Europeans' unease with the Camp David process and their belief that the American initiative was doomed to fail. Such recognition, along with diplomatic status accorded to the PLO, encouraged Arafat to pursue diplomacy as a major tactic. This in turn aroused intense Syrian hostility toward Arafat, as Damascus feared he might seek an accord in tandem with Jordan, still at odds with Assad. This would further isolate Syria in direct confrontation with Israel while its forces were divided between the Golan region and Lebanon.

Arafat consequently found himself under attack from various sides during the summer of 1981. The PFLP opposed his diplomacy. Syria undertook, through the sponsorship of a renagade Fatah official known as Abu Nidal, the assassination of the PLO representative in Belgium, who was the group's liaison with the European Economic Community. This killing followed by a month the murder of a leading Austrian Jew by the same Abu Nidal group. The pattern was not unusual. Abu Nidal agents had killed and would kill European Jews or Israelis abroad, and they also had a history of assassinating PLO representatives, usually associated with Fatah, who were involved in establishing diplomatic ties and fostering peace talks. Between 1978 and 1982, "nearly a dozen" Fatah representatives, some involed in dialogues with Israeli leftists, were killed by agents identified with Abu Nidal.[61]

As Arafat pushed his peace option, Fatah operations against Israel seemed to decline, although there still were numerous clashes between PLO groups and the Israeli-supplied militia of Saad Haddad in the strip controlled by him contiguous to Israel's northern border. There was a series of Israeli raids during April and May in conjunction with the Syrian missile crisis. The PLO retaliated with rocket barrages against northern Israel, no casualties resulting. Matters remained relatively quiet until early July when Israeli forces again raided Palestinian positions. A war of escalation immediately resulted. Artillery and rocket shells fired into Israel led Israel to intensify its attacks, culminating in an air strike against Fatah and the PDFLP headquarters in a crowded suburb of West Beirut, causing casualties estimated at about two hundred dead and six hundred wounded. Nearly all were civilians, with about thirty assumed to be members of the PLO. The result was a massive PLO rocket bombardment of northern Israeli settlements that paralyzed the region for several days and killed six Israeli civilians and wounded fifty-nine.[62] The intensity of these exchanges and the numerous civilian casualties in Beirut caused the United States to intervene. Philip Habib was again dispatched to the region. On 24 July he gained a cease-fire, mediated separately with the PLO and Israel, agreeing to a cessation of hostilities in southern Lebanon and along Israel's Lebanese border.

The PLO–Israeli cease-fire, though negotiated indirectly, appeared to pose a major threat to Israel in the eyes of many Israeli analysts. First, it suggested Israel's implicit recognition of the PLO. Second, it permitted the PLO to resume its buildup of forces in Lebanon, arms that might be used against Israel. Third, the United States' willingness to deal with the PLO was itself alarming, although Washington's position regarding the need of that organization to accept Resolution 242 remained unchanged. Here Israeli and Palestinian perspectives seem to mesh, as Arafat apparently hoped to use this accord to strengthen his own contacts with Washington in pursuit of diplomatic exchanges.

In this regard the Palestinians posed more of a challenge to Israel as a peacemaking organization than as a military one, with the continuance of the cease-fire more unsettling than its collapse. This was particularly the case as Arafat seemed unable or unwilling to denounce PLO incursions into Israel from Jordan; he held that the cease-fire applied only to Lebanon, whereas Israel argued that it was all-embracing. The result, however, was that Menachem Begin became more convinced than ever following the cease-fire that the PLO should be destroyed rather than permitted to exist behind a truce.

THE ISRAELI INVASION OF LEBANON, ITS BACKGROUND AND IMPACT, AUGUST 1981–SEPTEMBER 1982

The inauguration of the second Begin-led cabinet in Israel (August 1981) coincided with a series of developments that indicated the likelihood of increasing pressure from various Arab states for peace initiatives that would be aimed at

Washington. While in the American capital from 4 to 8 August, Sadat had called for the use of the PLO–Israeli cease-fire as a steppingstone to "mutual and simultaneous recognition" of each other than could form the basis of lasting peace. Begin had rejected the idea outright, saying that Israel would never deal with the PLO, and Washington stated its established position that the United States would negotiate with the Palestinian group only after it had accepted Resolution 242 and recognized Israel. Though consistent with previous positions, this stance posed a dilemma for Israel because of the American commitment to deal with the organization in the case that such recognition was offered.

Jockeying for influence continued. On 7 August, during Sadat's stay in Washington, Crown Prince Fahd of Saudi Arabia issued his proposals for peace. He called for the scrapping of Camp David, Israeli withdrawal from all territories occupied in 1967, and the creation of a Palestinian state with its capital in East Jerusalem. He dealt with Israel by stating that "all states in the region should be able to live in peace."[63] Some saw this statement as a major step forward, implying Arab recognition of Israel, but the only state mentioned specifically was that proposed for the Palestinians. Israel denounced the plan. Washington treated it more cautiously, hoping to use Saudi Arabia to encourage Syria to become more amenable to peace talks, but Fahd's proposals in themselves would have undermined the Camp David process to which the United States remained committed. Sadat felt constrained to criticize Fahd's remarks, obviously designed to upstage his visit, if only because he would regain all of the Sinai in April 1982 only as part of the Camp David agreements. Nevertheless, Fahd's overtures, despite their implicit and direct criticism of Israeli policies, seemed to indicate movement in the Arab camp toward a negotiating forum, something that itself could challenge Begin's desire to consolidate his control over the West Bank. Consequently, he and Ariel Sharon, now his defense minister, seem to have begun planning for Israel's invasion of Lebanon as early as September 1981.

Sharon's goal was to destroy the PLO military infrastructure and, if possible, the PLO leadership itself; the latter meant attacking West Beirut where the PLO headquarters and command bunkers were located. In addition, Sharon envisaged a major confrontation with the Syrians, driving them out of Lebanon. The outcome would be a new Lebanon in which the presidency of Bashir Gemayel would be ensured, elected under Israeli auspices. Such a scenario obviously appealed to Gemayel. Whatever the ongoing chaos of Lebanese politics and the continuing fighting and bombing in Beirut, he would probably not win any free election because of his bloody reputation gained while consolidating his power; many Maronites of other factions would likely vote against him. But Sharon wanted Gemayel, demanding in return that the latter express his willingness to sign a peace treaty with Israel, thus stabilizing, presumably forever, Israel's northern frontier. Gemayel and his aides reciprocated, seeking an Israeli intervention as soon as possible. Sharon visited Maronite headquarters north of

Beirut several times during 1981–1982, as did the Israeli staff assigned to coordinate arrangements for the attack.

The idea in its totality seems to have been Sharon's, though he had the support of Begin, Foreign Minister Yitzhak Shamir, and Chief of Staff Rafael Eitan. But there were disagreements. Eitan wanted to avoid a direct clash with the Syrians and to focus on the PLO. He was far more concerned about the Palestinian threat from Lebanon and on the West Bank than with Lebanese politics and the fortunes of Bashir Gemayel. Many high-ranking officers seem to have expressed strong reservations about parts or all of the plan, preferring a sweep of the southern region akin to the invasion of 1978. The Israeli cabinet remained uninformed about any plans until December 1981 when the scheme was placed before them for approval. They then expressed strong reservations, leading Begin to table the idea.[64]

Cabinet unease did not deter Sharon from proceeding with his arrangements which included informing American diplomats, who also responded negatively. In February 1982, Begin and Sharon dispatched the chief of military intelligence, Yehoshua Seguy, to Washington to consult on the expanding PLO military infrastructure in southern Lebanon and apparently to seek approval for a strike against the PLO under appropriate circumstances. Secretary of State Haig stressed that there could be no assault unless there had been a major provocation from Lebanon, apparently under the impression that such an operation would be restricted to the south. This condition met Israeli expectations; they had already considered the need to provoke the PLO into firing into northern Israel, thus justifying an attack, by bombing PLO positions in Lebanon. What remained uncertain from this time onward was whether Begin personally backed the full invasion plan, as he had previously, or whether he favored a limited strike that would satisfy his cabinet. What is clear is that Sharon and Eitan continued to prepare for the larger-scale invasion, whereas Begin decided to present the cabinet with proposals for a limited attack in order to gain its assent.

On various occasions during the spring of 1982 the Israeli military command sought approval for strikes that might lead the PLO to retaliate forcefully enough to justify to the world Israel's right to attack. Incidents creating the opportunity included the assassination of an Israeli diplomat in Paris in April and the death of an Israeli officer in Lebanon. The first air strike produced no response. Another, on 9 May following the discovery of explosives on a bus in Israel, caused a controlled PLO rocket barrage that was deemed insufficiently provocative to justify an attack. In none of these cases was there evidence that Arafat had ordered the incidents, but they could be used to justify seeking to do away with Arafat. By this time, awareness of Sharon's strategy existed, and news reports had appeared in both Israel and the United States from March onward noting the likelihood of an Israeli assault.[65] In late May, Sharon arrived in Washington where he met Haig and his staff. He showed them maps and detailed plans for two invasions, one restricted to south Lebanon and the other going north to

Beirut. Haig informed Sharon that no such undertaking was justifiable unless there was a major provocation, one acceptable to the international community. Depending on the source, the admonition could be seen as a warning, as Haig argues, or as tacit approval of a strike into Lebanon if the circumstances seemed to justify it, as Sharon seems to have interpreted Haig's remarks. Haig, in a subsequent private meeting with Sharon, may have been more positive than he was in front of his aides.[66]

The catalyst for the Israeli invasion of Lebanon came with the attempted assassination of the Israeli ambassador in London on 3 June. British intelligence sources identified the act as that of the Abu Nidal group, now probably sponsored by Iraq. Israeli intelligence evaluations apparently agreed, but Begin, Sharon, and Eitan were uninterested in this information. They had their excuse and ordered Israeli jets to attack West Beirut, strikes that resulted in over a hundred casualties. These air attacks were intended to cause PLO gunners to shell northern Israel, thus providing the justification to invade. They succeeded. With the PLO rocket and artillery barrage the Israeli cabinet met to approve the invasion. But what they were told and what was planned were two different things. Sharon informed them of a plan for an invasion of twenty-five miles to wipe out PLO positions in southern Lebanon, whereas he and Eitan had actually ordered the armed forces to proceed directly toward Beirut, as they did once the invasion began on 6 June. From then on, the cabinet was briefed in piecemeal fashion as Sharon carried out his design. Warned not to clash with the Syrians, he apparently ordered his troops to fire on Syrian positions to provoke a response that he could use to justify an attack. In this manner he and Eitan escalated the cabinet-approved limited strike to fit his prearranged design.[67]

By 15 June the Israeli forces were on the outskirts of Beirut consolidating their positions, and Sharon hoped to coordinate plans for the Maronite forces, quiet until now, to enter the Palestinian strongholds in West Beirut. His advisers rejected this proposal, regarding Maronite military capabilities with contempt. The alternative, an Israeli assault, seemed equally unpalatable given the expected casualties, although Sharon seems to have retained the option. With a stalemate resulting, the United States began pushing for an immediate PLO withdrawal of all forces from Lebanon. Sharon ordered air strikes and indiscriminate bombardments of West Beirut and adjacent areas, with heavy loss of civilian life, not always Palestinian. Haig approved these tactics, viewing Israeli actions as a means of pressuring Arafat to agree to leave. Sharon may have seen them as a means of evacuating or eradicating the civilian population, making it easier to attack the PLO and its leadership, which he preferred to destroy rather than permit to escape.[68] Negotiations over terms for withdrawal dragged on, Arafat seeking to gain guarantees for the Palestinian civilians left behind and to salvage some political gain from the crisis.

For its part the White House approved Israel's objectives, removal of the PLO from any role in future peace talks, but U.S. officials came to disapprove

Israeli tactics and disregard for noncombatants, leading to Haig's arranged resignation, announced on 25 June, though he remained in charge for several more weeks. Washington dispatched Philip Habib once more, now to try to gain agreement on the terms of withdrawal. He succeeded on 12 August, but only after a Sharon-ordered day-long bombardment of West Beirut that many observers interpreted as a last-ditch attempt to undermine the cease-fire; if it broke down, the only alternative would be to send in Israeli forces to destroy the Palestinian units. Strong cabinet reaction to his preemptive initiative, taken without consultation, and even stronger American criticism led to affirmation of a truce. A multinational peacekeeping force arrived, including American troops, whose mission was to oversee the departure of the PLO and to guarantee the safety of civilians in the refugee camps. By 1 September all Palestinian forces had left Beirut for other Arab countries, and American forces were withdrawn.

On the same day, 1 September, President Reagan proposed a new initiative designed to reinvigorate the Camp David accords. The Reagan Plan called for a freeze on Israeli settlements on the West Bank and denied Israeli claims of sovereignty over either that area or Gaza. At the same time Reagan rejected the idea of an independent Palestinian state. Instead he called for "full Palestinian autonomy," to be realized through confederation with Jordan in such a manner that "the legitimate rights of the Palestinians" would be realized without compromising the "legitimate security concerns of Israel." Reagan repudiated the basic PLO and Israeli positions. He pointedly remarked that in America's view, "the withdrawal provision of Resolution 242 applies to all fronts, including the West Bank and Gaza," thereby rejecting Begin's claim that these areas were excluded from the resolution. At the same time he implicitly, and the new secretary of state, George Shultz, explicitly in clarifying remarks, rejected the right of Palestinians to "self-determination," as it meant to them an independent state.[69]

Reagan's remarks concerning the Palestinians were ambiguous. He was unwilling to recognize the PLO, but he seemed amenable to an initiative treating the case of the Palestinians. Shultz, during his confirmation hearings, had declared that "the legitimate needs and problems of the Palestinian people must be addressed and resolved—urgently and in all their dimensions."[70] Designed to influence discussions at an upcoming Arab summit, scheduled to be held in Fez, Morocco, on 9 September, the Reagan Plan had a negative impact, as it never mentioned the PLO. Both Reagan, and Shultz in later remarks, stressed that the PLO had left Beirut, leaving the way open for consideration of the needs of the "Palestinian inhabitants of the West Bank and Gaza." Having informed Arab leaders that the United States would address the Palestinian problem in its entirety, Reagan had presented a plan supposed to aid Arab moderates that sought to remove the PLO from the peace equation. In so doing, the administration, whether deliberately or otherwise, accepted Begin's formula as expressed to Carter following Camp David, namely, that the inhabitants of the territories were the only Palestinians to be considered under the agreement.[71] On the other hand, references to Palestinian rights to full autonomy, presumably in a relationship with Jordan, clashed with Israeli designs to deny them any political rights. Thus both sides opposed the plan, with the Arab summit reaffirming the Rabat declaration of 1974 that the PLO was the sole representative of the Palestinian people.

The stand taken by President Reagan, to be the basis of future American policy, publicly disapproved of Israeli intentions for the West Bank while providing definitions of terms that backed Israel's positions. The principal victim of the speech was King Husayn, who had praised it before the summit and hoped to gain official Arab consent as a means of forestalling Israel's settlement policies. Husayn was willing to abandon Arafat if it meant that he could get American backing for the West Bank, but he needed general Arab approval to do so. The Reagan Plan seemed to have been intended to squeeze the Arab states, forcing them to abandon the PLO if they wished to save the West Bank or otherwise acquiescing in Israeli de facto annexation, American protestations to the contrary. In such circumstances the United States did not appear as the honest broker it claimed to be, especially because Sharon had already declared that the removal of the PLO from Beirut created the possibility for agreement between Israel and "moderate" Palestinians, a clear reference to the West Bank aspect of the invasion of Lebanon.[72]

In Lebanon, however, Israel's ambitions encountered unexpected obstacles that culminated in the assassination of Bashir Gemayel on 14 September. Gemayel's relations with Begin and Sharon had been strained. He resisted their demands for an immediate peace treaty between Lebanon and Israel and resented their insistence that Saad Haddad and his forces remain under Israel's military authority once Lebanon's national unity was reestablished. But they had reached agreement on 12 September that Phalangist forces would enter the Palestinian camps outside Beirut, supposedly to clear out some two thousand PLO fighters reputed to be there.[73] Now Gemayel's death set in motion a series of events that led to the massacres in the Sabra and Shatila refugee camps.

After paying their condolences to the Gemayel clan and consulting with their staff and Phalangist leaders, Sharon and Eitan—without informing the Israeli cabinet—ordered Israeli troops into West Beirut in violation of the truce negotiated by Philip Habib; the justification was that this was necessary to ensure peace, and the cabinet approved the move retroactively. The Israeli military command then arranged for Phalangist militias, numbering about two hundred, to be transported to the area surrounding the Shatila camp, which they entered at 6 P.M. on 16 September. Though the purpose was ostensibly to wipe out an estimated two thousand PLO fighters, the small number of Maronite forces suggests differently. Aided by Israeli flares to assist them at night, the Phalangists undertook a massacre of Palestinians which continued until the morning of 19 September. Although word of the atrocities emerged on

17 September, high-level officers ignored the news. There was sufficient information to cause it to be passed to Chief of Staff Eitan when he arrived in Beirut on the afternoon of the eighteenth, but he seemed to pay little attention to it. In a subsequent meeting with Phalangist officials, he and his staff approved a Phalange request to remain in the camps until the next morning. The Maronites exited on 19 September, leaving behind at least eight hundred dead, none apparently members of any PLO unit and a possible majority of them women and children. A subsequent Israeli commission of inquiry rejected the military's initial claims that the Phalange entered the camps without the assistance or even the knowledge of the Israeli command. The Kahan Commission found Israeli officials, especially Sharon and Eitan, indirectly responsible for the massacre, in that they should have known what would occur: the Phalange had repeatedly declared what they intended to do with Palestinians they found, and some Israeli leaders had stated candidly that they hoped to "purify" Lebanon of Palestinians.[74]

CONCLUSION: ILLUSIONS OF PEACE, SEPTEMBER 1982–FEBRUARY 1984

In the massacre's aftermath, the United States reintroduced its troops as part of the multinational force, aware that its original mission had been intended to protect Palestinian civilians. U.S. policy statements reflected sympathy for Palestinian aspirations, with George Shultz declaring that they were fully justified in seeking "a place with which they can identify" and that Israel would have to cede territory to gain peace in accordance with Resolution 242.[75] During the fall the Reagan administration tried to bring King Husayn into the negotiations. He negotiated with Arafat, something not to Washington's liking but to Husayn a necessary step to avoid isolating himself in the Arab world. He hoped to gain Arafat's permission to act on behalf of the Palestinians. The United States offered enticements, asking Congress not to increase aid to Israel in light of recent events and to approve shipment of sophisticated jet fighters to Amman. Congress rejected the latter and upped Israeli assistance, moves that reflected "the continued political advantages of supporting Israel" and Congress's demand that Husayn negotiate directly with that country without the PLO, a stipulation that mirrored Israel's conditions.[76] In the Middle East, administration efforts were stymied by inter-Arab rivalries. Various PLO groups objected to Arafat's willingness to discuss terms with Husayn, backed by Syria which opposed any unilateral accord. This combination of Israeli and Syrian opposition to American policies, coupled with PLO factionalism, succeeded in foiling Husayn. Arafat had nothing to offer without an American invitation that he could use to sway PLO opponents. Washington, however, insisted on his taking the initiative, a move Husayn encouraged for tactical reasons, as it would put Washington on the spot. His failure led Husayn to break off the talks and then to refuse in the spring of 1983 to negotiate directly with Israel.

Frustrated by the collapse of the American overture to Husayn, Shultz undertook negotiations to resolve the Lebanese crisis. After much wrangling over terms, he engineered a Lebanese-Israeli security agreement, signed on 17 May 1983, that provided for Israel's withdrawal from Lebanon, conditional on a similar commitment to do so by Damascus, which had been excluded from the American briefing on the talks. The treaty indicated American anger at the Arabs' recalcitrance and at the Soviet rearming of the Syrians more than a realistic assessment of the pact's chances for success. Ostensibly egalitarian in its terms, it in effect ratified the continued Israeli control of southern Lebanon through proxies. Haddad's forces would be integrated with other troops from the southern region into the reconstituted Lebanese army that would oversee the area; no troops from central and northern Lebanon could enter the south. If implemented, the treaty would have forced Syria to concede the loss of any influence in Lebanon, but Israel would retain a major foothold through Haddad.

Not the least of the pact's ironies was that this arrangement violated the provisions insisted on by Bashir Gemayel before his assassination, namely, that Haddad, whom he despised, be subordinated to his authority as head of Lebanon. Israel had rejected his request.[77] Bashir's successor, his older brother Amin, lacked his charisma and accepted the conditions as a means of gaining American backing against both Israel and Syria while trying to weave his way through the literal and metaphorical minefields of Lebanese politics. He hoped to use the United States to evade any obligation to redress imbalances within the confessional system, as agreement to such a course would weaken his support within the Maronite community.

The signing of the agreement followed by a month a bomb attack on the American embassy in Beirut that had caused extensive casualties. Possibly Syrian sponsored, it indicated both Assad's and Lebanese Muslim anger at the changing American role in the country. Supposedly neutral, American representatives now seemed intent on securing Maronite paramountcy. The security pact reinforced that impression, as it seemed designed to secure for Israel what it had not gained by its invasion. Non-Christian groups in Lebanon began to snipe at American military positions, identifying them with support for Gemayel. American marines became more vulnerable when the government of Yitzhak Shamir, who had replaced Begin as prime minister, decided in September to pull out of the Shouf Mountains overlooking Beirut, despite Washington's strong objections. The withdrawal exposed American forces to increased harassment as the Druze regained control of their traditional stronghold. The White House, over the objections of the marine commander in Beirut, responded by ordering naval bombardments of Druze positions, which resulted in numerous casualties, mostly noncombatant.[78] This response seemed a success, as a cease-fire ensued and a conference was arranged in Switzerland in which Lebanese leaders would seek to resolve their differences, but the respite was only temporary. The reply to the bombardments came in the form of the suicide bombing of the marine-naval barracks outside Beirut in October, causing 241 deaths.

The demolition of the barracks and its aftermath reflected the disparity between Arab and Reagan administration perceptions of its causes. Druze leader Walid Jumblat warned of further incidents if the United States pursued "its hostile policy towards the Arab and Islamic world. . . . " Reagan argued that keeping the marines in Lebanon was "central to U.S. credibility on a global scale" and to stopping the Middle East as a whole from being "incorporated into the Soviet bloc."[79] In the renewed clash between regional issues and global anti-Soviet perceptions of their significance in Washington, the latter again emerged victorious, to Israel's benefit. Shultz and Reagan, over Defense Department objections, decided to offer Israel a strategic agreement aimed at increasing "military and political cooperation" to counter "the threat to our mutual interests posed by increased Soviet involvement in the Middle East. . . . " The agreement also offered advanced military technology and favorable aid terms.[80] No conditions applied, and Israel did not restrict its settlement activities on the West Bank that the United States opposed. In Lebanon itself, the United States escalated attacks on Syrian positions in Lebanon, culminating in air strikes and bombardments by the battleship U.S.S. *New Jersey* at the turn of the year, which led to extensive civilian casualties and renewed domestic criticism in the United States. With his aides divided on the merits of confrontation, Reagan played both sides of the issue. Having accused his critics of seeking to surrender American interests, he decided to remove the troops from Lebanon and to deploy them on ships off-shore. He then ordered renewed shelling of Druze and Shi'i positions, causing more casualties and more animosity but creating a facade of militancy behind which the American navy sailed away in February 1984, leaving Lebanon an open battleground for regional competitors.[81] With Syria the apparent victor, Amin Gemayel now declared the security agreement with Israel to be dead. Assad would be the new broker of a Lebanese political pact if any could be achieved.

As American forces departed from Lebanon's shores in early 1984, the U.S. policy lay in ruins, the victim of the perceptions of its policymakers as well as the entangled web of regional and communal hatreds. Both the Carter and Reagan administrations had tried, from opposing vantage points, to seek to resolve conflicts in the area. Carter had hoped to conclude the entire regional dispute by including the PLO as well as the Soviet Union. This approach failed because of Israeli opposition and PLO recalcitrance at the terms offered. The Reagan administration placed itself in a contradictory posture, finding itself forced to try to resolve local tensions by negotiating with the very state, Syria, that it was trying to exclude from its strategic alliance aimed at expelling Soviet influence from the region. Though opposed to Israeli actions in principle, the administration either willingly or unwittingly became captive to Israel's strategic designs encompassed within the framework of the 1982 war. Frustrated by Israeli excesses and those of its clients, the Reagan government then tried to restore the internal balance in Lebanon by gaining the withdrawal of both Syria and Israel but did so in terms clearly supportive of the latter's goals. American failure to impose its will on Syria created more wrath, resulting in bombardments that indicated petulance more than strategy. The retaliatory bombing of the marine barracks signaled the bankruptcy of America's attempt to force the issue, though the administration did not concede defeat easily. What remained was a return to a total global perspective dominated by the polarization of American and Soviet interests and clients in which Israel played a willing and prominent role.

NOTES

1. William B. Quandt, *Camp David, Peacemaking and Politics* (Washington, D.C., 1986), p. 37.
2. Joel S. Migdal, *Palestinian Society and Politics* (Princeton, N.J., 1980), pp. 39–45. See also Don Peretz, *The West Bank: History, Politics, Society, and Economy* (Boulder, Colo., 1986), p. 39ff; and Pamela Ann Smith, *Palestine and the Palestinians, 1876–1983* (London, 1984), p. 87ff, who has a good discussion of these developments.
3. Meron Benvenisti, *The West Bank Data Project: A Survey of Israel's Policies* (Washington, D.C., 1984), p. 12.
4. Ibid., p.10. Compare Migdal, *Palestinian Society*, pp. 45–47, and Mark Heller, "Politics and Social Change in the West Bank Since 1967" in Migdal, *Palestinian Society*, pp. 185–211, who seem to emphasize the benefits derived from Israel's policies.
5. Migdal, *Palestinian Society*, pp. 67–73.
6. Benvenisti, *Data Project*, p. 10.
7. See the discussion of conditions in which these workers reside overnight, in Rafik Halabi, *The West Bank Story: An Israeli Arab's View of Both Sides of a Tangled Conflict* (San Diego, 1981), pp. 275–279. Increased Arab assaults on Jews following the killing of at least eighteen Arabs by Israeli police and troops near the Dome of the Rock and al Aqsa Mosque (Temple Mount) on 8 October 1990 have led to reinforcement of these restrictions.
8. Benvenisti, *Data Project*, p. 10.
9. Sammy Smooha, *Israel: Pluralism and Conflict* (Berkeley and Los Angeles, 1978), p. 103. See also his discussion of Ashkenazi attitudes toward oriental Jews and Arab-Jewish relations, pp. 86–95, 135–207. Smooha's discussion of the Labor elite's giving preference to European Jews in order to build the country is treated also by Tom Segev in his analysis of the attitudes of Israel's founders, *1949, The First Israelis* (New York, 1986), in which he shows how assumptions derived from perceived necessity to build a state quickly became entrenched as part of general social relations. An excellent study of Israel and Israeli Arabs is Ian Lustick, *Arabs in the Jewish State: Israel's Control of a National Minority* (Austin, Tex., 1980).
10. Asher Arian, *Politics in Israel: The Second Generation* (Chatham, N.J., 1985), pp. 136–144. Efraim Torgovnik, "Likud 1977–81: The Consolidation of Power," in Robert O. Freedman, ed., *Israel in the Begin Era* (New York, 1982), pp. 7–27, has a good overview of the first Begin government.
11. Lilly Weisbrod, "Gush Emunim Ideology—From Religious Doctrine to Political Action," *Middle Eastern Studies* 18 (1982): 265.
12. Lustick, *Arabs in the Jewish State*, pp. 130, 167; and Sabri Jiryis, *The Arabs in Israel* (New York, 1976), p. 80ff, 127 and tables in the appendix. See also Elia T. Zureik, *The Palestinians in Israel: A Study in Internal Colonialism* (London, 1979) for a broader overview of issues pertaining to this discussion.
13. Lustick, *Arabs in the Jewish State*, p. 258.
14. Meir Kahane, *They Must Go* (New York, 1981). Two unsympathetic but accurate portrayals of Kahane and his views are Yair Kotler, *Heil Kahane*, trans. Edward Levin (New York, 1986); and

Robert Friedman, *The False Prophet: Rabbi Meir Kahane, from FBI Informant to Knesset Member* (New York, 1990). Kahane was assassinated in New York City in November 1990.

15. Lustick, *Arabs in the Jewish State*, p. 129.
16. Ibid., p. 168.
17. Ibid., discussion on p. 186 and the map on p. 187, outlining plans for state-funded development of industrial zones that included the new Jewish town of Nazareth but excluded the adjacent old Arab city of the same name.
18. Walid Khalidi, *Conflict and Violence in Lebanon: Confrontation in the Middle East* (Cambridge, Mass., 1979), p. 42ff.
19. Ibid., p. 42, and p. 164, note 42.
20. Rashid Khalidi, *Under Siege: PLO Decisionmaking during the 1982 War* (New York, 1986), p. 10.
21. Walid Khalidi, *Conflict*, pp. 68–72. A good general account dealing with various factions is John Bulloch, *Death of a Country: The Civil War in Lebanon* (London, 1977).
22. In addition to Habash's PFLP and Ahmad Jibril's PFLP General Command, the Rejection Front included the Iraqi-backed Arab Liberation Front and the somewhat obscure Palestinian Popular Struggle movement. See Helena Cobban, *The Palestinian Liberation Organization: People, Power, and Politics* (Cambridge, England, 1984), p. 149.
23. This discussion relies on Walid Khalidi, *Conflict*, pp. 84–85; and the collection of essays in P. Edward Haley and Lewis Snider, eds., *Lebanon in Crisis: Participants and Issues* (Syracuse, N.Y., 1979), especially L. Snider, "Inter-Arab Relations," pp. 179–206, Mohammed Moghisuddin, "Egypt," pp. 133–146, John Cooley, "The Palestinians," pp. 21–54, and Lawrence L. Whetten, "The Military Dimension," pp. 75–90, along with Anthony Sampson, *The Arms Bazaar; from Lebanon to Lockheed* (New York, 1977), pp. 5–15. For estimates of Israeli military aid to the Maronites ranging from $100 million to $150 million, see Whetten, "The Military Dimension," p. 290, note 46; and Ze'ev Schiff and Ehud Ya'ari, *Israel's Lebanon War* (New York, 1984), p. 18.
24. The preliminary talks between American and Israeli officials are discussed in Cyrus Vance, *Hard Choices: Critical Years in America's Foreign Policy* (New York, 1983), p. 207ff. Vance was secretary of state under President Carter.
25. For the Shi'ite population of the south and the formation of their paramilitary group, Amal, see two studies by Augustus Richard Norton: "Harakat Amal (The Movement of Hope)," in Myron J. Aronoff, ed., *Religion and Politics, Political Anthropology*, vol. 3 (New Brunswick, N.J., 1984), pp. 105–132; and his broader study, *Amal and the Shi'a: Struggle for the Soul of Lebanon* (Austin, 1987). A broader discussion of the Lebanese Shia is Fouad Ajami, *The Vanished Imam: Musa al-Sadr and the Shi'a of Lebanon* (Ithica, N.Y., 1986). For Israeli efforts to create a free-fire zone by terrorizing civilians into flight, see Walid Khalidi, *Conflict*, pp. 129–130; Lewis P. Snider, P. Edward Haley, Abraham R. Wagner, and Nicki J. Cohen, "Israel," in Snider and Haley, eds., *Lebanon in Crisis*, pp. 95–103; and Frederic C. Hof, *Galilee Divided: The Israeli-Lebanon Frontier, 1916–1984* (Boulder, Colo., 1985), pp. 87–93. Compare Ezer Weizman, *The Battle for Peace* (New York, 1981), pp. 272–279.
26. Vance, *Hard Choices*, p. 209. The United States also sharply criticized Israel for its use of cluster bombs against civilian targets.
27. Quandt, *Camp David*, pp. 41–44, where he also states, footnote 22, that Israel's chief of staff thought that security requirements on the West Bank could be met with a limited military presence.
28. *Los Angeles Times*, 10 August 1977. Begin repeated these references to the Palestinians in his banquet toasts to the Egyptian delegation in January 1978.
29. Itamar Rabinovich, *The War for Lebanon, 1970–1985* (Ithaca, N.Y., 1985), pp. 48–49 and appendix.
30. Cobban, *Palestine Liberation Organization*, p. 84, quoting Farouq al-Qaddumi, responsible for foreign affairs in the PLO.
31. I rely for my discussion of Camp David primarily on Quandt, *Camp David*; Vance, *Hard Choices*; Weizman, *Battle for Peace*; Zbigniew Brzezinski, *Power and Principle: Memoirs of the National Security Adviser, 1977–1981* (New York, 1983); Moshe Dayan, *Breakthrough: A Personal Account of the Egypt–Israel Peace Negotiations* (New York, 1981); Steven L. Spiegel, *The Other Arab-Israeli Conflict: Making America's Middle East Policy, from Truman to Reagan* (Chicago, 1985); and Melvin A. Friedlander, *Sadat and Begin: The Domestic Politics of Peacemaking* (Boulder, Colo., 1983). Friedlander is generally more sympathetic to Begin than the other sources are, including Weiz-

man and Dayan. Spiegel is much more critical of Carter than of previous presidents and depicts Brzezinski as "arrogant," using personal criteria he has not heretofore employed. Spiegel appears upset that the Carter administration refused to give the Jewish community as much input or to view its lobbying as favorably as had other administrations. He strongly implies that Carter should have allowed Jewish leaders to try to have an impact on policy, even though when discussing Lyndon Johnson, he argued that the sympathy Johnson's aides felt toward Israel did not influence policy. Compare pp. 129 and 331 where Spiegel states that presidents should stay away from preliminary discussion of issues to provide "opposing American groups and foreign emissaries an opportunity to intervene before positions . . . hardened," in the context a clear reference to American Jewish and Israeli officials.

32. For a good discussion of Arab rivalries and Saudi attempts to mediate, see Nadav Safran, *Saudi Arabia, The Ceaseless Quiet for Security* (Cambridge, Mass., 1985), pp. 253–255.

33. Cobban, *Palestine Liberation Organization*, pp. 89–90; and Quandt, *Camp David*, pp. 48–103, for a detailed treatment of these matters.

34. Quandt, *Camp David*, p. 111.

35. Galia Golan, *The Soviet Union and the Palestine Liberation Organization: An Uneasy Alliance* (New York, 1980), pp. 113–142. Golan's study is the best available on the topic.

36. Quandt, *Camp David*, p. 132. The conversations had been tense, with Dayan threatening to go to the American Jewish community and complain about Carter's policies if the president did not publicly reiterate American commitments to Israel. Carter in turn said he would also have to appeal to American Jews. Brzezinski, *Power and Principle*, p. 108, uses the term *blackmail* to describe Dayan's tactics, but his overall account is less detailed than Quandt's is, pp. 126–131. Dayan, *Breakthrough*, pp. 65–71, stresses Carter's threat of confrontation rather than his own.

37. Dayan, *Breakthrough*, pp. 68–70. The interpretation of Israel's reasons for fearing Soviet involvement is mine.

38. Dayan, *Breakthrough*, pp. 38–54, discusses his meeting with Hassan Tuheimi, deputy prime minister of Egypt.

39. Weizman, *Battle for Peace*, pp. 142–147, criticizes the Begin cabinet for acting like stereotypical Jews and then attacks the Egyptian newspapers that depicted them that way, thereby intensifying the already growing mutual animosity.

40. Quandt, *Camp David*, pp. 168–205. Spiegel, *America's Middle East Policy*, pp. 346–349, discusses the arms sales furor and notes that Carter pushed the Saudi deal at a time when the Saudis had not requested it.

41. The quotation is from Quandt, *Camp David*, p. 256.

42. For information about Begin's interpretation of the word *people* as inhabitants of the West Bank and Gaza, see Yehoshafat Harkabi, *The Bar Kokhba Syndrome: Risk and Realism in International Politics*, trans. Max D. Ticktin and ed. David Altshuler (Chappaqua, N.Y., 1983), p. 171. Quandt does not discuss this particular issue, but the text of the U.S. response to Jordanian questions concerning the accord indicate that the Carter government included Palestinians from outside the territories in the term *people*: *Camp David*, Appendix H, p. 388.

43. For the dispute over the proposed freeze on settlements, compare Quandt, *Camp David*, pp. 247–251, and Spiegel, *America's Middle East Policy*, p. 362. Spiegel argues the Israeli position, stating that the notes of one Israeli adviser, Aharon Barak, proved that the freeze was tied to peace negotiations, not autonomy talks. Quandt contradicts Spiegel, saying that Barak's notes prove just the opposite. Spiegel's argument seems somewhat specious in his statement that "it is simply not plausible that Barak—soon to become an Israeli Supreme Court Justice and recognized by Carter for his integrity, moderation, and precision—would have been wrong about such a critical point."

44. Spiegel, *America's Middle East Policy*, pp. 375–379, where he states that Vance's position on the settlements angered Carter and intensified a growing rift between them that culminated in Vance's resignation because he opposed the abortive rescue mission into Iran. Vance makes no mention of the settlement flap in his memoirs. Another furor had arisen over unauthorized contacts made by the American U.N. ambassador, Andrew Young, with PLO representatives which were discovered by Israeli espionage and leaked to the press. Young initially denied the contacts and subsequently was asked to resign.

45. Spiegel, *America's Middle East Policy*, pp. 401–402.

46. *Washington Post*, 15 August 1979, p. 25; quoted in Spiegel, *America's Middle East Policy*, p. 406.

47. For Christian fundamentalist support of Israel, see Grace Halsell, *Prophecy and Politics: Militant Evangelists on the Road to Nuclear War* (Westport, Conn., 1986), who covers the activities of men such as Jerry Falwell and Pat Robertson. Many Christian fundamentalists support Israel in the belief that its policies will lead to a nuclear war in which the Arab states and most of Israel as well will be destroyed, thereby clearing the way for the fulfillment of Christian biblical prophecy. Although such views are not particularly sympathetic to Israel or Jews, they do establish a basis for strong financial backing for Israel, particularly because Israel serves as a bastion against the Anti-Christ that the Soviet Union represents, thus tying together anti-Soviet and pro-Israeli policies in a way quite compatible with Reagan's views. For Reagan's apparent sympathies with Jerry Falwell and others, perhaps without realizing their ambitions for the Middle East, see Halsell, pp. 171–173, 191. For the political activities of groups such as the Moral Majority and their connections with Israel, see also Paul Findley, *They Dare to Speak Out: People and Institutions Confront Israel's Lobby* (Westport, Conn., 1985), pp. 238–264, and Nimrod Novik, *The United States and Israel: Domestic Determinants of a Changing U.S. Commitment* (Boulder, Colo., 1986), pp. 86–93. Novik shows how Menachem Begin used his ties to Falwell to seek acceptance of Israeli actions.

48. Joel Brinkley, "Iran Sales Linked to Wide Program of Covert Policies," *New York Times*, 15 February 1987; and Doyle McManus, "Private Contra Funding of $32 Million Disclosed," *Los Angeles Times*, 6 March 1987.

49. Brinkley, "Iran Sales." For Israel, Argentina, and Nicaragua, see Aaron S. Klieman, *Israel's Global Reach: Arms Sales As Diplomacy* (Washington, D.C., 1985), p. 96, and especially pp. 156–157; Benjamin Beit-Hallahmi, "U.S.-Israeli-Central American Connection," *The Link* 18 (November 1985): 8–12; Milton Jamail and Margo Guiterrez, "Israel in Central America: Nicaragua, Honduras, El Salvador, Costa Rica," *Middle East Report* (MERIP) 16 (May–June 1986): 27–30; *Newsweek*, 3 November 1986; and Bishara Bahbah, *Israel and Latin America: The Military Connection* (New York, 1986).

50. This discussion relies on Ian Lustick, "Israel and the West Bank after Elon Moreh: The Mechanics of De Facto Annexation," *Middle East Journal* 35 (Autumn 1981): 562ff; and Peter Demant, "Israeli Settlement Policy Today," in Naseer H. Aruri, ed., *Occupation; Israel over Palestine* (Belmont, Mass., 1983), pp. 143–164.

51. Benvenisti, *Data Project*, p.34.

52. Ibid., pp. 34–35. The World Zionist Organization allocated $30 million for purchases for the period 1983–1986.

53. Ibid., pp. 43–45.

54. Ibid., pp. 46–47; and *The Karp Report: An Israeli Government Inquiry into Settler Violence against Palestinians on the West Bank* (Washington, D.C., 1984). The Karp Report notes that military officials on the West Bank appeared to delay investigations into incidents, cooperating with settlers and hindering Israeli police inquiries. This collusion between the military government and the settlers led to the latter's demanding a military, as opposed to a police, investigation of Arab complaints, something "tantamount to civil rebellion and a casting of aspersions on the civilian echelons of the Israeli police, the state attorney, and the courts of the state of Israel" (p. 46).

55. I rely on the following sources for the bulk of my discussion on the events leading up to the Israeli invasion of Lebanon in 1982; Schiff and Ya'ari, *Israel's Lebanon War;* Shai Feldman and Heda Rechnitz-Kijner, *Deception, Consensus and War: Israel in Lebanon*, Jaffee Center for Strategic Studies, Tel Aviv University, Paper no. 27 (October 1984); Jonathan C. Randal, *Going All the Way: Christian Warlords, Israeli Adventurers, and the War in Lebanon* (New York, 1983); Rabinovich, *The War for Lebanon; The Beirut Massacre: The Complete Kahan Commission Report* (Princeton, N.J., 1983). For an Israeli analysis of the Begin government's alarm at Arafat's peace initiative and the former's determination to deal with the PLO only "through the barrel of a gun," see David Bernstein, "The Worm in the Apple," *Jerusalem Post*, 15 June 1982.

56. Haim Shaked, "The Nuclearization of the Middle East," in Colin Legum, Haim Shaked, and Daniel Dishon, eds., *Middle East Contemporary Survey (MECS)* 5 (1980–1981): 192, where he states that "of necessity all governmental decisions were either made or judged in light of the election campaign."

57. Norton, "Harakat Amal," pp. 122–123.

58. Itamar Rabinovich, "The Lebanese Crisis," in *MECS* 5 (1980–1981): 171. Rabinovich is less

explicit about the nature of this commitment in his *The War for Lebanon*, saying only (p. 117) that Israel had promised to "not allow the Syrian air force to operate against it [the Maronite position]."

59. Schiff and Ya'ari, *Israel's Lebanon War*, pp. 31–34, treat this as a threat of military escalation which the Begin government had not clearly thought through. Rabinovich, *War for Lebanon*, pp. 117–118, suggests that the Israeli air strike was actually "a message that Israel was willing to accept Syrian hegemony in Zahle," a rather odd way of doing so and a message that Assad interpreted differently.

60. See Saadallah A. S. Hallaba, *Euro-Arab Dialogue* (Brattleboro, Vt., 1984) particularly Chapters 2 and 3; and D. Allen and A. Pijpers, eds., *European Foreign Policy-Making and the Arab-Israeli Conflict* (The Hague, 1984).

61. Cobban, *Palestinian Liberation Organization*, pp. 96–97; and Offer Yarimi, "The Palestine Liberation Organization (PLO)," *MECS* 5 (1980–1981): 301.

62. Moshe Gammer, "Armed Operations," *MECS* 5 (1980–1981): 214–220.

63. Idem, "The Middle East Peace Process," *MECS* 5 (1980–1981): 159–164, covers the Sadat and Fahd proposals, including the text of Fahd's interview.

64. Schiff and Ya'ari, *Israel's Lebanon War*, pp. 38–51, discusses the December 1981 meeting, and Feldman and Rechnitz-Kijner, *Israel in Lebanon*, pp. 54–55, note Eitan's differences with Sharon over the war's aim.

65. Feldman and Rechnitz-Kijner, pp. 22–23, and Rabinovich, *War for Lebanon*, p.134, note Israeli, Arab, and American news comments on Israeli plans up to three months before the invasion.

66. Schiff and Ya'ari, *Israel's Lebanon War*, pp. 67–77, discuss Haig's attempts to qualify Sharon's open revelations in such a way as to leave the Israelis with little doubt of Washington's tacit approval of the latter's plan. Rabinovich notes, *War for Lebanon*, pp. 125–126, that Haig may have opposed the plan in principle, as others in the Reagan administration did much more forcefully, but he believed that if inevitable, the attack should be supported as an opportunity to restabilize Lebanon and get rid of the PLO. This would be his position once the invasion commenced. Haig, on the other hand, presents himself in his memoirs as very forceful in his opposition to Sharon's designs when they met, emphasizing that there had to be a clear-cut provocation. See Haig's *Caveat, Realism, Reagan, and Foreign Policy* (New York, 1984), pp. 334–335. Doubts about Haig's continued opposition to Sharon's plans were shared by his own staff, including his chief negotiator, Philip Habib (private communication). And in an interview with Rashid Khalidi, Habib accused both Sharon and Haig of collusion and of lying regarding the process of negotiations for the PLO withdrawal from Beirut in the summer 1982. See Khalidi, *Under Siege*, p. 172, and especially note 10, p. 212.

67. Schiff and Ya'ari, *Israel's Lebanon War*, pp. 111–115, 163–166; and Feldman and Rechnitz-Kijner, *Israel in Lebanon*, pp. 25-41.

68. Rashid Khalidi, *Under Siege*, p. 135 and note 8, p. 209, where he observes that the editors of the *New York Times* censored the word *indiscriminate* from an article by Thomas Friedman describing the bombardments of 4 August. See also John Bulloch, *Final Conflict, the War in Lebanon* (London, 1983), especially pp. 86–89, 119–136; and Randal, *Going All the Way*, p. 219ff.

69. See *The Quest for Peace: Principal United States Public Statements and Related Documents on the Arab-Israeli Peace Process*, U.S. Department of State (Washington, D.C., 1984), pp. 108–129. Shultz refers to self-determination on p. 118.

70. Quoted in Spiegel, *America's Middle East Policy*, p. 419, who discusses U.S. actions but leaves unclear the American motives regarding the PLO.

71. See ibid., p. 412 and note 46.

72. As reported in the *Washington Post*, 30 August 1982; and noted in the "Chronology" of the *Middle East Journal* 37 (1983): 70, listing for 29 August.

73. Schiff and Ya'ari, *Israel's Lebanon War*, pp. 230–246.

74. For the chronology of events, see *Kahan Commission Report*, pp. 6–50, which also refers to Israeli awareness of Phalangist attitudes toward the Palestinians. For a critical evaluation of the Kahan report, see Ammon Kapeliouk, *Sabra and Shatila: Inquiry into a Massacre* (Belmont, Mass., 1984), Kapeliouk refutes the commission argument that Israeli observers could not see into the camp from their post high above it, a point made also by journalists there at the time. For example, Loren Jenkins in the *Washington Post*, 20 September 1982; and Thomas Friedman in the *New York Times*, 26 September 1982. American officials believed that Sharon and Eitan had to have known

a massacre would occur when they arranged for the Phalangists' entry but that they rationalized it by their desire to "purify" the Beirut area. See Wolf Blitzer in the *Jerusalem Post*, 24 September 1982. For other references to "purifying" and "purging" the camps of Palestinians, see Kapeliouk, *Sabra and Shatila*, pp. 34 and 83, and the transcript of an Israel Defense Forces Radio Announcement broadcast on 16 September 1982, before the massacre. These and many other journalistic references can be found in *The Beirut Massacre, Press Profile*, Claremont Research and Publications (New York, 1984).

75. Quoted in Spiegel, *America's Middle East Policy*, p. 422.
76. Quotation is from ibid., p. 423.
77. Hof, *Galilee Divided*, pp. 105–111, analyzes the agreement; Schiff and Ya'ari, *Israel's Lebanon War*, pp. 131, 231–234, treat Gemayel's dislike of Haddad.
78. Spiegel, *America's Middle East Policy*, p. 426.
79. Jumblat is quoted in the *New York Times*, 25 October 1983. Reagan's remarks were reported in the *Washington Post* on 25 and 28 October, 1983. See the "Chronology," *Middle East Journal* 38 (1984): 286.
80. Fred J. Khouri, *The Arab-Israeli Dilemma*, 3rd ed. (Syracuse, N.Y., 1985), p. 450. For U.S. defense contractors and their relations with the Israeli military and defense establishment, see Sheila Ryan, "U.S. Military Contractors in Israel," *Middle East Report* (MERIP) 17 (January–February 1987): 17–22. See also the breakdown of military aid to Middle Eastern countries generally, pp. 23–26.
81. See Spiegel, *America's Middle East Policy*, p. 428, for an account of Reagan's intervening to settle a major dispute among his advisers as to what course they should follow.

CHAPTER 10

The "New World Order" and Its Implications for the Middle East, 1984–1991

The years since the failure of the United States's intervention in Lebanon have witnessed major transformations in the world order, as well as within the Middle East itself. Since 1985 the Soviet Union has embarked on a process of political and economic liberalization under the guidance of its president, Mikhail Gorbachev. Extensive political and economic reforms within the U.S.S.R. paralleled Soviet willingness to divest itself of its Eastern European satellites, controlled as buffers against the West since the end of World War II. In some cases this led to the installation of democratic governments in countries such as Poland and Czechoslovakia and, at times, to revolutions where the overthrow of dictators seemed to result in political chaos and the recapturing of power by communist factions, as in Romania. The Soviets approved the reunification of Germany, which occurred in December 1990, in return for a massive aid package from Bonn that will total nearly $15 billion.

The Soviet opening to the capitalist world was designed to revamp its economy and to encourage outside assistance by demonstrating its capacity for political pluralism. But this pluralism opened a Pandora's box of conflicting demands at the heart and the periphery of the Soviet empire. The Baltic republics, annexed during World War II, demanded independence. Lithuanian assertiveness was particularly disconcerting because it inspired similar demands in other republics that had been under Soviet rule since 1919 but still identified themselves in terms of specific nationality; Armenia, Georgia, Azerbaijan (Turkish Shia Muslim), and the Ukraine all called for varying degrees of autonomy with regional strife erupting between Armenians and Azerbaijanis. In addition the Russian republic, headed by the radical politician Boris Yeltsin, challenged Soviet authority.

By the end of 1990 these tensions were no longer bearable. January 1991 saw a Soviet military crackdown in Lithuania, which Gorbachev supported but admitted he did not order. A new Soviet tack seemed apparent, one in which openness in external relations with former rivals was continued but at the expense of internal political liberalism, especially with regard to the claims of ethnic groups seeking greater if not total independence from Soviet rule. In his resignation speech in mid-December the Soviet foreign minister, Eduard Schevardnadze, warned against the reimposition of dictatorship within the U.S.S.R., and it seemed clear that conservative forces in Moscow were determined to take advantage of the disarray of their opponents to assert the primacy of the Soviet empire and quell dissent. These tensions led to the abortive coup of August 1991. The coup's failure appeared to ensure the advance of democracy, but may also result in the disintegration of the U.S.S.R. as dissident republics proclaim their independence.

In the Middle East, a war ended and a revolution began: the consequences of both developments remain at the heart of tensions in the region and serve as a test of the new set of relationships supposedly created by the end of the Cold War and the introduction of the post–Cold War era.

The revolution was the Palestinian *intifada* (literally a "shaking off" of a condition) that erupted in Gaza in December 1987 and that led to a popular uprising in the occupied territories against Israeli rule. By the end of 1990 an estimated nine hundred Palestinians had been killed by Israeli troops and settlers, with an additional two hundred suspected collaborators put to death by fellow Palestinians. The uprising galvanized a moribund PLO and encouraged it to take the historic steps of declaring an independent state of Palestine and recognizing the existence of Israel in November–December 1988. With great reluctance and after much agonizing and public demands for more proof of good faith, the United States acknowledged the shift in PLO direction, evident for years if never openly stated, and opened a dialogue with that organization through its embassy in Tunis where the PLO had established itself after leaving Lebanon.

In June 1990 the United States, under President George Bush, suspended the U.S.–PLO talks following an abortive Palestinian raid on Israel that was condemned by Yasir Arafat in terms deemed unacceptable by the administration. This suspension of the dialogue followed a period of increased violence in the occupied territories and an American veto on 31 May of a Security Council resolution calling for an investigation of the treatment of Palestinians under Israeli domination. These developments came at a time of growing desperation for the PLO because of the failure of American-sponsored overtures for negotiations with Israel regarding the territories and because of a major repercussion of Soviet *glasnost*, namely, Moscow's willingness to permit massive Soviet Jewish emigration. Thousands of Jews, averaging 10,000 a month, went to Israel where they immediately became a significant factor in the struggle for control of the territories. The Likud Party and its backers proclaimed the salvation of the territories for Israel because of the room needed to house these new immigrants.

The war that ended was between Iran and Iraq with the latter victorious, albeit with few tangible gains once a cease-fire was imposed on 20 July 1988. The Iraqi ruler, Saddam Husayn, soon found himself beset with debts to those who had financed his war against Iran, especially the oil-rich shaykhdoms of the Persian Gulf, and unable to finance the rebuilding of his military and economy as he wished because of lowered oil prices. In addition his regional ambitions were frustrated by his isolation in the Arab world. The Soviet withdrawal from the Cold War arena encouraged Syria, Iraq's arch rival in Arab affairs, to tilt toward the U.S. in early 1990. Hafiz Assad sought access to the peace process in the face of Soviet Jewish immigration into Israel and his own relative isolation in the Arab world because he had sided with Iran against Iraq. Syria therefore aligned itself closer to Egypt in announcing its willingness to settle outstanding issues with Israel.

Saddam Husayn chose to threaten those Arab states, principally Kuwait and the United Arab Emirates (UAE), whom he believed to be deliberately overproducing oil and driving down its price, thereby depriving him of needed revenues. In July 1990 he sent troops to the Kuwaiti border to intimidate that country and gain agreement for a price rise in oil. While deploring his tactics, other OPEC members, including Saudi Arabia, sided with him against Kuwait regarding the question of oil pricing. When Kuwait scorned further approaches regarding territorial questions, Iraq invaded that nation on 2 August and Saddam Husayn announced it had become a province of Iraq. This led to the formation of an American-sponsored military coalition, which included Egyptian and Syrian troops, designed to oust Iraq from Kuwait. When Saddam Husayn refused to obey a United Nations' resolution calling upon him to leave Kuwait by 15 January 1991, forces from that coalition, mainly American, attacked Iraq and Iraqi installations in Kuwait, liberating that country by the end of February. The political ramifications of the crisis will be discussed below.

One by-product of these developments was Syrian assertion of total control over central Lebanon, ousting General Michel Aoun, who had sought to retain Maronite paramountcy and the status quo. Israel retained its enclave in the south, but the rest of Lebanon now fell under the aegis of Hafiz Assad, and most Lebanese politicians welcomed the promise of a new political order.

LEBANON: A RESTRUCTURED MOSAIC?

With U.S. forces withdrawn from Lebanon in early 1984, the situation in that country seemed little changed. Rival factions struggled for control of neighborhoods or strongholds. Car bombings intended to fan communal hatreds recurred, often timed to foil negotiations designed to settle outstanding issues. Syria strove, by both persuasion and intimidation, to bring the leaders of major factions to agree to a plan that would retain a Maronite presidency but divide the parliament equally between Christians and Muslims, erasing the six-five ratio of long standing. This arrangement, given Christian communal rivalries, would have effectively checked Maronite dominance, because it also provided that the president could not dismiss his cabinet without parliamentary approval. Initially proposed by the Syrians in early 1976, it still had the backing of the Franjiyahs, but Maronite paramilitary groups, backed by the monastic establishment, refused to abandon their vision of complete Maronite ascendancy. Amin Gemayel remained president, but with little ability or inclination to curb his principal military factions who suspected him of being too amenable to compromise.

Fissures began to appear within even the Phalange. Elie Hobeika, intelligence chief under Bashir Gemayel and closely linked to the Israelis and to the direction of the Sabra-Shatila massacres, went over to the Syrians in support of political reform in September 1986.[1]

In the south, Israeli troops withdrew gradually from Lebanon under assaults from Shi'ite militias, their withdrawal to their enclave in southern Lebanon not completed until June 1985. The Shi'ites had originally welcomed Israel's invasion as a means of ousting the PLO, but they and most southern Lebanese became angered at Israeli exploitation of the region, which included blockading access to northern markets and dumping Israeli goods on the local economy to undercut indigenous merchants. These measures, plus Israeli round-ups and abductions of suspected "terrorists," ignited attacks and suicide car bombings, directed locally as well as from Damascus. Israel retaliated with an "iron fist" whereby Israeli terror squads invaded villages and assassinated individuals they claimed were involved in or backed these assaults.

The situation was complicated further by divisions within the Shia camp. Amal, the largest political-military organization, strove to manage the hostility, opposing Israel but focusing its attention on Beirut where it hoped to gain greater political representation commensurate with the now-acknowledged Shi'ite status as the largest religious community in Lebanon. But Amal was challenged by an Iranian-backed Shi'ite force, Hizbollah, that was far more militant religiously, and that often took the initiative against Israeli troops, using the backlash against their repression to gain supporters.[2]

On the other hand, Shi'ite anger at Israel did not diminish its animosity toward Palestinians. Shia leaders were determined to bar the return of PLO units to the south or to camps around Beirut. During 1985 and 1986, Amal forces surrounded these camps and attacked them, inflicting heavy casualties among civilian residents but failing to eject the PLO completely. Amal's actions against both Israel and the Palestinians were undertaken in cooperation with Syria. Angered at Arafat's willingness to negotiate with King Husayn, Hafiz Assad had backed rebel Fatah units that drove Arafat out of his newly acquired base in Tripoli in northern Lebanon during November 1983. Arafat then fled to Tunis where the PLO headquarters had been installed, but PLO cadres remained in Lebanon and were then strengthened, leading to the Shi'ite-PLO strife just noted.

In the midst of this anarchy Syria strove to impose a solution based on the 1976 proposals. Druze, Shi'ite, and some Christian leaders, including the Maronite head of the Lebanese Forces, linked to the Phalange, accepted them in an accord signed at the end of 1985. Maronites intent on retaining the status quo of Maronite primacy rejected it. With the end of Amin Gemayel's presidential term in 1988, the government split into two factions. One, led by Prime Minister Salim al-Hoss, accepted the 1985 agreement and had Muslim and some Christian backing. Many Maronites followed General Michel Aoun, the commander of the

Lebanese army, who was determined to defend Maronite interests and oust the Syrians from Lebanon. Aoun found a new and unexpected ally, Saddam Husayn of Iraq, who provided him with military aid in order to counter his rival, Syria's Hafiz Assad.

The ensuing carnage led Arab heads of state to recommend a solution, a peace plan proposed at the Saudi Arabian town of Taif that reflected the 1976 principles. The Lebanese parliament accepted the Taif Accord in late October 1989. General Aoun did not. When a moderate Maronite was elected president by the parliament on 5 November, Aoun repudiated him; the new president was assassinated by a bomb on 22 November. At this point Lebanon, especially Beirut, became engulfed in fratricidal warfare between rival Maronite factions. Many moderates and the leader of the Lebanese Forces, Samir Geagea, supported the new president, Elias Hrawi. Aoun, defending Maronite supremacy, proclaimed himself president, and vowed to fight Syria. Assad of Syria backed Geagea while Saddam Husayn of Iraq supplied General Aoun. Christian forces and neighborhoods suffered the types of casualties formerly identified with Muslim quarters.

The stalemate was finally resolved in October 1990, in the midst of the American-backed mobilization of forces in Saudi Arabia against Iraq, a coalition that Syria had agreed to join. With attention focused on the Gulf, Elias Hrawi invited the Syrians to oust General Aoun from the presidential palace that he had occupied since 1988. The move succeeded, with Aoun ultimately taking refuge in France which bitterly protested the decline of the last symbol of Maronite supremacy it had backed for over a century. Though denied by officials, it seemed that the Syrian move had been cleared with Washington, part of an attempt to settle the Lebanese situation and to acknowledge Syrian paramountcy for the moment, one of the many payoffs one can expect from U.S. efforts to form the alliance against Saddam Husayn. One week later, on 21 October, Dany Chamoun, son of Camille and backer of Aoun, was assassinated with his family. Old scores were being settled, whether by die-hard Maronites or pro-Syrian factions being unclear; Chamoun had survived an assassination attempt by Bashir Gemayel in 1980.[3]

With a national unity government founded on the Taif Accord in office, efforts to reassert national authority, nonexistent for over fifteen years, were inaugurated. Militia forces, including those of Hizbollah, agreed to leave Beirut. It remained uncertain, however, if all of the militias would give up their arms, although some, including Amal, had declared their willingness to do so by May 1991. The departure of these fighters from Beirut resulted in their dispersal throughout the south of Lebanon, increasing the likelihood of conflict with Israel and its clients in its enclave just north of the Israeli border. Israel, for its part, declared it would not recognize Lebanese authority over that territory, but there is evidence that tacit Israeli-Syrian cooperation exists, with the goal of controlling both PLO and Shia activities in the south.

PEACE GAMBITS, TERRORISM, AND INTERNAL POLITICS, 1984–1987

With the PLO established in Tunis, Yasir Arafat attempted to salvage something from the Lebanon disaster of 1982. He remained the titular leader of the organization but with increasingly less real influence over its many factions, even though loyalists still dominated the Palestine National Council (PNC), the PLO's governing body. Arafat's opponents condemned him for both the defeat at the hands of Israel and for considering a diplomatic option rather than adhering to the strategy of military confrontation.

Beset by such opposition in his own ranks, Arafat found little encouragement outside. His interest in diplomacy had been recognized by Israel and had incited them to drive the PLO out of Lebanon. Having succeeded, official Israeli policy remained that espoused by Begin and reiterated by Yitzhak Rabin: The PLO should be denied a role in negotiations "even if it accepts all the conditions of negotiations on the basis of the Camp David agreements (in addition to Resolutions 242 and 338) because the essence of the willingness to speak with the PLO is the willingness to speak about a Palestinian state, which must be opposed.[4]

The United States seemed to agree with this position. Its official stance was that it would not talk to the PLO or consider any role for it in negotiations until it "publicly and unequivocally" accepted Resolution 242. On the other hand, when Arafat sought American recognition of the Palestinian right to "self-determination," even if in the context of a confederation with Jordan, the Reagan administration objected, holding to the president's position of 1982 that self-determination meant a Palestinian state, which the U.S. refused to consider. Arafat found himself caught between an apparent American-Israeli alliance designed to block any overture he made that implied Palestine self-rule and the calls of PLO rejectionists for continued "armed struggle" to regain all of former Palestine, a reference to the strategy outlined in the 1968 charter. From the rejectionist standpoint, seeking a dialogue with the United States would lead nowhere and weaken the PLO position.

Apparent U.S. backing for Israel did not mean complete agreement however. The Reagan administration wanted a Jordanian solution to the West Bank, one that envisaged Israel giving up more territory than any Israeli politician seemed likely to do. It also seemed willing to accept as negotiators Palestinians from the West Bank and Gaza who were linked to the PLO, provided they were acceptable to Israel. This stance induced a situation where the administration seemed to be pressuring Israel to be forthcoming while permitting the latter a veto over its own proposals.

The results of Israeli elections in July 1984 further muddied the waters. The Labor Party, led by Shimon Peres, won a slight plurality, but he was unable to form a coalition government from among the fifteen minority parties that gained seats in the Knesset. Peres was forced to accept a coalition with Likud in which power would be shared and posts distributed equally. Labor would govern for the first eighteen months with Peres as prime minister and Yitzhak Shamir of Likud as foreign minister; Yitzhak Rabin, Peres's rival, was defense minister and Ariel Sharon reemerged on the Likud side as minister of commerce and industry. (Shamir would become prime minister in October 1986.) Peres hoped to achieve a settlement with King Husayn of Jordan while excluding the PLO. Success might enable him to call for new elections before he had to hand over the prime ministership to Shamir. But he had to tread cautiously so as not to be accused by the Likud of caving in to the PLO. For their part Shamir and Sharon opposed any negotiations with Jordan, hoping to annex the West Bank to Israel. They encouraged further settlement activity, which Peres tried to restrain in order to bring Husayn to the peace table.

Diplomatic bargaining intensified in 1985 along with equally determined efforts to derail that process. In February, King Husayn and Yasir Arafat reached agreement on their terms of dialogue and objectives. They called for a Palestinian state on the West Bank, to include East Jerusalem, but this "state" would exist in confederation with Jordan whose ruler would have final authority. Israel would withdraw completely from the occupied territories in return for peace. Negotiations towards these goals would be held at an international conference sponsored by the United Nations, with the PLO attending as the representative of the Palestinian people. Jordanian officials said that Arafat, by accepting inclusion in a confederation with Jordan, was implicitly abandoning the 1968 PLO Charter that called for Palestinian statehood in what was now Israel; this meant acceptance of Israel's existence, to be acknowledged openly if a settlement were reached.

The Husayn-Arafat accord seemed to be a major step towards accommodation, but it was fraught with pitfalls. Husayn preferred to regain the West Bank without Arafat but needed an alliance with the PLO to legitimize his aspirations in the eyes of the Arab world as well as in those of West Bank Arabs, most of whom remained loyal to Arafat. For his part the Fatah head had no love for Husayn but saw him as a possible vehicle by which to gain American support for PLO involvement in the negotiating process. Both saw American approval of their agreement and overtures as a way to stop further Israeli settlements from being implanted in the territories. But Arafat's gambit was restricted by obligations to his constituency. He would not recognize Israel openly *before* being himself, as head of the PLO, accepted into the international diplomatic arena; to do so would prejudice his position within PLO councils. Thus he would not take the one initiative that would have forced the American hand, namely, open acceptance of Resolution 242 which Washington insisted was the precondition for even considering a dialogue with the PLO, let alone its participation in diplomacy.

Arafat's hesitation to recognize Israel before a negotiated settlement suited the United States. American officials preferred direct Jordanian-Israeli talks without the PLO, under U.S. sponsorship, during which they would supposedly pressure Israel to make territorial concessions, thereby indicating their good faith to the Arabs. Also, they opposed an international conference not simply because of possible PLO participation, but because the Soviets would necessarily be involved. The Reagan administration was determined to control Middle East diplomacy and to block any Soviet role in a settlement. In Israel the Likud Party unilaterally condemned the idea of any talks regarding the West Bank, rejecting Peres's Jordanian option which had American backing. Likud and the settlers were determined to obstruct and undermine prospects for any agreement.[5]

Given these obstacles and circumstances little progress was made, despite Egyptian and Jordanian arguments that Arafat's overture was welcome and should be encouraged by the Reagan administration. Many believed that a major reason for the stalemate was the United States. The administration treated the Husayn-Arafat initiative with studied indifference, dictating terms it knew were impossible to meet rather than encouraging consultation. American conditions seemed designed to back Israel unequivocally while officials promised friendly Arabs that U.S. sponsorship, not an international conference, was the best way to regain land and achieve a settlement. Among those disenchanted with Washington were most West European countries including the government of Margaret Thatcher of Great Britain, normally Ronald Reagan's staunchest defender. Seeking to break the deadlock she invited two Fatah members of the PNC to meet with her in October 1985. This decision, announced in mid-September, was "a calculated gesture designed to distance Britain from both the U.S. and Israel. It is the clearest possible hint to the Americans, who have so far refused to talk to the PLO, that they should stop making difficulties and start making peace in the Middle East."[6] Intended also to encourage Mubarak and Husayn in their attempts to back Arafat, Thatcher's announcement was made while the two Arab leaders were visiting Washington where, in an unprecedented step, they publicly criticized American policy.

The upcoming meeting between Thatcher and Fatah representatives posed a serious threat to those who opposed Arafat's participation in the peace process, as it was to include a statement approved by him that would recognize Israel's existence more definitively. This alarmed Arab radical groups such as the PFLP and PDFLP who pledged to seek to destroy any accord, and Israel because such a statement might place pressure on the United States to modify its hostility to the PLO. A series of events took place designed to wreck such chances in which Arab radical and Israeli governmental interests coincided.

On 25 September a Palestinian assassination squad (including one British citizen) killed three Israelis in Cyprus. When captured the group claimed to belong to an elite PLO group linked to Fatah and Arafat, Force 17, although he and other PLO spokesmen denounced the affair. Nevertheless the incident gave the Peres government the opportunity to humiliate if not kill Arafat, fostering further militancy rather than conciliation towards Israel. On 1 October Israeli planes bombed the PLO headquarters outside Tunis, killing nearly fifty and wounding more, including Tunisians. According to Israel the attack was retaliation for the Arafat-sponsored killing of the three Israelis in Cyprus. It was definitely designed to derail Arafat's peace offensive. The United States cooperated. Whereas European, as well as Arab, leaders depicted the Israeli strike as intended to destroy the peace process, President Reagan called it a "legitimate" response, later toned down to "understandable but unfortunate."[7]

The American reaction particularly angered the Tunisians. The United States, a week before, had pledged to defend Tunisian air space and territorial integrity against Libyan overflights, calling such actions against "all norms of international behavior." As the Tunisians had agreed to house the PLO in 1982 at the request of the United States, American acceptance of Israeli violation of Tunisia's air space was all the more galling. On the other hand the raid buttressed Shimon Peres's image in Israel as he tried to entice King Husayn into direct talks, opposed by his Likud partners; one Israeli analyst declared on 3 October that "nobody will accuse Labor of being soft on the PLO or soft on terrorism now."[8]

The disintegration of the peace initiative continued. On 8 October PLO members commandeered a cruise ship in the Mediterranean, the *Achille Lauro*, apparently intending to disembark in Israel and take revenge for the Tunis bombings. Arafat condemned the undertaking and asked the hijackers to surrender, but they did so only after murdering a crippled American Jew and dumping his body overboard. At worst, especially in American eyes, Arafat had proved his terrorist tendencies. At best, he had been shown to lack control over units supposedly under his command: the head of the *Achille Lauro* operation was also based in Tunis. Lost in the uproar was recognition of the underlying reality governing the original chain of events. The Cyprus killing was intended to provoke an Israeli response that would make it impossible for Arafat to accept Israel's existence. Israel seized the opportunity, seeking to assassinate Arafat and put an end to the viability of the PLO, a continuance of the logic behind its 1982 invasion of Lebanon; it too opposed any PLO recognition of its right to exist.

Arafat's last-minute refusal to permit his representatives in London to sign the prearranged statement recognizing Israel went almost unnoticed in the furor. The British Foreign Office then cancelled the meeting, ending the Thatcher initiative amidst Jordanian charges that Arafat had violated his agreement. As in 1981–1982 official Palestinian interest in peace was more menacing to many than its pursuit of war, with Arafat further discredited by his unwillingness or inability to act decisively in the face of his Arab and Israeli opposition. The culmination of this episode was Shimon Peres's address to the United Nations on 21 October where he called for peace talks with Jordan. The U.S. approved the Peres overture, a stance suggesting implicit acceptance of the Israeli assault on the PLO headquarters. In Israel, on the other hand, Peres's speech was immediately vilified by the Israeli right which had no intention of ceding any territory.

In February 1986, Husayn abruptly abandoned his attempts to shepherd Arafat into the diplomatic arena. He had been unable to persuade him to accept Resolution 242—if only to force the United States' hand—and feared that further delay would jeopardize any chance for the return of West Bank lands to Jordanian jurisdiction. The Reagan administration welcomed Husayn's decision and sponsored private Israeli-Jordanian conversations as the year progressed toward an October deadline when the rejectionist Likud party would take over with Yitzhak Shamir as prime minister. Faced with this specter, both sides made concessions. Peres accepted the idea of an international conference espoused by Husayn, and the latter agreed to joint actions with Israel on the West Bank designed to foil Likud once Shamir took office. Late September and early October saw the appointment of Arab mayors in three West Bank towns and the reopening of a Jordanian bank closed since 1967. The timing suggested that Washington encouraged this tentative rapprochement in the hope of preventing Likud from unilaterally annexing the area while establishing a precedent for future Israeli-Jordanian cooperation.[9]

The sequence of events during this period illustrated certain constants of policy pursued by various actors. Arafat, opposed by factions within Fatah and by other PLO cadres after Israel's Lebanon invasion, had been unable to reassert the primacy of his leadership within that organization. His 1985 overture to Thatcher had been undermined by both Abu Nidal (the Cyprus assassinations) and Israel (the Tunis bombings), a combination seen previously in the events surrounding the Israeli invasion of Lebanon in 1982. Rival Fatah factions backed by Syria's Hafiz Assad opposed his leadership as did George Habash of the PFLP, all dedicated to undermining PLO peace initiatives. When an Arafat loyalist, Zafir al-Masri, accepted the mayoralty of Nablus in early 1986 to foster relations with Israeli authorities, he was soon assassinated by the PFLP. These events suited the Reagan administration, Israel's Labor Party, and eventually Jordan. An accord on an international conference under whose cloak they could have reached agreement on a condominium for the West Bank would have been a slap at both Arafat and Likud's Shamir. It would have blocked Likud from annexing the West Bank and the PLO from having access to a broader international forum where it might have called for a state with Arab and European backing.

There were other factors, however. The Reagan administration had viewed Israel as a strong component of its anticommunist crusade from the time the president took office. Burned by his foray into Lebanese politics in 1983, Secretary of State George Shultz had pushed hard for a closer strategic alliance with Israel that included technological exchanges related to the Strategic Defense

Initiative (the SDI or Star Wars project). Shultz declared in late 1986 that the goal of American-Israeli strategic cooperation was "to build institutional arrangements so that eight years from now, if there is a secretary of state who is not positive about Israel, he will not be able to overcome the bureaucratic relationship between Israel and the United States that we have established."[10] This cooperation could have domestic benefits as well. The administration encouraged Israel's involvement in the Star Wars project in part to overcome congressional opposition to it from liberal members of congress who usually backed Israel: "White House officials have not been shy in expressing hope that this Israeli cooperation will help shore up support for the programme among Israel's many influencial friends in the U.S., especially in Congress and in the Jewish community. Their hopes are being met."[11]

These goals transcended administration objections to Likud policies on the West Bank. They promised close ties whatever the nature of Likud actions toward Palestinians or the potential clash of Israeli and American interests elsewhere. Revelations about U.S.-Israeli arms shipments to Iran during the mid-1980s suggested to the Tower Commission that "Israel had its own interests, some in direct conflict with those of the United States, in having the United States pursue the initiative." The commission report noted also that one goal of Israeli actions had been "to distance the United States from the Arab world and ultimately to establish Israel as the only strategic partner of the United States in the region," an Israeli objective since the early 1950s.[12]

None of this disturbed the administration or its advisers during 1986–1987. The PLO seemed isolated from major bases of support. Arab heads of state virtually ignored Arafat at a summit held in Amman, Jordan, in November 1987. Concurrently, the Palestinians residing in the occupied territories had deeply resented Arafat's alliance with Husayn as a violation of his mission to liberate them; whatever his failing fortunes outside the territories, he was still the major hope of those within. Beset from all sides, Arafat seemed to American officials to be left with one option, an alliance with Jordan. Beyond this "The PLO [had] no military option and [lacked] an effective political strategy beyond perpetuating its own survival."[13] Given that any PLO military option was immediately deemed as "terrorist" by Israel and American spokespersons, this accusation of failure seemed self-serving and designed to perpetuate the status quo.

But circumstances were about to change. The PLO was to be given an option by the Palestinians within the territories as a result of their rebellion against Israeli rule. The intifada would create a new set of circumstances both within the territories and outside, challenging the foundations of American policy that had been based on the Jordanian option. These foundations would then be shattered by subsequent events that derived in part from the intifada, the Iraqi invasion of Kuwait, and the American decision to oppose it militarily in the hope of reasserting American power globally, not merely in the Middle East.

THE INTIFADA AND THE GULF CRISIS

INITIAL REFLECTIONS

Analysts agree that the intifada, the Palestinian movement to throw off Israeli rule in the occupied territories, began on 8 December 1987. It was on that day that an Israeli tank-transport truck crashed into several Arab cars in Gaza, killing four Palestinians and injuring several others. The demonstrations that erupted during the funerals of the victims were the first signs of an upheaval that spread rapidly to the West Bank and inaugurated a new phase in Palestinian Arab resistance to military rule designed to deprive them of their land and ultimately in Likud's eyes to oust them from the territories.

Comparisons can be made to the 1936-1939 Arab Revolt in Palestine, itself a popular uprising that the established leadership attempted to control and one that the occupying forces, British troops in that instance, finally quelled. In both rebellions Islamic groups were important though not crucial to articulating popular discontent. In both cases the eruptions occurred as the result of growing frustration and anger at the ongoing expropriation of land that had the tacit acceptance of local and outside authorities as a "legal" process: just as Zionists had a right to buy land and have Arab peasants expelled from it in mandatory Palestine, so did Jewish settlers have a "right" to expropriate land, often with government connivance, and work to reaffirm an ongoing Jewish presence in the territories. Many settlers talked openly of "transferring" the Arabs, a euphemism for ousting them by force from the West Bank to confirm Jewish control. Politicians sympathetic to settler goals gained or reattained prominence; in the latter case the reappearance of Ariel Sharon was particularly noteworthy.

In both cases these processes were designed to "create facts," to establish a presence that could not be repudiated and that could serve to negate future calls for compromise. In both cases the recognized Arab leadership seemed helpless to stem these efforts and was discredited by developments related to them. And in both cases economic grievances played an important part. Nevertheless, comparisons are only that and circumstances are never identical. Both the outcome of the intifada and the future of the PLO and indigenous leadership in the territories are still uncertain. Although the intifada was spontaneous in origin, PLO control and direction was achieved, contrary to the lack of direction characterizing the 1936-1939 Revolt. Much will depend on the resolution of tangential events that impact upon the issue; at present the political repercussions of the 1990–1991 Gulf crisis, just as the resolution of Arab grievances in the later 1930s was finally decided by World War II, the Holocaust, and British-American rivalries after the war.

An ultimate determinant will be the policy pursued by the dominant great power, in this case the United States. Here some similarities exist. In 1939, after crushing the Arab Revolt, Great Britain declared a White Paper apparently ensuring an Arab state in order to appease Arab heads of state on the eve of World War II. In the fall of 1990, after suspending talks with the PLO the previous June, the United States, in order to gain the agreement of Arab heads of state to participate in military action to oust Iraq from Kuwait, appeared to promise them that it would sponsor an international conference to consider the Palestinian question. In both cases the actions were taken to bolster the power's imperial status, and with little apparent real commitment to Arab goals per se; in the latter case Washington may have made a contradictory comment to Israel, promising it will not push quickly for an international conference, in order to keep that state out of the war. And in both cases, the promises were made to Arab rulers, not to representatives of the Palestinians. Here differences are equally revealing. British statesmen felt an obligation to Zionism but did not always believe it served their imperial interests. American politicians' commitment to Israel and their belief that it serves their geopolitical interests may waver, but they recognize the domestic political benefits of the alliance and use pro-Israeli groups to back their goals elsewhere—for example, in mobilizing domestic support of operations in the Gulf, as will be illustrated.[14]

The ultimate dilemma for the Bush administration may not be its conflicting promises regarding the fate of the territories in themselves but its conflicting obligations to allies *cum* client states. The Gulf regimes, especially the Saudis, may prove far more crucial to American interests in maintaining regional security than Israel could be or has been, in a period when the Cold War justification of Israel's use as an ally has faded. But Israel and her backers will oppose added military aid to the Saudis as a threat to her security, while simultaneously asking for additional aid to maintain military paramountcy in the region. This opposition, coupled with further repression of the intifada, will weaken the base for regional defense in the Gulf that the U.S. is so eager to create. Administration officials seem to equate Arab condemnation of Arafat for his initial support of Saddam Husayn with lessened Arab concern for Palestinian rights. The resolution of these matters awaits the future, but they are intertwined even if their origins are quite distinct from each other.

THE INTIFADA: ITS ROOTS[15]

The intifada was a spontaneous eruption of hatred and frustration incited by a specific incident, the tanker-truck collision of 8 December 1987 in Gaza. However it represented years of anger directed mostly at Israel but to some extent at the external Palestinian leadership also. This resentment contained economic as well as political grievances, some based on Israeli treatment of Arab labor, some the product of developments elsewhere, especially in the Gulf. Much of the anger resulted from personal factors beyond those issues related to politics or economics—the daily harassments, arrests, and beatings that the ordinary Palestinian could face and had faced for years.

As noted in previous chapters the benefits derived from Arab employment in Israel after 1967 were considerable and during much of the 1970s constituted a boom in living standards for Palestinians, especially in the West Bank. The advantages served to deflect attention from the costs of the occupation: subservient working status; the loss of salary, already low, through deductions for services available only to Israelis, not Arabs. For example, most Israelis in comparable positions earned twice as much in base salary as Arabs. Israelis received benefits from Histadrut and social and medical services while paying a lower tax rate than Arabs. The latter were assessed one percent of their wages by Histadrut but were ineligible to receive benefits and were denied membership to Histadrut. Much larger amounts were deducted for health, pension, and other funds for which Arabs received little in return. In effect, Arab labor in Israel helped to subsidize not only the occupation but Israeli costs and services for the Jewish population as well.

This situation seemed acceptable during much of the 1970s because wages were better than under Jordanian rule and were often supplemented by funds repatriated from Palestinians working in the Gulf where a thriving economy existed. In addition, Israeli occupation, until 1977, did not seem particularly threatening to the lives of most Arabs in the territories. Jewish settlements were relatively isolated from Arab communities and the rate of growth of these settlements was slight, especially when compared to that which occurred once Menachem Begin took office. At this point changes in policy occurred that soon seemed to constitute a major threat to Palestinian existence. As noted previously, the growth of settlements intensified: whereas an annual average of 770 Israelis settled in the territories from 1967–1977, that average increased under Likud to 5,960 annually from 1978 to 1987.[16] Settlements were often designed to abut Arab communities and often took over their lands, constituting a visible threat designed from Ariel Sharon's point of view to intimidate Arabs and encourage them to leave.

The 1980s witnessed the intensification of this strategy. The village leagues created at the end of 1981 to install Arabs willing to collaborate with Israel were accompanied by an "iron fist" policy proclaimed by Sharon and Chief of Staff Rafael Eitan as the best means of crushing Palestinian Arab resistance. Arab demonstrations in the spring of 1982 were met with arrests and beatings, though not the scale of imprisonment that would emerge later. The period immediately following the Israeli invasion of Lebanon, until 1985, was relatively quiescent, but aggressive land requisitions again aroused Arab resistance. It was not unusual for the military authorities to simply fence off Arab land and declare it Jewish with the owners having no legal recourse: the military administration was the law in the territories as it had been when administering the absentee property law in Arab sectors of Israel immediately after independence. The Israeli military, now under Defense Minister Yitzhak Rabin, responded in August of that year with a new "iron fist" campaign that intensified hatred on both sides.

For the Arabs, Israeli expansionist goals seemed on the verge of fulfillment in the vista of new bedroom communities for Israelis in the West Bank; settler harassments increased. At the same time one saw a new generation of Arabs emerging in the territories who had always lived under Israeli rule and who questioned their parents' submission to the daily humiliations they witnessed. This submission in the eyes of the youth had always been seen as fortitude or endurance, *sumud*, by their elders who had placed their hopes in the PLO leadership. For the youth, still loyal to that body, hope began to fade with the decline of the PLO in the mid-1980s, and the justifications for merely enduring seemed less convincing. Recession and inflation in Israel had caused economic decline for all sectors during most of the 1980s. As the Palestinian economy was tied to the shekel, its revenues and the purchasing power of individuals also suffered. Concomitantly, a steady decline in oil prices and economic growth in the Gulf, affected to some degree by spillover from the Iran-Iraq war, meant that jobs in Gulf states and remittances back to the territories were hit.[17]

In such circumstances, *sumud* gradually came to suggest capitulation to a set of conditions where one's future was endangered. Demonstrations increased from 1985 onward as did random violence by Arabs, including stone throwing and isolated assaults on Israelis. This, in turn, resulted in more controlled reprisals by Israelis, either Jewish settlers on a raid or military patrols. Arrests of Arabs spiraled and a punishment used initially by the British in the 1930s, demolition of the homes of suspected rioters, was reinstituted. Rabin restored the practice of administrative detention, where Palestinians could be held for six months without trial. Whereas only sixty-two Palestinians had been held without trial during the period 1980–1985, one hundred and thirty-one were consigned to that status in the last five months of 1985. Many more were arrested and later released but only after brutal treatment. According to an Israeli lawyer who sought to defend Palestinians: "If you are arrested, the general rule is: after you confess you can see a lawyer. Everyone is beaten when they are arrested or to get a confession out of them. You must be very tough not to break in these circumstances."[18] Some did break and were turned to become informers against their fellow Palestinians. Many others did not and used the prison experience, as had their predecessors in the 1970s, to formulate ties and strategies for the future: "Some of us died but a Palestinian personality was being built up. . . . Prison was like an education."[19]

In retrospect, this experience was a turning point for many Palestinians of a younger generation in the territories. In the past they had frequently been victims of Jewish terrorism that responded to Arab terrorism initiated from outside. In the early 1980s a particular flash point had been Hebron, site of the massacre of many Jews in 1929 and a focal point of Israeli settler attention from the mid-1970s when a Jewish (Gush Emunim) community reestablished itself in that city under military protection. An attack on settlers in May 1980 by Palestinians from outside the territories, killing six and wounding sixteen, led to a Jewish response, the car-bombings of several Arab mayors. The stabbing death of a yeshiva student in Hebron in 1983 resulted in random booby-trapping of Arab schools by a Jewish terrorist ring which before it was caught had planned to blow up the Dome of the Rock/Haram al-Sharif areas on the Temple Mount. A bombing of an Israeli bus, killing several Jews, resulted in the machine-gunning of an Arab bus. Arabs in the territories admitted they felt some satisfaction from Arab attacks; in one poll of Jews, nearly thirty-two percent of those questioned approved assaults on Arabs. Prison sentences for Jewish terrorists were often commuted following intense pressure from settler groups and right-wing politicians.[20]

From 1985 onwards Arab violence in the territories was more likely to be inspired from within, rather than by groups or individuals sent into the area from outside. To be sure, many Palestinians had ties to PLO groups, but they seem to have had little influence on stone-throwing youngsters. Also different was the Israeli reaction. Now it was official action as well as unofficial actions under the guise of settler or military retaliation, that sought to crush disturbances and impose retribution. Arabs in the territories came into increasing daily confrontations with Israeli troops, whether the former were involved in riots or not. Nowhere was tension more rife than in Gaza.

THE GAZA STRIP

Conditions in the Gaza Strip have always been constrained owing to the extraordinary population density of the area, perhaps second in world statistics only to Bangladesh. Refugees, from 1948 and 1967, make up about seventy percent of the population in an area one-fifteenth the size of the West Bank. The Palestinian population has been further squeezed by Israeli expropriation of forty-two percent of Arab land since 1967. As Sara Roy has shown, "One [refugee] camp, Jabalya, is home to sixty thousand people living on one-half square mile of land, giving the camp a population density . . . double the density of Manhattan. The Strip's population is very young, with nearly 50 percent comprised of children 14 years of age and younger."

With such a dependent population whose economy has been severely restricted by circumstances including loss of land to Israel, the strip has become the major source for cheap labor in Israel. On the other hand, sixteen settlements have been created out of land taken from Arabs with a total of approximately 2,500 Israeli settlers compared to a Palestinian population of 750,000. Water use restrictions imposed on Arabs in order to benefit Israeli settler agriculture have resulted in a severe decline in the productivity of the Gaza citrus industry; given population imbalances set against resource allocations, "individual Israelis consume seven times the amount of water consumed by individual Gazans" with more settlements intended for the area.[21]

Gaza has had a long tradition of resisting Israeli rule. The Israeli occupation of 1967, followed by announcements that Israel would retain control of the area in any subsequent peace agreements, led to armed resistance. This intensified in 1971 following Israeli deportation of families. A successful Israeli retaliation directed by Ariel Sharon saw sections of camps bulldozed to open roads for military access. Hostilities erupted again at the end of 1981 following the imposition of "civilian" administration into the West Bank and Gaza. Special taxes and curfews led to continued violence in resistance to Eitan's "iron fist" tactics and a number of Gazans were killed by soldiers stationed outside mosques during Friday prayers in early 1982.[22]

The place of Islam in the Gaza Strip has always been more significant politically than in the West Bank. This has been due in part to the influence of the Muslim Brotherhood derived from its base in Egypt, but it has also reflected the socioeconomic environment of Gaza where Muslim groups could provide social and moral alternatives to the alienation imposed by circumstances. Various offshoots of the Muslim Brothers have appeared, some more militant against Israel than others, with most calling for personal reform (jihad) as the dominant moral imperative. As a result these groups did not present themselves in the eyes of the populace as an alternative to the PLO whose goals of a Palestinian state were approved. Most Gazans, like West Bankers, were loyal to Arafat and Fatah. An Islamic University was created in Gaza and two universities, dominated by the Muslim Brothers al-Najah and Hebron, arose on the West Bank.

Islamic militancy appeared only with the formation of al-Jihad in the mid-1980s, another offshoot of the Muslim Brotherhood that argued that armed resistance against Israel was the only means of achieving liberation. Its appearance indicated frustration at the doctrine of self-development fostered by the Brotherhood during a period of increasing socioeconomic repression under Israeli rule, but it also showed that Israeli policy towards the religious groups had turned against itself. Israeli occupation and intelligence officials had encouraged the growth of the Muslim Brothers from the later 1970s, occasionally through funding but usually by imposing fewer restrictions on their movements than they did on known PLO sympathizers. The logic was that increasing adherence to Islam would undercut loyalty to the PLO and its secular political goals. Militant students were permitted to travel from Gaza to Bir Zayt University in Ramallah, outside of Jerusalem, for example, to rough up PLO supporters.

Though successful to a small degree, these Israeli tactics were compromised by the general tenor of Israel's approach to the territories and confiscation of land. Furthermore, devout Muslims could readily distinguish between Mossad backing for militants and Israeli army destruction of mosques and killing of attendants at prayers during periods of strife. As a result no real rift occurred between members of Islamic groups and PLO sympathizers who found common accord in their analysis of conditions within the territories.[23] In the meantime, the decline of PLO prestige during the mid-1980s enabled local militants to assume more authority and initiative. Locally-inspired violence increased in the territories, especially in Gaza, from 1985 onward. A cycle of protest and re-pression intensified during 1987. On 7 December an Israeli was stabbed to death by a Gazan. When the tanker-truck crash occurred the next day, rumors spread immediately that the driver was a relative of the deceased seeking revenge. The funerals for the Arab victims of the crash initiated the massive demonstrations that inflamed the West Bank as well. The uprising had begun.

INTIFADA: THE FIRST TWO YEARS, DECEMBER 1987–DECEMBER 1989

As we have seen, the intifada originated as a spontaneous outburst of anger, undirected by any higher committee or organization. As such it spread rapidly from Gaza to the West Bank and sustained itself through the cooperation of local committees and neighborhoods who organized for mutual assistance. It was only a month later that any semblance of direction from PLO headquarters in Tunis appeared, although local committee heads affiliated with various PLO factions had contacted them once the uprising began. At its heart the intifada was an uprising of the poor and the youth, the less-advantaged sectors of the population who organized popular committees which PLO representatives then sought to direct.

Various decisions seem to have been made on the spot. One was to restrict the protests to demonstrations and stone-throwing, and not to use weapons such as knives or guns. Those seeking to direct the protest realized that the image of the Palestinian populace confronting the Israeli military that strove to repress them by armed force was one that would affect world opinion. Violence, con-trolled and restricted in its weapons, was an important means of asserting open opposition to Israeli hegemony for many Palestinians. But a political agenda quickly appeared, inspired and possibly instigated from Tunis. In January 1988, the leadership in the territories called for an independent Palestinian state, led by the PLO, that would coexist with Israel. Resolution of issues should await an international conference sponsored by the U.N. Security Council, a program suggested by the PLO in April 1987. Within the territories, special taxes im-posed on Arabs should be rescinded.[24]

These principles, called the Fourteen Points, were initially announced by individuals not connected to the intifada, men more widely known to the outside world as "moderates" who had their own ties to the PLO in Tunis: Sari Nuseibeh and Faysal Husayni, for example. As members of a social elite they were viewed with suspicion by both the popular leadership and PLO committee heads when these points were first declared. Subsequently, with direction from Tunis, the Fourteen Points became the official agenda of the intifada. The process of integration among the various levels of leadership was never fully completed, but they collaborated successfully. While the moderates had their own ties to Tunis, PLO directives from Fatah, the PFLP, and the DFLP were being sent to their representatives in the territories. These local committee heads formed the unified command, UNL, which in general agreed on tactics and issued joint directives that were then taken up at the street level. The need to coordinate activities, coupled with general agreement on the political objective, an independent state, overrode incipient differences: frequently coordination within the territories between factions surpassed the tendency of their leaders to agree when meeting in Tunis. The Islamic Jihad, organized on the basis of cells, followed the UNL lead, mainly through its ties to Fatah.

The intifada radically affected the relationships of Arabs in the territories with both the PLO leadership and the Israelis. The former had always feared and tried to repress local leadership independent of its control in the territories, even if such individuals identified themselves with PLO goals. Now necessity demanded cooperation and reliance on information and advice from the territories. This interactive balance would prove crucial in encouraging the leadership to move towards diplomatic compromise once the resistance in the territories demanded it.

For Israelis, and the government leadership in particular, the popular uprising was interpreted in light of previous approaches to relations with Arabs, including at the state level. This was unacceptable behavior; for some, such as defense minister Yitzhak Rabin, it was "terrorism," and it should be dealt with accordingly. Arabs understood force, nothing else, and it was only when they experienced Israeli force that they would desist. Military repression, including shooting at demonstrators, was acceptable; also acceptable and encouraged was the beating of prisoners to "teach them a lesson." Given the colonial nature of the Israeli-Arab relationship, it was quite understandable that many soldiers who had grown up with Arabs in servile positions to them reacted with fury to Arabs who defied them. Mass beatings occurred during patrols and tear gas came to be used frequently in closed as well as open settings, a violation of the Geneva Convention. Houses adjacent to the site of stone-throwing were routinely vandalized and tear-gassed without evidence of the complicity of the occupants or regard for the frequent presence of pregnant women and children.

What Rabin explained as a policy designed to break Arab will, "beatings never killed anybody," turned into soldier-inspired riots against the populations of areas at times. Those arrested could expect serious beatings; those stopped, whether aged adults or children under five years of age, might experience the same. As one Israeli journalist explained it:

> There is democracy in Israel but none in the territories. A whole generation of Israelis grew up with a non-democratic system next to them, as non-democratic rulers. There is a difference between the arrest of Arabs and Jews. When you [a Jew] get arrested, the police or secret service people will say "We will give you Jewish treatment." You will be slapped around perhaps but not tortured. Arabs who are arrested are beaten and tortured. It is difficult to convince Israelis that this undemocratic way of ruling and treating Arabs is wrong or evil. Israelis see it as a normal practice [towards Arabs, not themselves].[25]

Eventually the excesses would become so great that public criticism within Israel, let alone outside, would lead to recrimination and in some cases legal actions against soldiers who were charged with exceeding their orders. Their defense, that they were following orders issued by superiors, including Rabin, was denied, causing accusations of lying to be hurled at the military leadership and Rabin by officers as well as soldiers.[26]

The Israeli response aroused international criticism—in the first five weeks of the intifada thirty-three Palestinians had been killed and over two hundred and fifty wounded; nearly two thousand had been imprisoned. There had been no Israeli fatalities, with sixty soldiers and forty civilians, mostly settlers who joined the fray, wounded. The threat to Israel was twofold.[27] Firstly, Israel had to suppress the uprising in order to control territories its rightist government hoped to keep. Secondly, the government had to stem any hope of a political resolution to the uprising. In April 1988 the coalition cabinet approved the assassination of Khalil al-Wazir (Abu Jihad) at his home in Tunis. Many Israelis considered this an act of desperation. Wazir was believed to be directing the intifada and to be counselling refusal to use arms. The cabinet's decision to kill him, fully supported by Likud members but also by defense minister Rabin of Labor, reflected the hope of quelling the uprising, but it also indicated a willingness to tolerate revolt so long as peace efforts were stymied. The timing of the assassination served to undercut calls for an international conference that had the approval of Shimon Peres.[28]

From the Palestinian perspective the intifada had two sides: a popular resistance to Israeli oppression; and an offer of coexistence once a Palestinian state was created. Both tracks had the same goal, getting rid of Israeli domination, but the second was just as threatening to Israeli rightist politicians as the first. The Israeli-Arab relationship could not be one of equality. Those Arabs who espoused such views should be punished. For example, two Arab lawyers from Gaza who defended demonstrators in Israeli courts were invited to speak on the goals of the intifada at a gathering at Tel Aviv University in the spring of 1988. They did so, advocating peaceful coexistence in separate states. Within two weeks each had been arrested and sentenced to six months detention without legal recourse in Ansar 3, a new prison built in the Negev to house such individuals. The Israeli organizers of the conference had no doubt as to the reasons for such detention; advocacy of peace was again more threatening than pursuit of violence.[29]

The Israeli repression had the opposite effect from that intended. Rather than crushing the uprising it unified it, solidifying ties that had been tenuous. As noted, the uprising had been one of the youth and the poor, usually an inclusive category in Gaza. When the intifada spread to the West Bank it also attracted the youth from the refugee camps, but many members of the middle class, and elders, questioned their motives. What united them with the younger generation ultimately was the fact that Israeli troops retaliated indiscriminately—you were beaten because you were Palestinian whatever your status or what you happened to be doing at the time the demonstration began. General, though not universal, cooperation developed regarding acts of civil disobedience. Boycotts of Israeli goods occurred as did refusal to pay Israeli taxes designed to finance the occupation. The UNL-sponsored strikes and shutdowns of businesses survived Israeli attempts to break them. Israeli counter-tactics, principally the denial of food supplies to villages, full quarantines and the like, were countered by striving for self-sufficiency in food. Family gardens became popular and a symbol of resistance to Israeli authorities who at times arrested Arabs for growing their own food, as happened in the Christian village of Bayt Sahur.

The first two years of the intifada, to the end of 1989, can be characterized as a period of intensified violence on both sides. The primary means of Arab resistance were stones and strikes, along with civil disobedience in the form of nonpayment of taxes and boycotts of Israeli goods. Israel retaliated with both violence and preventive administrative measures. Rules for military response were stretched to permit snipers to be stationed, in civilian clothes, where disturbances might erupt in order to assassinate stone throwers. Computerized tax lists led to confiscation of property, often automobiles, and village raids frequently resulted in destruction of gardens and orchards to force economic dependency on Israel. By the end of 1989 an estimated 626 Palestinians and 43 Israelis had been killed, 37,439 Arabs wounded, and between 35,000 and 40,000 arrested.[30] Increased pressures on Arab society led to individual acts of violence beyond those sanctioned by the leadership during 1989. Knifings and the use of grenades occurred along with retaliatory vengence such as the commandeering and deliberate crashing of an Israeli bus by a Palestinian in July.[31] These incidents encouraged assaults by individual Israelis on Arabs. In addition, Palestinians turned against their fellow Arabs suspected of collaborating with Israeli intelligence. Most observers believed in the existence of such spies because of the number of people arrested and threatened with torture who were then turned by Israeli police to work for them.

Individual Palestinian militancy was buttressed by the growing prominence of an Islamic resistance organization, Hamas (*Harakat al-Muqawama al-Islamiyya*) that had been formed in February 1988 at a time when the Islamic Jihad had been broken. Hamas was formed by members of the Muslim Brotherhood who rejected that organization's passive approach to Palestinian issues. Hamas posed an alternative to PLO political guidelines in that it called for the creation of a Palestinian state, founded on religious principles, in all of former Palestine; it thus rejected the compromise solution bruited about by Arafat for several years before being officially proclaimed in December 1988. For the time being, however, Hamas and Palestinians tied to secular groups overlooked their differences in order to combine their efforts against Israel. Estimates of Hamas affiliation varied, being 20 percent in Gaza and much less in the West Bank although pockets of strong identification existed, as in Nablus, a nearly totally Muslim town, where the incidence of Arab-Israeli atacks was higher than elsewhere. Gaza's militancy was not simply Islamic however. Khalil al-Wazir had been raised there and his assassination by Israel provided new impetus for opposition in the camps.

THE INTIFADA AND INTERNATIONAL POLITICS, 1987–1991

The eruption of the intifada engendered major changes in international politics relating to the Middle East and to the Palestinian future. The PLO, moribund on the eve of the uprising, took new life inspired, if not forced, by the initiatives coming from the territories to alter its hesitant posture toward peace with Israel. Arafat, through his deputy Bassam al-Sharif, presented a position paper at the Arab League Emergency Summit that met in Algiers in June 1988 to consider the uprising. In it he called for mutual recognition of the right of Palestinians as well as Israelis to peace and security. Arafat also insisted that the PLO recognized Resolutions 242 and 338 but only in the context of other U.N. resolutions referring to Palestinian national rights, mention of which is excluded from those resolutions. Sharif's paper argued that the PLO's *"raison d'être* is not the undoing of Israel but the salvation of the Palestinian people and their rights, including their right to democratic self-expression and national self-determination."[32] The paper generated a muted response although the league did call for an international conference to reach a settlement. League members, however, refused to contribute to a fund to support the intifada and to sustain workers who had lost jobs. Hence, though the PLO was accepted as a full member of the league, that did not stop Arafat from accusing Arab states of not backing the uprising.

Despite the tensions between Arafat and Arab heads of state, those leaders with close ties to the United States worked to restore contacts with the PLO leader and to encourage steps towards a dialogue between him and Washington. Husni Mubarak of Egypt was particularly instrumental in establishing a rapprochement between Arafat and Jordan's King Husayn in October. In November, a meeting of the PNC in Algiers declared the existence of "the state of Palestine . . . with its capital in the holy Jerusalem." In addition the PNC announced its readiness to negotiate with Israel on the basis of Resolutions 242 and 338 under the aegis of an international peace conference, with the condition that mutual recognition occurred, that Israel recognized Palestinian rights also. Particularly interesting was the document's stress on close ties between a future Palestinian state and Jordan, with the former existing in confederation with the latter. Four months earlier, in July, King Husayn had openly renounced any claims to Palestine and rescinded subsidies Jordan had paid into the West Bank for years; he had reacted with anger to the fourteen points issued by the UNL leadership that ignored Jordan.[33] Now Husayn strove to foster support for the Palestinian pronouncements, out of concern for the strong sympathy for the intifada shown by his own Palestinian constituency that comprised 60 percent of Jordan's population and because rightist Israelis such as Ariel Sharon were calling for the ouster of Palestinians from the territories to Jordan. Suddenly King Husayn's political security seemed to rest on the advent of a Palestinian state.

Arafat's efforts to gain international recognition of his peace proposals met finally with success in December 1988 when Washington agreed he had met their conditions of renouncing terrorism and accepting Resolution 242. This came after the State Department under George Shultz denied Arafat a visa to address the United Nations in New York, forcing the transfer of the meeting to Geneva where the PLO head again appealed for peace. With American acceptance of Arafat's overtures, a dialogue was established with the PLO through the American ambassador in Tunis where PLO headquarters remained. Nevertheless, the apparent legitimization of Arafat by Washington reflected little enthusiasm for backing PLO participation in serious negotiations unless the Bush administration felt it had popular support for doing so. A frequent criticism of the organization in 1989–1990 was its lack of interest in a public relations campaign designed to win American backing which, officials implied, would help their task. Left unsaid was the assumption that such backing would help politicians deflect criticism from Israel and American Jewish organizations supporting its stance. Indeed, one reason the PLO gained acceptance had been precisely because various American Jewish groups and individuals called for acceptance of Arafat's pledges and criticized Israeli tactics in suppressing the uprising.[34]

In the Middle East there was a distinct lack of enthusiasm for the new PLO line in many quarters. Both Likud and Labor Party leaders condemned it. So did Syria's Hafiz Assad who had backed Fatah opponents of Arafat since 1983. Within the PLO various factions expressed reservations. The PFLP under George Habash was opposed to any peace overtures that gave away recognition of Israel without the latter's reciprocation. Nayif Hawatmah's DFLP (no longer the PDFLP) also had reservations. The overwhelming vote of approval for the initiative at the November PNC meeting gained their adherence to the policy. However, several factions indicated their expectations that Israeli opposition would result in failure and that Arafat was staking his reputation on false premises, that the United States could bring Israel to the table.

Attention now focused on prime minister Shamir of Israel who had already attracted American criticism during 1988 as Washington began to show alarm at the ramifications of the intifada. Secretary of State George Shultz had pushed a peace plan during the spring and summer that called for recognition of "the legitimate rights of the Palestinian people," the same phrase he had used in 1982 when sworn in as secretary of state. This entailed Jordanian-Israeli negotiations under the umbrella of a U.N.-sponsored international conference, a concession to King Husayn. Palestinians would be part of the Jordanian delegation and the United States would provide a draft agreement for consideration. This was a rerun of the Jordanian option advanced by Washington in 1985–1986, with the addition of the international conference and Palestinians as part of the Jordanian delegation. Shamir opposed both ingredients and had no intention of negotiating the status of the West Bank, in contrast to his foreign minister, Shimon Peres of Labor, who welcomed the initiative and was praised by Washington in return. The only point of agreement between Washington and Jerusalem was their mutual opposition to the involvement of the PLO at this time.[35]

With the advent of 1989, however, many new factors had emerged. The U.S. had agreed to talk to the PLO, at a time when a new administration headed by George Bush was about to take office. Pressure on Shamir, whose obstinacy had greatly annoyed Shultz, could be expected. On the other hand, he had been strengthened by Knesset elections in early November 1988. Although Likud barely beat Labor in the polls, the strength of religious parties helped Shamir to form a new National Unity Government where Likud controlled the most important cabinet posts. Rabin of Labor remained as defense minister, responsible for quelling the intifada, but Shimon Peres was demoted to the ministry of finance with Likud now directing the foreign ministry.[36] Faced with requests from Washington for proposals to take to the PLO, and with strong hints from the American Jewish community that steps should be taken, Shamir proposed an election plan for the territories that was designed to stall the negotiating process and enable further consolidation of Israeli power in these areas. The stalemate would last until June 1990.

Shamir and Likud, over bitter opposition from rightists such as Ariel Sharon, gained Knesset approval in May 1989 of a plan calling for "free and democratic elections" among Palestinian Arabs in the territories, with the ultimate goal of autonomy that would grant them authority over their [unspecified] "affairs of daily life." Israel would retain control of security, foreign affairs and all aspects of policy pertaining to the settlers in the territories. While Israel declared itself "prepared to discuss any option which is presented," Shamir revealed his real intent when he responded to rightist critics charging that any promise of autonomy would lead to Palestinian independence: "We shall not give the Arabs one inch of our land, even if we have to negotiate for ten years. We won't give them a thing. . . . We have the veto in our hands. . . . The status quo of the interim arrangement will continue until all parties reach agreement on the permanent arrangement," which presumably would ratify acceptance of the territories as part of Israel. No restrictions on further settlements would be imposed.[37] These points were reaffirmed in a codicil of the government proposals that asserted the principle that no change in the status of the West Bank or Gaza was permissible and that Israel would never talk to the PLO, let alone permit a Palestinian state in the territories.

Palestinian spokesmen in the territories rejected the plan, as did the PLO. Both affirmed their goal of coexistence which required a state. The U.S., however, welcomed the proposal as a working document because it established linkage between elections in the territories and resolution of their status in final negotiations. The administration looked to the ending of Israeli occupation of the territories, something Israel would not accept, but decided to give Shamir a year to find Palestinian leaders in the West Bank or Gaza who would discuss his proposals. Given that no one would come forward, this gave Israel a year to suppress the intifada and expand more settlements while fending off American efforts to broaden the scope of Shamir's offer. Despite Shamir's bellicose statements in Israel, the administration apparently deluded itself into thinking he would be forthcoming if given the chance. This of course was the impression Shamir wished to impart while pursuing his own goals.

The Bush administration, while pressing Shamir to accept its proposals, was not eager to include the PLO in any talks. On the other hand it had to give the impression of concern for the latter's views while leaving open the options to be employed in future negotiations. Secretary of State James Baker, working closely with Egypt's Mubarak, strove to broaden the scope of the Shamir directive by establishing the principle that Palestinians exiled from the territories or who had residence in East Jerusalem could be members of the negotiating team that would meet to discuss election procedures. Jerusalem had not been mentioned specifically in the Israeli government proposals. Shamir violently opposed this idea as it contradicted Israel's position that East Jerusalem, annexed immediately after the 1967 war, was forever a part of Israel and non-negotiable. The official American stance was that East Jerusalem's status was still subject to negotiation. In return for this American attempt to enlarge the scope of Palestinian representation, Arafat had to concede the non-involvement of the PLO in such talks, if held. He had committed himself to American sponsorship of a dialogue. He thus severely undermined his credibility within his organization because Israel resisted American attempts to broaden the scope of representation and various politicians acknowledged they were trying to drive a wedge between Palestinians in the territories and PLO leadership.

The only concessions made were by Arafat at a time when harsher steps taken by Israel during the summer of 1989 took a greater toll on Palestinian lives in the territories. Israel held fast, though Peres would have accepted Arab representatives from Jerusalem. By March 1990 the plan was dead although Shamir did not reject it officially until June when he took office as head of a Likud government, without reliance on Labor participation. In the meantime, however, regional developments combined with events within the territories to end the U.S.-PLO dialogue.

The sequence of events began with President Bush stating on 3 March that the United States opposed further Israeli settlements in East Jerusalem, the West Bank, and Gaza; Shamir immediately replied that Israel intended to settle as many Soviet Jews in East Jerusalem as it could. The Labor Party, with presumed American encouragement, then threatened to dissolve the coalition unless Washington's points for negotiation, including the participation of East Jerusalem Arabs, were accepted. Shamir, as prime minister, then fired Peres, his finance minister, and Labor left the coalition as of 15 March. Tortuous negotiations for formation of a new cabinet ensued with Labor's Peres given the first chance. He ultimately failed, leaving the field open to Shamir; by mid-June he had put together a Likud cabinet without Labor. At that point, having rebuffed the Bush administration in March, Shamir now officially rejected on 28 June the plan for negotiations he had originally offered in May 1989.

The three-month period, mid-March to mid-June 1990, was a crucial one for Palestinians and Israelis. With Labor out of the coalition, Likud ran an interim government alone and used the opportunity to press its policy of settlements, in the territories and in East Jerusalem. At the same time, Yasir Arafat, sensitive to criticism of his policy of rapprochement after unofficial Likud rejection of the Bush settlement stipulations in March, began strengthening his ties with Iraq's Saddam Husayn in the hope of forcing negotiations based on power, rather than the conciliation advocated by Egypt's Husni Mubarak. Saddam Husayn himself, in early April and at an Arab summit in Baghdad from 28–30 May, would call for a more militant posture towards Israeli intransigence and American tolerance of that posture, especially in light of the massive Soviet Jewish immigration into Israel. By this time major developments had seriously poisoned the negotiating atmosphere.

On 11 April, Good Friday eve, militant Jewish settlers occupied a Greek Orthodox hospice adjacent to the Church of the Holy Sepulchre in East Jerusalem, claiming they had purchased a lease from the owner. It transpired that Likud, with Labor out of the coalition, had pushed this act, with the housing ministry providing 40 percent of the money and the remainder coming from a holding company in Panama. The latter funds seem to have originated with one of two possible sources: from profits gained from arms sales to Colombian drug barons organized by retired Israeli officers linked to the Israeli arms industry; or from profits gained from the Israeli Mossad contract to train the Panamanian defense forces, the same forces whose presumed threat to public order was one justification[38] for the American invasion to overthrow Manuel Noriega. This action, defended by Ariel Sharon as necessary to get all Arabs, whether Muslim or Christian, out of East Jerusalem, intensifed general Arab alarm at a time when the U.S. Senate, opposing the Bush administration, had on 22 March passed a resolution recognizing a unified Jerusalem as the capital of Israel.[39] Arab protest demonstrations and deaths due to Israeli military responses intensified as did growing concern elsewhere for conditions in the territories.

Negotiations at the United Nations in early May indicated American sympathy but no agreement for an Arab-sponsored resolution criticizing Israeli settlement policies, especially regarding that of placing Soviet Jewish immigrants in the territories. On 20 May an Israeli lined up and killed seven Gazans waiting for rides at Rishon le Zion to go to work in Israel. During the ensuing demonstrations and military reprisals at least seventeen more Arabs were killed and an estimated 600–700 wounded. The PLO immediately requested that Arafat address the U.N. Security Council on conditions in the territory. The

U.S. government rejected Arafat's visa application, refusing to permit him into the country; the meeting was held in Geneva on 25 May. There Arafat asked that the Security Council order an international team to the territories to investigate Palestinian complaints and conditions, a request that received backing from fourteen of the fifteen members; the U.S. opposed it because Israel would not accept it, despite assumptions by observers that it had initially promised to approve the resolution.[40]

The Arab summit took place in Baghdad from 28–30 May. Those attending, including Mubarak, approved a harsh statement criticizing American support for Israel. On 30 May Israelis intercepted a Palestinian attack from the Mediterranean backed by Abu al-Abbas, author of the hijacking of the *Achille Lauro* and now based in Baghdad. On 31 May the United States vetoed the Security Council Resolution calling for an investigation of conditions in the territories that had the support of all other members, apparently using the attack the day before as justification. The European Community (EC) would call for such an investigation on 2 June, when it also voiced its support for an international conference with the PLO in attendance as representative of the Palestinian people, a stance the U.S. opposed. On 13 June, Secretary of State Baker strongly criticized Shamir for rejecting U.S. peace proposals and Arafat for refusing to condemn and punish those who ordered the 30 May raid in terms acceptable to the U.S. These conditions included dropping al-Abbas from the PNC Executive Committee. On 20 June the Bush administration suspended its dialogue with the PLO, offering to resume it if U.S. terms were met.

American responses to this series of events suggest a growing recognition of its isolation in the Middle East and in Europe with regard to its approach to the Arab-Israeli conflict. President Bush acknowledged this in his 20 June statement suspending the PLO dialogue, noting that his "strongest allies" in Europe and the "most reasonable and moderate" Arab states disagreed with the U.S. course.[41] Bush's remarks came after a series of exchanges with Arab representatives in May in which Washington called on the Arab states to stop criticizing the United States by name and to accept its opposition to the call for an international conference at that time. The Arab League response, issued on 30 May, mirrored in tone the statement that concluded the Arab summit in Baghdad the same day. It condemned U.S. aid to Israel and promised to stop direct criticism of the United States when the latter "abandons its policy of total bias towards Israel and opens a new page in relations with the states in the region—one of coordinating efforts to implement international resolutions on the Middle East."[42] Arab statements also defended Iraq's military buildup and criticized what they called America's one-sided reaction to this problem because Washington refused to stop military assistance to Israel and did not call for its participation in regional disarmament, a step the Arab heads of state endorsed.

The EC stance was much closer to that of the Arab League than to Washington. U.S. allies such as Egypt and Saudi Arabia joined in the statements issued on 30 May. From the general Arab perspective, the U.S. veto of the Security Council resolution on 31 May proved the points made in the statements issued the day before. From Washington's perspective, such criticism did not reflect a constructive "moderate" approach to the region's problems. Arab and European perceptions of administration policies indicated concern for an apparent double standard in the American approach. Although the Bush administration criticized Shamir harshly, it restricted itself to asking that he be more forthcoming. When Arafat, before the guerrilla attack, asked to address the United Nations in New York, the administration ordered that his visa request be denied even though it was holding a dialogue with him and had acknowledged that Arafat was adhering to his opposition to terrorist attacks.

In light of subsequent developments, it is clear that Shamir emerged from the transition period in a highly strengthened position, much more capable of resisting American overtures. He was head of a cabinet either supporting his policies or trying to push him further to the right. Arafat, however, had been considerably weakened even before the suspension of the dialogue. Reports that Hamas and the PFLP were forming an alternative leadership to the Unified Command in the territories appeared from April 1990. Hamas delegates won a majority of seats on a UNRWA staff council in Gaza in June.[43] Control of the intifada seemed to be slipping away, as was any hope of progress in talks brokered by Egypt and the United States. These factors led Arafat to edge closer to Iraq. From the PLO perspective Israeli actions and American responses indicated that only Baghdad's growing military strength and political influence in the region, following the May summit, could "[create] the material base for a balanced settlement in the region . . . which is not accepted by the Israelis or the Americans."[44] A just settlement could not be achieved until Israel faced a credible military challenge, and only Iraq could pose that challenge; Egypt was too dependent on American aid to risk forcing the issue. This position threatened Washington's long-standing goal of controlling talks. It might force an international conference where U.S. policies would be criticized by its allies, let alone its foes.

This Palestinian shift towards Iraq, based on anger at U.S. actions, also indicated acceptance of the logic of Saddam Husayn's arguments made in April and repeated during the Arab summit. He threatened reprisals against any Israeli preemptive attacks but he also contended that

> so long as Arabs remained economically and militarily weak they would not be able to dislodge Israel from the occupied territories and establish a Palestinian state. An Arab approach to peace . . . must be coupled with a pan-Arab military and material build-up. Oil revenues must be invested in the Arab world rather than abroad; wealthy Arab governments must aid poor ones, and special pan-Arab funds should be set up to help the Palestinian intifada.[45]

In addition to undermining American efforts to direct the peace process through its own agents, this agenda, if successful, might also cause a rise in oil prices at a time when the United States was importing 50 percent of its oil, half of that from Persian Gulf states that included Iraq, and when its economy was confronted with an imminent recession.

In this context Iraq's invasion of Kuwait on 2 August was both a threat and an opportunity. It was a threat to the oil reserves of Kuwait, and possibly Saudi Arabia, that were major components of Western and Japanese economic stability. But it was also an opportunity to assert American power and possibly to destroy the challenge that Saddam Husayn posed, not only to the Gulf but to American influence in the region and over its allies, European as well as Arab.

THE GULF CRISIS: A SYNOPSIS

The diplomacy, and subsequent political and military alignments, that followed the Iraqi invasion of Kuwait on 2 August 1990 were enormously complex.[46] After extensive preparations, coalition forces led by the United States recaptured Kuwait and destroyed much of Iraq's military and civilian infrastructure in a campaign that began on 16 January 1991. A cease-fire was imposed on 28 February. The scale of the military triumph was unquestioned; less clear was the anticipated political resolution of the conflict, with respect to both the Persian Gulf and Arab-Israeli issues. Indeed, it is not certain that the Bush administration devoted much attention to precisely what set of alignments it wished to see emerge after the crisis, although it immediately initiated efforts to achieve an Arab-Israeli dialogue.

The Iraqi invasion of Kuwait was preceded by a confrontation in mid-July in which Iraq threatened Kuwait unless the latter agreed to raise oil prices which had been lowered through generally acknowledged overproduction by Kuwait and the United Arab Emirates (UAE). At an emergency meeting, Kuwait and the UAE agreed to Iraqi demands under pressure from all other states attending, especially Iran but also Saudi Arabia, who backed Iraq. Following this crisis, during which the U.S. sent air force squadrons to the UAE, the U.S. Central Command, responsible for the Persian Gulf, mounted a staff war-game exercise that "postulated a major threat to U.S. interests in the Middle East requiring a swift and massive military commitment"; this exercise ended on 29 July. At the same time, Washington instructed its ambassador in Baghdad to tell Saddam Husayn, in a 26 July meeting, that the United States had "no opinion" about his quarrels and relations with neighboring states, "like your border disagreement with Kuwait."[47]

Once Iraq had invaded Kuwait on 2 August, the U.S. immediately responded with military aid to Saudi Arabia, the dispatch of Secretary of Defense Richard Cheney to the region to gain Arab agreement for the positioning of large numbers of American troops, and the calling of emergency sessions of the U.N. Security Council to condemn the aggression. As early as 6 August reports appeared noting President Bush's determination to overthrow Saddam Husayn.

The administration refused to talk to the Iraqi leader and decided not to send its ambassador, then in London, back to Baghdad for discussions because "We don't have anything to say to him."[48] These efforts resulted in an American-led coalition force, dominated by American troops, that gained U.N. sanction for an invasion of Kuwait after 15 January 1991 if Iraq had not withdrawn from Kuwait or agreed to withdraw by that deadline. An extensive and sustained air bombardment of Iraq as well as of Kuwait, inaugurated on 16 January, resulted ultimately in a land assault on the evening of 24 February that met little Iraqi resistance and gained a cease-fire by 28 February.

The oil supplies of the Persian Gulf states have long been a primary strategic concern of the United States for two reasons: because of the reliance of American allies on these reserves; and because it was deemed imperative to block the Soviet Union from the potential to control these reserves and restrict their use by the United States and its allies. Both justifications for this concern therefore had a Cold-War rationale underlying them, beyond the actual value of oil imports to certain states—Japan relies on the Gulf for 70–80 percent of her oil. In recent years two developments have occurred. The end of the Cold War seemed to mean that the Soviet Union was no longer a threat to the lifeline of the West and its allies; and the United States itself became more dependent on Gulf oil. The U.S. in the past decade has increased its dependence on foreign oil to 50 percent of its total use, 25 percent of that coming from the Gulf with Iraq supplying 8 percent of that total and Kuwait less than 1 percent. These resources were important not only for domestic consumption, but also for servicing American military fuel needs abroad, especially, but not solely, in Asia; it is in the latter sphere that Kuwait and the UAE provided larger amounts, especially jet fuel. In recent years, therefore, low oil prices served perceived American strategic interests overseas and were particularly important as the American economy began to decline. Kuwait possessed additional importance in American eyes because of its investment assets in the U.S., totalling between $45–50 billion with major gold holdings and treasury securities, although this was only a fraction of Kuwaiti holdings in Britain.[49]

Since the Carter Doctrine of 1979 openly defined Persian Gulf reserves as of primary strategic value to U.S. interests, the United States and allies such as Great Britain have gradually built up a network of military alliances and agreements for the stationing of troops and material in time of crisis. Air bases have been built, armament storage depots constructed, and military technology such as AWACS have been sold to Saudi Arabia, ostensibly against an Iranian threat, but also to counter any Soviet thrust. These arrangements existed with smaller Gulf states such as Oman and Bahrain as well as the UAE before the crisis. Kuwait was the only Gulf state without such an agreement, but when threatened by Iran in 1987–1988, it requested outside assistance for securing the transport of its oil. After an initial request to the U.S. was ignored, Kuwait guaranteed an immediate response from Washington by asking the Soviets to intervene.

The American reflagging effort was successful from the military viewpoint and presumably contributed to the conclusion of the Iran-Iraq war after the U.S.S. *Vincennes* shot down an Iranian civilian airliner with heavy loss of life. When the crisis came, the infrastructure and plans, both political and military, were in place for a rapid American response. What remained was the justification for a massive troop deployment which went beyond the scope of these arrangements.[50]

The initial American explanation for its reaction to the invasion was to defend Saudi Arabia from an Iraqi attack, and then to force Iraq out of Kuwait. Over time, however, other reasons appeared, from an early claim to be defending the "American way of life," to staving off the threat to the economy, to destroying the Iraqi military machine and, if possible, Saddam Husayn himself. There is little doubt that oil played a major role in triggering an American response. As one "key policymaker," explained the matter, "if a country less important than Kuwait had been invaded and if the principal product of Kuwait and Saudi Arabia were artichokes instead of oil, we would not have proceeded as we did."[51] But although the United Nations approved the imposition of economic sanctions against Iraq very quickly, officials in Washington believed from late August that they might require too much time to take effect, and that military action against Saddam Husayn might not only be necessary but desirable.

In this framework, the White House played a particularly important role with National Security Adviser Brent Scowcroft and his assistant, Robert Gates, reinforcing the tendency of President Bush and Secretary of Defense Cheney to build a case for military action. The military and the State Department were far more reticent about the need for force and apparently preferred a diplomatic solution. It seems clear however that the president disagreed and sought to establish a diplomatic climate of confrontation that would discourage compromise and ensure a stalemate that would justify the military alternative.[52]

The reasons for this interest in a military response are rooted more in American concern for the global implications of the crisis than worry over its regional ramifications. Reports of the relative decline of the American economy vis-à-vis its major allies had circulated for months, as had related articles on the lessened political clout concomitant with this development.[53] Iraqi dominance of major oil reserves with the potential for higher prices would further weaken America, given its added dependence on these sources. At the same time, the Soviet withdrawal from the Cold War opened up opportunities hitherto obstructed, most importantly the ability to act unilaterally to enforce America's will without fear of Great Power confrontation. In this regard, the United States seems to have acted to fulfill traditional Cold War goals, American paramountcy, despite and indeed because of the end of the Cold War. Consequently, while the administration proposed rather early that "a new world order" was in the making, its actions suggested that its conceptions were based on the parameters of the old world order.

Administration officials stated in late August of 1990 that "the conflict in the gulf . . . may be the defining moment of this new order."[54] As a result the global, rather than the regional approach, precisely the old preference, now took priority once more, and area specialists again were deliberately excluded from consultation about policy. Administration spokespersons explained that

> The president sees this not as a traditional Middle East crisis but as the first post-Cold War crisis. . . . It requires new thinking and new concepts and there is a feeling that it is better to talk to people who see things in global terms rather than regional specialists whose thinking has been much slower to catch up with this new kind of situation.[55]

But this "new kind of situation" contained the roots of old problems which would have to be dealt with later, the regional security of the Gulf and attempts to resolve Arab-Israeli issues.

The Arab response to Saddam Husayn's invasion of Kuwait was nearly unanimous. Most heads of state condemned it and called for his withdrawal. Reports of atrocities and dispossession of property from both Kuwaiti and non-Kuwaiti workers, especially Palestinians of whom there were approximately half a million in Kuwait, gave the lie to Saddam's claims that he acted on behalf of the Palestinian cause. Ironically, the only prominent leader to defend his actions was Yasir Arafat, hoping to use Saddam to pressure the U.S. and its allies into concessions; it was a major miscalculation that severely weakened his standing in Arab capitals, not to say elsewhere.[56] But at the same time, many Arab leaders who called for Saddam's withdrawal also attacked the United States for engaging in a power play for its own purposes. Particularly galling to these leaders and their subjects was what appeared to be an American double standard, vetoing United Nations resolutions in order to protect Israel and refusing to punish her despite her treatment of Palestinians under the intifada, but suddenly calling on the U.N. to back its own immediate response to an Arab transgression. Attention was also called to the fact that the very U.N. principles Washington declared it was defending in confronting Saddam, the sanctity of national territory against aggression, were those it had violated in its 1989 invasion of Panama.

The primary expositor of this view was Jordan's King Husayn who in trying to mediate the crisis found himself upstaged by the American-led coalition and confronted by an embargo whose sanctions threatened Jordan's economic survival. Strongly dependent on Iraq for oil and for revenues from its own trade with that country, King Husayn now found himself adrift, with Saudi monetary subsidies cut off because of Jordanian criticism of its actions, while confronted with a massive refugee problem caused as hundreds of thousands fled Kuwait. Finally, King Husayn's criticism of the U.S. led to severe cuts in American aid being proposed as punishment, a tactic already employed against Yemen when that country defied the U.S. in the United Nations in December. From his perspective, however, Husayn had little choice. His population, over 60 percent Palestinian, supported Saddam out of anger against American allies while Israel's

Ariel Sharon spoke repeatedly of Jordan as the state of Palestine, strongly intimating that all Arabs from the territories should be removed to Jordan to overthrow Husayn and create the state for which they longed. Conversely, Husayn's defiance of his traditional Great Power ally brought him more domestic approval than ever before.[57]

The motivations of Washington's principal Arab allies in the coalition, Egypt, Saudi Arabia, Kuwait, and Syria were clear-cut, if diverse in inspiration. Egypt and Saudi Arabia had sympathized with Saddam's criticism of the United States in May and the latter had backed his pressure on Kuwait to raise oil prices in July. But neither could accept the sudden escalation of Saddam's power, despite his claims that he needed the additional revenues to rebuild Iraq following the Iran-Iraq war, or that Kuwait should quit its requests for repayment of billions of dollars in loans given to defeat Iran; furthermore, sympathy for his demands for two islands off Kuwait to extend his coastline could not countenance his violation of Kuwaiti sovereignty and the looting and killing in which his troops engaged.[58]

Saudi Arabia in particular could not tolerate a challenge to her own oil fields, let alone a greater rival for dominance in Gulf affairs, however much sympathy might be felt for Iraq's grievances. Egypt had its own reasons for opposing Saddam, viewing him now as a rival for primacy in the Arab world and as recreating the Iraqi-Egyptian axis that had split that world in the 1950s. Egyptian dependence on American aid meant that Cairo could not easily reject Washington's advice, but there is little doubt that Husni Mubarak and King Fahd were as eager as the Kuwaitis for Saddam to be overthrown and his military machine destroyed. Syrian incentives were equally clear. Saddam's downfall would be Assad's triumph over his old adversary, relieving him of pressure from his northern flank as he turned to seek a peace agreement with Israel under American auspices. In return, major arms sales were promised to the Saudis, later scaled down because of Israeli opposition.[59] Egypt was relieved of obligations totalling $7 billion to Washington for past economic and military assistance.

Israel was equally desirous of American-led military action that would destroy the Iraqi military machine and Saddam Husayn personally, and encouraged American military plans, calling for Saddam's overthrow from the beginning. The Bush administration viewed the Israeli position as both a threat and a stance to be exploited. Officials feared that Israel would intervene in the war, thereby undermining the Arab coalition backing the United States. This fear increased once Iraqi Scud missiles landed in the Tel Aviv-Haifa coastal strip, and resulted in visits to Israel by Under Secretary of State Lawrence Eagleburger to ensure no Israeli response. On the other hand, the administration exploited Israeli backing for an assault by quietly mobilizing pro-Israeli politicians in December to call for an American attack as being in U.S. national interests; it did this to put pressure on liberal congresspersons to support war rather than the continuance of economic sanctions, a tactic similar to that used by the Reagan administration to get backing for the SDI program in 1985. Also encouraging this group, The Committee for Peace and Security in the Gulf, was Prince Bandar, the Saudi ambassador in Washington who pushed for an assault. The influence of this group was such that Stephen Solarz, congressman from Brooklyn and a leading member of the committee, met with Brent Scowcroft, the National Security Adviser, to consult on the draft resolution whereby Congress would authorize the use of force.[60]

Left outstanding was the question of what efforts would be made to resolve Arab-Israeli matters after this crisis, including the future of the Palestinians. Saddam Husayn had frequently linked the possibility of his withdrawal from Kuwait to Israeli withdrawal from the occupied territories. It was this stance that gained him much Palestinian support. The administration repeatedly and emphatically rejected this linkage while promising, Secretary of State Baker more specifically than President Bush, that attention would be given to these issues at a suitable time once the Gulf crisis had ended. There can be little doubt that Washington's Arab allies expected such an effort to be made as part of the compensation for their participation in the coalition which legitimized the American presence. There is equally little doubt that Israel anticipated such pressure and that the Shamir cabinet prepared itself to resist it. Shamir brought the head of the Molodet Party into his cabinet; it advocates the forcible ouster of Arabs from the territories and identifies with the policies linked to the Kach Party founded by Meir Kahane. Shamir rejects the idea of territory for peace and has stated that "I don't think that the conditions for peace involve concessions on the land of Israel." Efforts to promote an Israeli-Syrian rapprochement based on the return to Syria of the Golan Heights, which would be demilitarized, were consequently rejected outright by Shamir in the aftermath of Baker's March 1991 trip to the region. When the retiring Israeli chief of staff declared that land could be given up for peace, including the Golan, Shamir was infuriated. He then reiterated his position:

> We can talk about peace, about the ways of peace, about economic cooperation. . . . We say we are ready to negotiate unconditionally with all the Arab states—nothing more than that. . . . Syria has the right to ask us to withdraw from the Golan Heights . . . If Syria does ask we shall say we do not agree to withdraw.[61]

The question remains what steps the United States will be prepared to take if obstacles persist at a time when the territories and Israel have seen increased violence and when America's Arab allies seem much more willing to recognize Israel so long as a satisfactory settlement of the Palestinian question is reached, one in which most if not all of the territories would return to Arab hands. Secretary of State Baker's visits to the Middle East in March and April 1991 ended in a stalemate. Arab states, Syria especially, wanted an international conference sponsored jointly by the U.S. and the Soviets to oversee direct negotiations with Israel for return of the Golan Heights. As noted, the Likud leadership refuses to consider this option. It thus pushed for a temporary international conference resulting in immediate face-to-face talks with Syria with no further international input. Such a framework would enable Israel to continue settling the territories and to refuse Syria's demands for land in exchange for peace, while simultaneously claiming that Syria had implicitly recognized Israel by negotiating with it.

Baker persevered however. In July he gained Syrian, Lebanese, and Jordanian agreement to participate in talks. Here Syria, the key player, agreed to direct talks with Israel under the guise of a one day international conference that would be sponsored by the U.S. and the U.S.S.R. Israeli objections to United Nations involvement would be met by granting the participants the right to veto suggestions of resorting to the U.N. if stalemates ensued, but the right of review by the United States and the Soviet Union was granted. The latter condition met Syrian concerns and offered the possibility of outside input. In addition, Syria's Hafiz Assad received U.S. assurances that the latter considered Israel's 1981 annexation of the Golan Heights to be illegal, and that S.C. Resolution 242 applied to the Golan and the West Bank, interpretations counter to those offered by Israeli rightists who seek to contravene the original meaning of the resolution. In another development, Saudi Arabia, Syria, and Jordan joined Egypt in agreeing to support the end of the Arab economic boycott of Israel if she would stop building settlements.

These developments aroused consternation in Israeli government circles. Rightist minority parties vowed to leave the Shamir cabinet, bringing it down, if he agreed to enter talks; the possibility of American refusal to fund housing of Soviet Jewish immigrants loomed if he rejected the U.S.–backed Arab overtures. As for the Palestinians, Baker has told West Bank leaders that the PLO must be excluded from any talks, but that Palestinians linked to the PLO and from East Jerusalem might be part of a joint Jordanian–Palestinian delegation. In short, major decisions faced Palestinian and Israeli leaders, but Arafat was on record as supporting American peace efforts. News items reported PLO willingness to remain aloof from talks so long as Palestinians from within and outside the territories were permitted to represent Palestinian interests.

The sticking point may well be East Jerusalem Palestinian representation, even if only on a Jordanian negotiating team. Israel refuses to accept international objection to its 1967 annexation of that part of the city. If West Bank Palestinians agree to negotiate without reference to East Jerusalem, it could destroy their credibility. For an Israeli government to appear to agree that its status is negotiable might be fatal to its continuance in office. As it is, right–wing parties object to any idea of returning the Golan Heights to Syria in return for peace, and a poll taken in June showed only seven percent of the Israelis questioned to be willing to give up all of the Golan in return for guarantees of peace and security. Shamir has acknowledged a major change in Syria's stance toward Israel, but whether that will induce a willingness to negotiate remained to be seen at the end of July.[62]

CONCLUSION

The outcome of the Arab–endorsed U.S. initiative may decide the fate of Arab politics, Arab–Israeli relations, and the status of the Palestinians for years to come. The United States has expressed more open dissatisfaction with Israel than with Arab leaders, but the fact remains that the status quo serves Israel's perceived interests. Conversely, King Husayn's acceptance of inclusion in talks brought a statement of condemnation from the Jordanian Parliament.[63] Democracy and parliamentary systems can often obstruct peace efforts and be used to undermine them, contrary to the assumption often voiced in the United States.

Failure to begin talks will increase the likelihood of renewed violence in the territories, already high as a consequence of developments during the past year. In September 1990, an Israeli army officer was killed in the Gaza Strip. On 8 October, at least seventeen Palestinians were killed and over one hundred wounded by Israeli border police in the Haram al-Sharif precinct on the Temple Mount overlooking the Wailing Wall. The Shamir cabinet defended the action and declared that hundreds of Arabs had been hurling stones on Jewish worshippers below, endangering their lives. Independent reports, including that of an Israeli human rights group, contradicted this testimony and charged the police with indiscriminate attacks on Arabs, a conclusion buttressed by the findings of the Israeli judge assigned to investigate the tragedy.[64] On 5 November Meir Kahane was assassinated in New York City by an Egyptian-American. On 14 December three Israelis were stabbed to death by people believed to be members of Hamas which had called for jihad (holy war) against Israel following the Haram al-Sharif killings; in their aftermath both Hamas and the UNL had ordered increased attacks on Israeli soldiers and civilians.[65] In January 1991 the second-in-command of the PLO, Salah Khalaf (Abu Iyad) was assassinated in Tunis by a bodyguard identified with Abu Nidal and Iraq, although Israeli infiltration of Abu Nidal and Arab intelligence services has long suspected.[66]

It seems clear that the intifada has changed direction under the impetus of events both within and outside the territories. Israeli analysts attribute the transition toward advocacy of violence and attempts to kill, as opposed to stone throwing, to the Rishon le Zion killings of May 1990 and the Haram al-Sharif killings of October, coupled with the influx of Soviet Jews. Prominent Palestinians "say the real turning point came in March [1990] when Shamir rejected the U.S.-backed formula for Israeli-Palestinian negotiations," eventually leading to the formation of the Likud cabinet of June when the peace process collapsed.[67] The United States has condemned Israeli reprisals, and tensions exist between the White House and the Shamir government, but the administration may lack the will or political courage to confront Israel with sanctions. AIPAC, the pro-Israeli lobby, has threatened to cut contributions to Republican 1992 campaigns unless they back Israeli requests for $1 billion in war-related costs. Reports from Israel indicate that plans to build new housing units for Soviet Jews in the territories have been implemented despite contrary promises to the U.S. as a condition for aid, promises that in some cases were later denied in Israel.[68] Shamir has rejected any linkage between the end of the Arab boycott and Israeli suspension of settlement–building. Such expansion encourages more violence from Palestinians already tending to such acts in an atmosphere of increasing desperation.

At the same time, America's allies expect that a joint effort to resolve the Palestinian question, quite possibly excluding the PLO, is forthcoming and essential. British, French, and Italian officials have expressed themselves on this matter, noting Arab warnings that with the end of the crisis "we . . . will demand that the UN impose exactly the same sanctions on Israel as on Iraq. They have a right to do so and plenty of reasons. . . ."[69] The French foreign minister declared to the National Assembly on 10 October, following the Haram al-Sharif killings, that "What happened in Jerusalem . . . is the result of an absence of a settlement of the Palestine problem and the maintenance for over twenty years of an occupation which the people of these territories reject."[70] Some allies, certainly the French, have adhered to the coalition in order to claim a right to have a voice in peace efforts that will follow regarding the territories, not simply the Gulf. France and Great Britain, like the Soviet Union, favor an international conference opposed by Israel and the United States.[71]

In the aftermath of the war, James Baker stated that the U.S. would consult allies but would not push or impose a solution, whereas France called for immediate peace talks sponsored by the U.N. Security Council.[72] If Baker's mediating efforts fail, he and the administration are unlikely to insist on an international forum opposed by Israel which recognizes general international opposition to its policies. The U.S. must then attempt to reconcile its acceptance of the principle of land for peace, advocated by some Arab states also, with its alliance with Israel who rejects that principle and demands unstinting American backing.

In such circumstances American expectations of hegemony, based on its ability to forge a U.N. coalition against Iraq, may soon confront their allies' (European as well as Arab) insistence that such cooperation and reliance on the United Nations apply to the Arab-Israeli conflict as well as to the Gulf. There is no doubt that, for the moment, Washington's Gulf strategy worked. The U.S. has recaptured the dominant world role it seemed to have lost, exemplified by the strength of other national economies exhibited at the Houston summit in July 1990; the London summit a year later reflected the prominence of the United States as a result of its success in ousting Iraq from Kuwait.[73] But the Bush

administration has assumed it could bring Arabs and Israelis together, symboliz-
ing its renewed prestige and power. Failure to do so may weaken its claims and
revive calls for an international forum, contrary to U.S. objectives in the Gulf as
well as with respect to Arab–Israeli issues.

Hawks in the National Security Council envisage an increased American
presence in the Gulf and in general view the crisis in geopolitical terms. These
terms now include acceptance of Saddam Husayn as ruler of an Iraq bombed back
to the preindustrial age because he can hold the Iraqi state together, forestalling
threats from neighbors. And such terms came to mean that Washington viewed
the revolts in Iraq, especially by the Kurds, as nuisances hindering American
policy goals even though the administration had encouraged the Kurdish rebellion from January onwards.[74] In addition, the United States intends to establish
the forward headquarters of the U.S. Central Command, based in Tampa,
Florida, in Bahrain and to station a permanent garrison of American ground
forces in Saudi Arabia itself, policies pushed by Chief of Staff Colin Powell and
Defense Secretary Richard Cheney.[75]

At the same time the Bush administration has proffered an energy program
that envisages nearly the same reliance on foreign oil in the year 2010 as now,
40–45 percent. This projected reliance on external supplies suggests that Washington assumes it can rely on if not impose its will to achieve cheap oil from the
Gulf, a scenario that presumes overall agreement on objectives in the region.[76]
These assumptions may be badly misplaced with respect to future oil prices and
the security of the American economy. Saudi Arabia, for example, must seek
loans to help repay its promised share of funding for the coalition's efforts. At the
same time the rebuilding of Kuwait, whose infrastructure was damaged initially
by the Iraqis and destroyed under allied assaults, will require more than loans.
American officials foresee lower oil prices in the future because needy Gulf states
will have to increase production to gain more revenue and privately boast about
how the war may show a profit for the U.S.[77] But the reverse could also be true.
OPEC could agree to hold prices at certain levels, and further financial assistance
might be needed from outside sources if the Saudis and Kuwaitis are expected to
finance a regional alliance designed to prevent any further threat to their reserves. Lower prices will not serve their interests, especially those of Kuwait if
damage to its oil facilities is greater than anticipated, not to mention the apparent
ecological impact of this destruction. In short, the American assumption that it
can impose its will on the Gulf states for the sake of its own economy may
confront indigenous needs that require higher oil prices.

These considerations must be placed alongside the implications for regional
disorder stemming from the crisis. The stabilization of social and political order
in Iraq may take years, given the need to resolve the status of the Kurds in Iraq.
Even more significant may be the lasting hatred caused by Saddam's suppression
of the Shi'ite revolts in the south that resulted in the destruction of shrines at the
holy cities of Najaf and Karbala. Such acts must heighten Iranian anger and

suggest the potential for Iranian revenge in the future. Moreover, an increased American military presence in the Gulf will also strain relations with Iran and may encourage closer ties between that country and branches of the Saudi ruling family, unhappy at such a visible American presence on Saudi soil; diplomatic ties between the two Gulf powers were restored in June.[78] An indication of Saudi unease surfaced in late April when the Saudi general who commanded Arab and Islamic forces in the anti-Saddam coalition suggested that his government did not want an increased American military presence in the Gulf and objected to Washington's plan to store large quantities of military supplies in his country.[79]

As for Kuwait, several hundred thousand Palestinians formerly resident in that country may be permanently ousted and must seek refuge in Jordan which could be destabilized. Kuwait itself may be faced with unrest as exiles, calling for democracy, seek more access to political freedom and challenge the ruling house of al-Sabah; reports of potential armed conflict between Sabah backers and the opposition have increased, and there has been an attempted assassination of a leading opponent of the regime. The ruling house is aware of its poor public image and spent over $11 million in public relations from the beginning to the end of the war. The forcible ouster of the Palestinians and continued absence of many Kuwaitis are only the most visible signs of a damaged economy whose recovery remains uncertain.[80]

Consequently, Iraq may not be alone in experiencing political upheaval in the aftermath of war, and popular sympathy for the Iraqi populace in the broader Arab world can be expected to intensify once the real number of civilian casualties is known, possibly putting pressure on leaders who have backed the American coalition. American admission that over 70 percent of its bombs missed their targets, a sharp contrast to the carefully cultivated public relations campaign maintained during hostilities, suggests that Iraqi fatalities among noncombatants will be in the tens of thousands. Israel also might see political fragmentation in party ranks. Elements within Likud, David Levy or Ehud Olmert in particular, seem ready to manuever for greater flexibility in talks and are strongly opposed to the inclusion of Molodet in the government, deeming it racist.[81] Leadership will come from Likud or factions to its right as Labor politicians seem increasingly discredited. These developments may serve to delay or obstruct talks on the Palestinian issue at a time of renewed unrest and repression in the territories.

The ultimate problem and contradiction is that Washington may focus on its unilateral power and might as a means of attempting to impose its own vision of world order by military more than political means. In contrast, American justification of internationalism and reliance on the United Nations has been welcomed by its allies and anticipated by others concerned with outstanding issues elsewhere. Future vetoes of otherwise unanimous Security Council resolutions on Palestinian questions will once again raise the charge of a double standard and of a refusal to apply the principles defended in confronting Saddam Husayn when addressing the problem of Likud intransigence. Whereas an international conference aimed at a Palestinian state may be impossible, such a conference to consider real Palestinian "autonomy" in conjunction with Jordan is conceivable. Here, administration anger at King Husayn may well be tempered by their need for his cooperation, especially if Arafat and the PLO are to be removed from the negotiating framework. Nevertheless, a Jordan burdened with thousands of additional Palestinian subjects forced out of Kuwait will push harder for Arab rights in the territories than Washington may expect. Conversely, Gulf Arab anger at Jordan's King Husayn as well as the PLO may encourage a willingness to ignore a resolution of Palestinian matters.

The settling of accounts between states has been suspended as various factions watch U.S. attempts to bring Arabs and Israelis together, but they will resume. In addition, Gulf Arab States differ on the importance of a heightened American military involvement in the Gulf. Saudi caution may result in friction among the allies. The United States seems eager to assert its power as visibly as possible, whereas British and Soviet leaders prefer a United Nations-sponsored security force. Washington's weaker Arab allies, such as Bahrain and Kuwait, accept the open assertion of American strength, via a military presence in the Gulf, that stronger powers, the Saudis and Iran especially, view warily.[82]

There are strong currents in the United States arguing for this visibility and assertiveness, justifying it on the basis of American power and claiming that only the United States can prevent regional arms races and achieve world order. In the words of one advocate

> International stability . . . , when achieved, . . . is the product of self-conscious action by the great powers, and most particularly of the greatest power, which now and for the forseeable future is the United States. If America wants stability it will have to create it. . . . Our best hope for safety is in American strength and will—the strength and will to lead a unipolar world, unashamedly laying down the rules of world order and being prepared to enforce them . . . Averting chaos is a rather subtle call to greatness. It is not a task we are any more eager to undertake than the great twilight struggle [against fascism and communism] just concluded. But it is just as noble and necessary.[83]

This is Rudyard Kipling revisited, the taking on of the white man's burden with all the paraphernalia of imperial and racial assumptions attached to it.

The United States has now destroyed much, though not all, of the military arsenal compiled by Iraq (including nuclear technology) and viewed by Washington as a potential challenge to its handling of Arab-Israeli issues and its need for cheap oil. In the process, it may have contributed, in the words of a distinguished historian, to "the end of the Franco-British settlement of the Middle East which began in World War I; it was always flimsy but it may be better and more lasting than anything the United States will try to put in its place."[84] U.S. efforts to retain unilateral control of these problems may exacerbate rather than alleviate them, and may well collide with the multilateral structure it created to resolve the Gulf crisis. In seeking to assert ourselves as the true great power in the region and the world, we may ultimately destroy the basis on which we wished to construct that claim. To continue to assert unilateral rights in the aftermath of collective war could ultimately alienate our European and Arab allies, as well as the peoples of the Arab world, especially if U.S.–sponsored Arab–Israeli peace talks fail to develop. The next eighteen months will serve to illustrate the ramifications of the course the United States has chosen to take.

NOTES

1. For articles on attempts at political reform in Lebanon, see the *New York Times*, 29 December 1985; and the *London Observer*, 17 March 1985. For Elie Hobeika's break with the Phalange leadership, see both the *New York Times* and the *Los Angeles Times*, 28 September 1986. As Itamar Rabinovich notes, *The War for Lebanon, 1970–1985* (Ithaca 1985), pp. 50–51, 76–77, the Druze also rejected this plan during the mid-1970s because they considered it too lenient.
2. Fouad Ajami, *The Vanished Imam: Musa al-Sadr and the Shia of Lebanon* (Ithaca, 1986); and Augustus R. Norton, *Amal and the Shia of Lebanon* (Ithaca, 1987) are the best sources for this subject. For treatment of Lebanon during the civil war and Israel's role in it, including its 1982 invasion, see Robert Fisk, *Pity the Nation: Lebanon at War* (London, 1990).
3. Nora Boustany, "Lebanon Says U.S. Approved Syrian Move Against Aoun," *Washington Post*, 16 October 1990; and idem, "Lebanese Christian Leader Slain," Ibid., 21 October 1990.
4. Quoted in Noam Chomsky, *The Fateful Triangle: The United States, Israel, and the Palestinians* (Boston, 1983), p. 112.
5. Thomas L. Friedman, "Seeking Peace in the Middle East," *New York Times*, 17 March 1985; and the "Chronology," *Middle East Journal* 39 (Autumn 1985): 800; along with Dan Fisher, "Israeli Right Assails Peres' Peace Bid to Jordan," *Los Angeles Times*, 23 October 1985.
6. Nigel Hawkes, "Thatcher Takes a Big Risk over PLO Talks," *London Observer*, 22 September 1985.
7. The sequence of events can be followed in the "Chronology," *Middle East Journal* 40 (Winter 1986); 115–117. For the *Achille Lauro* hijacking, see the articles in the *New York Times*, 10 October 1985.
8. Quoted in *Facts on File*, 4 October 1985. The Reagan administration was obsessed at this time with Muammar al-Qadhdhafi of Libya and provoked conflict in early 1986 that would justify an attack on his headquarters, carried out in April 1986. These verbal and military assaults on Qadhdhafi were then exploited by Reagan to pressure Congress to fund contra operations in Nicaragua, charging that the Libyan "arch terrorist" had "sent $400 million and an arsenal of weapons and advisers into Nicaragua to bring this war home to the United States." Ibid., 14 March 1986 and 18 April 1986.
9. "U.S. Acting as Go-Between in Jordan Talks, Peres Says," *Los Angeles Times*, 8 October 1986; and Dan Fisher, "Israel, Jordan Stepping Up Cooperation on West Bank," Ibid., 2 October 1986.
10. Quoted in *The Link* 19 (October–November 1986).
11. Wolf Blitzer, "Why the U.S. Wants Israel in the Star Wars Project," *Jerusalem Post International Edition*, 2 February 1986.
12. *The Tower Commission Report*, Bantam and Times Books (New York, 1987). The quotations are on pp. 83 and 23 respectively. For Ben-Gurion's hope of alienating the U.S. from Arab ties, see Chapter 6 of this text.
13. Aaron David Miller, "The PLO in Retrospect: The Arab and Israeli Dimensions," in Yehuda Lukacs and Abdalla M. Battah, eds., *The Arab-Israeli Conflict: Two Decades of Change* (Boulder, 1988), p. 130.

14. For an article on this subject with occasionally different emphases, see Kenneth Stein, "The Intifada and the 1936–1939 Uprising: A Comparison," *Journal of Palestine Studies* 19, 4 (1990): 64–85.

15. I rely on several books that have appeared since the intifada began. All are useful, with different emphases. A good general introduction is Don Peretz, *Intifada: The Palestinian Uprising* (Boulder, 1990). An Israeli analysis, highly critical of government policy, is Ze'ev Schiff and Ehud Ya'ari, *Intifada: The Palestinian Uprising—Israel's Third Front*, translated by Ina Friedman (New York, 1990). Two volumes containing excellent essays are Zachary Lockman and Joel Beinin, eds., *Intifada: The Palestinian Uprising against Israeli Occupation* (Washington, D.C., 1989); and Jamal R. Nassar and Roger Heacock, eds., *Intifada: Palestine at the Crossroads* (New York, 1990). Finally there is Robert Hunter's *The Palestinian Uprising: A War by Other Means* (Berkeley and Los Angeles, 1991), the best sustained analysis of the intifada, Israeli efforts to suppress it, and Palestinian strategies to maintain it. I am grateful to Professor Hunter for providing me with a copy of the manuscript prior to publication. Good background treatment appears in David McDowall, *Palestine and Israel: The Uprising and Beyond* (Berkeley and Los Angeles, 1989); and Ann Mosely Lesch and Mark Tessler, *Israel, Egypt, and the Palestinians from Camp David to Intifada* (Bloomington, 1989); the latter, a collection of articles written for the Universities Field Staff Service during the early and mid–1980s, is particularly valuable for the immediacy of its pieces. Most of these studies rely heavily on the volumes produced if not written by Meron Benvenisti under the rubric of *The West Bank Data Project* and *The Gaza Data Project*. In addition to sources cited earlier under these titles, see in particular Benvenisti, *The West Bank Handbook: A Political Lexicon* (Jerusalem, 1986); and his *1987 Report: Demographic, Economic, Legal, Social, and Political Developments in the West Bank* (Jerusalem, 1987); Benvenisti and Shlomo Khayat, *The West Bank and Gaza Atlas* (Jerusalem, 1988); and Sara Roy, *The Gaza Strip* (Jerusalem, 1986). Finally the ongoing coverage in the *Journal of Palestine Studies*, articles, chronologies, and documents, is indispensable.

16. Hunter, *Palestinian Uprising*, p. 48.

17. See the articles in George T. Abed, ed., *The Palestinian Economy: Studies in Development under Prolonged Occupation* (London, 1988).

18. Hunter, *Palestinian Uprising*, p. 55.

19. Ibid., p. 27.

20. The best single treatment of this subject is still David Shipler, *Arab and Jew: Wounded Spirits in the Promised Land* (New York, 1986) which deals with both Arab and Israeli self-images set against images of "the other." For violence, see his Chapter 4, "Terrorism: the Banality of Evil."

21. Both quotes come from Sara Roy, "From Hardship to Hunger: The Economic Impact of the Intifada on the Gaza Strip," *American-Arab Affairs*, Fall 1990, pp. 109–110. I rely mainly on Roy for my discussion here, but see also Ziad Abu-Amr, "The Gaza Economy: 1948–1984," in Abed, ed., *Palestinian Economy*, pp. 101–120, and two articles by Ann Lesch, "Gaza: History and Politics," and "Gaza: Life under Occupation," in Lesch and Tessler, *From Camp David to Intifada*, pp. 223–254.

22. Lesch, "Gaza: History and Politics," p. 235.

23. Peretz, *Intifada*, pp. 100–106; and Hunter, *Palestinian Uprising*, pp. 34–35. For Palestinian institutions and political developments in the West Bank, see Emile Sahliyeh, *In Search of Leadership: West Bank Politics since 1967* (Washington, D.C. 1988).

24. The points or demands also called for Israeli adherence to Geneva Conventions covering treatment of civilians, release of Palestinians in Israeli prisons, and trials of Israeli soldiers for crimes against Arabs. See the text of the Fourteen Points in the *Journal of Palestine Studies* (Spring 1988), pp. 63–65, and reprinted in Peretz, *Intifada*, Appendix 3.

25. Hunter, *Palestinian Uprising*, p. 107, quoting Tom Segev of *Ha'aretz*. For broader treatment of these questions, see Hunter, Chapter 4. A recent reported case of a Palestinian arrested and charged with spying who worked for Western newspapers is Joel Brinkley, "Israeli Court Extends Gaza Journalist's Detention Without Charges," *New York Times*, 19 February 1991. The Palestinian and his Israeli lawyer charged that he had been "the victim of physical abuse in prison" and Brinkley stated that "the defense lawyer . . . had to urge the court stenographer to continue taking notes for the record when he was presenting his case."

26. "Officer Claims General Mitzna Lied," *Jerusalem Post International Edition*, 10 November 1990, discussing orders given to deliberately break bones when beating Arabs.

27. Hunter, *Palestinian Uprising*, p. 81.
28. Peretz, *Intifada*, pp. 60–62.
29. Private communication with members of the peace group "Ad Kan."
30. Hunter, *Palestinian Uprising*, p. 215.
31. According to Hunter, the Palestinian responsible for the crash had had several relatives killed by Israeli troops and he and his bride had been beaten by them on their wedding day: Ibid., p. 202.
32. Peretz, *Intifada*, pp. 208–210.
33. Ibid., pp. 109–110, 184–187.
34. Ibid., pp. 173–181. I heard concern expressed at PLO lack of interest in public relations while holding interviews with American officials in both Washington, D.C. and in Tunis during the summer, 1989.
35. Ibid., pp. 167–168.
36. Two articles on this election and the role of religious parties are Don Peretz and Sammy Smooha, "Israel's Twelfth Knesset Election: An All-Loser Game," and Robert O. Freedman, "Religion, Politics, and the Israeli Elections of 1988," *Middle East Journal* 43, 3 (Summer 1989): 388–405 and 406–422 respectively.
37. Peretz, *Intifada*, p. 154. See also Hunter, *Palestinian Uprising*, pp. 178–179.
38. Israel's housing ministry gave about $1.8 million to the Hinmutta Company, a branch of the Jewish National Fund, with the remaining $2 million funneled through Panama. For housing ministry aid see Daniel Williams, "Israel Helped Buy Greek Church Buiding Lease," *Los Angeles Times*, 23 April 1990. For the Israeli connection to the drug barons through retired Colonel Yair Klein, see the following sources: Jeff Gerth, "Israeli arms, Ticketed to Antigua, End Up in Colombian Drug Arsenal," *New York Times*, 6 May 1990; Bill McAllister and Jackson Diehl, "Israeli Arms Tied to Colombian Cartel," *Washington Post*, 7 May 1990; Lee Hockstader, "Weapons Scandal Undercuts Antigua's Ruling Family," Ibid., 12 June 1990; Douglas Farah, "Israeli Rifles Leave Tortuous Trail, Turn Up with Colombian Trafficker," Ibid., 18 July 1990; and Farah, "Colombia: U.S. Arming Traffickers," Ibid., 12 June 1990, where Colombian intelligence officials state that Klein, the leader of the Israeli mercenaries, "had close ties to the Israeli embassy." Information on Israeli training of the Panamanian Defense Forces was acquired through private sources in Panama for several months prior to the American invasion.
39. For Sharon's remarks see the *Jerusalem Post Daily Edition*, 13 April 1990.
40. See the "Chronology," *Middle East Journal*, 44, 4 (Autumn 1990): 674. The Israeli was sentenced to life imprisonment in March 1991.
41. Excerpts from news conference held at Huntsville, Alabama, 20 June 1990, *Journal of Palestine Studies*, 20, 1 (Autumn 1990): 187.
42. Ibid., p. 152.
43. "Chronology," *Middle East Journal*, 44, 4 (Autumn 1990): 676.
44. Abdullah Hourani, member of PLO Executive Committee, quoted in "Chronology," Ibid., p. 675.
45. This paraphrase is from Joe Stork and Ann M. Lesch, "Why War?," *Middle East Report*, (November–December 1990), p. 15.
46. My sources are necessarily journalistic. I have relied mainly on articles from the *New York Times* and the *Washington Post*, broadcasts of National Public Radio, and have found Elizabeth Drew's "Letter from Washington," in *The New Yorker* to be particularly insightful.
47. The staff war exercise is discussed in Bob Woodward and Rick Atkinson, "Mideast Decision: Uncertainty over a Daunting Move," *Washington Post*, 26 August 1990, and in the Associated Press report by Richard Pyle, "U.S.-led war plan one for the texts," *The Daily Progress*, Charlottesville, Virginia, 27 February 1991. The text of Ambassador April Glaspie's conversation with Saddam Husayn is in the *Journal of Palestine Studies* 20, 2 (Winter 1991):163–168. Glaspie refers to Secretary of State James Baker's instructions on p.166. Since the Iraqi invasion, the administration has ostracized Glaspie and fostered the impression that she personally bore responsibility for misleading Saddam Husayn. The conjuncture of these plans and American actions in mid-August that seemed to block Arab-sponsored negotiating proposals for an Iraqi withdrawal have given rise to theories that the U.S. prepared itself for an invasion in advance and then blocked compromises to enable it to confront Saddam Husayn. The evidence, though intriguing, is circumstantial; it is probed in Milton Viorst, "The House of Hashem," *The New*

Yorker, 7 January 1991, pp. 32–52, stressing U.S. distaste for an Arab-sponsored compromise in early August. What is clear is that "Administration officials are understandably defensive about what they knew and what they did just before Iraq attacked Kuwait, because there is a growing body of evidence that by their actions, or inaction, in the weeks leading up to the attack, they may have led Saddam Hussein to believe that he had a green light." Elizabeth Drew, "Letter from Washington," *The New Yorker*, 24 September 1990, p. 104; Drew also notes, p. 105, how the administration has used April Glaspie as a scapegoat. Glaspie appeared before a Senate Foreign Relations Committee hearing in late March where she stated that the Iraqi version of her interview with Saddam omitted statements where she warned him against any military action against neighbors. The State Department argues that its "official" version of the interview will not be available for thirty years, the normal interim period for official documents.

48. "U.N. Votes Embargo on Iraq," *Washington Post*, 7 August 1990; and "Bush Orders Effort Aimed at Destabilizing, Toppling Iraqi Leader," Ibid., 6 August 1990.

49. A good survey of American concern for the Gulf and Indian Ocean strategic matters is William Stivers, *America's Confrontation with Revolutionary Change in the Middle East, 1948–1983* (New York, 1986). The classic work on strategic relationships in the Gulf is Anthony Cordesman, *The Gulf and the Search for Strategic Stability: Saudi Arabia, the Military Balance in the Gulf, and the Arab-Israeli Military Balance*, (Boulder, 1984). For U.S. imports see Matthew L. Wald, "U.S. Imports Record 49.9% of Oil," *New York Times*, 19 July 1990; and idem, "For This Oil War, the Ground Rules Are Different," Ibid., 3 August 1990, where he notes that the U.S. imported more oil from Iraq than from Kuwait. The Kuwaiti portfolio is discussed in Clyde H. Farnsworth, "Bush in Freezing Assets, Bars $30 Billion to Hussein," Ibid., 3 August 1990; and Steven Mufson, "Kuwaiti Assets Form Vast Frozen Empire," *Washington Post*, 6 August 1990, who notes that Kuwait "is a major player in world currency markets, a major customer for U.S. Treasury securities and has stock in scores of major blue chip companies around the world."

50. In addition to Cordesman cited in the preceding note, see R. K. Ramazani, *The Gulf Cooperation Council: Records and Analysis* (University Press of Virginia, 1988); and Steve Coll, "U.S. Gulf Ties Eased Buildup: Co-Development of Strategic Facilities was Decades-Long Effort," *Washington Post*, 14 August 1990.

51. Elizabeth Drew, "Letter from Washington," *The New Yorker*, 24 September 1990, p. 106.

52. David Hoffman, "White House Counts on Military Buildup to Force Saddam's Hand," *Washington Post*, 15 August 1990, where Hoffman notes White House interest in provoking a confrontation rather than letting the embargo drag on; Thomas L. Friedman, "How U.S. Won Support to Use MidEast Forces," *New York Times*, Sunday Edition, 2 December 1990, where he reports official views that "the [proposed but not implemented] Baker mission [to Baghdad] . . . was intended largely for domestic considerations—to try to convince Congress and the American people that the president was doing everything possible to avert a war." This view is corroborated by Elizabeth Drew, "Letter from Washington," *The New Yorker*, 4 February 1991, pp. 82–90 who states that some high administration officials "saw sanctions and diplomacy as the necessary precursors of war—that each would be—as one official put it, 'a box to check.' In the early days, an official said to me that by the time we went to war the president would be able to say that he had tried sanctions and tried diplomacy. They were also the necessary logistical precursors of war: the military needed time to build up its forces in the Gulf region." (p. 82) Drew also reports it being known (p. 83) that John Sununu, White House Chief of Staff, "was telling people that a short successful war would be pure political gold for the president—would guarantee his reelection." In February Republicans began positioning for attacks on Democrats over opposition to the war: David Broder and Thomas B. Edsall, "GOP Seeking to Exploit Public Support for Bush: Democrats' Opposition to War Will Be Target," *Washington Post*, 24 February 1991. See also the 2 November 1990 interview in the *New York Times* with General Norman Schwarzkopf where he expresses his distaste for the military alternative. For the increased influence of Scowcroft and Cheney see Andrew Rosenthal, "Scowcroft and Gates: A Team Rivals Baker," *New York Times*, 21 February 1991, and Michael R. Gordon, "Cracking the Whip," *New York Times Sunday Magazine*, 27 January 1991, a study of Cheney that stresses Cheney's reinforcement of Bush's own inclinations for military action.

53. See R. W. Apple, Jr., "A New Balance of Power: Compromise Was Theme at Summit Talks as Kohl Breaks Washington's Domination," *New York Times*, 12 July 1990 where President Bush is

quoted as saying that "in a rapidly changing world other countries should not have to clear their policies with Washington . . . any more than Washington clears its policies with them." Also David Hoffman, "Summit Dynamics Reflect Shift to Multipolar World," *Washington Post*, 15 July 1990; Steven Erlanger, "U.S. Policies Criticized by Allies in Asia," *New York Times*, 25 July 1990.

54. Dan Balz and David Hoffman, "Bush Urged to Clarify U.S. Mission," *Washington Post*, 29 August 1990.

55. The quote is from John Goshko, "Bush Seen Seeking Little Advice from U.S. Experts on Arab World," *Washington Post*, 25 November 1990. Similar behavior characterized the formulation of the Eisenhower Doctrine and our perceptions of the 1958 Lebanese crisis and the 1970 civil war in Jordan. See above, pp. 174, 183, 222.

56. For a Palestinian Arab analysis of the crisis highly critical of Saddam, see Walid Khalidi, "The Gulf Crisis: Origins and Consequences," *Journal of Palestine Studies*, 20, 2 (Winter 1991): 5–28.

57. Ann Devroy, "Bush, in Saudi Arabia, Says U.N. Will Meet on Kuwait," *Washington Post*, 22 November 1990; and Valarie Yorke, "Hussein Fights to Save Country and Throne," *Middle East International*, 23 November 1990. Administration anger at King Husayn appeared when Secretary of State Baker deliberately omitted Jordan from the itinerary of his post-war tour of the region in mid-March "in protest over King Husayn's support of Iraq during the gulf war," and Congress approved a denial of $55 million in aid to Jordan with the condition it can be restored if president Bush decides Jordan is helping to advance the peace process: see Thomas L. Friedman, "Baker Sees Arab 'New Thinking' and Urges Israel to Reciprocate," *New York Times*, 12 March 1991; and Martin Tolchin, "Congress Withholds $55 Million in Aid to Jordan," Ibid., 23 March 1991.

58. An article that covers some of these issues is Ann Mosely Lesch, "Contrasting Reactions to the Persian Gulf Crisis: Egypt, Syria, Jordan, and the Palestinians," *Middle East Journal*, 45, 1 (Winter 1991): 30–50.

59. The "Chronology" in the *Journal of Palestine Studies*, 20, 2 (Winter 1991) covers these issues. The Egyptians were particularly angry at Iraq. Mubarak felt Saddam Husayn had lied to him about his intentions; and Egyptian workers in Iraq had been treated brutally by Iraqis returning from the Iran war, with government connivance. Several thousand Egyptians seem to have been killed or injured.

60. Elizabeth Drew, "Letter from Washington," *The New Yorker*, 4 February 1991, p. 86, states that the White House was "instrumental" in creating the committee headed by Richard Perle and Stephen Solarz, and that "AIPAC turned loose its nationwide network of contributors, prominent businessmen, and social friends of members [of Congress]." Michael Massing, "The Way to War," *The New York Review of Books*, 28 March 1991, pp. 17–22 argues that the committee coalesced without White House initiative in October, but that it had close ties to Scowcroft through Richard Haas, Scowcroft's Middle East adviser, who identifies American security in the Middle East as closely tied to Israel. Haas argues against concern for swift resolution of the Palestinian issue, a stance that encourages Israel to push for further settlements as a means of consolidating its hold over the territories during a period of benign American interest.

61. Joel Brinkley, "Israeli Army Chief Talks of Return of Golan Heights," *New York Times*, 20 March 1991. See also Brinkley, "Shamir's Move: Post-War Leverage?" *New York Times*, 7 February 1991; and Jackson Diehl, "Israel Vows to Resist Concessions in Post-War Mideast Peace Effort: Shamir Tells Party Occupied Arab Lands Will Not Be Given Up," *Washington Post*, 27 February 1991.

62. For these developments see articles in the *Washington Post* and the *New York Times* from 19 July 1991. Two good analyses are David Hoffman and Caryle Murphy, "Assad Tells Baker He Accepts U.S. Plan on Mideast Talks," *Washington Post*, 19 July 1991, and Thomas L. Friedman, "Israel Tells U.S. It Will Consider Mideast Conference," *New York Tims*, 23 July 1991.

63. Ibid.

64. See the file "The Haram al-Sharif (Temple Mount) Killings," *Journal of Palestine Studies* 20, 1 (Winter 1991): 134–159. In July 1991 an Israeli judge concluded that the police instigated the violence, a finding that contradicted the government-appointed panel's conclusions: Joel Brinkley, "Israel Judge Says Police Provoked al-Aksa Violence that Killed 17," *New York Times*, 19 July 1991.

65. Linda Gradstein, "3 Israelis Stabbed Dead: 2 Fundamentalists Sought," *Washington Post*, 15 December 1990.
66. Michael Wines, "2 or 3 Agents Are Believed Killed after Rare U.S.-Syrian Contacts," *New York Times*, 7 February 1991, notes the theory that Mossad may have infiltrated Abu Nidal. A later article by Wines reports Bush Administration officials as saying that the undercover agents killed by Syrians last fall worked for Jordanian intelligence and that Jordan shared their information on Palestinian terrorist activities with the CIA and other Western intelligence services: "Jordan Link Reported for Spies Slain in Syria," Ibid., 12 March 1991. If this is true, it is likely that this information would have reached Israel through the CIA. A good summary noting these issues and general PLO attribution of blame to Abu Nidal is Jonathan C. Randal, "Document Suggests Abu Nidal Was Behind Slaying of Arafat Aide," *Washington Post*, 23 July 1991.
67. Jackson Diehl, "A Radical Shift in the Intifada," *Washington Post*, 8 December 1990.
68. Rowland Evans and Robert Novak, "AIPAC's GOP 'Alert'," *Washington Post*, 6 March 1991. Tensions over Israeli denials of commitments have arisen previously. James Baker ordered publication of a letter from Israeli Foreign Minister David Levy promising that no new apartments would be built in the territories after Levy, in Israel, denied he had ever written such a letter.
69. "Chronology," *Journal of Palestine Studies*, 20, 2 (Winter 1991): 218.
70. Ibid., p. 151.
71. William Drodziak, "French-U.S. Relations Blossom Amid Desert Storm," *Washington Post*, 26 February 1991.
72. George Lardner, Jr., "Baker Rules Out U.S.-Imposed Solution in Arab-Israeli Conflict," *Washington Post*, 4 March 1991; and William Drodziak, "France Urges Middle East Peace Talks: Mitterand Seeks Palestinian State 'Secure' Borders for Israel," Ibid.
73. Stephen Kinzer, "Weakened Kohl Frustrated by Summit Colleagues," *New York Times*, 19 July 1991.
74. An excellent summary of these issues is Elizabeth Drew, "Letter from Washington," *The New Yorker*, 6 May 1991. Drew notes administration concern for a balance of power in the region superceding alarm at the Kurds' fate, and refers to reports of C.I.A. broadcasts encouraging rebellion. I have been told by intelligence analysts that a "finding" approving this C.I.A. policy was signed by President Bush in mid-January.
75. See two articles by Patrick E. Tyler, "Powell Says U.S. Will Stay in Iraq 'For Some Months'," and "U.S. and Bahrain Near Pact on Permanent Military Base," *New York Times*, 23 March and 25 March 1991 respectively; and Barton Gellman and David Hoffman, "Grip on Southern Iraq Offers Leverage to Allies," *Washington Post*, 26 February 1991.
76. Matthew Wald, "Bush Asserts Need for Foreign Oil," *New York Times*, Section D., 21 February 1991.
77. Eric Schmitt, "Saudis Reported to Look for Loans," *New York Times*, 13 February 1991. For assumptions of low oil prices, see Peter Passell, "The Big Spoils from a Bargain War: Cheap Oil for Years to Come; A Quicker End to the Recession; The Pentagon Might Even Show a Profit," *New York Sunday Times*, Section 3, 3 March 1991.
78. Dan Balz and Al Kamen, "U.S. Seen Lacking Policy on Post-War Goals," *Washington Post*, 24 March 1991; and William Drodziak, "Iran Reasserts Influence in Gulf: Rafsanjani Backs Iraqi Rebels, Woos Saudis," Ibid.
79. Judith Miller, "Saudi General Sees No Need for Big American Presence," *New York Times*, 29 April 1991. As Miller notes, "American officials have made stockpiling of weapons in the kingdom a key element in their strategy to improve security and defense in the gulf after the defeat of Iraq."
80. Philip Shenon, "The Refugees Envision a Transformed Kuwait," *New York Times*, 13 February 1991; Caryle Murphy, " 'Hit List' Allegations Heighten Tensions in Kuwait," *Washington Post*, 6 March 1991; Gary Lee, "The Selling of Kuwait Moves Into New Phase," Ibid., 17 March 1991; and John H. Cushman, Jr., "Most of the Kuwaiti Economy Is Still in Suspension," *New York Times*, 23 July 1991.
81. Jackson Diehl, "Levy Links Palestinian, Arab Talks," *Washington Post*, 1 February 1991. There

is great rivalry within Likud with Levy positioned against both Shamir and Moshe Arens, the defense minister.

82. Michael Dobbs, "Soviet, Briton Press for U.N. Role in Gulf," *Washington Post*, 6 March 1991.
83. Charles Krauthammer, "The Unipolar Moment," *Foreign Affairs*, 1990/1991, pp. 29 and 33.
84. Albert Hourani, private communication.

CHAPTER 1

1300–1200 B.C. Jews and Philistines invade Palestine, then known as Canaan.

1000 B.C. Kingdom of Israel founded.

140–63 B.C. Independent Hasmonean Dynasty of Israel.

63 B.C.–638 A.D. Palestine under Roman and Byzantine rule.

638–1918 Palestine under Muslim rule.

1099–1244 Palestine under Crusader control.

1453 End of Byzantine Empire; Ottoman Empire begins.

1699 Treaty of Karlowitz.

1798–1802 French occupation of Egypt.

1854–1856 Crimean War.

1869 Suez Canal opens.

1882 Egypt occupied by the British.

CHAPTER 2

1516–1918 Palestine under Ottoman rule.

1839 Hatti Sharif of Gulhane.

1856 Hatti Humayun.

1861–1918 Autonomous status for Mount Lebanon under international guarantees.

1881 Hibbat Zion founded in Russia.

1896 Theodor Herzl's *Der Judenstaat* published.

1897 World Zionist Organization founded at first Zionist Congress.

1901 Jewish National Fund established.

1908 Young Turk Revolt.

1908, 1911 Palestinian Arab Papers, *al-Karmil* and *Filastin,* founded.

CHAPTER 3

1914–1918 World War I.

November 1914 Ottoman Empire enters war on German side.

February–December 1915 Gallipoli campaign.

March 1915 Constantinople Convention.

July 1915–January 1916 Husayn–McMahon correspondence.

May 1916 Sykes–Picot Agreement.

June 1916 Arab revolt begins.

March 1917 First Russian Revolution; British take Baghdad.

November 1917 Balfour Declaration; Second Russian Revolution.

December 1917 General Allenby takes Jerusalem.

June 1918 Allied Declaration to the Seven.

November 1918 Armistice ends war in Europe.

January 1919 Faysal–Weizmann agreement; Peace Conference begins.

March 1920 Syrian Arab National Congress proclaims Faysal King of Greater Syria.

April 1920 San Remo Conference.

May–August 1920 Iraqi rebellion.

July 1920 French take Damascus, oust Faysal.

March 1921 Cairo Conference.

CHAPTER 4

July 1920 British military administration in Palestine ends.

December 1920 Histadrut created.

April 1921 Hajj Amin al-Husayni appointed Mufti of Jerusalem.

January 1922 Supreme Muslim Council (SMC) created.

August 1929 Zionist claims to Wailing Wall leads to Muslim riots; 133 Jews and 116 Arabs killed; many more wounded. Hebron Jewish community evacuated.

March 1930 Shaw Commission Report.

October 1930 Passfield White Paper.

January 1933 Hitler becomes German Chancellor.

April 1936 Arab Revolt begins.

July 1937 Peel Commission recommends partition.

November 1938 Woodhead Commission Report.

May 1939 British White Paper.

CHAPTER 5

September 1939 World War II begins.

May 1942 Biltmore Conference.

November 1944 Jewish terrorists (LEHI) assassinate Lord Moyne.

March 1945 Arab League formed.

April 1945 Roosevelt dies; Truman becomes president.

May 1945 War ends in Europe.

August 1945 Japan surrenders.

November 1945–April 1946 Anglo-American Committee of Inquiry investigation and Report.

July–August 1946 Morrison–Grady Committee.

July 1946 Irgun bombs King David Hotel.

February 1947 London Conference; Britain to submit Palestine question to U.N.

June–July 1947 UNSCOP visit to Palestine.

November 1947 U.N. General Assembly approves partition; Zionists accept; Arabs reject.

April 1948 Haganah takes the offensive.

May 14, 1948 State of Israel proclaimed.

May 15, 1948 Arabs invade Israel; war ends July 19; Israel later takes Negev.

September 1948 Count Bernadotte assassinated by LEHI.

January–July 1949 Israel and Arab states reach armistice agreements.

CHAPTER 6

May 1950 Tripartite Declaration.

July 1952 King Faruq overthrown; Egyptian

army officers led by Gamal Abd al-Nasser take over government.

July 1954 British troops agree to withdraw from Suez Canal Zone by June 1956.

August 1954 French-Israeli arms deal.

February 1955 Baghdad Pact. Israeli raid on Gaza.

September 1955 Soviet-Egyptian arms deal.

July 1956 Nasser nationalizes Suez Canal.

October 1956 British-French-Israeli attack on Egypt.

CHAPTER 7

February 1958 United Arab Republic formed; lasts to September 1961.

July 1958 Iraqi revolution. U.S. Forces land in Lebanon.

January 1964 Palestine Liberation Organization (PLO) formed.

May 1967 Egypt closes Straits of Tiran.

June 1967 Six-Day War.

CHAPTER 8

August 1967 Khartoum Conference.

November 1967 Security Council Resolution 242.

July 1968 PLO Charter revised at Palestine National Council meeting.

February 1969 Yasir Arafat elected head of PLO.

March 1969—August 1970 Egyptian-Israeli war of attrition.

September 1970 Jordanian civil war. Nasser dies and is replaced by Anwar al-Sadat.

November 1970 Hafiz al-Assad becomes Syrian president.

September 1972 Fatah's Black September group takes Israeli Olympic athletes hostage in Munich. All die.

October 1973 1973 War (Egypt and Syria attack Israel). Faysal applies an oil embargo. Cease-fire leads to Security Council Resolution 338.

January 1974 Egypt-Israel "Disengagement of Forces Agreement" signed.

May 1974 Syria-Israel disengagement pact regarding Golan Heights.

October 1974 Arab summit (Rabat) declares PLO legitimate representative of Palestinians.

September 1975 Second Egypt-Israel disengagement agreement.

CHAPTER 9

April 1975—October 1976 Lebanese Civil War.

March 1977 Carter endorses a Palestinian "homeland."

June 1977 Begin becomes prime minister of Israel.

September 1978 Camp David Agreements.

January—February 1979 Shah leaves Iran; Ayatollah Khomeini returns.

March 1979 Egyptian-Israeli peace treaty signed; Egypt expelled from Arab League.

November 1979 American hostages taken in Teheran.

December 1979 Soviets invade Afghanistan.

June 1980 Venice Declaration.

September 1980 Iraq invades Iran.

January 1981 Reagan becomes president; American hostages in Iran released.

July 1981 PLO-Israeli Cease-Fire.

October 1981 Sadat assassinated, replaced by Husni Mubarak.

December 1981 Israel annexes Golan Heights.

April 1982 Israeli pullback from the Sinai completed.

June 1982 Israel invades Lebanon; surrounds Beirut.

August—September 1982 PLO leaves Beirut; multinational forces arrive.

September 1982 Reagan Plan; Fez Plan; Gemayel assassinated; his brother succeeds.

August 1983 Begin resigns, replaced by Yitzhak Shamir.

October 1983 241 U.S. Marines killed in Beirut.

November 1983 U.S.-Israeli strategic agreement.

February 1984 U.S. forces leave Lebanon.

February 1985 PLO-Jordanian peace plan.

CHAPTER 10

December 1987 Outbreak of the intifada.

July 1988 King Husayn renounces claims to West Bank. Iraq-Iran War armistice.

November 1988 PNC proclaims Independent Palestinian state.

December 1988 PLO accepts Resolution 242, ronounces terrorism, recognizes Israel's right to exist. U.S. agrees to dialogue with PLO.

May 1990 An Israeli killing of seven Palestinians leads to more deaths during protests in territories. Arab summit (Baghdad) condems U.S. policy towards Israel; Israel intercepts Palestinian attack; U.S. vetoes Security Council resolution to investigate Israeli treatment of Palestinians.

June 1990 U.S. suspends dialogue with PLO.

August 1990 Iraq invades Kuwait.

January 1991 U.S.-led coalition bombs Iraq and Iraqi positions in Kuwait.

February 1991 Coalition land assault begins. Cease-fire declared after four days.

March 1991 U.S.-encouraged uprisings by Kurds and Shi'is in Iraq are crushed with U.S. acquiescence.

July 1991 Jordan, Lebanon, and Syria agree to U.S.-sponsored peace talks with Israel.

SELECT BIBLIOGRAPHY*

Abed, George T., ed. *The Palestinian Economy: Studies in Development under Prolonged Occupation.* London: Routledge, 1988.

Ajami, Fouad. *The Arab Predicament: Arab Political Thought and Practice Since 1967.* New York: Cambridge University Press, 1982.

Aronoff, Myron. *Israeli Visions and Divisions: Cultural Change and Political Conflict.* New Brunswick, N.J.: Transaction Publishers, 1989.

Avineri, Shlomo. *The Making of Modern Zionism: The Intellectual Origins of the Jewish State.* New York: Basic Books, 1981.

Benvenisti, Meron. *The West Bank Data Project: A Survey of Israel's Policies.* Washington, D.C.: American Enterprise Institute for Public Policy Research, 1984, and later supplements.

Brand, Laurie A. *Palestinians in the Arab World: Institution Building and the Search for State.* New York: Columbia University Press, 1988.

Braude, Benjamin, and Lewis, Bernard, eds. *Christians and Jews in the Ottoman Empire: The Functioning of a Plural Society.* Two Volumes. New York: Holmes and Meier, 1982.

Brynen, Rex. *Sanctuary and Survival: The PLO in Lebanon.* Boulder: Westview, 1990.

Cobban, Helena. *The Palestinian Liberation Organization: People, Power, and Politics.* New York: Cambridge University Press, 1984.

Cohen, Amnon. *Palestine in the 18th Century: Patterns of Government and Administration.* Jerusalem: The Magnes Press, 1973.

Cohen, Michael. *Palestine, Retreat from the Mandate: The Making of British Policy, 1936–1945.* New York: Holmes and Meier, 1978.

Cordesman, Anthony H. *The Gulf and the Search for Strategic Stability: Saudi Arabia, the Military Balance in the Gulf, and Trends in the Arab-Israeli Military Balance.* Boulder: Westview, 1984.

Dawisha, Adeed, ed. *Islam in Foreign Policy.* New York: Cambridge University Press, 1983.

Dawisha, Karen. *Soviet Foreign Policy towards Egypt.* New York: St. Martin's Press, 1979.

Dessouki, Ali E. Hillal, ed. *Islamic Resurgence in the Arab World.* New York: Praeger, 1982.

Ellis, Marc H. *Beyond Innocence and Redemption: Confronting the Holocaust and Israeli Power.* New York: Harper & Row, 1990.

Fisk, Robert. *Pity the Nation: Lebanon at War.* London: Andre Deutsch, 1990.

Garthoff, Raymond L. *Detente and Confrontation: American-Soviet Relations from Nixon to Reagan.* Washington, D.C.: Brookings Institution, 1985.

Ghabra, Shafeeq N. *Palestinians in Kuwait: The Family and the Politics of Survival.* Boulder: Westview, 1987.

Golan, Galia. *The Soviet Union and the Palestine Liberation Organization: An Uneasy Alliance.* New York: Praeger, 1980.

Golan, Galia. *Yom Kippur and After: The Soviet Union and the Middle East Crisis.* Cambridge, England: Cambridge University Press, 1977.

Gresh, Alain. *The PLO, the Struggle Within: Towards an Independent Palestinian State.* Translated by A. M. Berrett. London: Zed Books, 1985.

Harkabi, Yehoshafat. *Israel's Fateful Hour.* Translated by Lenn Schramm. New York: Harper & Row, 1988.

---

* This bibliography, expanded from that in the first edition, is designed to introduce readers to various subjects. Whenever possible I have chosen books according to the quality of their bibliographies in order to encourage further examination of a topic. Several of these do not appear in the notes, either because of recent publication or their general coverage of a subject. More extensive citations are found in the footnotes.

Harris, William W. *Taking Root: Israeli Settlement in the West Bank, the Golan, and the Gaza-Sinai, 1967–1980.* New York: Research Studies Press, 1980.

Hart, Alan. *Arafat: A Political Biography.* Bloomington, Indiana: Indiana University Press, 1989.

Held, Colbert C. *Middle East Patterns: Places, Peoples, and Politics.* Boulder: Westview, 1989.

His Majesty's Stationery Office. *A Survey of Palestine.* Two Volumes. Prepared in December 1945 and January 1946 for the information of the Anglo-American Committee of Inquiry. Jerusalem, 1946. With a *Supplement to the 'Survey of Palestine'.* June 1947. Reprinted by the Institute for Palestine Studies: Braun-Brumfield, Inc. Press, 1991.

Hunter, F. Robert. *The Palestinian Uprising: A War by Other Means.* Berkeley: University of California Press, 1991.

Kepel, Gilles. *The Prophet and Pharaoh: Muslim Extremism in Egypt.* London: Zed Books, 1985.

Kerr, Malcolm. *The Arab Cold War: Gamal 'Abd al-Nasir and His Rivals, 1958–1970.* New York: Oxford University Press, 1971.

Kerr, Malcolm, ed. *The Elusive Peace in the Middle East.* Albany: State University of New York Press, 1975.

Khalidi, Rashid. *Under Siege: P.L.O. Decisionmaking during the 1982 War.* New York: Columbia University Press, 1986.

al-Khalil, Samir. *Republic of Fear: The Inside Story of Saddam's Iraq.* Berkeley: University of California Press, 1989.

Klieman, Aaron S. *Israel's Global Reach: Arms Sales As Diplomacy.* Washington, D.C., 1985.

Kushner, David, ed. *Palestine in the Late Ottoman Period: Political, Social, and Economic Transformation.* Leiden: E. J. Brill, 1986.

Lewis, Norman N. *Nomads and Settlers in Syria and Jordan, 1800–1980.* Cambridge, England: Cambridge University Press, 1987.

Liebman, Charles S., and Don-Yehiya, Eliezer. *Religion and Politics in Israel.* Bloomington, Indiana: Indiana University Press, 1984.

Louis, Wm. Roger. *The British Empire in the Middle East, 1945–1951: Arab Nationalism, the U.S., and Postwar Imperialism.* Oxford: Oxford University Press, 1984.

Lucas, Noah. *The Modern History of Israel.* New York: Praeger, 1975.

Lustick, Ian. *Arabs in the Jewish State: Israel's Control of a National Minority.* Austin: University of Texas Press, 1980.

Mandel, Neville. *The Arabs and Zionism before World War I.* Berkeley: University of California Press, 1976.

McCarthy, Justin. *The Population of Palestine: Population Statistics of the Late Ottoman Period and the Mandate.* New York: Columbia University Press, 1990.

Miller, Ylana. *Government and Society in Rural Palestine, 1920–1948.* Austin: University of Texas Press, 1985.

Morris, Benny. *The Birth of the Palestinian Refugee Problem, 1947–1949.* New York: Cambridge University Press, 1988.

Muslih, Muhammad. *The Origins of Palestinian Nationalism.* New York: Columbia University Press, 1988.

Newman, David, ed. *The Impact of Gush Emunim: Politics and Settlement in the West Bank.* London: Croom Helm, 1985.

Norton, Augustus R. *Amal and the Shia of Lebanon.* Ithaca: Cornell University Press, 1987.

Owen, E. R. J. *The Middle East in the World Economy, 1800–1914.* New York: Methuen, 1981.

Peretz, Don. *Intifada: The Palestinian Uprising.* Boulder: Westview, 1990.

Peri, Yoram. *Between Battles and Ballots: Israeli Military in Politics.* Cambridge, England: Cambridge University Press, 1983.

Porath, Yehoshua. *The Emergence of the Palestinian Arab National Movement, 1918–1929.* London: Frank Cass, 1974.

Porath, Yehoshua. *The Palestinian Arab National Movement, 1929–1939: From Riots to Rebellion.* London: Frank Cass, 1977.

Quandt, William. *Camp David: Peacemaking and Politics.* Washington, D.C.: Brookings Institution, 1986.

Quandt, William. *Decade of Decision: American Policy Toward the Arab-Israeli Conflict, 1967–1976.* Berkeley: University of California Press, 1977.

Richards, Alan, and Waterbury, John. *A Political Economy of the Middle East: State, Class, and Economic Development*. Boulder: Westview, 1990.

Sahliyeh, Émile. *In Search of Leadership: West Bank Politics since 1967*. Washington, D.C.: Brookings Institution, 1988.

Sampson, Anthony. *The Arms Bazaar: From Lebanon to Lockheed*. New York: Bantam, 1977.

Schiff, Ze'ev, and Ya'ari, Ehud. *Israel's Lebanon War*. New York: Simon & Schuster, 1984.

Seale, Patrick. *Asad of Syria: The Struggle for the Middle East*. Berkeley: University of California Press, 1988.

Shafir, Gershon. *Land, Labor, and the Origins of the Israeli-Palestinian Conflict, 1882–1914*. New York: Cambridge University Press, 1989.

Shipler, David. *Arab and Jew: Wounded Spirits in a Promised Land*. New York: Times Books, 1986.

Shlaim, Avi. *Collusion Across the Jordan: King Abdullah, the Zionist Movement, and the Partition of Palestine*. Oxford: Clarendon Press, 1988.

Smith, Pamela Ann. *Palestine and the Palestinians, 1876–1983*. London: Croom Helm, 1984.

Smooha, Sammy. *Israel: Pluralism and Conflict*. Berkeley: University of California Press, 1978.

Spiegel, Steven. *The Other Arab-Israeli Conflict: Making America's Middle East Policy, from Truman to Reagan*. Chicago: University of Chicago Press, 1985.

Stein, Kenneth. *The Land Question in Palestine, 1917–1939*. Chapel Hill: University of North Carolina Press, 1984.

Teveth, Shabtai. *Ben-Gurion: The Burning Ground. 1886–1948*. Boston: Houghton Mifflin, 1987.

Wasserstein, Bernard. *The British in Palestine: The Mandatory Government and the Arab Jewish Conflict, 1917–1929*. London: The Royal Historical Society, 1978.

Waterbury, John. *The Egypt of Nasser and Sadat: The Political Economy of Two Regimes*. Princeton: Princeton University Press, 1983.

Whetten, Lawrence L. *The Canal War. Four-Power Conflict in the Middle East, 1967–1974*. Cambridge, Mass.: Harvard University Press, 1974.

Wilson, Jeremy. *Lawrence of Arabia: The Authorized Biography of T. E. Lawrence*. New York: Atheneum, 1990.

Wilson, Mary C. *King Abdullah, Britain, and the Making of Jordan*. New York: Cambridge University Press, 1987.

INDEX